ANDREA SHULMAN

Love and Marriage

Love and Marriage

F. ALEXANDER MAGOUN

with the collaboration of
RICHARD M. MAGOUN

Revised Edition

Harper & Brothers: Publishers: New York

*Where actions are rooted in love, nothing
but goodness can flower therefrom.*

Goodnight

(For Husbands and Wives)

This day is almost done. When the night and morning meet it will be only an unalterable memory. So let no unkind word; no careless, doubting thought; no guilty secret; no neglected duty; no wisp of jealous fog becloud its passing. For we belong to each other—to have and to hold—and we are determined not to lose the keen sense of mutual appreciation which God has given us. To have is passive, and was consummated on our wedding day, but to hold is active and can never be quite finished so long as we both shall live.

Now, as we put our arms around each other, in sincere and affectionate token of our deep and abiding love, we would lay aside all disturbing thoughts, all misunderstandings, all unworthiness. If things have gone awry let neither of us lift an accusing finger nor become entangled in the rationalizations of self-defense. Who is to blame is not important; only how shall we set the situation right. And so, serving and being served, loving and being loved, blessing and being blessed, we shall make a happy, peaceful home, where hearts shall never drop their leaves, but where we and our children shall learn to face life joyfully, fearlessly, triumphantly, so near as God shall give us grace.

Goodnight, beloved.

F. ALEXANDER MAGOUN

Contents

Contents

Figures

Preface

THERE are three problems which are fundamental to a well-lived life: the achievement of a good social adjustment, based on emotional maturity; the selection of, preparation for, and carrying out of some worthwhile way of earning a living which uses one's aptitudes to one's emotional satisfaction; and the achievement of a happy family. In our culture, mature happiness depends more upon finding the right choice of a mate and subsequent good interpersonal relationships in marriage than upon any other single factor.

Happy marriage is important to a person's career as well as to his physical and emotional well-being. Business rightly puts increased valuation on the happily married individual, for he does better work, is more dependable, and is more socially adequate. Married people are better citizens; they live longer, and they usually have more to live for. The most lasting satisfaction is a happy marriage.

But how can one be sure his marriage will be happy? The only absolutely valid test is probably five years of marriage. Sometimes even that is not enough, for the real factors affecting success or failure are subconscious. These are always operative but often are apparent only after an adequate period of time.

There is, then, an inevitable element of risk, which an intelligent person will reduce to a minimum by using available good methods in arriving at discriminating judgments. This is particularly necessary at the present time, because modern young people—starting out with the same devotion, the same determination to build a happy home, the same abilities and virtues as those possessed by their grandparents—have less chance of achieving success. This is because marriage was once largely an economic partnership. It is now equally concerned with personal, emotional reassurance. Physically, home life has become much easier for us; emotionally, it is more difficult. In our present culture husband and wife are expected to be, and sometimes almost are, all things to each other. This requires a high order of emotional maturity.

The great problem of our civilization, aside from staying alive, is to become emotionally mature. It is easy enough to say that in order to select the right mate, or to be happily married, one must be emotionally mature; must be willing and able to make flexible readjustments; be capable of accepting mature responsibilities; know how to take criticism; be reasonably calm and unafraid in the face of suspense and uncertainty; possess a balanced personality because of a deep inner acceptance of whatever life does to one, based on the conviction that one has the ability to sense and to carry out the appropriate (not the vengeful) thing in response. Of course! *But how?*

This book is an attempt to give some answers to that question, though they can be no more than intellectual answers. Nothing is an effective answer until the individual has the emotional feel of it in his viscera; until he can use it without having to think about it. *Theory is worthless until it has been utilized in experience which leaves a deposit of wisdom.* Ideas will not work until the individual puts them to work. Nothing is of value until the individual discovers its truth, through his own experience, and so begins to change his inner feelings. Emotions are what matter; not the ability to repeat the answers in the book.

We know that learning is a function of its emotional consequences. But alas, we know little of how to teach a person to want to learn. It takes most of us half a century to find out what we could have known by our middle twenties if only our education (far more than mere schooling) had been right. One of the most tragic things in life is the lag and the difference between being able to repeat an important truth, and living by it.

Words are puny; feelings are powerful. Seed cannot be planted in frozen ground, but when the earth yearns to bring forth fruit, good seed can replace weeds.

So, the 657 courses on marriage and parenthood currently being taught by 1968 professors in 550 colleges seem to me to be worth while. Unless we provide for the next generation a record of the cumulative experience of the past, we can hope for little more than trial-and-error marriage. It is possible to ruin a marriage in the process of learning how to be married, and it is equally possible to teach those who have a strong and urgent desire what it is that they should try to learn.

Even an old dog can learn new tricks when the desire is urgent. A man of worldwide scientific reputation recently told me that intelligent effort has corrected the tangled condition of his marriage, which for twenty years has had him frantic and cornered. Two years ago he and his wife attended the lectures on preparation for marriage, finding out at last what they ought to work for together and how to go about it.

Youth should, of course, be allowed to make decisions of its own. It should also have available in readily usable form for critical study, revision, or adoption the best thinking of the preceding generation. Marriage is too serious for gambling.

Most of the individuals who read this book will be young people who are contemplating marriage and who consider themselves already in love. To them I would say, "The question of whether or not you are in love, or even understand the nature of love, is one which should be scrutinized critically and with unflagging search until the very moment you approach the altar. When you love someone, you have to love him enough to include all of him—and all of yourself too." To the other readers I would say, "Fix where you think you are in the succession of courtship, love, and marriage. Then read the rest of the book in an attempt to discover whether or not you are where you thought you were. Is your self-classification real or only imagined? What are the things you think you want, and do you want them for the reasons you thought you wanted them?"

Every reader will, I hope, come to realize that a happy marriage is not something to be taken for granted, or to be possessed by desultory effort. Many people enter marriage with a mixture of casual assumption, gurgles of pleasure, and resentment suppressed by the proud intention not to show it. The result is misery. Happiness must be earned through intelligent work, and kept through unrelenting effort which appreciates and cherishes the uniqueness of the home. Conscientious attention to business every day is as necessary to the family as to the office. Otherwise there will be failure. As my friend, the Jaffrey sculptor says, "Marriage is a hard job, but it is the best job anybody can get."

Some people will be of the opinion that I have overemphasized the importance of knowing what one really feels and the effect of childhood training on this knowledge. But it is of great importance to emphasize what is important. There are fields in which it is calamitous to be ignorant, none more disastrous, as far as happy marriage is concerned, than the emotional immaturity of not knowing what the actual feelings are that lie behind one's behavior. Most of what most of us think we know about ourselves is false. This is worse than ignorance. We accept as true many emotional things which are not so—exactly as we believed the sun went around the earth—and our belief is based on the same sort of obvious, superficial evidence.

The sex relation is by no means the most important element in marriage, as a careful study of Chapter 1 or Chapter 11 will show. But the subject is important because, of the five areas of married life—religious, social, economic, emotional, and sexual—with the possible exception of religion, sex is the one in which sound information is hardest to come by. This need for an objective, accurate, uninhibited approach is doubled by the fact that there are so many active, mis-educative forces, including movies, plays, jokes, and advertising, as well as the back alley.

Instead of sex being a natural, normal thing, fitting into the business of living with proper perspective, it has become almost an obsession in our civilization. Authoritative information, given without embarrassment or ribald reference, will correct this. The chief obstacle, as others before me have pointed out, is the well-meaning effort of adults who do not perceive that instead of their attention being on trying to help young people make a proper sex adjustment, their efforts actually are focused on a guarantee that whatever adjustment is made comes about in ignorance . . . or as a result of what was unfortunately learned in the gutter school.

Ignorance and good taste are by no means the same thing. I have had students in nine different colleges beg me to help them achieve a clean, understanding approach to the pre-marital problem of sex, and to good bedroom manners. On four occasions an eight o'clock lecture, followed by a question period at nine, has lasted until two o'clock the next morning, when I could talk no longer.

This thirst for decency as well as for knowledge is no surprise to anyone who remembers that when the Lynds inquired at the Middletown Library as to where the residents could find authoritative sex information, the librarian replied, "Not here!"

Nothing dies harder than prejudice, but when prejudice and fact collide, eventually prejudice has to give in. It is no more sensible for us to withhold the results of sex experience from a new generation, than for us to do so in physics or chemistry. Wisconsin offers frank sex instruction to 90 per cent of its high school students. The syphilis rate among its drafted men in World War II was 6.3 per thousand as against 170.1 per thousand in some other states. Oregon has recently passed a law that education concerning preparation for marriage—including comprehensive sex education in its appropriate place—shall be given in every grade of every school in the state, from kindergarten to high school.

"Wait," said Emerson, "to see what the centuries say. Never mind what the hours say."

I am, as is every author, indebted to other people for ideas, criticism, and encouragement. Wallace M. Ross, for twenty-nine years the general secretary of the Technology Christian Association, has been gentle, yet neither timid nor yielding in his efforts to give recurring opportunity for the lectures for which this material has been gathered over a period of nineteen years. Dr. James C. Janney, gynecologist and president of the Marriage Study Association, has tried to preserve me from ambiguity and error in the chapter on the sex relation. Izette de Forest, psychoanalyst and cherished friend, has done her best to help my understanding of the dark labyrinth of our subconscious. She has also given me many ideas.

The inner springs of diligence can be unremitting over so long a time as nineteen years only when one has a sense of worthwhileness in his effort. This sense is renewed when former students testify to their increased happiness. It is also renewed when a great and good friend, long able to point out a disagreeable truth with no loss of togetherness, believes in the rightness of what one is trying to do, and proves it with constructive suggestions as well as with words of encouragement. Such a friend R. Carter Nyman of Yale University has been to me these many years.

If life's superlative satisfaction is the rearing of a healthy, happy, emotionally mature family, then moments of special satisfaction come when, in collaboration with a son—himself a specialist in human relations—one can examine the slippery surfaces and the empty spots of his own ideas on marriage and the family. There is an added debt to both Richard and his brother, for when they were in their teens they helped me to cut down the trees and to build the log cabin where this book has been written. What could be more conducive to that composure of spirit one must have in order to write than days uninterrupted except by the chatter of some chipmunk, peering bright-eyed out of the maple tree, or the young McKeons, scampering barefoot over the country road to beguile me from my desk for the delightful refreshment of a late afternoon swim; the little spruce trees leaning on the dusk; and the long evenings of exquisite silence when ink flows, as the thoughts come fast enough to write a page an hour.

And there is, of course, my wife. It is so empty and inadequate merely to say that she has typed the manuscript, finding her way without a single error through the confusion of my inserts and deletions. Her contribution is far greater than she, or anyone else, can ever know. But her wisdom, her courage, and her co-operation —enlarging my heart and quickening my understanding—are alive in every good paragraph in this book.

F. ALEXANDER MAGOUN

Jaffrey, New Hampshire
July, 1948.

Preface to the Second Edition

An author reconsidering himself will now and then become restlessly aware that ink has flowed down his pen in places where the pen might better have been dry. He may also find convincing passages which seem to him better than anything he could have written. If the intervening years have given him added perspective, there surely will be places where he sees the need to roll up his sleeves and work.

The precipitate of the decade of experience which has almost gone by since the first edition was in long hand, is an increased realization of the solid relationships between emotional maturity and love. Hence, the new chapter. Every chapter has had some revision, but chapters 1, 5, 6, and 13 have been carpentered the most.

There is renewed acknowledgment justly due son Richard in spite of his untimely death in 1952. He left the preliminary work for a book of his own from which I have not only benefited but copied a few things. Given a little more experience, a few years of further reflection, he might have contributed significantly to our understanding of what love is. He had so much to give, so much to live for, and he loved in a way to fill one's heart with quiet rejoicing.

Environment has a significant effect on the quality of one's work. Although half of my week is spent amid the unavoidable pressures of massed humanity and industrial grime, how fortunate I am to have a place to write where it is impossible to think that nothing matters. Outside my window beautiful shafts of moonlight are stabbing through the trees. Below is the dell—to me a kind of sanctuary—where my grandsons and I found life mysterious and good this afternoon. The chicadees that lighted on my outstretched hand are sound asleep in the comfortable refuge of the spruces, while the wind is brushing a few clouds over the mountain, and I am filled with gratitude for so tranquil a spot.

Once again, as over all these years and through the multitudinous pages of a half dozen book manuscripts, I owe so much to her from whom I have learned the superior power of sheer womanliness. Twice she has saved my life. May this book be a partial justification.

F. ALEXANDER MAGOUN

Jaffrey, New Hampshire
March 26, 1956

Love and Marriage

1

The Nature of Love

Significance of the Concept of Love

THE literature, the poetry, the art, the song of all civilizations bear witness to man's deep yearning to love and to be loved. But so rare a thing is this mysterious and beautiful experience that not only does every human being know the empty depths of loneliness; many never know real love in an entire lifetime.

What is love? The questions concerning its nature have been as persistent as the yearning to possess it. "I can't give you a satisfactory definition, but everybody knows what love is," only covers an unwillingness to recognize ignorance. The more accurately a thing is understood the more readily it can be defined. Without a clear concept of what love is, how can anyone approach marriage intelligently?

Much that is labeled love has nothing to do with love. Indeed, part of it is hate. We have made love a hopelessly ambiguous word. We talk about love in contexts as varied as a moonlight night, a Sunday sermon, a popular song, a psychoanalytical diagnosis, and a book like this. We say, "I love lobster thermidor," "Don't you just love that hat?" "If you love me, you will do this for me," "Her death was such a tragedy. They were deeply in love,"

1

"God is love." Obviously the gourmet, the milliner, the domineering parent, the old acquaintance, and the clergyman mean different things by the word "love."

Is love an emotional response created in an individual? Is love a feeling one person has toward another person? Is it an atmosphere two people create together? The confusion resulting from this uncertainty is an index of our failure to understand the nature of love. It would be hard to imagine any more complete success in misleading us than has been accomplished by the jumble of false concepts and half truths resulting from misconception compounded upon misconception.

Many young people—or older ones for that matter—have no way of knowing that the Hollywood representations of the chase and its successful accomplishment, two hearts beating as one amid stardust, physical beauty, poetic passion, emotions almost at the breaking point, are not love. By fallacious algebra it is possible to prove that two equals one, but even though we may lack the wit to see where the fallacy lies, our other experience tells us instantly that something is wrong. Because of the unrealistic influence of the movies, popular songs, novels, national advertising, and the like—which imply that the birth of passion is love itself—an erroneous concept of love looks as though it were right. That which is exciting, thrilling, dreamy, romantic is only infatuation. Deep and abiding love is calm, patient, comforting, satisfying, delicate but never fragile. Love at first sight is impossible. It cannot blossom instantly any more than a rare flower does. Fascinating attraction at first sight is commonplace. There is no way to discover this short of painful experience, or of education, leading through insight to the truth.

Almost everyone who marries thinks, at the time, that he is in love. Still, the painful struggle of our search for love, our fear of not finding it, or of not deserving it, or of being unable to create together the conditions which will nurture it, cry out that many of us do not know how to love because we do not know what love is. This ignorance and inability are probably the most costly of all human frailties. It is even a root cause of war.

Mankind is barely on the threshold of understanding love. We know far more about water in its three physical states than we know about human relations. Our need to learn is obvious.

In a book on courtship and marriage there is no avoiding the word love. It is, therefore, essential not only to define it, but to discuss the definition until what is meant becomes clear. Where such definition has to do with a mystery which most people mistakenly believe they understand, this is difficult.

Certainly many definitions which appeal to young people offer neither insight nor truth. For example:

"Love is an itchy feeling around the heart that you can't scratch."

"Love is the inward inexpressibility of an outward all-over-ishness."

"Life is one darn thing after another. Love is two darn things after each other."

"Love is a feeling you feel when you feel you are going to feel a feeling you never felt before."

Nor is there enlightenment in an intellectual quagmire such as, "Love is a verbal symbol for an extremely complex variety of interpersonal behavior and feelings, and there are multitudinous degrees of this interpersonal relationship."

This inability to distinguish between abiding love and an emotional chocolate sundae is imposed upon us early in life. The music of romance becomes familiar, dear, irresistibly touching. Instead of recognizing romance as a daydream, a phantom, a will-of-the-wisp, a delight in what is thrilling and mysterious, it becomes a synonym for love, as though romance were a part of the heritage of youth, and life would be impoverished without it. This, despite the easily observable fact that no matter how busily Aladdin rubs the lamp, only those people who do not know each other intimately can feel romantic. Ignorance of reality makes the necessary daydreaming possible.

The struggle to put the glowing romance of courtship into marriage, as though it were love, leads to untold heartaches. As Truxal and Merrill say, ". . . the extreme cult of romance in American society inevitably leads to a growing proportion of disillusioned marriages."* No wonder, for though we teach children the mysteries of long division and perhaps even the secret of extracting a square root, few of them are ever taught, either by precept or example, the true nature of love. Much of what is taught about love is not worth its weight in hot air. The real thing must be passed on by behavior, not in words, and it has to be entirely recreated for each new generation.

Thus do most of us grow up with disastrous misconceptions. Love is some kind of trap to ensnare the unwary. Love is a thrilly feeling that makes delightful little squiggles run up and down the spine. Love is an indefinable mystery, yet easily identifiable when it comes. Love is something that solves all problems. Love is an all or none feeling without variations of degree, to be determined by the "she loves me, she loves me not" absolute of the daisy petal test. Love is largely sexual. In this big, wide world there is a "one and only." Love is easy to recognize because it makes the heart beat faster. (So does scarlet fever, fear of an income tax investigation, acute indigestion, or even strong drink.) Love is blind. (Infatuation is blind in one eye, but not love.) Perhaps the most common misconception is that being in love with the feeling of being loved is love.

College students, asked to define love, will often err on the side of romance, or on the opposite extreme of self-abnegation and unreasonable forbearance. "The rapture, the thrill, the sparkle an individual feels when in close association with the object of his love," writes one. A second says, "Love is the deep emotion by which a person places another's happiness, well being, or even life itself above all else, to the exclusion of self." Occasionally there will be a more emotionally honest and perceptive definition such as, "Love is a feeling of tenderness and devotion toward someone, so profound that to share that individual's joys, anticipations, sor-

* A. G. Truxal and E. E. Merrill, *The Family in American Culture* (New York: Prentice-Hall, 1947), p. 36.

rows, and pain is the very essence of living." Observe that word
share. Definitions will vary, but a good definition is essential.

The thrill over beauty, breathing invitation; the immaturity of
a grown-up search for mother; the transitory solace of sweet and
mad vibrations which banish loneliness; the spurious reassurances
of infatuation or dependency; no one of these is love. Equally false,
but often asserted by well-intentioned adults, is the idea that to
live for others, without regard for self, is to love; that goodness
requires a tremendous but unending effort because, being born in
sin, evil is he who does not overcome himself; that to want happiness for others is virtue, to want it for one's self is base; that "I try
to be as you (parent, husband, wife) desire me" is the song of love;
that the loving person keeps on loving with forbearance no matter
what effrontery he suffers.

This is all wrong. "You and I are one, but *you're* the one," is just
as evil and destructive, though not as annoying to others as "You
and I are one, but *I'm* the one."

Such concepts involve, at least on the subconscious level of
feeling, an idea which denies our individual independence, either
at the expense of the spouse (sadism), or at the expense of one's
self (masochism). Such concepts ignore the fact that, "Man's main
task in life is to give birth to himself, to become what he potentially is. The most important product of his effort is his own
personality."* Such concepts ignore one of the two great commandments of Moses, later quoted by Jesus, "Thou shalt love thy
neighbor as thyself,"** a clear implication being that one must
love himself before he can love anyone else. We now know this to
be a fundamental truth. Such concepts ignore the bribery on the
one hand and the domination on the other inherent in, "He will
think I am lovable if I do what he wants." Evil and hatred are the
end products of unfulfilled powers denied a chance to grow.

What concept could be more contrary to the fact of our biological individuality than the idea that one person should continually

* E. Fromm: *Man For Himself* (New York: Rinehart, 1947), p. 237.
** Leviticus 19:18. See also Deuteronomy 6:5.

sacrifice himself to the wishes of another, ignoring his own emotional and intellectual needs! Voluntary slavery, selfless devotion, is a sentimental concept. It cannot be love, for it lacks respect for the facts of our proper interpersonal relationships. Any attempt at unity without a concurrent cherishing of individuality is destructive. It results in the idea that, "If you do not do what I want, you do not love me."

To belittle one's self, to be bowed down by a sense of sin (especially if pretended), to feel powerless and unworthy, is not to love either God or man. Nevertheless, the idea has been widely taught and widely successful in gaining power over people, an obvious example being Hitler's secular use of it in, *"Der Staat is alles. Sie sind nichts."**

Separateness, while important, is, of course, not all. The togetherness of, "What will be best for us both?" is fundamental, each knowing how the other is concerned that he too be fulfilled. No domination, no unwilling giving in, no running away. Together!

No one can be happy with someone who does not allow him to be himself. Any self-sacrifice which damages the personality, or harms the genuine togetherness of people, is not virtue. The more warmth and sincerity of affection a person has for himself, the more he can bestow on others. The selfish person has to be self-centered because he hates himself, impossible as that may seem to the uninitiated. Selfishness and masochism are both failures in solving the problem of togetherness, for each tries to deny the fact of *separate individuality to be respected in the togetherness.* We shall have more to say about this later.

The true song of love is, "Because I was born good, when I am my real self, not some false imitation, I have a wonderful power to love and to be loved. If you can respect my uniqueness and dignity, as I respect both mine and yours, we can love each other . . . at least to some degree."

Sharing is the word, not selfless giving.

Love cannot be based on unrealistic ideas which are ignorant,

---

* "The state is everything. You are nothing," which is exactly opposite the essence of the teaching of Jesus.

delusive, and false. It must be understood and defined in terms of the reality of its conscious or subconscious purposes. In order to understand the significance of any concept it is necessary to examine its consequences in action. What love might be, or ought to be, or someday may be, matters not. What is the actual purpose behind the behavior of loving people in our culture? To know that is to understand what love is.

DEFINITION OF LOVE

Love is the passionate* and abiding desire on the part of two or more people to produce together the conditions under which each can be and spontaneously express his real self; to produce together an intellectual soil and an emotional climate in which each can flourish, far superior to what either could achieve alone. It is an intimate relatedness based on the mutual approval and affirmation of the character and integrity of the personalities involved. It is not a situation where two partners think more of each other than they do of themselves. That idea is idealistic. Except for rare, short intervals of misunderstanding, it is a situation where two partners think more of the partnership than they do of themselves. It is an interweaving of interests and a facing of sacrifice** together for the sake of both, for love is not love unless it is expressed in action. It is the feeling of security and contentment that comes with the adequate satisfaction of each person's emotional needs through their mutual efforts. It is man's superlative method of self-realization and survival.

When the five-year-old says he loves his dog he may mean, as most grownups do, that he is fond of the animal, or he may really love the dog because of a reciprocal self-fulfillment in which to-

---

* Passion is being in the grip of an emotional experience so big that it possesses you and you can do nothing about it, like the feelings which possess a person in the presence of birth, or death, or love.

** Sacrifice comes from two Latin words, *sacra* and *ficio*, meaning "to make holy." Thus, an individual gives up something highly desirable to him for the sake of protecting, of developing, but especially of improving a person, end, or ideal dearer to him than the thing given up. Sacrifice usually involves self-denial, but it has no implication, as is commonly supposed, of being exploited, dominated, imposed upon, or victimized.

gether they have a richer and a broader experience of their potentialities for living. Does one ever forget an experience like hearing a child say, "I love my dog because *he* listens to me." To think that statement is selfish is to be insensitive.

But no one "loves" lobster thermidor; he only likes the taste of it. There is no mutual relationship, no response of the one to the other, no creating together. It is not even a live relationship.

Love is a mutual responsiveness. It says, "I perceive in your feelings the sort of evaluations and responses to life I believe to be characteristics of the real me. Because we are alike in this way, we can accept each other as we are and for what we are; we can grow in the same intellectual soil and the same emotional climate. There is a sincere purpose behind our lives, as behind every life, which begs to be expressed. Our purposes are so close together they can spontaneously unite to the advantage of each of us."

Spontaneous action is free of pretense, embarrassment, or premeditated attempts to impress. It is a sparkling expression of honest feeling, without any sense of "ought-to-feel," or coercion of any kind. Consider how a dog shows joy by jumping up on his master, barking, wagging his tail, running back and forth in a genuine reaction. How different from the falsification and the deadening of feelings we are taught in the name of good manners, despite the fact that our real selves can relate genuinely only insofar as our responses are genuine. Real selves can relate to neighbors, store clerks, children, and mates, but there is a difference in the breadth and depth of the relation. The more area the genuine responses cover, the deeper the affection, because the more complete the union of real selves.

Spontaneity and impulsiveness are not the same thing. True, they are alike in that neither comes about by deliberation. But where impulse is involuntary, forced by emotion, actuated impetuously under the stress of the feelings of the moment, spontaneity is voluntary, natural, expressive of the true nature of the individual. A young child, enthusiastically telling about the planning and successful carrying out of some activity, is being spontaneous. An impulsive action is sudden; a spontaneous one is genuine. Impulse is always the warped expression of some blocked spontaneity.

Spontaneity is possible only when one has mastered the underlying principles of what he is trying to do. The foreigner, restricted in vocabulary, uncertain in pronunciation, bewildered by grammar, cannot express himself spontaneously. But once he becomes familiar with the language, free because now able to obey the rules without thinking, he can express himself naturally, and without hampering restrictions. Spontaneity, like freedom, is a matter of voluntary obedience to law. No experienced motorist wants to disobey the rules of the road. No author rebels against the rules of grammar. Neither of these is a restriction on behavior, for both result in the possibility of spontaneous self-expression, unthreatened by violence or misunderstanding.

We are happiest with people who give us a sense of personal fulfillment. Loving behavior is natural wherever a person can be his real self. There is no other way to be free from the conflicts and the repressions which destroy the spontaneous, creative self-expression that underlies love. *The more completely one can express his real self to another person, the more deeply he can love.*

Love carries through the whole gamut of emotions, producing a kinship of body, mind, and spirit. It is not an occasional tingling with anticipation. It is not the idealistic, emotionally dishonest self-denial which proclaims the essence of love and morality to be the subordination of one's individual satisfactions to the service of someone else. This is self-abdication, and where there is someone surrendering himself, there is also someone collecting the offering. Such a relationship is closer to slavery than to love.

"When love awakens dies the self," sings the poet. Nonsense! When love awakens comes self-fulfillment, enhanced, beautified, strengthened by reinforcement in the beloved person. Love is never continued selflessness. Such self-frustration sooner or later turns to hate. Love is not doing things only for the sake of the other person, it is doing them because of the happiness and creative self-expression it gives to provide together the intellectual soil and the emotional climate in which *both* can flourish.

The idea that love consists of surrendering one's self for another's benefit was devised by those who could benefit. They, in turn, had previously suffered so from the exploitation of others as to be unable to give of themselves without careful calculation of the cost. Love does come at a price. It is not to be had for nothing. But it cannot be earned by so many hours at the dishpan, the kitchen stove, the brokerage office, or the factory. It cannot be produced by ordering it. No sense of duty can force it. It can come only where the conditions exist which will create it.

There is no virtue in giving up something in order to feel unselfish. Virtue comes from having *enjoyed* making someone else happy. When two people try to give in to each other in order to feel exemplary, they end by pleasing neither. But each feels he has a special claim to consideration next time, and subconsciously hates the other for having taken advantage of him. The end result is prolonged anxiety, partly due to the insincerity of the giving up, but also due to never knowing how severely one's values may be threatened by the assumed martyrdom of a wife who says, "I gave up for you . . ." or a husband who claims, "If it hadn't been for you. . . ."

Thus two people love each other when they naturally and honestly fulfill each other's emotional needs. There must be a mutuality to loving behavior. The satisfaction-seeking efforts of each must, to a large extent, provide simultaneous satisfaction for the other. This is why love intensifies with time, not by domination or submission, but by mutual development; two people singing to one music, sometimes in unison, sometimes in parallel harmonic intervals, sometimes in pleasing counterpoint, sometimes in acceptable dissonances—but always at least two, and always together.

Love recognizes the sacredness of personality, both of the self and of others. After birth, the survival of any individual is not absolutely dependent on any other. Only a healthy degree of independence, keeping co-operation from becoming a dependency or a protectorate, can be a basis for healthy emotional unity.

When we react to stimuli which concern other people's needs, it is because at the same time our needs are involved in some direct or indirect way. Our own happiness is a prerequisite for making other people happy. Is happiness to be found in forgetting one's self? By no means. The alcoholic, the psychotic, the drug addict are all seeking self-forgetfulness. The only road to complete self-forgetfulness is suicide. Happiness comes through giving one's self, freely and completely, to a cause emotionally satisfying to one's self.

Some individuals are usually takers and seldom givers. Why? No one can give of himself until his own basic emotional needs are satisfied. It is not possible to give from poverty. Many people are incapable of loving because they dare not give of themselves for fear they will be cheated out of what little emotional satisfaction they have. These are the individuals who were brought up in the "love is self-surrender" school. But the battle to live ignoring one's self, as well as the battle to live unto one's self alone, is a battle in which no one can win a decisive victory.

The nourishment and preservation of the personality of a beloved individual is of such importance to the loving person that the way to maintain his own best satisfaction is also through a genuine concern for the other's happiness; mutual appreciation leading to mutual self-expression through loving behavior. To each the satisfactions of the loved one are usually as important as his own. Where there is love the lover not only experiences happiness himself, he experiences happiness in the happiness of his beloved. Thus the personality of each is recognized, respected, strengthened through the intimate feeling of belonging together without any withholding or restrictive possessiveness.

Real love cannot be withheld.

THE EXPRESSION OF LOVE

The fundamental drive in every life is self-preservation—even more emotional than physical.* How this is worked out in behavior

---

* If physical self-preservation were the first law of human nature no one would ever commit suicide.

is largely in terms of the dynamic relationship between self-expression and self-evaluation. This needs to be explained.

Self-expression consists of finding uninhibited outlets for one's true nature in imaginative thought, or spontaneous action which uses aptitudes to one's emotional satisfaction.

Self-evaluation consists of personal judgments as to one's capacities and worth. It lacks the objectivity and definiteness of a financial appraisal, but determines subjective deductions and conclusions as to one's abilities compared with those of other men; one's honesty, freedom from emotional conflict or hypocrisy, genuineness of feeling, wholesomeness, intelligent use of opportunity or aptitudes, steadfastness, fidelity. Self-evaluation is what an individual honestly thinks of himself as a person compared to other people.

Love, like all the rest of life, cannot reveal itself except through the interaction of self-evaluation on self-expression, and vice versa. But here the situation is complicated by the fact that two individuals are involved. It is not only John's self-evaluation operating on his own self-expression, but his self-evaluation influencing and reacting to both Mary's self-expression and Mary's self-evaluation and so on indefinitely. Consider how she becomes a cheer leader because he plays basketball. Consider how her self-evaluation may act on both his self-expression and his self-evaluation when she says, "I'm not that kind of a girl!"

Thus, love requires a complicated dynamic structure of four elements and twelve possible avenues of emotional relationship, including the self and the beloved. Hence its sensitivity and its need for a capacity to integrate the behavior of the lovers, naturally and without strain, so love can build on the changes that come instead of being destroyed by them. The self-expression and the self-evaluation of each must be secure, both within the individual and with the other person. How this operates will be made more clear by a study of Figure I.

Force traveling along any one of the twelve possible routes must be an acceptable component of the system, or it may tend to disrupt and to destroy the system. How is self-expression or self-evaluation sought? Does it lead to satisfaction or to frustration? The self-expression of one lover will often bring pleasant self-expression or self-evaluation to the other. The giver may be engaged in activity which expresses himself, and at the same time indicates his high evaluation of the receiver. Thus there will be mutual self-expression resulting in mutual appreciation through devotion to a common cause, each being able to give himself freely to the other without fear of being hurt, imposed upon, or misunderstood. This gives a zest to living because each has something to belong to outside himself and much bigger than himself; someone to live with and to live for; someone to share joys and thus double them, to share sorrows and thus halve them; someone to be courageous with him; someone to comfort him and to be comforted by him.

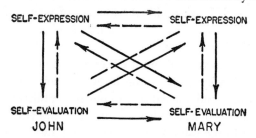

Fig. 1. Avenues of Emotional Relationship in Love

It is not a separate, isolated Mary whom John loves, but their relationship. And yet it is always a relationship in which the unity equals two. Paradoxical as it sounds, both are separate and at the same time bound together, united and yet distinct, on a basis which preserves and nurtures each individual self. Each physiological entity remains separate, but the entities respond, reach out, interact. A one way relationship is possible, but that is devotion, not love. "What we love in others is not so much the individual as the possibility of a bond of affection, not so much the friend as the friendship,"* says Piaget. Love is not an "inter-emotion." No one can feel another person's feelings. Love is an "intra-emotion."

* J. Piaget, *The Moral Judgment of the Child* (London: Kegan Paul, 1932), p. 354.

All of us hunger for inner feelings of fulfillment based on enjoyable self-expression and satisfactory self-evaluation. Many achieve them only fleetingly because of their internal civil wars. Their desires are demanding, their conscience is threatening, their discrimination is weak and vacillating, their self-respect is starving. So they become uneasy, lonely, yearning to feel loved.

Just being with other people is not a cure. One can be more lonely in an hilarious group than alone in the unspoiled loveliness of the woods. Loneliness is an emotional sickness which feeds upon itself. Love is outgoing. Loneliness is ingrowing. The lonely person sometimes feels that he would sell his soul to be loved. He does not realize that no one can be lovable until he is strong enough within himself to pour out loving behavior with no calculation as to its return. "Though I speak with the tongues of men and of angels, and have not love (*without asking for it*) I am become as sounding brass, or a tinkling cymbal."*

In our self-expression we must either love some other person or become emotionally twisted through the blocking of our emotional outlets and the resultant damage to our self-evaluation. Liking or admiring other people, and having them like and admire us is not enough. Just loving is not enough. Just being loved is not enough. The achievement of our real selves is impossible unless there is a free flow of loving relationships through the twelve possible avenues of communication which connect our own self-evaluation and self-expression with those of at least one other person.

As Izette de Forest has said to me, *a free flow of loving relationships can be achieved only when each discovers and lives by his REAL emotions, which are inescapably in harmony with the true reality of human relations, simply because he is a human being.* As we shall see, impulsive behavior or rebellious behavior is not behavior in terms of the real self.

Because love is a mutual experience of increased self-fulfillment, loving and being loved cannot be separated for long. This leads to the realization that if a person is lovable he will be loved . . .

* First Corinthians, 13:1.

though not by everyone. "I will be loved because, despite my human shortcomings, I am mostly lovable," is no more conceited and no less true than, "Because I am a good workman I will be hired."

Many psychologists will insist that loving and being loved are not concurrent as far as a mother and baby are concerned. Their belief is we are born wanting to be loved, but the ability to love has to be beaten into us by some system of rewards and punishments. I protest! Because a new baby is entirely dependent does not mean that he is egocentric. Surely he tries hard to unite with his mother in an effort to create together the intellectual soil and the emotional climate in which each can grow. He never cries unless something is wrong. He cherishes to the utmost of his ability a togetherness which is by no means one-sided. Few adults produce the rewarding facial expressions of joy and affection with which a three-month-old child greets a loving parent. His desire to give in terms of his capacities is as real and as vital as his desire to receive in terms of his needs.

Every child is born good, not in the sense that he obeys the mores of his culture, but in the more important sense that he has the innate urge to grow, to establish relationships of confidence and cooperation with other people, to discover truth for himself, to possess worthwhile capacities of significance and value to himself and to his fellowmen. For the baby, whatever obstruction clogs the avenues of emotional relationship shown in Figure 1, or builds a dam across the confidence stream of Figure 4 (of which more later on pages 77-80), is always due to adult ignorance, impatience, emotional immaturity, maladjustment, or fatigue. It is never created by the baby. Endeavoring to force a child too fast, or in the wrong direction, of course produces rebellion. Then, in our colossal blindness, we say he has to be taught how to love.

Baby requires tender affection in order to develop. Without it, his sucking response is poor, for he can sense rejection as well as helplessness. Mother, however, does not always respond to his need. He gets pushed away instead of being allowed to grow away by the enlargement of his confidence and capabilities. His realization of rejection is as disruptive and as intolerable to him as any adult's. The result is anger, fear, and a "selfishness" which is nothing more than the baby's only way of attempting to preserve himself despite an overpowering attack and a terrible emotional wound. This becomes especially true when he is subjected to forced weaning or to premature toilet training.

The baby's loving is not yet mature love for exactly the same reason that his hating is not yet mature hate. Heartfelt human relations do not spring up already matured. They require a long period of testing and development to reach full flower.

Need for Understanding Our Emotional Nature

Few of us understand our emotional natures. We do not perceive our feelings accurately enough to recognize sentimental friendliness as a cover for aggression. We do not recognize that a self-conscious person is a frightened individual who has concentrated on defending himself. Yet behind all thought is emotion, and if the emotions are hostile the thinking will be hostile. The reasoning powers of the mind are used in different ways, depending upon whether the emotional drive is love, anger, hate, fear, or whatever it may be. If the feeling is not a loving feeling, the thinking cannot be a loving thought, no matter how much we disguise it in the attempt to fool ourselves or someone else. To think one is in love when the real feeling is not there is hypocrisy, and subconscious hypocrisy is even more deadly than the conscious variety because it results in greater loss of internal consistency.

The deceit usually stems from having learned as a child that in the presence of a powerful parent it is safer to act lovingly despite a hateful emotion. But we cannot try to deceive others about our feelings without soon deceiving ourselves, and deceiving ourselves results in becoming less lovable because less sincere. At last we do not know what we feel, for pretended feelings lead to self-deception as lying leads to beliving one's own falsehoods.

Most of our conscious feelings are a ready-made pattern taken over from our parents (or some other significant person in our early life). We were brought up to believe that unless we felt these feelings we were lost souls. The result is a hopeless muddle of true self and counterfeit self, incapable of feeling honestly and, therefore, incapable of love. No wonder love is such a rare commodity! This is a dire picture, but a true one.

Love is feeling, and much of feeling cannot be expressed in words. To say, "I love you," is not necessarily to love. The word is not the thing. Words are puny; feelings are powerful. Words are only the trivia that convey ideas—usually somebody else's ideas. Feeling is life itself, and fullness of life depends upon breadth, and depth, and reality of feeling. It is relatively easy to share ideas. Many emotions are difficult to share. Nevertheless, love is impossible until one can *feel* differences and similarities in people, and feel a respect for them.

Most of us do not correctly feel what is going on within ourselves or within anyone else. Because of our childhood conditioning, what we feel is convention and social obligation. We were brought up to obey convention for fear we would obey our impulses. To know what one is feeling does not mean that it will be expressed impulsively. To know what one is feeling makes it easier to wait until one knows how he wants to express it. The breaking through of impulse is proof of repressed feelings. *There can be no explosion unless first some force has been imprisoned.*

Nothing can be truly known until it has been experienced and assimilated on the level of feeling. To know what one wants and needs requires first an understanding of what one's feelings are. What is one's fundamental nature? What is one seeking to express in living his particular life in his particular environment? Of the great variety of emotional impulses which continuously come to everyone, and which no one can avoid, which does one genuinely desire to develop and to express for his own, best, long-run satisfaction? To discover one's self is to discover what human nature is like, and therefore, to have an understanding of what people are like and the purposes for which they were created—including the need to love and to be loved.

Love between two people who cannot sense and share each other's emotions is impossible. Though they may be devoted and actively loyal to each other, they cannot be in love. To love is to feel with fidelity to the facts, and thus to know what each wants and needs in order to produce together the conditions under which each can grow into his real self.

The loving person is completely self-respecting. The loving person does not fear what other people may think of him. *The more genuine and self-respecting he is, the less he cares about any opinion of himself except his very own.* He does not feel himself unique or degraded because he experiences anger, hate, jealousy, sensuality. He does not feel hopeless or unlovable because of traits he dislikes in himself. He recognizes these as emotions experienced by all men. He acknowledges that as a human being he cannot be perfect. The best he can do is on the one hand to cherish the constructive qualities in his personality; on the other to understand, accept, and control to the best of his ability the negative qualities. He is disturbed by whatever evil he may do, particularly evil toward himself. He handles it by facing his responsibility for it and correcting it, not by ignoring his responsibility or by covering himself with the sackcloth and ashes of self-abasement.

We cannot love someone else while we still hate ourselves. The idea that a person who loves himself cannot love anyone else is mistaken. This is the only condition under which it is possible to love. The unlovable people are those who despair of ever loving themselves. The loving person must first have tolerance for his own hostile and evil thoughts, concentrating on how to handle them constructively; not on how to strangle them (and himself) destructively. Only then can he be tolerant of another person's shortcomings.

Without tolerance and self-respect love is impossible. We must find our own reality, accept it, live by it. Only then can we be happy. Only then will another person become an individual in whose existence we can take delight for himself alone. Only then do we know ourselves and other people honestly enough to face our inability to get along with everyone, and to identify the relatively few individuals with whom we can spontaneously create conditions superior to what we could achieve alone.

Not knowing, as is the case with most of us, what we are really feeling, it is no wonder that we are successfully duped by the various counterfeit emotions which masquerade as love.

Every day there are people who find the temporary lift and the self-centered ecstacy of infatuation has turned to ashes. Any culture where love is passionately sought and grossly misunderstood is bound to be strewn with the charred wreckage of burned-out memories.

Counterfeit Emotions which Masquerade as Love

There are many false emotions which mislead us, the most dangerous of which, at the outset, look like love. All of them are difficult to recognize at first; most of them are brutally unmasked by time. Among them are: mistaking romance—which stresses glamour and adventure rather than character—for love; a parasitic dependence upon another person because of being too weak or too afraid to stand alone; sexual desire aroused by physical beauty or perhaps sheer energy and zest for life; need to exploit someone to gain self-assurance through money, prestige, or power; living life vicariously through another person because of inability to be one's self; a compulsive desire to feel needed; a man intent upon the conquest of a woman to mother him; a woman determined not to be an old maid, or in search of a meal-ticket; either or both craving the rapturous feeling of reassurance which comes when an individual is treated as though he were, in fact, that which in his glorified fantasies about himself he would like himself to be. Naturally the greater the discrepancy between the fantasy and reality, the greater the need for outside reassurance of its reality. The greater the reassurance, the bigger the thrill of feeling "I am lovable after all"—until reality brings the deception to an end, as it always does, in the headache of the morning after.

Romance is an attempt to overcome in action the painful experiences of infancy and early childhood which convinced a person he was not only helpless but unworthy, and therefore separated from others with whom he yearned for a close relationship. Romance is the hope of at last having such a relationship despite not knowing how to cherish the individuality which must be cherished in any duality which becomes a loving unity. The romantic who thinks he is in love comes to the same ultimate frustration as the hen sitting on a china egg. In both instances there is no reality to the imagined relationship.

Each of these counterfeits is based on some kind of self-centered, irrational reassurance. In no one of them—no matter how one may temporarily fool himself to the contrary—is there a sincere, consuming desire to produce *with the other person* the conditions under which *each can be and spontaneously express his real self*. In no one of them is there a sincere desire to produce together an intellectual soil and an emotional climate in which *each* can flourish, far superior to what either could achieve alone. To fail in this is to fall short of love.

Love is a different thing from romance, for it is created by a sense of the other individual's worth, not by how the other individual makes the lover feel. *Love is not emotional nourishment for a hungry time*. Romance is. But, alas, how can post-adolescent puppy love, in which sex attraction is the most important factor, fulfill so exacting a demand?

Where there is belief in romance, the parentally arranged marriages of China and India seem unfeeling and harsh. Nevertheless, despite other objections, the parentally arranged marriage does make husband and wife, from childhood on, face the emptiness of romance and the inevitability of their need to work together to make the marriage successful. Happiness must be earned. In marriage, as in dancing, the happiness does not stem from the way the individual himself moves, but in the togetherness of the movement.

We think we are in love because of the way another person makes us feel. This is a desire for the blissful emotions created in us by the other individual *at the moment*. It is not loving him. Love is not a method for keeping someone happy about himself. That is infatuation. Love knows not the underlying fear and uncertainty of the reassurance-seeking swain who hugs passionately and whispers, "You do love me, darling, don't you? You know you do." There is here a turbulent and fragile quality which love does not have, for though it is delicate it is never fragile.

Love is not delight in ME, love is self-realization together in US. Two mutually infatuated people can want each other desperately without love, and without sensing the emotional insincerity which consumes them during the delicious and palpitant intimacy of necking in a parked car. Neither realizes how allergic he is to himself; neither perceives he is experiencing little more than a cheap reassurance. What seems to be love is but blind delight in being treated as though one were perfection itself, when actually one is dissatisfied with one's self. It often takes five years for a young couple to discover that "we do everything together" is sentimentality and not love.

So there is an engagement, probably of short duration, followed by a touching wedding ceremony. Sooner or later each partner finds that the other does not agree with everything he says and does. No one is always loving or always lovable. Quiet desperation is followed by panic. The reassurance of complete agreement is gone. Troubled faces confront each other across the breakfast table. By dinner time they may be angry faces, divided as only emotional distance can divide. Little do these two people realize that a man and a woman really in love are not concerned over disagreement. Differences of opinion are not the same thing as loss of emotional unity.

What happens to the romantic emotions when the bubble bursts and the reality of the total situation has to be faced? The idealistic nonsense of "living only for each other" shrivels beyond repair. It now looks as though love had changed into indifference, contempt, hate. The truth is that the desire to consume each other emotionally has now come to the surface.

Unless the person discovers how full of subconscious fear he is, and why, there is probably a divorce, perhaps followed by a second marriage in which the selfsame pattern is repeated. How tragic that emotional insecurity led the individual to suppose that the transitory, false value of how the other person made him feel was love. "She's my inspiration," can never be love, though "we inspire each other" may be. The idealism is only an unrecognized defense against any recognition of the underlying selfishness. Love is not so blind! In love the feelings of affection and security are fundamental. In infatuation the primary emotions are insecurity and a compulsive need for reassurance of one's own personal worth. It is often difficult to tell the difference until time has shown which is the wispy child and which the healthy one, but in time, or in a crisis, reality and sham are easily differentiated.

Those who love must love in terms of the total situation. Love is concerned with the realities of life; not with ideas about romantic idealism which cannot be embodied in life. Love sees faults as well as virtues. Love knows and unhesitatingly accepts the fact that no one is perfect. Love permits no deceiving of one's self or of anyone else. Love says, and says with honest feeling, "I know that I shall be irked by your inability ever to be on time, I know that you will be irritated by my smoking, I know that the differences in our energy and tempo will annoy both of us until we learn how to integrate them. But despite these difficulties, we see so much of value in each other that our emotional potentialities surely can create together an intellectual soil and an emotional climate far superior to what either of us could achieve alone. It is not necessary for you to share my interest in European history, or for me to understand why you enjoy Chinese checkers. What matters is that we each sense and like the kind of person the other is, and want to cherish him for what he is."

The infatuated individual is unaware of his assumption that the object of his emotions will do whatever he wishes, as though one individual had a right to use another for the achievement of his own desires, with no reciprocal exchange of effort. Love is no such tyranny and bondage. These do not develop and expand. These only restrict and destroy.

Love is never loss of freedom. It is willing self-restraint, at times, for the sake of another person. To think that there are no things to be given up *for* each other is to suppose that love costs nothing. It is what is suffered *from* each other which is a debit instead of an investment. Love is self-discovery and self-fulfillment through healthy growth with and for the other person. As long as an individual is really loving and lives in a loving environment, he cannot experience prolonged unhappiness. Nevertheless, the feeling that love entails giving in, being a slave, letting other people hurt one without resistance or revenge is not uncommon.

Nor is love a parasitic leaning of one person upon another. A relationship in which two people always have to be together smacks of mother and baby. This makes impossible the continued, spontaneous self-expression that must characterize a really happy relationship. Sometimes the dependent partner is domineering; in other instances compliant, and therefore encouraging the spouse to be his opposite. There is no mutuality to such a relationship; only domination and subordination. Many onlookers and even many participants think this is love. Actually it is weakness and fear.

A common mistake is to confuse physical attraction and affection. Attraction is possible with little knowledge of the individual's personality. Love needs to know a great deal. Is a sexual infatuation to be regarded as love? If sex is love, then the home is not as important as the boudoir, and the bust line is more important than the personality, both of which may be false. Freud contributed to the confusion between attraction and affection, for—as Reik pointed out*—he continually referred to the "love object," when what he meant was the "sex object." Sex is concerned with the enjoyment of another person's body as it is. Love is concerned with

---

* T. A. Reik, *A Psychologist Looks at Love* (New York: Farrar and Rinehart, 1944), p. 7.

enjoying and giving enjoyment to another personality as it is, with married people including the sex relation in varying degrees.

Once the novelty of intercourse between two people has worn off, little affection is exchanged unless it is earned by something more than an easy disposition, expressions of endearment, or laughter at a husband's jokes. There must be an enduring element which preserves and develops the individual personalities of both partners. The fact that sex is almost universal, yet love a rare and precious gift, should be proof enough that the latter does not originate in or draw its vitality from sexual gratification. Love stems from and is nurtured by an intimate emotional relationship, but physical attraction alone is not enough.

We sometimes call it love when two young people gaze soulfully at each other in the moonlight. Puppy-love is a more accurate nomenclature. This always has ridiculous aspects, particularly when the participants are no longer in their teens. Yet ridicule is probably wrong. Just because the emotion cannot be lasting does not mean that the feeling is not intense. To the adolescent it seems imperishable and poingnantly beautiful. Ridicule only compels him to attempt the defense of his emotions. Understanding may lead him to more solid reality.

Unrequited love has been the basis of some disturbingly beautiful stories, but in actual life it is not love. The indirect, disguised anger of self-pity which says, "I'll let other people see what you have done to me. I'll make them realize how you have impoverished my life by not feeling about me the way I feel about you," is not love. Unless there is a closed cycle, allowing the emotional currents to ebb and flow equally in both directions, the result is strangulated and lifeless.

The difference between infatuation, unrequited love, and love itself lies partly in this matter of how the emotional currents flow. Infatuation, which may be one-sided or mutual, reaches out to take what it wants (Figure 2). Unrequited love may give, but there is no return, and the system will quickly become unbalanced. Love provides for a two-way exchange which can be continuously maintained, and the ability to maintain it comes from honestly wanting to affirm the personality of the other individual *as it is,* honestly wanting to keep and to cherish it.

Love is a process, like evolution, or the ripening of an apple, or the erection of a building, or the living of a lifetime. Historical continuity is no guarantee of spiritual and emotional continuity, but if love cannot stand the test of time it is not love. This is not to say that love is unchanging. The idea of permanence in anything human is untenable. Love can shrivel if it is not maintained, or it can grow, nourished by constant thoughtfulness that is spontane-

INFATUATION   UNREQUITED LOVE   LOVE

Fig. 2. Infatuation, Unrequited Love, and Love

ous on the part of each lover and welcomed by each loved one. But in order for it to be lasting, love must be lastingly fulfilled.

COMPARISONS

Romance	*Love*
Feelings	
Genuine feelings often repressed. Superficial feelings masking hostility to people.	Genuine, deep feelings based on a liking for and faith in people as a whole.
An almost immediate feeling of emotional unity.	May be immediate attraction, but this grows gradually into love because both individuals try to make it wider and deeper.
Intense feeling of walking on air which wears off with time.	Quiet, calm, clear headed sense of well-being when together, which increases.

Comparisons—*Continued*

Romance	Love
Feelings	

"She makes me feel I am the kind of person I wish I were."

"She helps me to feel more accurately and completely the kind of person I am."

The feeling of emotional unity is soon subject to doubting spells.

An increasingly solid and reliable sense of togetherness.

Either fear of straining the relationship if sacrifices are asked, demanding them, or both.

Knowing requests are reasonable, or if not that they will be revised, and so asking without fear.

Doubts about the security of the relationship. Appearance of jealousy and fear that the other will be jealous.

A gradually increasing mutual trust allowing each confidence in being himself with everyone.

Inner doubts dishonestly suppressed, such as avoiding psychological tests of compatibility, or refusing to consult a marriage counselor.

The possibility of doubt honestly faced, welcoming any valid psychological test, and both wanting to talk with a qualified marriage counselor.

Hostile responses to criticisms from the other (it threatens the reassurance).

Calm consideration of criticism, knowing it is not hostile but an attempt to be helpful.

Feeling of catastrophe if the relationship breaks up, or ruthlessly breaking it up in a way which ignores the other's feelings.

Regret the relationship ending, but picking up the pieces and going on fearlessly, confidently. Separating in kindness, perhaps because of mutually recognized wisdom.

Action

Dependence on others, with a feeling of helpless worthlessness if rejected.

A healthy interdependence, without fear of worthlessness if the relationship is broken.

COMPARISONS—*Continued*

Romance	Love

Action

Pretended mutual interests and therefore hypocritically calculated reactions.	Actual mutual interest and therefore spontaneous, sincere reactions.
Mutual pretense, particularly about disagreeable things.	Mutual sincerity, even about disagreeable things.
Attention almost exclusively on the importance TO ME OF YOUR behavior.	Attention almost exclusively on the importance TO ME of YOUR AND MY behavior as individuals in a togetherness.
Appraise only the other person's action.	Concentrate on the other person's intentions.
Continual "I love you" and "Of course you love me."	"I love you and realize you love me" said in action more than in words.
Desire to be alone together to express the companionship of sex attraction by necking.	Enjoyment of each other with people as well as alone, in a companionship of shared interests.
Generous or unselfish acts accompanied by a need to be thanked.	Giving because of wanting to give, and no strings attached, no thought of reward.

Thought

Lack of concern for other people as a whole, or else a compulsive need to save the world, *your way.*	Genuine, calm concern for people with reasonable effort to contribute one's share in a modest way.
Unilateral approach to problems in an attempt to protect one's own happiness. Predominant "I" thinking.	Bilateral approach to problems resulting in mutual happiness and growth. Predominant "we" thinking.

Romance	Love

Thought

Romance	Love
Assuming desired characteristics exist in each other without seeing evidence of same.	Studying each other to understand each other in terms of objective evidence.
Relief that "someone cares about me at last."	Confidence that many people do and will care.
"We" thinking only when there is agreement. Anger and withdrawal in conflict.	"We" thinking, even in serious disagreement, and with no loss of emotional unity because both emotionally mature.
"I was happy tonight," or "I must find out what she wants."	"We were happy tonight," or "We work out together what is best for us."

LOVE AND HATE

All love is tainted at times with some anger and hostility.* The people we love the most are also the ones we hurt the most. We are more tolerant of those to whom we are indifferent than toward those we love. Man is ambivalent as a result of unresolved conflicts within him. He can love and hate the same person simultaneously, as well as concurrently, because he can do one consciously and the other subconsciously. Love says, "If I could only grow and develop with you, we could produce together the conditions under which each of us could become his best self." Hate says, "If only I could destroy this and that about you which threatens or frustrates me in one way or another!" Wanting to change another person is always wanting to destroy at least part of him because that part is felt to be dangerously inconsistent with one's own personality.

The hating person cannot join in creating an affectionate interpersonal relationship because he cannot respond in a loving way. He says in effect, "I will love you only on condition that you will

* K. A. Menninger, *Love Against Hate* (New York: Harcourt, Brace, 1942).

do all these things for me." This cannot be love, for love must be an unconditional, spontaneous giving of one's self; no bribery, no enticement, no duress.

Hate often masquerades as love. The woman driving a man by nagging or insinuation into a profession for which he has little inclination, "Because I'm thinking of your own good, dear," is trying to destroy part of him in the hope of getting in exchange more money, or more freedom, or more social prestige for herself. The self-righteous father, luring or compelling his son into study in a field for which the boy has no interest, is a destroyer. The husband and wife, continually attacking each other in such words as, "The trouble with you is . . . ," are bent on emotional murder.

Hate develops from a continuing state of repressed anger over fears we refuse to recognize. Like a boil, it is an attempt to concentrate an emotional infection, and to throw it out of the system. It is the symptom of something wrong, and it is also the attempt to get well. For example: doing someone an injustice, and allowing it to go uncorrected, results in hating him as a means of hiding and throwing off the subconscious anger and contempt one feels for one's self for being guilty of the injustice.

Thus, it seems to me, a person cannot *truly* love and *truly* hate simultaneously. Ambivalent emotions are perverted emotions, not honest emotions. The probability is that we do not want to hate, but are forced into doing so by some blocking (either inside or outside the personality) which interferes with interpersonal relationships of confidence, cooperation, and love.*

Most of us are taught not to hate. We might as well be taught not to love. In being taught not to hate, seeds are sown which curtail love because spontaneity and emotional honesty are impaired. Everybody hates. Hatred is only love "tortured by its own hunger and thirst."** Instead of trying to deny the hatred, it would be more intelligent to recognize and to understand it. Unidentified

* This is illustrated in Figure 4 and discussed in detail beginning on page 77.

** This idea is interestingly developed in I. D. Suttie, *The Origins of Love and Hate* (London: Kegan Paul, Trench, Trubner and Co., reprinted 1945).

or misunderstood it cannot be wisely handled, and therefore, always harms its creator. Unresolved conflicts between love and hate lead to neurosis in which the individual feels helpless and without hope because there is no inner unity to his personality.

No two human beings can possibly live together in the most intimate emotional relationship known to man without sometimes frustrating each other. When love is blocked it turns to anger and hate. But change the situation a little, remove the frustration and affection pours out once more. Then comes the sweetness of making up after a quarrel. Nevertheless, the Fates should not be tempted by allowing this to happen often. Calmer ways of meeting frustration need to be developed.

In Conclusion

It is not possible to live much of a life alone. To live alone is to half live. To live selfishly is to fear living. To love is to live two lives, one's own and that of one's beloved. All of us need other people. But when two people use each other chiefly for compulsive reassurance, the result is exploitation. Any selfish motive is destructive even to a friendly relationship. For love, each must be willing to give fully and freely of himself, and to accept the other for what he is, not for what he can give. This is only possible where both are so emotionally mature and so close together in their attitude toward life, that deviations by either from behavior expected or desired by the other will almost never be felt as a threat to the personality of the other.

Where there is love, its concept and functioning will grow as the years go by. *The very experience of loving will lead to the discovery of how to love better.* Each individual will perceive more clearly ways in which to love. Nothing is ever static. It either grows or disintegrates. Where love is involved, the decay begins whenever there is real need and no healthy fulfillment. Where the underlying purpose of either is no longer to create conditions for both, love has gone. When growth stops, death begins—leaving in live bodies dead hearts, lifeless minds, and decomposing spirits. Having the capacity to love means nothing. It is only the ability to put capacity to productive use that counts.

We rub shoulders with thousands; we can share our hearts with few. But there is no substitute for love, just as there is no substitute for sex, and no substitute for marriage. The need for love is as universal as the need for bread. Without it, men seek money, or power, or fame, or a succession of phyically beautiful women— poor, impoverished, starved souls seeking to benumb their loneliness by picking up shiny, frosted crumbs under the table of life. Few of them face stark reality as Turgenev did when he said, "I would give up my fame and all my art if there were one woman who would care whether I came home late for dinner."

Love will not solve all problems. It does not stay the stars in their courses, or remove the necessity for work, or give back one's youth. It does provide the most nearly perfect environment: one in which our emotional needs are best fulfilled; one conducive to the cooperative solution of problems; one in which frustrations are held at a minimum because of the compatibility of mutual needs; one in which optimum, mutual, creative, self-expression is possible because it can be spontaneous.

Two people do not suddenly "fall in love." They develop it together over a long period of time. It must first germinate, then take root, grow, blossom, and be nourished by the necessary intellectual soil and emotional climate until at last the fruit can ripen year after year. It is only by such continuing development that the dreams of youth can become the reality of maturity.

Obviously the process must go on while suitor and sweetheart, husband and wife, parent and child, are apart as well as together. Obviously there must be testing, searching, appraising, to know where the relationship is, where it is headed, and how fast it is moving. There is no such thing as a sure-fire, quick determination of love. Many young people think so, but the sooner they feel convinced they are in love the more probably it is only infatuation. Love is patient preparation for happiness. Infatuation is haste to mate.

Love comes gradually. Its development, like that of a tree or a lady's slipper, it not a steady process but an irregular one. Those who expect love always to be the same are doomed to a disappointment which may lead to quarrels, broken engagements, or even suicide. Chill winds bring intermissions: leaves fall, ground freezes, bulbs are dormant. The art of love is patience till the spring returns. But what we have once loved can never be lost. Its influence on our personality is always with us, and perhaps even death does not take it away.

The only thing in the world as strong as love is truth, and there are reasons to believe that as far as marriage is concerned they are different aspects of the same thing. A deep and abiding love is the emotional response to an intellectual recognition of the truth about another person.

2

The Nature of Marriage

COMPONENTS

MARRIAGE is one of man's most ancient institutions. No culture is known which did not have it in some form. It has survived war, pestilence, migration, prosperity, and change because, of all the things that have been tried, nothing else gives so sound a basis for a decent civilization.

The wide variety of patterns by which a family is set up in different cultures is so amazing as to deserve a few paragraphs. We are not instinctively monogamous any more than we are instinctively polygamous, or polyandrous, or promiscuous. As La Barre says, "Man, in fact, has all the forms of marriage he has been able to think up. Nor will we be disposed to belittle his imagination, when we take a look at the facts."*

Polygamy was common with most of the North and South American Indians, and their marriage ceremony consisted of merely setting up housekeeping together. A Moslem is permitted four wives, providing he can financially afford so chastening an exposure to the difficulties of intense human relations.

* W. La Barre, *The Human Animal* (Chicago: University of Chicago Press, 1954), p. 111. See also pp. 110-31 for what follows.

Among the Nayars of Malabar the daughters of an extended family (group of female kin) are all married before puberty to the same man, at the same time. Three days later all are forthwith divorced. No remarriage is permitted. The men with whom the girls mate later are never considered as husbands and fathers. The head of a resulting family is the woman's oldest brother, and the legal father is the absent divorced individual, who positively could not be the biological parent.

In Tibet, Abyssina, portions of Persia, and parts of Arabia, one finds "term marriages," which last for a specified period only: perhaps a month, maybe twenty-four hours. Offspring are legitimate. Among the Mentawei of Indonesia, a man cannot marry until after he has a family of which to become the head. Otherwise, they feel, there is no point in marrying. After the ceremony he formally adopts his own sons!

There are cultures where polyandry is the normal and preferred form of marriage. In southern India a man's brothers share his wife. Indeed, Murdock found forty-one social orders in which this kind of fraternal connubial liberality was true.*

Eskimos believe marriage to be a one-man one-woman affair, but because the man owns the woman, as he does his dog team, he can lend her. This is no sordid affair, but the result of a hunter's inescapable need to have a woman to take care of skins, repair clothes, chew boots, etc., when he is on a long trip. The included sexual privileges are merely incidental.

There are other interesting systems, but anthropologists agree no human group exists without its particular sex restrictions. Complete freedom to be promiscuous does not exist anywhere because it does not work satisfactorily anywhere. Each culture has worked out what, for it, appear to be the most satisfactory set of rules. What is considered normal is not a universal pattern, not an average of all cultures, but an adaptation to the particular circumstances. We are, therefore, rightly concerned with our own accepted procedures.

* G. P. Murdock, *Social Structure* (New York: Macmillan, 1949), p. 25.

Our society says that marriage is a legal question. State legislatures, through laws and the courts, lay down certain qualifications to be fulfilled before people can marry, such as the necessity for a license, the achievement of a minimum age, a witnessed ceremony conducted by a legally qualified person, no other marriage already in existence, no close blood relationship between bride and groom (in many states first cousins cannot marry). These requirements are important, but they are not enough.

Marriage is a many-sided relationship between a man and a woman, intended in our culture to continue until interrupted by death; the legal, social, economic, religious, and emotional aspects of which provide—theoretically at least—the best circumstances under which to conceive and to rear children; at the same time, offering the maximum opportunity for the greatest number of adults to live well-rounded, happy lives as individuals. Marriage also provides a way of inheriting property. My family has a farm in Maine which has come down from father to son since the land was first taken from the Indians.

There are many ways of being married. One can be married physically, or financially, or intellectually, or emotionally, as well as legally. In the ideal situation, wedlock includes bonds in all these areas. Unhappy indeed is the couple where the bond is only legal. "What God hath joined" expresses an unwarranted assumption which would surely be characterized as such by omniscient wisdom. The idea that an agreement and a legal bond automatically confer happiness, because marriages are made in heaven by some mysterious and divine predestination, is sentimental tommyrot. Marriages are not made in heaven, but in the childhood home. If marriages are made in heaven, why do so many married people live in hell?

Much trouble arises from a failure to face the fact that marriage takes two people, and is never only one. The idea that there must be complete unity without disagreement fails to recognize that here is a composite of two. Indeed, the word component which heads this section, rightly used, stresses the separate identity and the distinguishable character of the various parts which comprise a whole.

From the historical point of view marriage developed out of the sex relation, first into a purely economic family, begun while man still lived by hunting. This carried over into the agricultural civilization, and finally grew into the complicated emotional relationship of our industrial time. In the modern world there are still whole cultures where the relation between husband and wife is largely sexual and economic. She is not his companion, but his servant and his concubine.

Certainly over the greater part of its history, marriage has been largely concerned with the production of things: children, tents, flocks, clothes, patchwork quilts, mincemeat, vegetables, cordwood, smoked ham, wool. As recently as 1789, when George Washington became the first president, 75 per cent of us lived by the use of our own property. Now only 14 per cent of us do. Power machinery has largely destroyed the family as a unit of production. No longer is there a spinning wheel in the kitchen and a loom in the back shed. We do not produce our own cloth, or bake our own bread, or preserve our own winter supply of vegetables. As a result many families own no real property. We are no longer posterity-minded, and the whole structure of family life has changed.

Still, 90 per cent of Americans marry. It is the normal thing. We marry because through the ages no other arrangement has proved as satisfactory in the division of the labor involved in making a home, as sacred in the sex relation, as wholesome in the bringing up of children, as rewarding in companionship, or as enjoyable in the social life of the community. To be sure, we sometimes marry because of pregnancy out of wedlock, or to escape an unhappy home, or because of money, or social prestige, or physical attraction. But these are not the reason why the institution of marriage is ageless despite hard realities and the heavy blows of fate. A good marriage is the best reason why a child is born and grows up looking to the past with gratitude and to the future with anticipation.

People who do not get married may be undersexed, or inhibited by the unhappiness of their childhood home, or prevented by parental interference, or diverted by a compulsion to concentrate on a career, or thwarted by a training which made intercourse an evil thing to be repressed, or even shackled by the devotion of carrying a torch for an individual who died or married someone else.

The basic forces which enter into the successful establishment and functioning of a marriage are many and varied. Marriage is fundamentally a problem of living happily together; a man and a woman united in the achievement of common goals to which they give their hopes, their thoughts, and their best efforts. They are two parts of the same team, with interlocking functions and inter-dependent powers which will lead to quarreling unless successfully inter-related.

Marriage is essentially an adjustment between a man and a woman who are happy or unhappy because of what they ARE. Success or failure is largely in terms of the ability to interweave interests. Sharing the affection of a goodbye kiss in the morning; quiet enjoyment of a loving embrace at the evening homecoming, so that each feels this is the moment the other has been waiting for all day, and now his life is complete and overflowing once more; darting little affectionate glances at each other while sharing the day's experiences; sitting together in the lamplight in wordless understanding: these are the pattern into which marriage should be woven, but the threads must be held together by the strands of love. The stronger the strands, the wider and deeper the sharing of experience. Every act becomes an act of love: making a bed, baking a pie, ironing a shirt, running slender fingers through his hair; saving patiently to be able to buy the new china she would like to have; wiping the dishes for her after she has entertained a business colleague; doing the baby's wash because she is behind in her work through no fault of her own. Homemaking *is* more than mere housekeeping.

The establishment of a physical and emotional communion between husband and wife is a time-consuming process. Any long-range purpose must be achieved in steps, each step constituting progress toward and a partial realization of the final objective. There will be many mileposts, but an ultimate goal is never reached. Progress toward it consists in seeing the problem as a whole, in detail, thought through to the end without distortion, and then concentrating on one step at a time. In marriage the fundamental steps are:

(1) Establishment of the antecedent conditions
(2) Courtship
(3) Engagement
(4) Marriage
(5) Mutual emotional adjustments
(6) Children.

These things require an ever-increasing capacity to accept and to fulfill responsibilities. During courtship the emphasis can be on tenderness and enjoyment. (It had better be something more, as we shall see later.) An engagement acknowledges the acceptance of obligations and duties, some of which are already in force. The wedding greatly increases the breadth, depth, and scope of these, and so does the coming of a child.

In a nice division of effort the wife should become a good home-maker and the husband a good provider. Her problem is one of organizing her work, scheduling her time so the housekeeping is accomplished efficiently, improving her quality. In the beginning, and again much later, she has a freedom to plan with a flexibility few men ever enjoy. She is her own boss in choosing what to spend money for, when to do the ironing, how long to visit a neighbor. She can decide what is important to do today and what is not. If she is not a good organizer, or if she lacks the character to be self-directing, she will not be a good housewife.

She may find with weary spirit that her husband's profession takes her to an unfamiliar climate amid strangers. Perhaps her experience as a banker's daughter presents difficulties to her as a clergyman's wife, or her roots—deep in the soil of a New Hampshire farm—seem never able to find nourishment in the nomadic life of a naval officer's family.

When the children come there will be no star dust of romance in changing a diaper for a crying baby at three o'clock in the morning, or having her schedule for the day disrupted, because junior has an upset stomach while she is trying to help her husband get on at the office by having the boss and his wife to dinner. She may find the restrictive ball and chain of a baby virtual imprisonment compared to the carefree days at college. What now? Will she drive the snake of monotony from her paradise by redecorating the nursery, or learning to reupholster the furniture, or becoming an expert on Chinese cooking?

He too will have problems. No longer can he be as unconcerned over the loss of his job, nor can he change jobs as easily. What has been first person planning and thinking must now become plural planning and thinking. If the other bills are to be paid, perhaps there is not money enough for the fall hunting trips he so enjoyed. There may be sudden expense because of the wife's illness, or because a baby is expected for whom neither clothing, crib, nor carriage has been provided, to say nothing of medical expenses.

He too may find that his company wants him to go to a new location, or that his wife is unable to adjust to the present one. Nor will there be any romance for him in walking the floor at 2:00 A.M. while he burps the baby.

For a loving relationship each must live up to his responsibilities with a willing heart. These change with the years. They also change when physical or emotional illness take their toll of anguish. But they are gladly undertaken.

The most competent people are usually the most happily married, for quality is never an accident. It comes as the result of wise choices based on good methods.

One other component, sometimes overlooked, stems from the people who, though not present, are nevertheless involved. One does marry the other person's family, at least to the degree that physical inheritance, intellectual and emotional background, social standing, tastes, standards, and the influence of some family friends, are affecting the situation. Perhaps some professor in a woman's college creates a troubling spirit as an aftermath of her implication that the smooth administration of household machinery is a bit degrading to anyone who has dipped into the perfection of Browning's poetry. Almost inevitably the husband will bring home the emotional indigestion caused by some curt remark from the boss. And where marriages have crossed religious lines, many a perceptive physician recognizes the illness brought to his office as an internal struggle between the vanity of inflexible dogma and the bonds of affection.

Some Prerequisites

There is far more to marriage than the warm fire of romantic attraction. Two people who successfully spend upwards of fifteen thousand days and night of intimacy together require the opportunity to be their spontaneous selves in full security; a mutual understanding of mind and heart which develops, strengthens, and completes both personalities.

There are price tags on these relationships, and few bargains. Whatever road we choose we pay a toll. Those who are able to seek only self-satisfaction at every turn, feel cheated in the end. If an individual sets up conditions which must be met in order for him to be happy, his chances are a gamble. Life does not always meet our demands. Those who want a good marriage must learn what a good marriage costs, and work to pay for it. The girl who can square dance, and swim, and play golf, but who lacks the energy to wash dishes or sweep floors usually wants what she likes without earning it. A person's body is never too tired to do whatever his emotions really want to do. The man who pays ardent court until he is married and then takes his wife for granted, will have a rude awakening one day. We pay for what we get, and get what we pay for. Usually we pay more than we originally intended, either because in our first estimates we did not realize the cost, or because we find we want additional things. This is as true in building a marriage as it is in building a house.

Husband and wife must enter the marriage with honest unity of purpose. The more things they care about in common, the closer together they will be in mind and emotion. This does not mean husband and wife cannot have special interests of their own. It does mean there cannot be a major conflict of those responses to life which determine our standards of value, for the atmosphere of the home is determined by the interweaving of the self-expression and the self-evaluation of its members. Mere agreement is not to be confused with emotional unity. There can be agreement despite loss of emotional unity, as when someone tilts his nose at angle theta with a "now-she-sees-I'm-right" air of virtue. And there can be disagreement with no loss of emotional unity, as when husband and wife sincerely seek to explain to each other their respective positions, with no attempt at coercion.

Unless there is to be a difficult and perhaps an impossible period of adjustment for both, husband and wife must enter the marriage with a common background by which to understand each other. Human relationships are the joint product of the observer and the observed. Where the two are not operating on the same standards, annoyance, and even distrust are bound to result.

We cannot correctly interpret behavior until we understand the emotion which prompted it. If Kenneth slaps Mildred on the shoulder in anger, she may boil over with resentment. If he does the same thing in fun, she may say, "Hello, darling." To Ben, "I'll do it later," may mean exactly that. To Helen these words may be a polite way of saying, "I neither wish nor intend to do it." To Ben, her use of the statement sounds like plain lying. Helen may tell a neighbor she has no sugar, when what she means is "Yes, I have some, but I do not care to lend it for your purpose." Ben would have said, "I have some, but not enough to share." What he means is exactly what Helen meant, but again, her words have no ring of truth to him.

When Helen says, "I'll take you to the opera," she may mean,

"I will do so unless some unexpected interference comes up which will spoil our fun." When Ben says the same thing, he may mean, "If I say I'll take you, I'll take you, come hell or high water! But if it is inconvenient, I'll make you suffer because of my compulsion to keep my promises." It is not the act, but the meaning of the act which is important.

Because we have no fixed and measurable standard background, it is all the more important for husband and wife to have a sure sense of each other's emotions. Is Phoebe's little speech mere flattery intended to influence and beguile because she wants something? Are Edgar's words of acid criticism uttered as a self-defense in the hope of pulling himself up by humiliating Phoebe, though there is no real cause for complaint in her behavior? Is Phoebe merely tired out? Is Edgar transferring to his wife anger actually carried over from a repressed boyhood hatred of his mother?

The satisfaction-seeking behavior of the husband will inevitably interfere with the satisfaction-seeking behavior of the wife, and vice versa, unless both bring to the marriage an ability to understand and to make reasonable adjustment to each other. A man and a woman reared in different ways of living, with habit patterns developed in different backgrounds, cannot be happily married short of a rare capacity for major readjustments.

These things will be discussed in the chapter on the criteria for choosing a mate and the chapter on emotional adjustments.

Attitudes Toward Marriage

Without realizing it, many people have an emotional attitude toward marriage akin to, "Now I shall have again the protection I enjoyed as a little child." It is true that a happy family is the highest of all sources of emotional security. It is true that marriage is the best method for a well-balanced person to effect emotional completion. It is true that we do not live by bread alone; with it we need companionship, laughter, mutuality of value standards. But so many brides and grooms expect a marriage to provide solutions for all the difficult struggles within their personalities. So many assume that it will no longer be necessary for them to stand on their own feet because now they are to have sanctuary, and happiness will follow safety.

Marriage provides a new atmosphere, but both husband and wife meet the same old problems of life, as well as some new ones— and do it with the same old behavior techniques. Each now has a new title role, but the parts assigned them by their parents during childhood have so typed their acting that each will play almost the same character as before. If they have the emotional maturity to be able to accept personal responsibilities, they will create together a healthy atmosphere in which both individuals will flourish and develop even more inner strength with which to meet problems. If they are not emotionally mature, if there is not true internal consistency in their personalities, the resulting inner conflicts will produce an unhealthy atmosphere in which each individual will frustrate the other, thus denying both an opportunity for spontaneous self-expression.

Far too many young people approach marriage with a romantic and egocentric attitude, full of daydreams which are concerned with *getting*, never with *giving*. They have not progressed emotionally beyond the "gimme" stage. Such an attitude is not only wishful thinking, it is turning the church aisle into a warpath. Here the desire for a happy home is only a desire for the benefits of a happy home, not a readiness to accept the responsibility and the work of producing the necessary conditions to create a happy home. This is expecting too much. Of course it leads to bitter disillusionment. Daydreaming of the end result, with no regard for means, is only silly sentimentalism.

Daydreams about marriage often have to do with:
   (1) Escape from an unhappy environment
   (2) Sexual satisfaction
   (3) Devoted "mothering" for the man, or "fathering" for the woman
   (4) Economic security and social status (for the woman).
Where there is daydreaming, it is not the reality of Barbara that

Albert is marrying, but a fantasy Albert has pictured. Nevertheless, she can only be herself, as he will surely find out sooner or later. Then comes bewilderment, disappointment, anger. He thought Barbara was a goddess, and behold, she is only a human being, afraid of mice and thunderstorms, wanting to spend money for things which seem to him inconsequential, running the house in ways that backslide from the true faith exemplified by his mother, simmering in resentment on occasion, objecting to his habit of reading the paper at the breakfast table, telling him the neighborhood gossip but turning on the radio when he starts to talk about the office. It is a great shock to waken to this reality and to discover that marriage is not what he thought it would be. There is cruel tragedy in it. But the trouble is not with marriage. The trouble is with a civilization which permits, and to some degree encourages, the stupidity of believing happy marriage is given us like a Christmas present. Why think of marriage only in terms of pleasure? No one approaches a profession that way. Happiness is not a right we possess, it must be earned, and as always, the best rewards come after years of effort.

If a happy home is to be established, the attitude of its members toward each other must be like that of an ardent gardener toward a rare plant. In order to create the conditions most favorable to its growth he will draw on—or develop—a background of knowledge as to the conditions needed by the plant. He will joyfully fulfill these needs to the best of his ability, and rejoice in watching the precious thing grow—partially because of his efforts. He can appreciate and enjoy praise for his effort but the praise is not the thing he is seeking.

Anyone going into marriage with the expectation of being thanked for bringing home the bacon—even against dismaying odds —or for shining the ancestral silver tea service till it glistens from the buffet in little pinwheels of light, is headed for heartache. Doing anything in order to be thanked constitutes emotionally dishonest giving, and is a symptom of feelings of inferiority. Emotionally honest rewards are in inner satisfaction, not in exterior flattery. The more intently we expect a future reward for what we give, the more positive is the indication that we are not finding adequate self-expression and self-evaluation in everyday living. Unsatisfied inner emotions lead to forcing, or bribing, someone else to give us substitute outer satisfactions in the form of some kind of power. To remind a husband, or a wife, or a child of something which has been done for him, is an indirect way of accusing him of being ungrateful. Asking for gratitude is asking for admitted indebtedness, which is indirectly asking for power over someone. A person can properly want "to bite the hand that feeds him" when he is being humiliated because of this kind of subserviency.

On the other hand, where a person (like our gardener) is experiencing adequate self-realization, praise for his effort is relatively unimportant to him.

There are individuals who look upon marriage as a bondage. "A husband would throttle my personality. I want a career! I don't want to be dependent on a man," says Julia with mixed belligerence, bewilderment, and still unquenched hope. "Marry? Not me!" says Charles, "I want my freedom! I don't want any woman for a millstone around my neck." As though forty years in the wilderness were preferable to the responsibilities of a family! Anyone who has ever known the incommunicable companionship, the togetherness, the complete sharing of a happy marriage does not talk about "freedom" or "careers." Few of us—men or women—have careers. We just work. Few of us think beyond the adolescent notion that freedom is escape from the domination of some powerful and restrictive person. We forget that freedom implies the ability and the willingness to be responsible for ourselves.

The truth is that we give up one kind of freedom for the sake of a better one. We exchange our freedom to drive with thoughtless abandon across a busy street intersection for the more important freedom of immunity from accidents. We give up the irresponsibility of single blessedness to merit the far more worthwhile privileges of marriage.

Unfortunate childhood experiences have led the bachelor and

the career girl to believe that marriage is some sort of bondage. What they saw in childhood and adolescence was their inability to live a rich, full life in a family group because those around them were not working together for the same things in about the same way. Happiness and unhappiness are contagious, although resistance or susceptibility will influence the degree to which a person is affected. Neither the persistent bachelor nor the career girl experienced the freedom of togetherness. They must have grown up in families which operated on the principles of collectivism more than in the spirit of co-operation. Co-operation with a willing heart is the condition of real freedom. Marriage should be the completion of two people, not the competition of two people; husband and wife supplementing each other in creative self-expression by planning, overcoming obstacles, and contemplating results; a co-operativeness enriching every day with self-fulfillment. But beware confusing the business man whose wife is merely his social hostess, with two people thinking, yearning, developing, achieving together.

For togetherness, people must be on the same track, going in the same direction, at about the same rate of speed. Parallel tracks are not enough. They can be half a world apart. Give and take is not enough. Only sharing will suffice, because sharing requires the mutual participation of both to a degree beyond mere exchange.

Neither the perennial bachelor nor the determined career girl is able to participate, freely and fully, with someone else. The reason, as has already been pointed out, is that their own emotional needs have not yet been satisfied, and they cannot give from poverty. The paradox is that they cannot love until their needs are satisfied, and they cannot satisfy their needs until they do love.

The great human tragedy is this appalling trap which captures us. We cannot pour out our affection until we have received affection, and only the little child has the right to receive without pouring out. If only we were really loved in childhood! The hope of those of us who were not lies first in honestly facing our predicament, and then in finding competent help in the rare friend who cares and understands, or the wise counselor who can show us the way to salvation.

Whenever a person cannot achieve the freedom of togetherness, he will try to get his freedom by avoiding close relationships, yet pretending them in daydreams and rebellious reveries which involve, but do not in reality include, other people. The result is an even worse bondage. What self-deception and betrayal! Only . through constructive relatedness to other people is it possible to develop and to enrich the personality. In all proper relationships there is no surrender by anyone to anyone. Where there is domination or enticement, the result is frustration and rebellion—either overt or disguised.

Fundamentally, the real responsibility of husband and wife to each other lies in responsibility to the self. When Roger tries to give up drinking to please Nancy, he fails because of the false responsibility to her for his self-respect. This will lead to hating her. Where we are dependent instead of co-operative, we always hate. When Roger wants to stop drinking because *he* wants to change, never mind what anyone else thinks, success is possible.

But Roger will find it difficult to face himself as the villain of his own suffering. Until a person learns how to cope with it successfully, nothing is more terrifying than the need to admit responsibility for one's own unhappiness. We are mistaken in the appraisal of most of our thoughts and deeds because of the diabolically clever plots and rationalizations we create in order to transfer blame to someone else and thus keep from blaming ourselves.

A real marriage has as its basis permanent and harmonious attitudes of co-operation. These can flourish and grow only in terms of each partner taking full responsibility for his own emotional reactions. No life is completely serene and untroubled by frustration, inner sadness, or despondency. No marriage is strong at the outset. It starts to flourish and grow only after fusion begins. It has to be challenged by differences of opinion, obstacles, and disappointments in order to grow strong. Differences and obstacles and disappointments are not to be confused with suffering.

If the marriage is worth much, both partners will become happier, more emotionally mature, more self-confident and spontaneous. This is impossible unless they have the right raw materials to start with: a knowledge of sound principles of human relations, good method in applying them, and the vision of attainable objectives sincerely desired by both. Such developments are not random and confused, but planned and purposeful. Marriage cannot be expected to run by wishful thinking. The interlocking leadership and the interweaving responsibilities of husband and wife must be constructive, and this constructive action is part of a thought-out, adequate process.

ORGANIZATION

A home is an organized social unit and should be run by criteria of good organization. The prime mover in any organized effort is leadership with the vision of an objective, and the ability to influence other people to work together willingly for its accomplishment. But nothing happens until there is work done. It cannot be all executives and no production.

The art and science of good management, either at home or in the office, consists of bringing into effective unity the two major aspects of organization: right emotional relationships between the participants, and a formalized structure of responsibilities which makes for the optimum productive use of each person's abilities in a self-respecting status.

Much has already been said about emotional relationships because these precede and underlie the formalized structure of any organization. No two (or more) people can be in association without experiencing emotions, many of them unrecognized, which determine individual and group behavior. The most important adjustments in marriage, as well as in all other organized relationships, are emotional, but the resulting companionship, the spiritual loveliness that enriches every day with understanding, is rare outside the family circle. Where else is a person continually able to express his real self to other people, often given things without having to ask for them, and blessed with the courage to overcome many disappointments because of a feeling of togetherness?

As for responsibilities and authorities, husband and wife play many different and mutually overlapping parts—a worker here, the purchasing agent there, both worker and executive somewhere else, clear lines of responsibility for this, no lines whatsoever of authority for that. So many confused and interlocking parts, all involved in each other, make an organization chart practically impossible. But marriage can be made to work if husband and wife have a good sense of administration and are sincerely motivated by a desire for togetherness. Like a watch, the marriage works because of the right relationship of its parts, not just because the parts are there. The elements of a watch—springs, bearings, gears, castings, case, hands —can be gathered on a table, but until they are arranged in the co-operative relationship intended by their creator, and are properly lubricated and activated, they have no meaning.

Relatedness is the law of the whole universe. The stars in their courses are related by gravitational forces. The components of an atom revolve around a nucleus in definite kinship. The pull of the moon produces tides in the ocean, which create friction on the earth's surface and thus slow down its speed of revolution by a thousandth of a second per century. This, in turn, results in the moon pulling away from the earth seven feet a century. Failure of the rice crop in Louisiana brings hardship in China. Father finds outlet for his anger over a disagreeable incident at the office by an unwarranted attack on Junior at the dinner table. Good relatedness succeeds. Wrong relatedness fails. Isolation is impossible.

The family is an organization in which two sexes, and often two or more generations at a time, face this problem of relatedness in the creation of a common atmosphere. They exercise influence upon each other, varying from outright force, through calculated persuasion, to a spontaneous effort to find the truth together. They consciously and subconsciously impose difficulties upon one another. They invent outlets for individual self-expression. They undertake a wide variety of responsibilities.

FAMILY ORGANIZATION COMPARED TO FACTORY ORGANIZATION

If the members of a family are to work together with willing hearts, their efforts must be intelligently organized and inter-related. Improper inter-relation is like connecting the distributor of an automobile so that sparks enter the cylinders in the wrong sequence. The engine only backfires. Correctly connected, the distributor helps to produce power. Correctly interrelated the members of a family help to produce co-operative effort. But a definite structure of formalized responsibility, divided in agreed and acceptable ways, is as difficult and complex as that of any factory.

The production units of a family are commingled; mother in the kitchen, father in the office, children in the back yard, and all of them in the living room. There are divided responsibilities with an accompanying uncertainty as to authority. The family has vertical relationships, similar to those between executives and workmen, which sometimes turn vice versa as they never do in a factory. There are horizontal relationships—like those between factory manager and treasurer—which fluctuate between husband and wife because production and spending reside in either or in both. There are diagonal relationships, which are neither those of superior to subordinate nor of co-equals, but between individuals on different levels of differing lines of authority. The purchasing agent and the foreman of the machine shop would be a factory example. The husband doing an errand for his mother-in-law would be a family example. There are multiple informal relationships, like a "Good morning," in the factory or a goodnight kiss in the home, involving neither authority nor responsibility, but resulting simply from the fact that people are living or working together in intimate association. These informal relationships constitute a network of prime importance in the transmission of those emotional attitudes and influences which determine the prevailing mood of the family as well as the factory. They should be used as a means of developing constructive emotional attitudes, and therefore a stronger common willingness.

The impossibility of establishing harmonious relations amid such a tangled complexity of interlocking functions is at once apparent where there are immature emotional attitudes, a contest for power, no common background, or no common responsibility for results. Even in the office and the factory, those who successfully exercise authority to do so through their:

(1) Ability to make men want to follow them with a willing heart

(2) Technical knowledge of the job

(3) Desire to assume responsibility for the proper performance of the job.

Authority always stems from responsibility, never vice versa. These should also be co-terminous and co-equal. Many people think that authority can be conferred on a person by some superior. This is a delusion. What is conferred is responsibility. The authority must be earned. How much authority does a plant manager have during a strike? None. He still has the responsibility to run the plant. His authority must be earned from the men under him. If the wife is to have authority in the kitchen she must earn it. If the husband is to have authority in the cellar he must earn it. Otherwise there will be a domestic strike of more or less importance.

In the home, as in industry, the authority of leadership is accorded only where trust has first been earned, and trust is always dependent on accomplishment, both as to technical competence and acceptability of manner. Trust is slowly earned and easily destroyed. As husband and wife inspire trust, agreement will be given to each other's desires. What is trust? Confidence that the plans and procedures of the other person not only safeguard but embrace one's own.

There must be both good organizational design and right administration if the family is to produce the circumstances under which it can run smoothly. These include:

(A) Conditions which will assure

(1) A wholesome means of satisfying the reasonable desire of each member of the family

(2) Acceptable techniques for resolving what would otherwise be frustrating circumstances*

(3) Effective opportunities for and use of each person's ability to see each problem in its relation to the whole, leading to mutual understanding

(B) Relationships—physical and emotional—so organized that everyone has

(1) A self-respecting status

(2) Effective use of specialized abilities, including outlets for spontaneous, creative self-expression

(3) Valid interrelation with the other members of the family so that activities are correctly integrated and correlated.

Where this is successfully accomplished, even though the members of the family have common responsibility for results, each will stick to his valid functions. The marriage will operate like a factory in which the purchasing agent purchases, the production manager produces, the sales manager sells. There is no other way to guarantee everyone a self-respecting status, common understanding, and the resolution of conflict by good method.

In the family the problem is emotionally somewhat more complex than in the factory because, short of the tyranny of a patriarchal family, there is no objective point at which the wife ceases to be and the husband becomes the purchasing agent. Both occupy the office. There is also no single top executive who listens to the differing points of view of department heads, integrates them, ponders the situation as a whole, and determines what each member of the organization shall do regarding the matter in hand. Neither husband nor wife is the head of the house; they both lead— separately in some respects, together in others.

There must be a continual understanding between them of how any decision or action affects, or is in turn affected by whatever

* A recognized specialist in human relations has a dart game in the back yard for his children, the target being a caricature of himself labeled "Dad." The children can work off a frustration by throwing the darts . . . and they do!

else is going on. What needs to be done? In what order? Why?
What are the limiting factors inherent in the proposed procedure?
What factors facilitate it? How do they interrelate? Without a
clear concept of what these elements add up to, the family will
soon become confused, frustrated, and quarrelsome.

If the household machinery is to function smoothly, it must
follow an articulated procedure. The steps needed to carry out
any plan affecting the family must be so related as to produce a
logical, effective whole. The steps must be properly interrelated,
and in the correct order. Establishment of agreement as to what
is to be done and how will always precede the attempt to do it.
Nor is understanding at one level of the family enough. Everybody
should understand. This sometimes requires skill and effort on the
part of husband, or wife, or both. It is even more essential where
children are involved.

Like all successful executives, husband and wife must use good
method in analyzing their problems. They must:

(1) Get the facts, and be sure that the facts they get are valid,
objective, reliable, and reasonably complete

(2) Think about the facts inclusively enough and penetra-
tively enough to perceive the true relationship of the facts.
What is important and what is not?

(3) Determine the fundamental problem. (In human relations, *what seems at first to be the trouble is almost never
the real trouble.*)

(4) Determine the principles by which the problem can best
be solved

(5) Determine how best to apply these principles in this particular case.

The wife is a partner in all this, not just a mother, or a sister, or a
concubine, or the household manager. Husband and wife should
make hundreds of decisions together each month; some trivial,
some important. "Shall we go to the movies tonight or call on
the Smiths? Should Junior have his tonsils out? Is Betty to be
allowed to go out with the Jones boy again after his not seeing her

all the way home the other night? Shall we accept the business opportunity in Milwaukee?" . . . an intimate, personal relation of consultation and decision.

If the household administration is not an integrated effort, it fails because it is power politics, not sound management. It has changed the "develop, direct, and control" (in the sense of keeping within the bounds of what is necessary and proper) of good administration, into the "exploit, order, and dominate" of scheming self-interest. When administrative integrity is lost in one area, it is soon likely to be lost in all areas. Certainly the minute administrative responsibility is neglected, or administrative power is abused, it is not management any more, but merely the basis for fear, frustration, and conflict. This is as true in the home as in the factory.

Finally, if the family organization is to be run in such a way as to relax tensions and encourage spontaneous (not impulsive) behavior, it must be run through mutually instructive, cross-education; not by domination. Only in this way can each understand and appreciate what the others are up against and why. Where there is no coercion they will want to know.

THE PATRIARCHAL FAMILY

Clearly the organization of family relationships is a matter of great complexity. The only way to make it simple is by the use of domination, which is what happened in the old patriarchal family. The wife and children were subject to the authority of the husband, even in the disposition of their leisure time. In Western civilization the family has traditionally been patriarchal, but it now has undergone many modifications.

A dictator, be he on the throne, or on the threshold of a home, is creating a psychologically wrong situation. He says, in effect, "Be good, and I will reward you. Disobey, and you will be punished." If he gets his way by domination, the other members of the family will recognize the source of their frustrations, and hate him because they fear him. (What they want is to love and to be loved by him.) If he gets his way by enticement, it will be almost impossible for the family to recognize *consciously* what is happening. Subconsciously they will recognize the bribery. Below the level of awareness they will hate themselves for accepting and him for offering the bribe. Above that level they will feel they ought to love him—without knowing why they cannot.

This results in a demoralizing ambivalence which leads straight into loss of emotional unity within the personality. Within the family there is no interflow of ideas, no co-ordination of desires, no mutuality of decision; only exercise of power on the one hand, and subservience on the other. Here is intimacy, often without understanding or consideration. Here, too, are unsatisfied emotional needs which tend to dominate the character of the relationship between husband and wife (and children). *Intimacy cannot be separated from understanding without destroying love.*

For a family organization to hold together, the core values uniting its members must be strong enough and inclusive enough to withstand the disintegrative forces which attack it. The patriarchal family lacks any such strength with which to combat the individualistic trends of our culture. The "whither thou goest, I will go; and where thou lodgest, I will lodge; thy people shall be my people, and thy God my God," of Ruth to Naomi is not for our generation. No longer are there many exclusively masculine spheres or many restrictive feminine ones. Everyone, including the child, has power, and left to himself will go his own independent way, pursuing his own divergent interests.

THE INDEPENDENT FAMILY

In the attempt to escape from the subserviency and dependence of the patriarchal family, many of us have jumped all the way to the opposite error, thus missing the strength and joy of co-operation for the sake of pursuing the mirage of complete independence. We lack emotional relatedness to one another; we are not subject to the rules or control of the "head of the house"; we attempt to stand alone with utter detachment.

Under these circumstances it is inevitable that the home should be changing in America. It did in Athens during the Golden Age of Pericles, and it did several centuries after Christ among the Romans. Infidelity, divorce, abortion, and homosexuality are all on the increase as a result. The outstanding difference between what is happening to us, and what did happen to the Greeks and Romans is that they were honest about their behavior, whereas we hide the truth about ours.

The family should be a co-operative unit, uniting for the sake of mutual assistance, acting together for a common cause, willingly undertaken by its various members, and in the varying ways and varying degrees which are most advantageous to the individual as well as to the family group.

Nobody can be really independent. Thoreau sang the virtues of independence as he built his solitary hermitage by the shores of Walden Pond . . . using an axe made by the co-operative efforts of several other men! Nobody can be independent, particularly in a successful family organization. To attempt it is to lose both the strength and the freedom of togetherness.

THE CO-OPERATIVE FAMILY

The only valid basis for the existence of any organization— family, factory, or nation—is to create a mutually desired final result in terms of the coordinated action of its members toward their objective. This means:

(1) Coordinated desires (shared planning on appropriate levels, of what the objectives ought to be)

(2) Coordinated decisions (settlement, again on appropriate levels, of what, where, when, how, by whom the job is to be done)

(3) Coordinated action (each doing his job at the right time in the right way).

Under these circumstances, the operation of the family (or factory, or nation) would result from an interflow of ideas, attitudes, problems, and mutually arrived-at solutions which integrate them into the most reasonable and effective action *over the long run.*

This is co-operation. This is an emotionally secure relationship, not a threatening or frustrating one. This is respect for personalities and personality differences, so that each individual can work in the area of his aptitudes. This is equal concern for one's own legitimate interests and the further needs and desires of the others. This is properly relating people because it first distinguishes among their abilities, weaknesses, wants. This is achieving unity because it recognizes that the whole consists of separate and distinct parts which must be correctly related. This is mutual help, mutual encouragement, continual adjustment on each level of experience, stemming from—and in turn re-creating—right emotional relationships.

Using authority is no hallmark of a good administrator. Whenever an executive only wants to have his own way, he is no longer an executive but at best a manipulator, a contriver, a demagogue. At worst he is a tyrant.

Marriage should be two people (three the very day the first child arrives) working together for coordination of desires, coordination of decisions, coordination of actions. Let me repeat, this can only be done by respecting the criteria of good organization.

COORDINATION OF DESIRES

Man is a continuously wanting animal. Not only are most of his desires repetitive, they are inseparably interdependent. An individual is only half alive if physically fed and emotionally starved. Thus the physical and the psychological combine to make psycho-biological life on a cultural level—something more complicated than the mere animal level. The physical and the psychological are not always simultaneous in operation, but they are always concomitant.

Naturally some needs are ordinarily more important than others because more fundamental to the preservation of life or of the personality. Material well-being is necessary for contentment and happiness. But physical self-preservation is by no means invariably the individual's primary concern. If it were, there would be no suicides and no soldiers. A man will sometimes prefer to destroy himself physically rather than to suffer longer the psychological havoc and emotional demolition he is experiencing. But whatever the existing relationship between physical and emotional self-

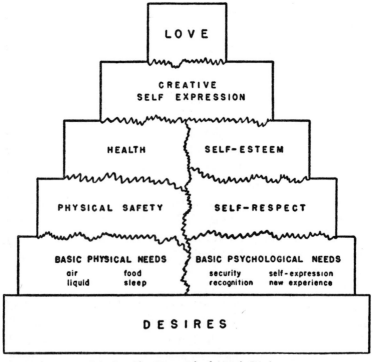

Fig. 3.   The Pyramid of Man's Desires

preservation, these two objectives are always the foundation stones at the base of man's pyramid of desires (Figure 3). The starving man has little concern for anything except food, air, water, and sleep. Something to eat becomes far more important to him than physical safety. His body begs to be fed, and his mind is filled with schemes—often involving great danger—to secure food. It is also filled with terror that his efforts will fail. The physical and the emotional cannot be separated, but have an interlocking relationship within themselves and with each other, as has been indicated by the irregular division lines in Figure 3.

Once these bare physical needs are reasonably sure of satisfaction, other desires will gradually emerge. It is not necessary for a need to be wholly satisfied before going on to the next. Gradually desires evolve from one another. Which need arises is based as much upon what the individual already possesses as upon what he does not have. Gratification can be as truly a stimulus as deprivation. After a meal, a person is not concerned with food unless he does not know where the next meal is coming from. He wants to go back to work, to read the paper, or to go for a ride with his girl.

When the needs for sustaining life have been reasonably met, what men want next is security; physical and emotional. Most of the individuals in America have had physical security, although now the atom bomb and rumors of more war have lessened our confidence in it. Men have not had an equivalent emotional security, the basis of which must be self-respect. Much of this is due to fears instilled in us during childhood. Because of the criticism, unfairness, domination, inconsistencies of parents, many of us grow up to see other people as threats instead of as co-operators. What should have been years of growing self-confidence, self-reliance, self-realization, trust in others, were years when fear bedeviled developing personalities. Frustrations built repressed anger. Emotional growth was sometimes a frantic endeavor to escape co-operation because it might conceal a threat.

In our culture many people resort to excessive expressions of security-seeking behavior. Over-eating, continuous talk, selfishness, psychosomatic illness are all examples.

Emotional security is compounded of many elements, the order of which would be a matter of controversy among the psychologists.* My feeling is that self-respect comes first. This belief in his

* A. H. Maslow, "A Theory of Human Motivation," *Psychological Review*, Vol. 50, No. 4 (July 1943), pp. 370-96.

own fundamental goodness is a quality with which every normal child is born, often to lose it when he is brought up on a battlefield. Certainly everyone has a lifelong desire to be given a self-respecting status. After self-respect, soundly based on an adequate expression of one's real capacities, the next unfolding need is for the respect of others.* We want the approval of the group to which we belong. We want to be appreciated, to feel important because we can participate—on our appropriate level—in the activities of our environment, and so to have a sense of belongingness, prestige, self-esteem. Whereas self-respect comes from confidence within the personality, self-esteem comes from the opinions of others.

Trouble results when self-esteem is used as a substitute for self-respect. Under these circumstances the center of gravity of the personality is outside the individual and in the keeping of the significant persons in his environment. What he thinks of himself is in terms of what they make him think they think, not in terms of what he feels is the truth. Self-esteem would never allow him to be disagreeable. Self-respect makes disagreeable behavior perfectly possible, provided that the individual feels it is right under the circumstances.

Is it not clear that he who replaces self-respect with self-esteem is a lost soul? The two qualities, like all the others in man's pyramid of desires, should be properly inter-related into a proper whole. When this happens, the individual achieves a feeling of self-confidence, worth, strength. When it does not, his feelings of weakness, inferiority, discouragement, uselessness will find compensation in habitual fighting, habitual submission, habitual detachment from other people, or some such neurotic behavior.

Given the satisfaction of bodily needs, physical safety, physical adequacy in the form of good health and stimulating exercise, self-respect, and self-esteem, the individual will then consciously want opportunity for creative self-expression, the chance to turn poten-

* Some psychologists believe the individual is not conscious of himself as a self until age two or three, and that his ideas of himself are made up of the reflected appraisals of others. Even if this be true on the conscious level, it certainly is not true on the subconscious level.

tialities into actualities. Creative self-expression is the highest manifestation of freedom. The hen lays eggs, the spider spins webs, the wood thrush sings songs. Each creates according to his inheritance. Similarly, where an individual does not face such disturbing hazards as lack of food or physical security, where he feels emotionally safe, he will want to become creatively self-expressive according to his talents. For most of us this will not go beyond modest accomplishments. Nevertheless, if they are to be happy together, it is of great importance that the interaction of what constitutes creative self-expression for the husband and for the wife be harmoniously correlated.

Direct, personal self-fulfillment resulting from the accomplishment of something worth while, leads to the final need in our pyramid of desires: the need for self-fulfillment through love and through the happiness of those we love. This has regenerative power which augments and intensifies all capacities upon which it rests.

All behavior tends to be influenced by *all* the basic needs. A dinner party can be far more than just the process of sustaining life. It may also involve creative self-expression on the part of the wife, the husband's self-esteem because of pride in her qualities as a hostess, increased emotional security because of a favorable reaction on the part of a business associate, and an expression of love between husband and wife because of their working together to make the dinner a success for both. In a single situation it is possible to find fulfillment of practically every requirement in the pyramid of desires.

Conscious desires are only symptoms of more basic needs. The wife's conscious desire for a fur coat may be no more than wanting to possess a warm garment. Subconsciously she may be wanting reassurance that her husband still loves her, or wanting added self-esteem at the Woman's Club. If the basic need is for a warm garment, whether or not the material is fur becomes relatively unimportant. If the basic need is for reassurance, fur seems of great importance. But she does not really need a mink coat. The only thing that needs a mink coat is the mink. For husband or wife to take every desire at it face value is to be misled into drawing mistaken conclusions. Desires can even be inconsistent on the surface and we must learn to distinguish between them.

When deprived of two or more needs, the individual will always seek whichever is for him the more basic at the time. Again, things have meaning only in terms of relatedness. The lesser needs are forgotten or perhaps renounced. But whenever one need is reasonably satisfied—together with reasonable expectation of continuing future satisfaction—the next higher need in the pyramid will beg for attention.

Man is not only a perpetually wanting animal, he is also an animal of many wants. To be "a good provider" is not enough to satisfy a wife or a child. To be a good housekeeper is not enough to satisfy a husband or a baby. We need emotional vitamins as much as we need groceries. To have food is to want something more, until the whole pyramid has been satisfied. If we cannot get good food, we will eat infected food, which sooner or later results in physical illness. If we do not have good emotional outlets, we will take psychologically wrong ones, which sooner or later lead to emotional illness.

The pyramid cannot be satisfied once and for all, because needs are recurrent. Today's breakfast or affectionate relationships will not suffice for tomorrow's wants. Thus, a person who is fundamentally satisfied will have capacity for further desires, but little imperious desire. He will be satisfied exactly as a continually watered garden will never be parched. Except in occasional passing moments he will have no imperative food needs, liquid needs, sleep needs, sex needs, safety needs, self-respect needs, self-esteem needs, creative self-expression needs, love needs.

On the other hand, greatly frustrated for any length of time, a person will become emotionally ill. Thwarting unimportant needs produces no trouble; thwarting basic needs always does. A physical threat at once also becomes an emotional one against which emotional defenses are erected.

Husband and wife have the responsibility of making reasonable and emotionally honest adjustments to, as well as contributions to, each other's pyramid of desires. The husband wants a combined companion, cook, hostess, dressmaker, purchasing agent, mistress, bridge partner, nurse, governess, and comforter among other things. The wife wants a combined lover, protector, household handyman, provider, squire, and father of her children. For either to fail in any one of these roles may result in frustration and trouble. What is just right for one, may be too much or too little for the other; what is satiation for one may leave hunger in the other. Husband and wife may develop mentally and spiritually at differing rates of speed, or in different directions. His enthusiasm may retain its spontaneity while hers stagnates—or vice versa. The happy family results when both desire to go in the same direction at nearly the same speed, and can co-ordinate their decisions and actions in doing so. This does not mean their views must be the same. It does mean they cannot be widely divergent in important matters to the point where intimate understanding is difficult or impossible. But there is always the necessity of understanding those who are not like ourselves, particularly in marriage.

That which is already complicated becomes increasingly complicated with the advent of children. Each member of the family desires many things from the others. In the beginning there are only two interpersonal reactions: husband to wife and wife to husband. With the advent of one child there are six: husband to wife, wife to husband, mother to child, child to mother, father to child, child to father. With two children there are twelve relationships, with three children there are twenty. No wonder the family experiences more than occasional tremors of dissatisfaction where its co-ordination of desires is not good.

COORDINATION OF DECISIONS

In the home, as in every other organization, decisions must be made, and it is necessary to decide who will be the decider in the several areas. Otherwise there can be no functional integrity. A husband reversing the wife's arrangement of her kitchen is like the sales manager of a manufacturing plant reversing the superintendent's instructions to the master mechanic.

On the other hand, people who love each other want to share many decisions because they affect the family. It must be so from the very nature of love. There is no other way in which family action can rest on family purpose, although it often takes time to arrive at an agreement on family purpose which coerces no one.

Where each person is concerned only in his personal domain, and is ignorant or indifferent to the family objective—or, worse still, there is no planned objective—there can be no co-operation. No family can achieve an objective in terms of coordinated action unless first there are coordinated decisions. These decisions should be participated in by all those who have responsibility "to get other people to do," and fully explained to those who, in the particular situation, have the responsibility of "doing."

With differing activities, the source of final authority should change from person to person. How the saucepans shall be stored is clearly the wife's department, although the husband may participate to the extent of tendering his knowledge of packaging, or of time and motion studies. Where the family is to live will be principally determined by where the husband's work takes him, although the whole family—children included—should be consulted. When father attempts to assist Junior in the construction of a tree house, Junior's decisions should be final except where matters of safety are involved. Father must be particularly careful here about making suggestions because the age difference and previous disciplining makes what to him is no more than a proposal seem a polite command to Junior. Each member of the household should have a voice in where the family goes for its vacation, or they will not be able to understand fully or to accept the decision easily.

Decisions should be based on the common problem, the long run problem, and the situation as a whole. If the problem is family-wide, the solution must be family-wide. To deny husband, or wife, or child the right to participate on his appropriate level, is to interfere with his self-esteem, and perhaps with his self-respect. This will influence all the blocks in his pyramid of desires which depend upon self-respect for their support and stability. Deprived of healthy self-respect, an individual will seek a spurious feeling of being worth while by dominating someone else, rebelling, retreating into daydreams, or becoming completely submissive.

Each member of the family should give attention to arriving at decisions which will contribute to the happiness of all. Some kind of reciprocity is the very basis of human relations. Happy marriage is not for the man or woman who cannot endure having his decisions disrupted or revised by someone else's plans. There must be attention to the interplay between desires, abilities, and goals. If any member of the group has to drive himself to the effort, it will not be a success.

There are, of course, always obstacles to be recognized and overcome. One must not expect too much of marriage. Minor disagreements are inevitable. But neither agreement nor disagreement are permanent, any more than success or failure are permanent. Disagreement or failure are fatal only when no one picks up the pieces and starts on again. Nevertheless, people, frustrated by each other, will punish each other in some way. If mother commands Junior to wear his rubbers, he may achieve an indirect revenge by forgetting to do her errand on the way home from school. She will scold, but this is proof that his forgetting hurt. Even if she compels him to go back to the store, he has had the satisfaction of annoying her and of temporarily defying her, although he will not usually be aware of this on a conscious level.

Once decisions are made, the mature individual will take full responsibility for them. He will recognize, admit, and correct mistakes without hesitation. Because the parents of some of us were critical and domineering, we fear the penalty of a mistake and shovel sand over our eyes by refusing to admit an error. Thus are the iniquities of the fathers visited unto the children. Thus everyone pays the double price of his parents' mistakes as well as his own, none more fully than those who refuse to recognize and to correct them.

COORDINATION OF ACTION

Where desires and decisions have been honestly coordinated, unity of action should follow as a corollary. But because actions are always motivated by feelings, unity may not take place. The reality of a marriage is a history of its actual behavior. It is what husband and wife feel and do, not what they say, that determines how the family develops. Reality is to be found in actions, not in theory, not in idealism, not in talk.

So often the young bride wonders, "What am I going to say to him to get him to clean up that cellar?" This gradually progresses toward, "What am I going to do to him?" The only effective long-run approach is to ask, "What am I feeling? Why am I feeling it? What do I want to feel? What should I do to have that feeling?" What she ought to want is a constructive sense of togetherness, and it may be that the only way to have it in this particular situation with this particular man is glady and without vindictiveness to clean the cellar herself. No doubt he has to do some comparable thing for her. This is not ideal, but neither are people.

There is some friction in the meshing of any machinery, mechanical or emotional, and therefore, the interlocking action of individual self-expression cannot be expected to take place without some disagreement. But there is such a difference between those who usually co-operate lovingly and those who usually snatch privileges while seeking to escape duties. When the husband has tried to save a little money, as well as perhaps to find creative self-expression, by making a needed set of shelves for the home, his wife may say, "You just gather up your tools. I'll take care of sweeping up the kitchen." Or, with melting glance and corrosive tongue she may snarl, "Why don't you clean up the mess you make!" The difference is colossal.

Co-operation offers survival value to every activity in the world. Co-operation is mutually benefiting from each other's capacities.

Crows take turns as sentinels; ants combine forces to move a dead beetle; husbands and wives should divide the responsibilities of the home in accordance with their respective talents. There is survival value in these things because each individual has supplemented what his abilities alone could achieve. But also each must constantly adapt to what the other is able to give. Asking someone to produce contrary to his abilities, destroys the relation. When a naturally quick person tries to hurry a naturally slow person the result is unsuccessful, and exasperating to both.

The seriousness of conflict between opposing channels of self-fulfillment, depends upon:

(1) The strength of individual habits, including habits of evaluating

(2) The significance of the particular channels in terms of inborn characteristics.

If Kate buys a cut glass bowl when what Hugh wanted was a record album of Beethoven's Ninth Symphony, the quarrel may center around music or around cut glass, depending on the balance of power. The real trouble was lack of common enjoyment, reflecting itself in lack of co-ordinated desires, decisions, and actions. The more intelligent the people are, the more they will suffer from such a mistake unless they learn from it, and the more damage is done to each other and to the children. In marriage, the only way to have a thing is to share it.

Little acts of consideration for each other in what sometimes seem insignificant ways are of great importance when lovingly performed, because they are such emphatic statements of intention. Getting his slippers and pipe, carrying the laundry downstairs for her, preparing cold lemonade when he mows the lawn on a scorching day, buying flowers that match her dress, remembering and celebrating anniversaries together—all of these help to keep togetherness verdant.

When every reasonable effort has been made to provide for the needs of the various members of the family, wherever direct means of satisfaction cannot be devised, the group will co-operate to find indirect ones. Where the basic needs of the family cannot be reasonably fulfilled through group action (food in war, famine, or depression is an obvious example), and where no indirect satisfaction can be devised (as it certainly cannot with food), the result is stark tragedy. How much can husband and wife endure? There always come times when all one can do is to stand and take it. For such occasions does the marriage have a reservoir of inner strength? What reserves are there to call upon?

The Emotional Security Reservoir

Family quarreling (not to be confused with disagreement), is evidence of failure to coordinate desires and decisions. The quarrel and the failure are just as much punishment for misuse of the laws of human nature as a broken hip is punishment for a violation of some physical law. Failure in marriage is evidence that we have used poor method, or are pursuing a wrong goal.

The solution of family disagreement and the ability to coordinate decisions depends, for one thing, upon the existence of a background of confidence in each other; a sort of generalized emotional security reservoir. How convinced is each person that he can discuss disagreements sincerely, revealing without hesitation just what he feels, thinks, sees? No pretense, no exaggeration, no insincerity; just complete trust and genuineness. How assured is he that in spite of differences of opinion, the others accept him for his real self, believe in him, wholeheartedly want the marriage and the home? How certain can he be this is not an "all-or-none" relationship? How genuinely does his conduct make the others feel he wants to build depth as well as length and breadth into their lives by contributing his share in the establishment of these conditions? In a crisis will he undertake more than his usual share?

If he does not want these conditions, the only way he can be brought to want them is through some crisis which leads (not compels) him to see the evil results on himself of his desire to take advantage of or to exert power over those he thinks he loves. He is trying to imprison and then to devour their lives. People can nourish each other, physically and emotionally, but they cannot long feed on each other. Emotional cannibalism is destructive even to the successful cannibal.

A continuing stream of confidence, swelling into a reservoir, provides a reserve of trust in each other by which to deal with actual or anticipated frustrations. It is a basis of accepting each other which transcends the misunderstanding of the moment. It provides assurance to each person that even though desires clash, decisions will not be final until they provide for everyone's legitimate needs in so far as is reasonably possible. It will not be done by taking a vote. Ballots show how people are divided, not where they agree.* It will be done by patiently working toward a unifying "sense of the meeting," as the Quakers do.

In order to build such a reservoir of confidence and security, husband and wife must bring to the marriage (or go through the agonizing pain of developing):

(1) Emotional maturity
(2) Mutual compatibility in fundamental standards of what is important and worth while, so that specific, evaluations will be seen as only specific, and therefore, not the "be-all" and the "end-all"
(3) Empathy, with which to *feel* each other's emotional responses
(4) Absence of undue irritation or interference from outside sources—in-laws, for example.

The security reservoir must be filled from streams of confidence welling up in many areas of the marriage. This is not a static thing. Like water, it will evaporate unless replenished. It can be drained by domination, or hiding resentment under cynicism, or camouflaging a need for loving and being loved with false independence, or even by excessive self-sacrifice. In what direction behavior will then turn is probably governed largely by generalized emotional attitudes.

* The people who vote in favor of something seldom vote for the same reason.

When heavy demands have been made upon the supply, the reservoir must be quickly replenished, for feelings of insecurity spread from one area to another faster and more powerfully than do feelings of confidence. We can always destroy more swiftly than we can create.

When the reservoir fills faster than it empties, love grows, until at last even the casual observer perceives that the marriage has strength in reserve when decisions are difficult to coordinate. It allows husband and wife to adjust to uncertainty because they have something to fall back on. It provides a dynamic security that is flexible. It guarantees an optimum of spontaneous self-expression.

If either husband or wife is habitually ill at ease unless sure of what the other is doing, the security reservoir is close to emptiness. Does the wife continually pry into what the husband is thinking? If so, whenever he wants to be alone with his thoughts he will try to get away from her. He may still be physically in the living room, but emotionally he has fled the bondage of his personal Egypt. There is now no possibility for spontaneous confidence because there is no reserve to draw upon. Scarcity makes hoarders of us all.

There is a definite relationship between the complex problem of mutual self-expression and self-evaluation on the one hand, and the establishment of an emotional security reservoir on the other. There are a number of reasons for this:

(1) Both husband and wife—like everyone else—are vitally concerned with feeling emotionally secure, and will be emotionally disturbed whenever they feel their self-expression or self-evalution threatened

(2) When the same situation threatens one but not the other, wise handling can contribute to the security reservoir; poor handling can be a drain upon it

(3) Serious threats to security due to such things as misunderstanding, conflicts between divergent desires, lack of initial patience in working toward common standards of value, the dependency of "take care of me" or of "praise me a lot," etc., may come before the security reservoir has

been developed. Anyone undertaking a marriage without the security of his own self-respect will find it almost impossible to build a generalized feeling of security through togetherness with anyone else.

A periodic examination of their security reservoir ought to be important to husband and wife. Sometime during every week he should stop to listen to her in the kitchen, coming out of the nursery, on the stairs. He should ask himself what life would be like without her. Empty? Then tell her so. Would she still have complete confidence in him no matter what malicious story she was told by the local Jezebel?

Meanwhile, the wife should ask herself whether her husband was in better physical, mental, and emotional shape when he set off for the office because he is married to her? Does she encourage him when he needs encouragement, and gently give him a better sense of perspective when he seems conceited? Does he have confidence in her judgment and listen to her counsel? Does she run the house as conscientiously as though she were employed in an office, at a good salary, by a man of her husband's ability? What satisfactions is she getting from the marriage? Tell him about them.

Each should make self-inquiry as to whether the other partner would genuinely want to continue the relationship if all marriages were suddenly dissolved by government edict. Each should continually ask himself what things he can joyfully do which will contribute to the happiness of the other. Each should continuously pay attention to the general factors which make for success in marriage, and thus continuously contribute to the filling of the security reservoir. Important among these factors are:

(1) Mutual effort toward the achievement and maintenance of emotional maturity

(2) Mutual effort toward the self-fulfillment of each personality through creative self-expression, and objective self-evaluations

(3) Mutual realization of the strength and freedom of togetherness, and what is necessary to maintain it

(4) Mutual effort toward good method in solving family prob-
        lems, including a respect for the principles of organization.

This soon becomes losing one's self in something greater than
one's self. The more it happens, the more humble a person is and
the less inferior he feels. True humility is seeing, with a proper
sense of perspective, where one fits into the total situation. False
humility is pretending that one is unimportant. (Such an individual would, no doubt, actually feel unimportant if he could see
the truth.) True humility comes to those who do not demand the
impossible of themselves or of anyone else. They are not permanently upset by either success or failure. They also have a sound
basis on which to develop an emotional security reservoir, for
security begets humility, which begets more security in an increasingly effective sprial.

In Conclusion

Successful marriage is a creative achievement. It does not come
because of a romantic thrill. It is not to be had by reaching out for
a marriage license as one would pluck a lovely flower. It comes
only with specialized knowledge and hard work.

There is no human situation in which all problems have been
solved. It is fantasy to think there is, or can be, perfect harmony
in marriage. Differences are always present, and they matter. But
they can usually be solved by facing them honestly, understanding
them, and wanting to work them out. Differences can even be
fruitful, as the glorious blending of a variety of tone and timbre
demonstrates when a great orchestra raises its voices with common
intention. When there is no unity of purpose and each musician
goes his own independent way, the result is only noise. The oboe
may be more plaintive and penetrating, the violin more brilliant,
but whether the oboe is superior or inferior to the violin is beside
the point. What matters is that each instrument plays its own part
well, and that the result is far superior to what any one instrument
could produce alone.

What matters is that each member of the family play his part well. Whether father or mother is superior to Junior is beside the point. Only a little child can bring a certain ring of laughter to the household; only an old person can contribute a certain unshakeable tranquility; and the only way for any member of the family to have something—Junior included—is to share it. The freedom of togetherness!

Each musician in the orchestra tries to do the right thing, at the right time, in the right way, in the right relationship with the other musicians. So does the mature person. He may even be able to look at a family problem as though it had happened to someone else, instead of to him. Certainly he will be able to keep the future present in the present. "How will this look to me in a year? Am I doing the right thing? Am I doing it at the right time, with the right individuals, and in the best way?"

When a machine, an organization, or a family fails to respond adequately with replacements or sound new sections for worn-out parts, breakdown is coming. There may be temporary rallies, but the end is near. Marriage can become drab. It does not take long for the new-found intimacy of the honeymoon to metamorphose into the reality of everyday living. Novelty gives way to routine, and, unless steps are taken, stagnation will set in.

A good marriage builds memories to cherish and cherishes them, for the great achievement in life is not money, or power, or fame, but a truly happy home. But as we said, there are price tags on a happy marriage, and few bargains.

3

Sources of Preparation for Marriage

WHERE PREPARATION BEGINS

THERE are those who behave as though preparing for marriage is little more than buying some new clothes, taking a bath, brushing the teeth, picking up the license, and going to the clergyman. Others, with enough foresight to say, "I'm planning to be married in six weeks. What should I do in order to insure our continued happiness?" usually consider themselves wisely superior.

Preparation for marriage actually begins in the cradle, for it consists largely of preparation for normal, co-operative living. Exactly as the extemporaneous speech is never extemporaneous, but prepared for by effort which was not labeled for the particular occasion, most preparation for marriage is not so labeled. By the time a baby is a year old his basic attitudes toward people are well under way. Long before he learns to walk, he acquires emotional reactions and patterns of response to other people, not only by observing how the significant individuals in his environment treat each other, but by feeling how they treat him. Aldrich is convinced that the personality is established by age two.* By the time the child is

* C. A. Aldrich and M. M. Aldrich, *Babies Are Human Beings* (New York: Macmillan, 1938), p. 61.

seven, his behavior patterns are certainly widely conditioned. By the time he is twelve they are deeply set.

Unfortunately, the sources from which we must learn our concepts of love and marriage are no guarantee of their validity. A person cannot drive an automobile until he demonstrates his fitness to do so. There is no such prerequisite for rearing a child.

During the war I was in a hospital for an operation. The room assigned me was occupied by a two-weeks-old baby, who was subsequently moved into the corridor. That evening the baby began to whimper: not the, "Please feed me because I'm hungry," complaint; not the, "I'm trying to be patient, but I'm wet and uncomfortable. Won't you give me some attention?" fret; but a plaintive, beseeching whimper that said, "Won't someone love me just a little bit? I'm anxious and afraid in this strange world. Please give me reassurance that I'm wanted. I can't fend for myself. Won't someone please love me? It's my birthright."

Because one of the patients was annoyed, the nurse rolled the crib down the corridor and into the operating room. Before she could shut the door behind her, the baby shifted vocal gears into a bellow of rage. For twenty minutes he cried in unrestrained anger. Finally he wore himself out and went to sleep, whereupon the nurse brought the crib back into the corridor. An hour later the whole performance was repeated: the whimper to be loved; the ostracism to the surgery; the roars of wrath.

Next morning, on being asked what the matter was with the baby, the head nurse replied, "We don't know. We can't find anything, but something is wrong. He should be gaining weight, and he's still losing. He fusses all the time. He shows no enthusiasm for his food. There's something the matter, but we can't find what." She did, however, corroborate the hypothesis that the child's mother did not want him, and his father had no interest in him.

This baby had sensed his lack of welcome, and as a result could not make up his mind that he wanted to go on living in so hostile an atmosphere. Already, at two weeks of age, his attitudes toward other people were being formed; attitudes which would surely carry fear and suspicion into a marriage unless somehow vigorously revised. The inborn sense that he was fundamentally adequate must have made not being loved all the harder to bear. Nevertheless, not being loved gradually leads a growing child to feeling unlovable, and to attack one's self as being unlovable is as evil as to think of one's self as perfect. In the wake of this insecurity comes some sort of aggressive effort to demand the needed love. The hostility of other people to this aggression then verifies the child's sense of unworthiness, and his life is likely to become a subconscious struggle against a tragic lie.

The significance of an action is never lost even though it is often not consciously remembered, and perhaps not even consciously realized. Preparation for marriage begins the day a person is born, for every experience becomes a part of his personality. He is what he is now, as the cumulative result of everything he has experienced and been from the moment of conception. We are the creatures of all our yesterdays. The past is ever present in terms of how we then felt and now feel about it. As Izette de Forest has often said, it is not water over the dam, but water behind the dam—pushing. Only the surface water goes over the dam. Even a piece of steel or a fiber of wool actually remembers its history of having been strained, and after a while will break from fatigue.

Our attitudes toward people and toward life are so early and spontaneously acquired that we are never conscious of them until we have intimate contact with someone reared in a different environment. The child in the home is a personality in the making. Is it not an unlovely piece of behavior to make much of the evils of divorce while we are still blithely bringing up little children on a domestic battlefield, and paying almost no attention to what constitutes good preparation for marriage?

Life itself, as well as marriage, is based on inner emotional attitudes toward other people, and we acquire these long before we reach our teens. Childhood experiences give us the premises we use to interpret human relations throughout the rest of our lives.

As a result, all of us are constantly imputing to other people characteristics which we read into them; constantly making subconscious assumptions that stick to us, and contaminate, with prejudiced emotions, the goodness of many of our opinions.

Preparation for marriage does indeed begin in the cradle. It depends largely upon the love relationship between the child and the parents, for this is first an example to the child, and second has a direct effect upon the child far greater than that of siblings, playmates, and relatives combined. Baby sees how father and mother treat each other and feels how they treat him. This gives him an emotional set toward other people. Thus is wrong childhood upbringing the albatross around the neck of most unhappy marriages.

THE LOVE STREAM AND THE HATE STREAM

As long as there is life, energy flows. As long as energy flows, emotions flow, and there are fundamentally only two kinds: responses to pleasure and to pain; feelings of happiness and confidence, or of unhappiness and fear. Even the little one-celled amœba, possessing no nervous system, no digestive system, no brain, will seek satisfactions and try to avoid pain. With an almost ferocious vim, every member of mankind endeavors to achieve the things he enjoys and endeavors to avoid the things that hurt.

Our response to pleasurable experience is positive. We become happy, friendly, co-operative, loving. Our response to painful experience is negative. We become miserable, suspicious, solitary, hateful. Thus emotional energy either flows down the love stream, down the hate stream, or down some combination of both. (Figure 4 will partially illustrate this.)

Fear leads to hate because hate has a few emotional compensations. Fear has none. Hate is also the great soothing syrup for guilt feelings. Thus, the more a person fears someone, the more he will hate him; the more ashamed he is of his own actions, the more he will hate. The trouble is not the fear or the shame. The trouble comes from bringing about the secondary perversion of these distressing feelings by exchanging them for a false satisfaction, instead of trying to find the disagreeable truth and to correct the situation.

Freud, and many others, believed it as natural to hate as to love. This seems to me inconsistent with our unquestioned preference for pleasure over pain. True, one sometimes experiences satisfaction from being hateful, but only as a secondary, perverted response when the love stream has been blocked. Every little child wants

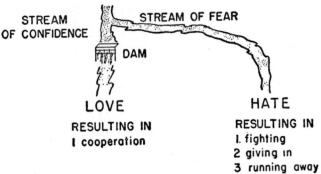

AS LONG AS THERE IS
LIFE
ENERGY FLOWS
DOWN ONE OR BOTH OF TWO
EMOTIONAL STREAMS

STREAM OF CONFIDENCE   STREAM OF FEAR

DAM

LOVE   HATE
RESULTING IN   RESULTING IN
1 cooperation   1. fighting
                        2 giving in
                        3 running away

Fig. 4. Types of Behavior

and tries the love stream first. The downfall of man stems from parents building dams across the child's creative outlets. Does not the baby himself have a more accurate idea of when he needs to be fed than some schedule-bound pediatrician? Experiments conducted by the Institute of Human Relations at Yale bear out the conclusion that we have insulted the intelligence of little children.

Frustration leads to rebellion. Loving emotions are forced underground, imprisoned, as it were, in the blackness of some subterranean cavern where they ferment and seek escape in grotesque behavior patterns. If energy is to flow down the love stream, parents must have the passionate desire to create for the child the conditions under which he can fluorish. This is not to be confused with allowing him always to have his own way. It consists of a sincere respect for the child's personality; the provision of opportunities for creative self-expression; discipline based on kindness with no trace of weakness; no attempt to dominate, coerce, entice or bribe *in order to gain power over* the child.

Only under these circumstances will the love stream remain open. There are many ways in which a dam can be built across it, interfering with the child's opportunity to be his real self. This is soon a defensive self in which he is driven to do things unrepresentative of his real self because he feels, "This is what I must do to protect myself."

No power on earth can build a dam across the hate stream. Its course can lie entirely within the individual. Denied outlet down the love stream, which must find outward expression, energy has to flow down the hate stream, even though it may never reach beyond the rills of annoyance. These must accumulate the run-off of large areas before widening and deepening into hate.

The usual procedure of trying not to hate is a mistaken one. To repress is not to destroy. Love cannot be achieved sincerely by denying the existence of hate. Everybody hates; make no mistake about that. Giving a child the idea that he is naughty whenever he feels anger or hate is making him feel guilty for feeling what all humanity feels. The individual does not exist who has only pleasant emotions and no disagreeable ones. The psychologically sound procedure is honestly to recognize energy going down the hate stream, to understand why it is present, to evaluate it, and to *feel out* what—in the light of the individual's own value standards —he wants to do about it. The right answer may be to express it vigorously in a way which may correct the conditions responsible for the feeling of hate. This is what Lincoln did when he saw a man sold into slavery.

When either love or hate is repressed the result is serious, for to repress one emotion is to be compelled to repress many others in order to keep the first *incommunicado*. When a child's emotional honesty is upset in one area, it is always upset in many other areas as a result. If he is led to refuse to feel one feeling, in order to cover up this lie, he can no longer honestly feel many other feelings. No one of us can pick and choose what he consciously feels, and still know what he actually feels. *We can only pick and choose what we want to do about what we feel.* When we do not know what we feel, how can we choose intelligently?

The Need For Emotional Honesty

Habitually happy, co-operative people are loving people. Habitually unhappy, quarreling people are full of hate. The difference is not that one group has loving emotions and the other group hates. Both groups experience both emotions. The difference is that one group was brought up to recognize what its emotions were, and allowed to feel through to the greater satisfactions of love; the other was taught, "This is what you ought to feel," and so lost the ability to feel honestly. Emotional energy was coerced, repressed, given feelings of guilt, denied the opportunity to flow down the love stream and, therefore, could only flow down the hate stream.

The foundation of character development is emotional development. All emotional development is the result of exposure and response to other people—not repressing emotions, not expressing them in counterfeit ways, but feeling deeply, honestly, and sincerely in one's heart. Denied the ability to feel honestly, a person will become emotionally stunted and twisted.

Attitudes cannot be effective unless they are based on reality, which is only another way of saying that to be a happy, well-balanced person one must have been brought up to be emotionally honest. This is the condition under which we can best perceive reality.

There are three kinds of honesty:

    (1) *Financial*, to which we pay a great deal of attention

    (2) *Intellectual*, to which we pay some attention, but which

is more important because no one can be truly financially honest until he is intellectually honest

(3) *Emotional*, to which we pay almost no attention, and yet it is the most important of the three because emotions underlie all thought and action.

We even deliberately teach children to be emotionally dishonest. Need one say more than "social conventions" to be convincing? We are taught to pretend to feel what we do not feel, and to pretend not to feel what we do feel, until in the end many of us do not know what we feel.*

To deceive one's self about what one is feeling is to betray one's self. This is what Fromm calls the unforgivable sin; the most destructive thing that can happen to a personality. Across the continent is a trail of wrecked marriages resulting from the wrecked lives produced because children have been made to feel that they are wicked and sinful unless they feel what parents, teachers, relatives, clergy say they ought to feel. The measure of whether an individual is good or evil ought to be his own considered opinion, not anyone else's. Virtue must be an honest feeling. Chemicals always react in terms of *their own true nature* no matter what the other chemicals do. Would God intend less for men, particularly since the first choice of behavior is to love? The evil of living life without doing what one ought to do is no greater than the evil of living without doing what one honestly wants to do.

Suppose a child discovers that he can never safely express his anger against his father. Does this mean that he will never be angry? Now, instead of having an opportunity to think out for himself what is and what is not, for him, worth being angry about, he can only try to stifle and to hide the anger; to express it in indirect ways, like bullying a playmate, being disobedient at home or unco-operative in school; at last to fool himself into thinking he does not get angry. To feel without acting is soon to be unable to act honestly and to be unaware of true feeling. The conscious and

* J. Macmurray, *Reason and Emotion* (New York: Appleton Century, 1938), pp. 13-66.

subconscious hate that develops under these circumstances is his pathetic attempt to protect what is left of his personality. But he has not been allowed to find out what he really felt beyond the aching need to feel accepted by the powerful people in his environment whom he wants to love if they will make it possible by first loving him.

All babies are emotionally honest. They express ecstasy or anger spontaneously and sincerely. With the passing of the years they often learn emotional dishonesty as a means of self-protection. They must adjust to their environment. They want physical and psychological satisfactions. They try to avoid pain. In order to do this, by the time they are adolescent some of them have almost stifled all feeling. Emotionally twisted and squeezed as children, they have felt so deeply and been hurt so much they try not to feel at all. What tragedy! An individual can grow emotionally—or be happily married—only insofar as he feels deeply and genuinely. When he stifles his real feelings, he kills his heart.

To destroy the sincerity of one's emotional life to is to destroy the most precious thing a person can possess, namely, his inner integrity. To pretend a feeling not really experienced, or to deny a feeling actually present, is to lose the capacity to know what one truly feels. There is no more sure way to destroy the capacity to be a loving personality.

As individual ideas need to be thought out, so individual values need to be felt out. Feeling requires even more honesty than thinking because, as already stated, feeling underlies thinking. Feeling out a value or thinking out an idea are both slow processes. But once accomplished, the emotional attitude toward a value, or the intellectual attitude toward an idea, can be reproduced with rapidity.

Despite the carelessness with which we distinguish between them, *feeling and thinking cannot be separated*. They are two interacting parts of the same thing. Both take place in the brain. Thinking without feeling is impossible. Feeling without discriminatory analysis is possible, but dangerous. Above the level of pure reflex action, feeling without any thought seems improbable. Feeling affects thinking; thinking affects feeling in a continuous merry-go-round which early in life can no longer be separated into head and tail.

But what we feel and how we feel is more important than what we think and how we think. Our true emotions are not illogical, and confused, and untrustworthy, a barbarous collection of impulses requiring to be subdued and guided by reason. Emotions acting on reason have their own logic and purpose, and will not only correctly guide but will intelligently govern us if given the opportunity. Failure to realize this explains why the philsophers have done so little for us.

Not only through example but by precept we teach emotional dishonesty. The Sunday School lesson was about Ruth and Naomi, with numerous references to the thirteenth chapter of First Corinthians. At the end of the lesson book were the usual questions, one of which was, "Does love show kindness or anger?" This clearly implies that the answer cannot be both, and that people are either good or bad. How can there be truth to an answer when there is not truth to the question? People are not good or bad; they are good and bad. Despite the dishonesty of the question, one ten-year-old felt and expressed the emotional truth. Bright-eyed and eager he gave his answer. "Love shows both kindness and anger. I had a fight with my sister this morning, but we love each other just the same." A host of people have paid the psychiatrists hundreds of dollars to get that truth back into their systems.

Controlling anger is a far different thing from denying the truth of the anger. We are not sinners because we experience anger against our loved ones, nor are we unlovable because they sometimes feel angry at us. The evil lies not in the anger, but in how it is understood and expressed.

There is a vast difference between emotional inclination and emotional honesty. The impulsive inclination may be to hate. Impulse, not subject to discrimination, may engender a shameful deed. The carefully felt out emotional value is likely to be something quite different. What a large percentage of the population mistakenly considers "doing as one pleases," is only rebellious behavoir against some previous domination. Such actions are carried out in ignorance of what the self is like and what it wants. Rebellion is only protest; it is never self-realization or creative self-expression.

No one need ever be ashamed of any *honest* emotion no matter what it is. The emotion is only a consequence; the cause is the thing that is making trouble. Causes lie in the conditions which produce emotions.

The problem of honestly recognizing our emotions is the most important single problem in preparing for a happy marriage—if indeed not in life itself. Until an individual knows how he feels and why, he cannot know what he is or what he thinks. And yet any one of us can diligently practice self-examination without ever perceiving facts about himself which are obvious to those who have lived or worked with him. Until an individual knows the truth concerning what he feels about himself, he cannot trust what he thinks about other individuals. How can he choose a mate wisely, or live with her intelligently? He cannot understand himself unless his inner emotional honesty is complete; he cannot trust himself unless he understands himself. Without knowledge of self how can he understand or trust another person, particularly in the intense relationships of marriage? He loses his self-confidence and his ability to co-operate when he loses his emotional honesty. He regains his self-confidence and his capacity to love and to be loved, once he gets back his emotional honesty.

Harmful Preparation

There is trouble when an individual's upbringing does not allow him to keep the emotional honesty with which he was born. The child may consciously hate the effect of his father's domination, yet without knowing it envy his father's power. He thus refuses to accept father's ideas as applied to himself, but dishonestly adopts the parent's technique toward other people.

There is another more inescapable reason for this. The only

way to defend one's self is in terms of the tactics by which one is attacked. To use Izette de Forest's illustration, the Red Coats could not fight the Indians as they had fought the French. The Indians soon adopted guns with which to fight the Red Coats. In so far as one adopts the Indian's or the Red Coat's tactics, one becomes an Indian or a Red Coat—without realizing it or intending it.* Father never admits being wrong? Neither will Junior. Father utterly refuses to admit Mother's point of view unless thoroughly overpowered? How natural for Junior to think a wife must be overpowered before she will be co-operative. How natural, but how tragic!

Here is the answer to the youth who says, "My father and mother really hated each other. They only stayed together for appearances. I know what hell marriage can be. That's why my marriage is going to be happy!" Possibly, but in having to live with the Indians, he subconsciously became an Indian. Because of what was perhaps father's brutality and mother's indirect deceiving, he may trust almost no one. Subconsciously he may regard everyone as an enemy. The sequence of his emotions will then be:

(1) Mobilize emotional defenses against potential attack. He will regard this as self-protection. Other people will recognize it as aggression

(2) Because of his attitude of attack, others will reject him. He will sense the rejection, feel hurt and humiliated. Being disliked because of an insecure relationship, also results in making the relationship more insecure

(3) Because of his false pride, rather than admit the humiliation and search for its reason within his own emotional responses, he will become defiant

(4) This makes love and even friendship impossible.

Thus will he betray himself by behavoir which prevents accomplishing the very thing he wanted. It takes deep self-understanding—

* If, as some psychoanalysts believe, we imitate our enemies more than we imitate our friends, then many children must defend themselves more than they express themselves. This might be a fruitful area of research into why people become unhappy.

or an unusually well-balanced and wise mate—to perceive and to correct such a train of events.

A little child is completely at the mercy of his parents because he must be dependent upon them. But *dependence need not mean subservience* unless the home is a little absolute monarchy or a nest of bribing, domestic politicians. What the child needs is a feeling of security. This can be destroyed by domination or by over-protection. These wreck the confidence of the child in his ability to think for himself. As a mature person facing marriage he will need to be able to test, to evaluate, and to react appropriately to reality. Is having someone make his decisions for him good preparation for reality? Is feeling that he must be bribed to be co-operative an advantage to him as a person? Is getting his own way most readily and completely by being a cry-baby a fruitful qualification for marriage?

There are myriad marriages in which husband, or wife, or both want to be treated like a baby. Unless mothered exactly as they want to be, some people get angry, and like a weak child express rage in a negative reaction such as, "I won't." The common refusal to talk (negotiate) is comparable to the baby holding his breath. This is defiance because of fear.

It is easy for a child to feel frightened and alone in a hostile world unless he is honestly loved and guided *in his own interest*, with rights and privileges of his own. Lack of self-assurance develops in the fighter a desire to dominate; in the spineless a willingness to give in. What his parents are offering him is a false self-development and a spurious security at the price of his emotional integrity, and his subconscious knows it.

Because he is dishonestly loved, his own love will become diseased. The real influence is what the parents *feel*. The words they use mean nothing, except perhaps hypocrisy. They may say, "We'll do this for you," at the same time feeling, "We do it only because we think we ought to, but see how unhappy it makes us." What the child then comes to feel is:

(1) No one can make him happy or even give him fun without self-abdication

(2) He cannot make anyone else happy without surrendering himself.

What kind of preparation for love and marriage is this?

Often the withholding of what the parent calls love is in terms of some power mechanism, such as, "If you love me, you'll bring home a better report card," or "If you love me, you'll come to the table with clean hands." This is not love, it is either a threat or a bribe. Doubtless the child already knows that he is not loved, but in the desperate hope of getting the parent to love him as he wants to be loved, he gives in to the threat or pays the bribe and thereby loses another increment of his integrity.

Sometimes the withholding of love is more overt. Consider this excerpt from a student letter. "My mother did not want me. She resented the responsibility of a child to rear. I would fight back with, 'I didn't ask to be born!' but she was too preoccupied with what sin of hers was responsible for this cross to bear, this vengeance of a child to raise, to sense the longing for affection in me." Imagine what a re-examination of evaluations could have done for both of them.

Here is another. "I am only eighteen, but have already become old and bitter. You could not pay me enough to live any one of those years over again, or to marry anyone after what I experienced as a child."

The parents in these cases were merely trying to dominate their children, and of all the things we hate and fear, being made subservient heads the list. Contrariwise, of all the things most people *think* they *want*, none is more common than the desire for power over others. For the ordinary person, the one time in life when he unquestionably has this power is during the years when his children are young.

The attempt to exert power over children finds many outlets, most of them indirect, for the individual with a lust for power seldom fights openly. His objective would be too easily recognized.

He might lose. So he makes his children feel guilty, robs them of their integrity, demoralizes them with conflicting emotions by which to divide and conquer the personality, and only once in a while plays the tyrant openly.

The most common technique is first to frustrate the child and then to give him some desired reward. Whereas a good frustration brings about rebellion or submission, this devil's brew of frustration and enticement demoralizes the child because of the inhibiting ambivalence. Half of him wants to fight, and half of him feels he ought to be grateful. The integrity of wholeness is lost, and he can only waiver indecisively between rebellion and gratitude like a lost sheep in dire need of a shepherd. This is exactly what the parent subconsciously wanted, because being a needed shepherd makes one feel important. It also means that because the sheep is pastured he will be shorn.

Some parents give lavish gifts, though not of themselves, to make the child feel indebted, and thus afraid to reject the parent. Such bribery to compel love destroys the integrity of him that gives and him that takes. There are also guilt feelings involved on both sides, as well as two kinds of guilt feelings:

(1) My family will dislike me because I did not conform (for example, not showing gratitude where it is expected)

(2) I have injured myself (for example, behaving in a way which destroys love, or one's emotional integrity).

Occasionally a child will become rebellious and aggressive in the attempt to seize the right to be himself, but short of revolutionary changes in environment, this is a struggle few children can win. Hating both himself and his rulers if he gives in, punished if he fights, he must readjust to wrong conditions by trying to protect himself. Instead of keeping the natural feeling that men and women supplement and reinforce each other, he comes to feel that there is an underhanded warfare going on between people. His attitude gradually becomes, "I cannot trust; therefore, I dare not love or I shall be betrayed. All I can hope for is some kind of reassurance." As he grows older, and perhaps establishes a home of his own, he will change the scenery of his acting, but not the plot of his behavior. His heart was so frightened when it was little that it did not dare to grow.

As Freud pointed out, we tend throughout our lives to see in the situations which confront us as adults the very things we could not handle successfully as children. Our developing personalities can stand a few emotional shocks (even death) fairly well. What demoralizes us is a repetitive series of emotional upsets like fear of domination, insecurity, or humiliation. As a downtrodden child grows up, the person with power or authority becomes to him a very significant person. In every situation the maturing youngster relives the persecution he suffered as a child. Must he suffer it again? The quickest way to find out is to create conditions similar to the ones in which father was a tyrant, and to watch what happens. The girl, unloved by her father, will try to force her husband into her father's pattern, and then try to compel him to love her. It fails, not only because her husband is himself and not her father, but also because her techniques are the same childish ones which failed when adopted in defense against her father. Her attitude toward her husband will be, "You have power and can use it to fight me if you want to. Now will you be reasonable!" What she should feel is, "What can we do together to help this situation?"

Prolonged tensions, lack of confidence, quarreling, unhappiness are all manifestations of personality problems which started in early childhood, and resulted in behavior which is in no way expressive of the person's true nature. Every day he is faced with evidence that he is not being his real self. But to recognize it would be to destroy the security of the counterfeit self he has built as a defense. This, he is not strong enough to do, so he must devise ways of refuting the damning facts; of getting a false feeling of confidence. The obvious one is to blame someone else for his troubles. Who more naturally than the person he marries? He cannot blame his parents, for his youth was surrounded by influences which conspired to make him feel he must honor his father and his mother or be in danger of hell. He cannot blame himself, for he is too weak. Like a fly squirming in a spider web, his false emotions entangle him more and more. He perhaps acts self-confident; actually he feels alone, cheated, unhappy, desperately afraid, bitterly at war with himself.

This loss of integrity will greatly damage his character. If he has sufficient intelligence he may achieve professional success, amass a fortune, acquire power, becomes famous, but the conflict and fear with him (or her) will result in neurotic behavior,* such as:

(1) Fighting—an attempt to dominate in a world of hatred, by force if possible, but by bribery where power fails

(2) Giving in—an attempt to appease and thus, though weak, to dominate by being a dependent clinging vine and an excessive self-sacrificer to whom others are indebted

(3) Running away—an attempt to escape both the dangers of fighting and the ignominy of giving in.

What his real self wants is to be constructively co-operative. What his conscious self wants is to feel important. He believes that to be important will mean to be secure, not realizing that his dominating efforts in seeking importance arouse antagonism and defeat his achievement of security.

His wishes are disunited and split; his ability to want wholeheartedly has gone. Here is an inner conflict which threatens to tear him apart. A house divided against itself canot stand. So he makes frantic effort to evade the battle. He takes refuge in idealism as a protection against the disillusionment he fears to face. This is particularly true of the adolescent. He builds a glorified image of himself as a defender of men; an unusually lovable person; an adored parent or teacher; a doer of great deeds; a thinker of great thoughts. He imagines himself receiving the plaudits of the crowds; discovering a cure for cancer; immortalized in bronze as a martyr to some saintly cause; so indispensable that an institution would collapse without his presence. He is likely to build an elaborate daydream of

* K. Horney, *Our Inner Conflicts* (New York: Norton, 1945), is an excellent book on neurotic behavior.

himself as happily married, for marriage is the Promised Land of adolescence.

This is hardly facing reality. It is covering emotional dishonesty with a seasoning of sentimentality so he can swallow the dishonesty. It devises an idealistic answer to, "What could I have been like had I been fortunate enough to have had parents who loved me?" It says, "See what a prize package I might become. Why don't you do something about it?" It ignores his responsibility to see that the situation has changed, and that now he is free to do something about it himself.

Over against this glorified image, because of his weakness he will build a degraded image in which he looks upon himself as worthless, unlovable, without hope, not only unwanted and unsung but devoid of a single redeeming characteristic. By implication this says, "See what I've been forced into by the significant persons in my life. What psychological murderers! They ought to be punished:"

These fantasies are usually referred to by the psychiatrists as the idealized image and the despised image. It seems to me that what I have called the glorified image and the degraded image are each both idealized and despised. Certainly an image which was only despised would not be devised or accepted by the personality. We never do anything without some reason for wanting it.

These image fantasies are the creation of individuals who were made self-conscious as children. Self-consciousness is not so much "How do I look to someone else?" That can be only superficial. Self-consciousness is the more fundamental, "How do I look to me?" which is necessitated by the guilt of not being the real "Me." In every situation there is an "I" and a "Me." "I" often pays little attention to "Me" because "I" pays so much attention to what other people think. But "Me" is the important thing and is quietly there all the time. "How do I look to Me?" must have honest answers, and when "I" is not an honest self, "Me" is deeply disturbed over it.

A child shapes the "I" of his character as a result of what the significant people in his environment expect him to be. "I" can hate father's tyranny, yet envy and idolize his power. Something deep down below the surface says, "This isn't the real Me." Then the child becomes sentimental and builds a glorified image; self-accusatory and builds a degraded image, because he has not been allowed to find out what he really feels about himself. There are false significances and no real values to his emotions. When he thinks he is in love, it rests on a slippery surface because he is befogged and full of guilt, trying to feel what he thinks someone else thinks he ought to feel.

The greatest feeling of guilt comes from the self-betrayal of being dishonest to one's self about one's self; the "I" preventing the "Me" from breaking through to consciousness with the truth that "I's" value standards and goals are not "Me's" own, but bogus ones imposed by and accepted from someone else, either directly or indirectly. These are the betrayers which lead to marrying a man for his money, or a woman for her social position, or either for any reason except love in its deepest and truest sense; these are the betrayers which lead to the fictitious goals, not the true, lasting goals.

Nevertheless, the real "Me" is down in the subconscious all the time, functioning continuously like the heart, or the lungs. In it is stored every experience from birth to the present. Whereas "I" may believe something is admired for its inherent aesthetic qualities, "Me" may be causing the approval because of a hatred of mother, who would have abominated it; or because of both.

Obviously it accomplishes nothing to emphasize how necessary it is for the individual to be loved as a child if he is to be happily married as an adult, without at the same time putting equal emphasis upon the fact that parents cannot love children unless they are themselves emotionally mature. Where they are not emotionally mature, the iniquities of the fathers are visited upon the children unto the third and fourth generation—in short, times enough for us to realize that something is seriously wrong and we should do something about it.

Effective Preparation

Let us imagine two individuals who achieve happy marriage together, and follow the steps of preparation which led to this result. In the begining each is a fetus, completely dependent physically upon its mother. After being born, each child at once begins to establish mental-emotional relationships with its parents in addition to the physical dependency. Bodily and emotional security are closely bound together. The satisfaction of needs depends on attention from other people. Unless carefully watched, this will arouse strong feelings that attention from others constitutes security. If this happens, the individual will develop a whole bag of tricks for getting attention, perhaps including temper tantrums.

As time goes by the physical bond gradually lessens, and the mental-emotional bonds widen and strengthen under conditions in which the children can flourish.

Before going on to the next steps, some examples would be useful in making the procedure clear. David was two years old. For months he had been put to bed at seven o'clock, but on this particular night he protested. He was not sleepy. He did not want to go to bed. Most parents would have said, "Come along now, David, and no nonsense. Mother knows best." But not David's mother. She had made a careful study of human emotions. She really loved the child and had respect for his personality.

"All right," she said. "When you want to go to bed you let me know."

By eight o'clock David was sleepy, but he would not give in. He wanted to know whether mother really had respect enough for his personality to wait until he asked, or whether mother would try to establish her superiority by saying, "It's eight o'clock. Don't you think you ought to go to bed now?" At nine o'clock, staggering and hardly able to keep his little eyes open, David asked to be put to bed.

The next night his mother made no move to put the child to bed at seven. About an hour later he asked to go. After that he settled into a routine of asking, and although he could not read a clock he would ask within ten minutes, one way or the other, of seven. David and mother were in agreement as to the proper time for him to go to bed. Now it was a joint decision. Suppose David had settled into a routine of seven-thirty? Then mother had been mistaken in sending him to bed a half hour earlier. If this seems hard to believe it is because we have so underestimated the intelligence of little children and so lost faith in the individual's capacity to sense his own needs correctly. Here was a search for truth, not a struggle to dominate. Contrary to the beliefs and predictions of power-seeking parents, David is growing into as co-operative, unselfish, and kind a child as can be found in a day's journey.

What an excellent preparation for marriage! On the other hand, the son of a domineering mother naturally has a hard time in marriage for he learns his "mother tongue" in emotions as well as in vocabulary.

Life is a process, characterized by continual change. But change is often only the superficial aspect of life. The boy *is* father to the man. The realities of his nature remain the same. If he was really loved as a child, he will have confidence in himself and achieve in marriage creative self-expression through good interpersonal relationships.

Virginia had stuffed the bulk of a peanut butter sandwich into her five-year-old mouth until each cheek was a bulging pouch. Then she tried to tell her father something, but the words died of strangulation before they reached her lips.

"You know better than to do a thing like that," her father said. "I can't understand what you are saying. It doesn't look well. And furthermore, you might choke. Now don't try to talk with food in your mouth, and don't push the food in as though you were stuffing a turkey."

Virginia swallowed the sandwich only to be filled with wrath. "I hate you!" she yelled, "I wish you were dead! I wish the dog would eat you up!" What she meant was, "You make me unhappy, and therefore, I wish I could be rid of you." Would punishment for this feeling lessen it one whit?

Being wise in the ways of human emotions, instead of scolding a second time, the father said with no suggestion of sarcasm, but rather with an acceptance of Virginia's emotion, "I know just how you feel. There are people I would sometimes like to be rid of too. But you know, in order for the dog to eat me, I would have to be cut into little pieces first." In two minutes father and daughter were laughing over whether a big toe would be a nicer piece than a thumb.

But Virginia did not stuff her mouth again, as she undoubtedly would have done had it become a symbol of her independence. She knew it was not the thing to do. Fortunately, father knew that little daughter ought to be allowed to get the anger out of her system instead of being made afraid to express it directly. As R. C. Nyman pointed out in discussing this with me, every individual has an indestructible power of making decisions for himself. Father might compel Virginia's action, but he could not possibly prevent her from making decisions based on her feeling about him and about the action. Life—and marriage—should be lived on a self-respecting basis, not on a coercive basis.

Children are extremely imitative, and Virginia had perhaps received a greater lesson in the values of civilization from the fact that her father had perceived and respected how she felt, than from the fact that her environment would not tolerate the repulsive appearance of bulging cheeks, or the inaudibility of throttled words. Understanding consideration breeds understanding consideration. In a few years, Virginia will be the kind of girl who will say to her father, "The boy who has moved next door is hard to play with because he thinks he doesn't have any fun unless he wins everything. But I figure we're likely to be neighbors for several years and maybe, if we can teach him good sportsmanship, after a while he will learn how to have fun together."

But to go on with the other steps of effective preparation. As little children, boys and girls play together indiscriminately, but with the approach of adolescence they pretend to ignore each other. The mental-emotional bonds to father and mother also undergo changes, for now our two young people have reached an age where they want freedom, but fear to undertake responsibility for themselves, which is the first requisite of freedom. The maturing self wants to be independent; the baby self wants to be protected. The adolescent is a vacillating mixture of both. These conflicting attitudes should at last precipitate out into a buoyant, natural confidence in one's self because of developing a true emotional consistency.

Some personalities stop growing during the teens and live out the rest of their days in suspended adolescence because the parent refused to allow the child to outgrow emotional dependence, refused to cut the emotional umbilical cord, usually called "Mother's apron strings." The young man who fails to make a good adjustment to girls is an excellent example. The probable trouble is that his mother did not want him to like any girl—she wanted to keep him for herself. Neither mother nor son may have any conscious awareness of this. Serious, and perhaps permanent, damage may result.

With the boy and girl successfully through the growing pains of adolescence, the developing experience of a number of friendships, and the preparation for earning a living, courtship may begin. The dependent bonds on parents have been broken; the co-operative bonds of marriage have not yet been established. What exist are the abidingly friendly mental-emotional relationships with the parents, and the developing mental-emotional-physical relationships between the lovers. At last, in marriage, these bonds grow into an enduring, integrated system which binds husband and wife together, not in a straitjacket of self-surrender, but with a girdle of strength (Figure 5).

If, however, the young people are not emotionally mature, if they lack a sound concept of the nature of love and marriage, the result will probably be a tragic tangle of confused effort and troubled emotions. They may have a veneer of mature manners which allows them enough self-deception to believe they are balanced personalities, and so never go through the struggle of becoming so.

Whether these two are attracted or repelled is influenced by the experiences each had in childhood. A man may be attracted to a girl because she represents what his mother was—or was not. A girl

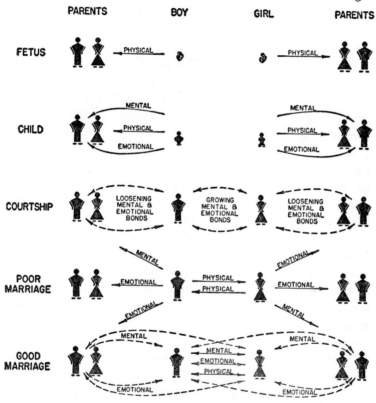

Fig. 5. Stages in Preparation for Marriage

may think she is in love with a man because he resembles her father, whom she loved devotedly.

Fortunate is the child who is allowed to develop and to retain his inner feelings, without corrosive unpleasantness. He will know that:

(1) Not everyone will like him, exactly as he will not like everyone
(2) It is not important that they should. All that matters is a few people loving him
(3) Nobody ever sincerely likes anything that is not genuine, particularly people.

COMPARISON OF METHODS

In order to carry still further the analysis of how our emotional preparation for marriage takes place in early childhood, let us consider the handling of a single incident in three different ways, and assuming these ways to be typical of the child's bringing up, examine their respective consequences.

When Bobby asked his mother for the materials with which to write a letter, she thought nothing of it, but the next evening on his way home from work the lad's father was accosted by an irate neighbor, waving an envelope in vicious pokes and shouting, "Look what your son wrote to me!" The document contained a youngster's-eye-view of the neighbor's characteristics, expressed in terms including "stinker," which were not greatly at variance with the body of more mature neighborhood opinion.

What often happens in circumstances like this is for father to say, "Junior, did you write this? Very well, young man, you march straight home and up to your room! I'll attend to you later!" The boy will now be faced with the threatening disapproval of a powerful father, as well as with his unsolved problem involving the neighbor. Instead of being allowed to feel the situation through, all he can possibly do is to mobilize his emotions in self-defense. *Because no attempt was made to examine his motives, he will be led to assume a pattern of motives in other people. Then, instead of looking for the motives behind an act, he will see only the act, and proceed to respond to it in terms of his previous assumptions. Thus will he reproduce in his own life, exactly the things his father is doing to him.*

Is a blind assumption of motives a good preparation for marriage? Or being afraid of people? Or believing that people are cruel? If Bobby adores his father and finds that his father has let him down, the cruelty will be all the greater. Certainly he will sense in his subconscious Mrs. de Forest's principle that nobody could want power over him until first the individual had despised him.

A second thing which may happen to Bobby is father saying, "Junior, did you write this? Well, so what?" Again the boy has no chance to feel the situation through. He only goes as far as "Goody, goody. I got away with something!" He becomes selfish and defiant because he still fears the threat of other people's power, and hopes to overcome it by a counterattack. This is the courage of desperation; not his real self.

What Bobby's father ought to say is, "Junior, did you write this? Well, let's go home and talk it over, son." Hand in hand, and with mutual confidence they reach the living room to occupy a comfortable chair—together. "Son," says father with kindness, but no trace of weakness. "There's always a reason for what each one of us does. Do you want to tell me what happened?" Junior begins explaining, and father adds comments. "Yes, you were playing ball in the street. . . . Oh, it went over her fence, and knocked over her geranium. Well, where's the ball now? . . . Then she seems to be a thief as well as a stinker. . . . You wrote the letter to get the ball back? Did you get it? . . . Tell me, are you better off or are you worse off now than you were before you wrote the letter? . . . What do you think you should have done? . . . Well, what are you going to do now?"

Here there is no threat, no punishment, no telling him what he ought to have done, no solving the situation for him, no putting him in a situation where he must defend himself; only patient and sympathetic questions to help the lad honestly to feel through, and therefore at the same time correctly to think through, the situation for himself. Unless he has previously been wrongly handled, he will see readily enough that his anger was unintelligently expressed. We have insulted the intelligence of children.

How will all this affect his marriage? The depressed and ferocious emotional climate of the you-march-straight-home-and-up-to-your-room school of thought will produce a stolid and secretive man, convinced that in a dog-eat-dog world the only safe place is to be top dog, and the only safe behavior is to be an efficient eater. As an adolescent he will have sullen and rebellious thoughts of running away from home. He will steal, fight, lie as all dominated children with originally strong integrities do. As a husband he will practice the hard selfishness that is the repayment for not having been loved as a child; selfishness that ignores cause and effect, and reacts only on impulse, *because he feels threatened*. The effect of his selfishness will not be pleasant, even to himself, and with each additional unfavorable effect he will feel threatened more and more. He will become increasingly desperate in his efforts to achieve satisfaction. He will be less and less able to restrain himself, or to think in terms of anyone but himself. His marriage will at last become a continuous fight to get by force the satisfaction he fears will be denied him. Where there should be an emotional security reservoir, will be only a parched, desert waste. The ultimate embrace will be for him, only enjoyment for *him*; never enjoyment of the giving of enjoyment. Having filled his own cup of animalism to animal overflowing, and with neither understanding nor concern for his wife's state of unsatisfied hunger, he will roll over and say, "Now go downstairs and make me a ham sandwich."* Thus do we transfer to a spouse punishment for the sins of a parent.

If the boy lacks the strength of personality to rebel, he will substitute compulsive submission for open resistance, and live the life of a doormat.

The "so-what" school of thought will produce a man with such subconscious contempt for other people he will flout the laws of good interpersonal relationships with amazing deliberation. He will be more dangerous than the first man because not so obviously brutal. What he thinks is love will be a mixture of selfishness and

* This is a direct quotation from the actual case of a well-educated man who achieved a degree of prominence.

sentimentality. He will invite guests to his home without asking his wife whether it suits her convenience. He will seldom share ideas with her, or respect any opinion not his own. He may be willing to listen. He will not be willing to learn. Like the first man, under it all he will be desperately ashamed. Nevertheless, the inconsiderateness of the father begot inconsiderateness in the son.

The let's-go-home-and-talk-this-over school of thought will produce a man of significant kindness. As an adolescent, instead of cursing when he loses a big one he will say, "Well—that's fishing." He will always be aware of emotional relationships and respectful of long-run values. He will not be content to play with mere pebbles on the seashore of emotional awareness. He will not be a fugitive from facts. Sometimes he will prepare his own breakfast because he senses what a half-hour of delicious semi-consciousness will mean to his wife after having been up during the night with the baby. When he comes home after a long, hard day in the office, he will not yammer about the tough breaks he has had until he has appraised what her condition is. Perhaps she has had an even more difficult day, in which case he may make a jail break with her from the prison of the here and now by whisking off her apron and taking her out to dinner. Or, if the family budget will not allow such reckless abandon, for a soda, or at least for a walk, arm in arm, to discuss their joys, to forget their troubles, and to renew their affection.

He will become the kind of husband who will sense what his wife is feeling. After she has done the work for a party at which he had a particularly good time because her conscientious effort gave everybody much happiness, he will not say, "Now we must have So-and-so to dinner." He will perceive that for the next week she does not want to hear a thing about entertaining, except a sincere word of appreciation for what she has just done. Thus does the lengthening shadow of a parent's ability to sense and to respect what a child feels, touch with gentle, protective kindness the life of whoever marries the maturing man. He will still be asking the questions he was taught to ask on his father's knee. "What should we have done?" "What are we going to do now?"

IMPROVING ONE'S PREPARATION

We cannot have a good marriage just because we want it, or just because our parents failed to achieve it. We can have it only where our preparation for it is adequate. Good preparation consists of learning co-operative ways of getting along with other people. These are most easily acquired where, from the day one was born, he was surrounded by and participated in loving behavior. Poor preparation consists of destructive ways of getting along with other people. These are acquired where one does not grow up in an emotionally mature, happy home. When father fluctuates from treating mother like an inferior child to wanting her to baby him, what can Junior learn about love?

As soon as a young person is able to stand on his own feet—and the sooner this happens after he has reached the stage where he should be ready for it, the better off he is likely to be—he should evaluate the way he was brought up. What methods was he taught for solving his interpersonal problems? How have these patterns succeeded? What have they gained? What have they cost? Will they be reliable in the future? Is behavior a matter of considered choice, or a matter of compulsive drives which represent ways of getting on with other people despite feelings of fear, hostility, helplessness, isolation, insecurity? If his parents were domineering, is he merely rebelling, or does he realize that all of us suffer some domination? Domination should be recognized for what it really is—a cover for feelings of weakness—and understandingly reacted to. If his parents were overprotective, can he shake himself loose from this enervating reassurance and stand on his own feet? *The only real security anyone ever knows is his own belief in himself.*

What has happened to him is not so important as what he does about it, although the readjustments attempted are almost sure to be in terms of the kind of bringing-up he had. Preparation for marriage takes place during childhood. The weak, maladjusted young people will need to see their own responsibility for dissipating their emotional energy *destructively* in cursing their parents and pitying themselves. The strong will perceive the sin against themselves of continuing not to be themselves, and therefore they will use their energy *constructively* in trying to save themselves. Naturally there is disillusion in this. Most of us experience disillusionments as we grow older. The strong adjust to it in their stride; the weak resent, rebel, become cynical, seek revenge on their parents, their children, their wives. The strong say, "Oh well, my illusions were not justified by reality. I'm glad to know the truth." The weak say, "What a dirty trick they played on me! I'll never believe anybody again."

When an individual does not understand the nature of love, or the nature of marriage, and knows not that he does not know, the result will be one of the bitterest and most frustrating disappointments of our civilization, often ending in the painful surgery of divorce. If, on the other hand, such an individual—approaching, or only recently initiated into the responsibilities of marriage—realizes the seriousness of his situation, he may well tremble, but should not feel without hope.

He has already taken the first step, which is to recognize his inability to love in the truest sense of the word, and his inadequate preparation for marriage. Far too few people possess the intellectual courage and the emotional honesty which so humiliating an admission requires, but nothing constructive can be accomplished until the individual *feels* deep within himself the distress which so many of us ought to feel because of our inability to love and because of our unfitness for marriage. Intellectual admissions alone are of no value. They must be felt with honest emotions. Then action, not just words, may follow.

The next step is to realize the fruitlessness of brave resolutions, of teeth-gritting will power, or talk without an unfettered desire to face reality. Millions of people have little contact with sound reality in many areas of life during their entire childhood. Our stupid secrecy about sex is a good example. Fear is the child of this failure to face reality, and the grandchildren are most of the emotional ills to which man is heir: stubbornness, egotism, indirect expressions of anger, habitual loneliness, morbid dependency, promiscuity, desire for power over other people, the emotional conflicts which make us prejudge situations.

Any unyielding, dogmatic idealism is fatal because it hides emotional immaturity from its possessor. He does not recognize on the one hand the difference between feeling physical attraction, or feeling the delight of being treated as though his glorified image were reality, and on the other feeling a deep and abiding desire to love in terms of the nature of real love. (Reread Chapter 1.)

Finally, there must be honest emotions, honestly expressed. We all see the mistake of emotions impulsively expressed. We do not see the even greater mistake of emotions habitually repressed, thus subsequently blighting adult life with spells of depression which the individual cannot understand, and which few people recognize as indirect aggression. The right procedure involves emotions which are recognized and given creative outlets through discriminating understanding.

Emotions, impulsively expressed, make enemies. Where emotions are repressed, conventions will be obeyed and the result may look like virtue, but under the surface, anger and hate are generating pressures which will find outlets in neurotic behavior. Such maladjustment before marriage will certainly show up after marriage. Emotions honestly recognized bring insight; the emotions are constructively released; the end result is happiness and freedom.

To improve one's preparation for marriage requires an understanding of the nature of love and of the nature of marriage, followed by character-changing actions which increase one's capacity to fulfill the requirements of love and of marriage. Do not be discouraged by the amount of time and effort needed. All change begins with the infinitesimal. But confusion concerning what to strive for, or how to do it is an indication of difficulty requiring help. Where such confusion exists it is probably wise to have the advice of a good psychiatrist, exactly as one would seek the counsel of a competent physician when physical health is in question. If the case is severe, an analysis may be necessary. Medium cases should be referred for remedy to the better Marriage Counseling Centers. This may involve traveling some distance to another city —a trifling matter where the success of a marriage is at stake. Mild cases may find sufficient help in a single psychiatric consultation, or in books such as this.*

Under no circumstances should anyone work with a psychiatrist whose intelligence and richness of personality does not exceed his own.

In Conclusion

All of us strive to find adequate ways to get along with each other. Good preparation for marriage results in the happy, constructive ways which succeed; poor preparation for marriage results in the malign, destructive ways which fail. Both patterns have roots which reach back to the very day a child was born. Which pattern is predominant depends upon the individual's heredity, his environments, and the time he was exposed to the respective environments—both as to *when* during his development, and as to *how long* a period.

"To produce a generation of emotionally mature citizens is the biggest and most necessary job any country could undertake, and the reward in saving of misery and suffering would be colossal."**
Is it not obvious that we were right when we said marriages are not made in heaven, but in the childhood home?

* See particularly the chapters on the nature of love, on the nature of marriage, and on emotional adjustments.
** G. B. Chisholm, "The Psychiatry of Enduring Peace and Social Progress," *Psychiatry,* Vol. IX, No. 1 (February 1946), p. 9.

4

Emotional Maturity

WHAT IS EMOTIONAL MATURITY?

MARRIAGE is not for children. Nor is it enough to be physically capable of caring for one's self. If the marriage is to be something more than the fragments of a broken rainbow, even an overflowing ability to support a family is not enough. Every sociological study of marriage that has ever been made has concluded, either directly or implicitly, that the most important factor in happy marriage is emotional maturity.

Of mankind's three maturities—physical, intellectual, and emotional—the latter is probably the most rare. Many people never achieve it. And yet I am convinced, to my amazement, by a small piece of research, that where a child is properly brought up he matures emotionally first.

What is emotional maturity? It is usually dealt with as an undefined concept, explained by enumerating some of its manifestations. Perhaps it would be well to begin that way before attempting a definition.

The emotionally mature person relies on himself, takes the responsibility for his own acts. He knows that what happens to him is not as important as what he does about it. He continually learns from the lessons of experience instead of suffering from a repetition of the same mistakes. Life is no meaningless, dead-end thing to him. There is purpose to it, and that purpose is self-fulfillment through growth.

He makes a good adjustment to other people, with a healthy respect for their rights and property. With real humility he recognizes his own fallibility. His attitude is, "I see myself as right from my point of view, but recognize that you, with equal logic, see yourself as right. When reality for me is not reality for you, of course we disagree. By further inquiry, together we may arrive at a point of view both of us will feel is right. Meanwhile, neither of us feels threatened. Each has a sense of self-direction, self-fulfillment, and self-respect." Thus, he can work toward reality, for he is not unmindful of nor imprisoned by his own personal feelings. To him, personality is something to be revered. He recognizes it as the result of the internal dynamic relationships between an individual's anatomy, biochemistry, and emotions which determine his unique consciousness and behavior.

He has learned to live with situations he cannot change or honorably avoid. He keeps his promises. He does not blame others for what goes wrong, nor attempt to get the credit for what goes right. His principal concern is for getting things done well. He is kind but with no trace of weakness; not just courteous, not just tolerant, certainly not unable to withstand strain or pressure. Genuinely liking other people, he wants to work with them and for them, even despite occasional provocation from people who are not emotionally mature. But whenever others represent ends which are intolerant, coercive, or dogmatic he resists vigorously in a sportsmanlike manner.

He is sincere, and therefore never a poser. He has found himself, accepted his own unique personality, and continued to develop his potentialities, free from the imposed bondages of anyone who would dominate him. He has learned to retain his inner emotional balance under trying circumstances, the while holding to the things that matter with a sound sense of proportion. He will resolve conflicts in the outer situation in a man-to-man fashion, face-to-face and eye-to-eye. He has few impulsive responses and no daydreams (not to be confused with purposeful, reflective thinking).

He has integrity, not only because he has standards and lives up to them, but because the whole of him wants to do this without ambivalence. Thus, his emotional responses are generally appropriate.

Flattery offends him. He neither makes mountains out of mole hills, nor mole hills out of mountains. Controlling other people is not emotionally necessary to him. He knows he cannot win all the time. Failure is no disgrace providing he did his best. He has the inner strength to assimilate criticism, disappointment, or grief. He has genuine values of his own, but also the flexibility to revise them whenever there is clear evidence to the contrary. He can perceive, understand, and sympathize with other points of view. He is devoid of moral arrogance.

Finally, he has a genuine capacity to love because he knows he is lovable despite all his human frailties.

The emotionally immature individual does not learn from the lessons of experience, but rebels against the past. He remains dependent on other people, either to take care of him, or because of his emotional need to dominate them. When he cannot have what he wants he loses his temper. (She may burst into tears.) He understands little of how other people feel. His value judgments are often poor. When things go wrong he will loose an exuberance of rhetoric, or clam up while he tries to soothe his wounds in the muddy waters of self-pity. He cannot tolerate criticism or aggression from anyone else because he cannot handle his own inner conflicts. He takes out these disturbances by attacks against himself and against other people. He often has trouble holding a job. (She cannot organize or manage a home.) Because his insides are rotted by bad emotional food he has the chronic need of the unfulfilled individual to smash something, even himself.

The tragic result is an inability to love; a defensive attitude resulting from the feeling that emotionally one should remain a hermit, for otherwise he will be tortured. In a rare moment of honesty without insight he will say, "To love would be to sell my soul. The price is too high. Don't love or you'll get hurt."

DEFINITION OF EMOTIONAL MATURITY

The difficulty with the above is not only its inadequacy as a definition, already mentioned, but its failure to distinguish between emotional control and emotional maturity. To assume that all people who are emotionally stable are also emotionally mature is like assuming that people with brains are always wise.

It can be argued that there is no such thing as an intelligent devil, for intelligence and the spirit of evil are incompatible. Nevertheless, there are evil men with bright minds, warped though they be. So also there are men, possessing no morals and knowing only expediency, who are emotionally stable. As Dr. Bush, who has more evidence to go on than most of us, said when we were discussing this, "Joe Stalin was undoubtedly emotionally stable." Certainly the old Bolshevik could choose what emotions he wanted to use, instead of being dominated by his impulses. But he never developed his tender emotions.

Emotional maturity is the ripened and developed ability to understand and to use all one's emotions in personally controlled ways.

This means that in any given situation the individual can deliberately choose what emotions he wishes to use, because he knows why he wants to use them.

Destructive emotions are hardly enough if there is to be happy marriage. It is rumored that Stalin murdered his wife. Perhaps, if he had really understood emotions, he would have seen what his ferocity, often concealed under formal politeness, was costing him. Can it be a fully comprehended emotional spectrum which sees only the infra-selfish and misses the ultra-together? It seems to me that maturity, in the sense we must consider it here, will embrace as a corollary to its definition a general statement orienting the manifestation of emotions toward creative and cooperative outlets, though no one of us will always achieve them.

Because of the inner strength and self-understanding which results from the sincerity of a developed and integrated personality, emotional maturity gives one the ability to perceive, with an accurate sense of proportion, the forces motivating him, the forces motivating others, and therefore to act creatively in terms of the reality of the situation. This is the ability to respect and to preserve mutual individuality within a togetherness, and can involve co-operation, opposition, or avoidance as the case may be.

"Once the realization is accepted that even between the *closest* human beings infinite distances continue to exist, a wonderful living side by side can grow up, if they succeed in loving the distance between them which makes it possible for each to see the other whole and against a wide sky."*

Just being unemotional is a long way from emotional maturity. One form of insanity is the inability to express emotion. Conformity to one's environment may be equally witless, as men like Socrates have shown.

No one is completely emotionally mature. However, most of the time we should be able to be our true selves with other people, in a relationship so full of trust and acceptance that each can spontaneously express himself without fear of rejection. Mature individuals respect differences on the intellectual and emotional level, as all of us do on a physical one. Who expects a man to suckle a baby, or a woman to sing bass? Who can "feel in his own body the pain which another suffers," or even know where he itches?

Being human, we all have the equivalent of Achilles heel. A person may be emotionally mature in most situations, but he has a weak spot somewhere, sometimes. This impairment in no way lessens our need to know what maturity is, how it is developed,

* Rainer Maria Rilke, as quoted from his letters; I. de Forest, *The Leaven of Love* (New York: Harper, 1954), p. 108.

what procedures threatens it. A good marriage is much more than two people relating to each other physically. It must be a relationship functioning in accordance with the insights of emotional maturity.

Reality, as well as beauty, is in the eye of the beholder, and there is no absolute reality in human relations. Our concepts change as we get clearer insights into the tangle of our fragmentary information. *To understand a person it is necessary to perceive what he is seeing as reality.* It is necessary to get inside him and to look out his particular windows of perceiving. Thus, common purpose amid differences becomes possible. To discover unity where there is disagreement is to learn togetherness without loss of individuality.

Love grows when emotions are shared, but only emotional maturity can be truly sharing. The more we disregard each others feelings, the more we provoke the consequences of conflict. This is equally true when we disregard our own feelings. Indeed, repressing honest emotions can be more damaging to an ability to think straight than anything else. To try to kill emotion is merely to drive it underground, where it becomes subversive. I am not suggesting impulsive action. I am saying that to become emotionally mature one must know what he is feeling. We need to put as much intelligent effort into the development of our emotions as we have given to the development of our minds. John Macmurray called attention to this when he said, "A merely intellectual force is powerless against an emotional resistance . . . we are intellectually civilized and emotionally primitive."*

No industry can sell emotional maturity, therefore it sells romance. Emotional maturity cannot be had from a book. It must be developed in living experience. But perhaps a book can help develop insight and understanding of what to work for and why. Certainly there is encouragement and hope in the fact that emo-

* John Macmurray: *Freedom in the Modern World;* (New York: Appleton Century Company, 1932), p. 47.

tionally and intellectually we are capable of new growth (as well as of arrested growth) at almost any age.

Perhaps emotional maturity is one of the two or three greatest achievements of mankind.

Sources of Emotional Maturity

Except for individuals who have suffered some malformation in the womb, or brain injury during birth, I believe every newborn baby possesses the capacity to achieve emotional maturity. Certainly whether or not he does is independent of sex, color, body structure, pulse rate, or intellect. With equal certainty, his childhood experiences will have a great deal to do with how mature he becomes.

Experience must precede any philosophy of behavior which is operational and not just empty words. We respond to our individual perception of how to get along in the world, and once an evaluation has been made it constitutes reality for the person concerned *unless invalidated and altered by further experience which he can correctly evaluate.* The whole animal kingdom continually substitutes past impressions for present facts. It is reactions to these impressions which largely control behavior.

When, untried and untested, we are made to adopt someone else's evaluations, we feel inferior and become haughty. Then, when something happens which shows that what we accepted as true is not true, we resist it, for we were denied the right to think for ourselves. Our intellectual and emotional flexibility has hardened, with no experience of working from uncertainty to increasing understanding.

Emotional maturity should be acquired in a loving environment during childhood. That is the natural way and the easy way. The alternative is a valiant struggle, often requiring competent help, persistently carried on in late youth or adulthood.

To begin with, the child's individuality should be cherished. A terrifying childhood develops rigid defenses which may last through life. All tender creatures, threatened in weakness and suffering an inability to flee, are compelled to develop some kind of hard or bristling exterior in order to survive, as the turtle and the porcupine demonstrated long ago. On the other hand, raised in an environment where their needs are fulfilled without the necessity of self-defense, the lion and the bear become tame.

A secure and affectionate beginning will give the human being an emotional maturity, even in the face of extensive misfortune. My grandfather, aroused in the night by a tumult in the street, looked down the hill from his bedroom window to see his warehouse and fortune going up in flames during the Boston fire of November 9-10, 1872. When grandmother asked him what he was going to do, he replied, "Go back to sleep. Tomorrow I shall need all my faculties."

The baby's realization of his separateness from his mother should come as gradually as possible. (Maternity wards please note!) At the time when he cannot use words it is particularly important that he feel the tender affection of cuddling. Let him grow at his own rate of speed. Neither hold him back nor force him forward. Renunciations should be introduced gently. To snatch the scissors from a baby may prevent *physical* injury, but the baby's interpretation is not the same as the parent's intent. To him it is a ruthless attack.

Secondly, as the child grows older, he should be helped to develop SELF-control under tension. The exteriorly imposed restriction of self-CONTROL is no good for, as Izette de Forest has pointed out, "without knowledge of our self, we have nothing to control."* The essential thing is for him to sense what he is really feeling. Then, in any given situation, he can decide whether or not it is *appropriate for him* to act on it.

Suppose five-year-old Peter is angry because his mother refuses to allow him to play outdoors in the rain. He shouts, "I hate you! I wish you were dead!" The emotionally immature parent, ignoring the child's small capacity for tension under strain, will

* I. de Forest, *op. cit.*, p. 167.

scold or even punish; a procedure which, if persisted in, will produce another emotionally immature individual; a little mind remaining numbed by the horror of past fights and the fear of future ones. Because of the immature parent's insatiable need for superficial emotional support, she denies the boy a chance to examine what he is feeling, and what he would really like to do about it. She merely impresses on him the realization that continuing approval can be had from her only at the price of his own individuality.

There is nothing in the experience to teach him that patience is worthwhile, or that mother is not trying to spoil his fun. Here we have a parent using a child to protect her emotional sore spots, and calling it love; gasping at words as the source of her personal worth without regard for the boy's integrity. Repeated conflicts with a parent, always an unequal battle which the child cannot solve to his satisfaction, become internalized on a subconscious level. Even after Peter has grown to manhood and the parent is dead, he will go on fighting battles with the ghosts of his emotional past, becoming submissive or defiant, masochistic or sadistic, depending on the strength of his personality.

Love is something better than this.

On the other hand, if mother remains calm until Peter's temper has cooled, she can tell him how much better it was for him to have exploded in words than in blows. She can help him to a more accurate understanding and expression of his emotion. Didn't you really mean, "I'm angry with you because you wouldn't let me go out? Well, why was it I didn't want you to go out?" Thus, in imaginative sympathy, she can provide his developing maturity with sources of nourishment.

Perhaps, without the slightest direct evidence, Peter complains, "Sister took my fire engine. I know she did." When the facts are discovered, however, it becomes apparent that baby brother pushed it behind the divan. Instead of ridiculing the accuser, which would produce fear and cut down his analytical powers, mother helps her son to conclude, "It *seemed to me* that sister did." Or, if she loses patience and scolds, she can help their togetherness by talking the incident over with him after she has cooled down. He will learn a valuable lesson if she points out that her calling him a naughty boy was influenced by a temporary loss of self-control and does not represent all she feels about him.

This way lies the happiness of emotional maturity. Love respects the child when he is bad as well as when he is good. Disobedience and rebellion are often a superb though subtle test of "Do you love me for myself, or only for behavior which pleases you?"

Again we see the fundamental problem of individual separateness within a togetherness which must be solved if there is to be emotional maturity. When a child is helped to find out what he genuinely feels (not to be confused with uncontrolled impluse), he can rest secure in an intimate relationship despite occasional antagonisms which are not constructively resolved. Love becomes possible when two people know what each is feeling and can feel together sufficiently to satisfy their individual needs in the relationship. Only the emotionally mature can do this.

Thirdly, the child's right to opinions of his own should be respected. He will then soon come to realize that all evaluations are personal, not absolute. He should be helped to find out what, *for him*, is worth being angry at, worth fighting for, worth devoting time and treasure to achieve. An effective way of crippling self-confidence is to insist that instead of basing evaluations on his own solid experience, he adopt the judgments of his parents.

"I just didn't have the strength to stand up for my own convictions until now I don't know whether I have any to stand up for." How frightening and how angering! No one can be emotionally mature until he has the courage of his own convictions, for only then can he act with self-confidence and without fear. To be dependent on the opinions of others is to be a slave. To honestly hold opinions they also hold may be desirable, but they must be opinions independently arrived at.

The little child should be taught that even in science evaluations are not absolute. Ideas accepted around the world are recognized by educated people as mere temporary approximations awaiting the further discoveries of subsequent observers. Copernicus, Galileo, Newton, and Einstein constitute one such sequence, and the end is not yet.

Most of us put too much emphasis on what other people think. For an evaluation to be valid it must be one's own, not a copied one. "What you seem to think of me," should not determine, "What I think of me." A child's need for a sense of togetherness is so necessary his unique awareness as an individual is often crushed by parents, teachers, or clergy who make him feel acceptance is dependent on subservience. He becomes alienated from his true feelings and thoughts. He matures physically but not emotionally. Other people may deceive, overpower, or abandon him, as well as love him. When he makes this discovery, especially if it comes suddenly and repeatedly amid painful experiences, at a time when he is helplessly dependent, it creates a desperate anxiety against which he will develop defense mechanisms in order to avoid unbearable heartbreak. One way is to fight; another is to try to kill all feeling.

In this, no one ever succeeds. The best he can do is to cling tenaciously to what he has been taught, or to its opposite. There can be no honest questioning, for in his insecurity he clings to the idea that his beliefs are the only right beliefs, and therefore are unalterable. Ideas concerning religion, politics, medicine, diet, etc. are blindly defended, no matter what the evidence to the contrary, for only such rigidity can offer survival value to so crippled a personality. When a person realizes that each of us has his own individual experiences, emotions, concepts, and *nobody thinks of himself as intellectually dishonest,* then he can be more humble. True humility is a characteristic of matured emotions.

Fourthly, the child should be helped to realize that ends are not separate from means, for means have consequences of their own. It is a commonplace that failure to achieve a goal often stems from the unexpected and destructive consequences of using the wrong means.

Not realizing this is a natural outcome of a child's limited experience. He can be helped to understand by parents who encourage him to analyze not only the successes and failures of his own actions, but what he observes around him. I once witnessed a contentious woman suddenly perceiving unpleasant truths about herself because a cat that scratched people was banished to the cellar. Similarly, by skillful questioning, Alan can be brought to see for himself that Jack refuses to play ball with him this afternoon because he hit Jack in the attempt to be first at bat.

Without clear awareness of our own part in creating human relations, we grow up longing to be loved and feeling helpless to do anything about it. The fact is that we influence ourselves by our behavior toward others. The emotionally mature person has learned this and looks for the origins of his difficulties *within himself*.

Clearly the natural and the easy road to maturity is to be brought up by parents who are themselves emotionally mature. But the good parent does not try to do things "by the book" (including this one). He memorizes no rules. He strives to become a better person by *perceiving how his fear of being dominated leads him to dominate (and his children to resist openly or sullenly); how his fear of isolation leads him to enslave (and his children to struggle for freedom); how his false pride prevents him from respecting his children as individuals (and them from trusting him)*. To face these things honestly is painful, but it is also an amazingly rewarding experience for parents as well as for children. It is equally applicable to husbands and wives.

Effect of Emotional Immaturity on Courtship and Marriage

Enough has been said to intimate the difficulties in human relations encountered by the emotionally immature. These can become a demoniac infestation in so intense a relationship as courtship or marriage. Unfulfilled responsibilities, imagined wrongs, tears, quarrels, demands to be understood without any accompanying explanation, and that worst of all techniques of weakness and venom—glum silence—are familiar to every adult observer.

Consider the agonies of an emotionally immature girl (or boy) following the breakup of a college romance. The truth is not that men are unchangeably hostile to her, but that she feels the rejection as surmounting all other emotions. The truth is not that he has broken her heart, but that she assumes the crumbling of their relationship an irremediable tragedy. Nor is the situation final, or wholly determined outside herself. By her clinging or her dominating behavior she participated in creating it, and therefore she can change it, or some subsequent relation, in some way. Behavior is never completely determined by one person. It is always the product of a relationship. Still she blames someone else because the original rejection (father or mother) was someone else. But refusal to take the inescapable responsibility to set herself right will be self-defeating.

Her torch-bearing really says, "I look upon myself as unlovable. Therefore it is unthinkable that anyone else will establish a loving relation with me. I am only pretending to love because I do not know how to love. Still, on the subconscious level at least, I must react to truth. You torture me by offering a love I know (1) is as insincere as mine, or (2) I do not deserve and therefore cannot accept."

Subconsciously she knows that in her present condition she is incapable of love, but she will accept romance because she knows she can return this fraudulent emotion. To the expert, down underneath may be indications of a rich and loving personality, begging to be allowed to grow, but fettered by the fear that if she expresses anger she will build walls that make her unbearably isolated.

Hostility and anger are part of our real selves, and require adequate outlet. Contrary to popular notions, the more we try to restrain and to hold in anger, the more intense it usually becomes, and the more false, vulnerable, and unhappy is the relationship from which it springs. Conflicts should be brought out into the open and settled in grown-up fashion instead of driven underground.

Disagreement can be a chance to set love on a more solid foundation. "I wish you wouldn't do that. It makes me angry," is an honest protest, which expresses underlying confidence in the relationship. "How can you be so deliberately mean!" is neither honest nor mature, for it attacks the other person's motives, ignoring all consideration of his intentions. Where disagreement becomes a fight and someone is defeated, the result is anger, fear, distrust, resentment, guilt.

Between emotionally mature people there can be virtue to battle, for in the end it contributes to togetherness by identifying and eliminating difference. This sometimes involves anticipating how a desired action will affect the spouse, and applying forethought to behavior. The mature attitude is, "I am able to give this up freely and can be happy doing it because in our increased togetherness, which I value, it contributes to me as well as to you. This would not be so if you tried to make me give it up, or if you were indifferent to my needs."

The emotionally immature husband (or wife) belittles the partner, tries to offend her, to anger her, to trick her into impatient disparagements, to frustrate her, all because of two subconscious convictions: *a conviction of the hostility and faithlessness of other people, and a conviction of his own personal unworthiness.* Both stem from his experience as a child, growing up in an environment where individual needs were not respected, and where he lacked an opportunity to create with other people the intellectual soil and the emotional climate in which, together, they could grow individually. Naturally he dare not trust, let go, share, contribute. Dragging the ball and chain of a wrong upbringing, he can only try to defend himself, for in his heart he knows he is inferior to what he should have become.

This feeling of worthlessness requires reassurance, which he seeks by attempting to enslave (or to be enslaved by) any partner in courtship, business, or marriage. His conviction of unworthiness is reinforced by his many failures, not only in love but in everyday human relations. He feels he must fight people (or give in) lest they destroy him, and yet he does not really believe this. The result is anger, desperation, and despair in his ambivalence.

The fury of an irascible husband on the one hand, and the unreasonable forbearance of a wife's meek selfless devotion on the other, have origins in common. The cause in each case is so great a need to feel emotional unity that evidence of emotional separateness cannot be tolerated. In childhood there was no cherishing of contrasting personalities. The fundamental problem of respect for individuality in a togetherness is still unsolved, hence the "I-cannot-let-you(me)-be-different" attitude. In the subconscious lurks a fear of aloneness and consequent helplessness. The result is a need emotionally to swallow (or be swallowed by) those who are nearest and dearest, for it is with them we feel the deepest need for emotional unity.

It is one of humanities greatest tragedies that those unloved and unloving people who most need to love and to be loved are the very ones who most vigorously resist learning how to love because they feel so unworthy. To express love for anyone else is, for them, to be terrified by the calamitous risk of rejection. Thus do they overwork their equipment for offense and defense when the circumstances do not warrant it.

Love allows a person to be free; to form his own opinions; to oppose without being emotionally separated from; to say, "I feel unhappy about this, for we share a wonderful relation. But my faith in myself, in you, and in our life together is not shaken."

Basically the trouble with an emotionally immature person is that he is an unfulfilled person and therefore not his real self. No one is able to discover whether he can experience a broad and rich union of real selves with another person when he does not know his own genuine responses. How, during a courtship, can he size up his probable affinity with someone else, or how can he nourish it in marriage? As a phony, unhappy, twisted, insincere self, which has been pounded out of shape by the cruel though well-meaning blows of other people, he is angry at what he sees in himself, and at mankind for allowing it to happen.

A person's real self is the sum total of the ways in which he can genuinely and wholeheartedly reveal himself to others when he is free of pretense, inhibitions, compulsions, and defense mechanisms. This is not altogether easy to fathom, for there is more than one reality in a person's behavior as observed by others, and there is the complicating factor of the subconscious. On the level of conscious awareness he may see an action as something he *wants* to do. Subconsciously he may simultaneously view it as a *must*. The conscious thought is therefore unreal, for the action will not be wholehearted and genuine.

How easy it is for two emotionally immature people at the outset to believe they are in love. The courtship is a romantic affair in which differences are not squarely faced. Since like seeks out like, here are two persons, each desperately needing someone to feed on emotionally, and neither capable of respecting or preserving individuality in a togetherness because of the mutual demand for personal reassurance. Each soon feels the indifference of the other, and reacts in disappointment. Then comes hostility and self-defense.

Obviously when something as precious as marriage fails to bring people together, not only as they had hoped but as they confidently expected, it drives them apart. Each hesitates to love because of a valid sense of impending conflict, a simultaneous need for loving human relations, and the fear of not knowing how, not finding out how, not being worthy to learn, yet struggling toward an unrecognized goal (emotional maturity) with means inadequate for its achievement.

With a strange combination of tenderness and anger he says in effect, "If I loved her completely without reservation or any effort to protect myself, I'd have to kick her out of my life before I got hurt." Her equivalent is, "I know now why people believe in heaven. They have to. It doesn't seem as though human beings are meant to live this torment within themselves or between each other. Something in me cries out that we need not live this savagery because we were not intended to."

Or, as a student, surprised by a sudden insight, once exclaimed, "When what *he* is really looking for is a good mother, and what *she* needs is a good father, and *they* have a baby, that's tough!"

Marriage should be a relationship in which a person loves as he has never loved before, is loved as he has wanted to be loved since first he discovered that he was separate from his mother. But as long as a person is emotionally immature he cannot achieve this. Nevertheless, emotional isolation is unbearable. He must have some sense of emotional unity even if he has to invent it. In despair he often turns to the supernatural where he manages to feel an imagined security by which to soften the many interpersonal failures he has experienced, or he declares that vanity of vanities, all is vanity in an area where he should have been able to co-operate in confidence.

To Be Born Again

When a person approaches, or has passed, physical maturity without having already become emotionally mature, he is in a bad way. With awakening apprehension many people are asking, "How can I become emotionally mature?" Others are struggling to help them, knowing there is no easy answer, and recognizing their own ignorance. Nevertheless, without the questing minds of courageous men there will never be light in our darkness.

Here, then, is a suggestion:

(I) Recognize your condition. Only the truth can make you free. Honestly face the fact and degree of your emotional immaturity. Recognize that you are not to blame for the condition, but with equal forthrightness acknowledge your inescapable responsibility—and yours alone—to correct it. Your happiness depends on it. (Alas, the more you need to do something, the less likely you are to face it.)

(II) Unless *you* want to change as desperately as you have ever wanted anything in your life, abandon the effort, for there will be discouragement, failure, opposition, and as many trials as John Bunyan's famous hero had. Part of you will struggle hard to preserve the *status quo*. In addition to your own opposition there will be the efforts of other people who want you to fail, for your success will embarrass, frustrate, and expose them (probably including members of your own family). These efforts—your own against yourself as well as those of others—will be persistent, direct, underhanded, and powerful. Nothing short of an unshakable determination to grow up emotionally will succeed.

And remember that it will be a long, long war. How many years (and they included the most plastic, impressionable years of your life) has it taken to become what you now are? Do you think you can undo that in as many weeks . . . or months?

(III) Get a clear idea of what the trouble is, and why it makes trouble for you.

    (A) Emotional maturity is the ability to respect and to preserve mutual individuality within a togetherness. This is impossible for anyone who is not his real self.

    (B) Despite the widely different ways in which emotional immaturity expresses itself—domination, subservience, boasting, excessive withdrawal, etc.—there are basically two strong and generalized subconscious convictions under it

        (1) Conviction of personal unworthiness;

        (2) Conviction of the hostility and faithlessness of other people. These convictions are not absolute. They are caused by the perversion of confidence into fear (see Figure 4), and are therefore capable of change with changed experience.

(IV) Intellectual understanding of the problem may be a good beginning, but nothing can be substituted for the convincing effect of emotionally charged experience. It was experience which made you believe yourself unworthy and people hostile. Only contrary experience can change it. Our opinions are not much influenced by argument or exhortation. Even if they were, the longest journey in the world is still from head to heart. *Finding the contrary experience and believing it is a long, arduous task.*

Even when he finds such experience, the emotionally immature will at first echo the college boy who said, "The evidence of your concern for me is so clear I cannot deny it. But I can't believe it either, though it doesn't seem possible for me to change it. I've tried and tried to break you down, to make you reject me. Then I could crawl back into my shell and say, 'See, I told you life was that way!' But I always fail to make you reject me. I don't know how to cope with this. I can bear rejection, though not in a happy way, by turning in on myself, feeling depressed, considering suicide. But how can I cope with this?"

The idea that nobody will accept him for himself, and therefore he cannot trust people, attacks his need for emotional survival. Therefore he will not abandon his defenses until he feels secure in some other procedure which is even more essential to him. Until he can be doubly sure the change will further, not threaten, his ability to survive emotionally and physically, he is compelled to refuse to believe what superficially seems, even to him, self-evident.

The difficulty encountered by the ordinary person in trying to help someone to become mature is an inability to understand the expressions of antagonism which develop when he begins to grow emotionally. These outbursts are not seen as a sign of increasing faith, for he does not explain, "Now, at last, I begin to dare to let go. I can almost say what I want to say and still feel safe." Nor is the antagonism seen as a valid test of the other person's sincerity. "Does he really care about me, or will he reject me if I get disagreeable?"

Anyone who has been dominated and abused most of his life is deeply impressed when his counselor calmly and repeatedly admits being wrong, or that he has in some way been guilty of an action which was unloving. Then, what began as a threat ends as a wonderful reassurance.

When a wife, struggling to grow up, says, "I think you are being awfully unfair to me, pretending my problems mean something to you, but not caring at all," to reply, "But I do care," is not convincing. For one thing, it is only words. More important still, it puts her on the defensive for it implies that she is mistaken. If her husband actually does care (but not otherwise) the effective way is to imply by voice and facial expression her right to criticize, saying, "To you, then, I seem an old fraud, behaving in accordance with a set of rules." This does not put her on the defensive, *because he does care*, and allows her to figure out for herself that she is the fraud. What she wants is a loving relationship.

To help an unloving person to love and to be loved it is necessary to provide for him experiences by which he can realize *by himself* the degree to which he expects rejection when he could find understanding and acceptance instead. But the initiative must be left to him. At first it will increase fear. Gradually it should develop confidence.

If an emotionally immature wife says, "May I turn off the radio?" the wise husband will answer, but with complete kindness, "You apparently think I would be angry if you did. I guess you'll have to find out for yourself." She will relate the actual result to the expected result.

There are three ways in which an immature person will try to keep his behavior consistent with his inner convictions. First, he will endeavor to control his experience, like the college boy who persistently tried to make his counselor reject him. Second, he will distort what he observes to make it fit his superficial conclusions, like the wife who said, "You pretend my problems mean something to you." Finally, he will change his concepts to fit his new experience.

This does not mean that he has necessarily come out into the bright, clear sunshine of emotional maturity, for he can change his concepts in three ways. He can *apparently* do it, saying, "You've done a lot for me. I don't need you any more," when the truth is he fears going on, sensing that it will soon compel him to face himself as he really is. He can do it *compulsively*, reacting with a dogmatic overcompensation which says, "Now I'm my worthwhile self," despite strong inner doubts. Or he can do it *genuinely*, wholeheartedly revising his concepts because now he knows some people will respond to him lovingly, and some should not be expected to.

It is remarkable how skillfully a person can go through life defending a phony self, once he has been hammered out of shape. The way to help him is to make his self-defense unnecessary, at the same time providing experiences by which he can see for himself that his need to love in a vital spiritual relationship is being fulfilled.

The effectiveness of overcoming fear and developing maturity varies with the degree to which the memories of past fears are reactivated and proved unnecessary, providing the reactivated fear is not so great as to be unbearable, and therefore becomes worse before it can be shown unnecessary.

Reactions to Loss

No other common problem in life brings as much pain as the loss of a loving relationship, or even of one thought to be loving. The most important single determinant of how such losses are met is emotional maturity, for it determines the quality of the love.

Paradoxical as it may seem, we can more calmly bear the loss of someone with whom we were truly happy, than someone with whom we desperately hoped to find happiness. Parting leaves one situation a fact; the other only a frustrated dream.

Whether the loss is due to a rival in courtship, a broken engagement, or death after years of happy marriage, love makes the situation more manageable, for the emotional maturity behind it has always recognized and accepted individual separateness in unity. The mature person does not want to go on alone, but knows he can. The infatuated, emotionally immature individual fears he cannot. Where there is love, even death cannot take away all. The sense of emotionally mature union lives on.

Infatuation	*Love*
Great pain over a long period, and no effort to recover.	Rapid recovery from what is at first great pain.
Frustration.	Acceptance of an utter finality.
Continuing despair and feelings of guilt.	Continuing self-confidence. Separateness regretted but bearable.
Transfer of sense of blame— "Why did God do this to me?"	Continued sense of the other's presence. The loss is not complete.
Passionate grasp at any substitute, or stubborn refusal to accept any.	Deliberate but calm effort to make helpful substitutions.

In Conclusion

In all of life there are few more rewarding experiences than the sense of having grown, for competence always comes from growth.

Years ago I sat in the rear of an auditorium while someone told a thousand high school students how hard it is to grow up. I wanted to shout, "Sir, you couldn't be more wrong! Growing is among our most happy experiences. What's hard is the struggle to grow straight after having been twisted crooked! Even a tree will show you that."

Each year we mark junior's physical growth on the jamb of his bedroom door. Periodically he brings home a report card intended to be a measure of intellectual growth. But in the area of emotional development, which is the most important of all, most of us let time stand still.

To grow always means there are things one can never do again, as well as things, impossible before, which can now be undertaken. When I was a very small boy it was a delightful experience to crawl in or out through the little door for the chickens in grand-father's hen house. That soon became impossible, but now I could drive a horse or carry in an armful of wood.

So it is with emotional growth. We cannot do the small thing anymore, but in its place can take responsibility and carry a load. Thus do we grow to a man's task. Robert Louis Stevenson has something to say about a man's task which is worth memorizing.

"To be honest, to be kind—to earn a little and to spend a little less, to make upon the whole a family happier for his presence, to renounce when that shall be necessary and not be embittered, to keep a few friends, but these without capitulation—above all, on the same grim condition, to keep friends with himself—here is a task for all that a man has of fortitude and delicacy."*

* R. L. Stevenson, "The Task Before Us; A Christmas Sermon," quoted in *Great Companions*, compiled by R. F. Leavens (Boston: The Beacon Press, 1927), p. 272.

5

The Pre-marital Sex Problem

SEX EDUCATION

ATTITUDES about sex are acquired in childhood. They become deeply set, and are likely to last, for they begin to form when the baby is in the cradle. Is he cuddled or ignored, loved consistently or made to hunger for affection? The circumstances under which we learn our close contacts with others are of great importance.

There are two biases with which people approach the subject of sex. Both are more evident in what we do than in what we say. The first is to treat sex as a subject for crude laughter and ribald jokes; a subject not to be seriously discussed, and certainly never to be talked about in public. That idea follows naturally from the primary premise. What person of refined sensitivity wants to raise a loutish whisper to a public shout?

An increasing group, possessed of deep regard for the values of civilization, feel that the important thing is not what one talks about, but the attitude with which one does it. Certainly a sacred and beautiful thing can be discussed in public.

The second bias can be summed up in the common expression that, "Nice people do not talk about such things." Here is an idea rooted in ignorance and violated in secrecy. It is essentially an attitude of prudery; it is the Puritan struggling to disown his emotions because he is subconsciously terrified to face what he thinks of himself, and so buries his true feelings under ideals which hide the disagreeable truth. It is identified with the behavior of a father worrying over his son's virtue, and not recognizing that the real anxiety has to do with a subconscious fear concerning his own morality. The prudery was subconsciously revealed by the Boston matron whose comment concerning the pencilings sometimes found on washroom walls was, "Oh, yes, and they are ungrammatical too!"

The psychiatrist at once recognizes the nice-people-don't-talk-about-such-things attitude as a reaction formation to protect the self from desires of which the self is ashamed. The Puritan conviction that all pleasure is of the devil gives even a layman an idea of what they thought was pleasure.

The Puritan morality, for which most of the modern generation has little conscious sympathy, was based on grim self-control by will power. This not only resulted in mouths merciless in their compression; it produced serious and hypocritical twists of character. More of this still remains in the world than one would think. Well-meaning adults who have counseled me to discuss sex, in my lectures for college students, only in terms of the birds, the bees, and the flowers, have not been amused when attention was called to the fact that these lovely things are largely promiscuous, or that a young person is not going out with a bee. During the late 1930's I was invited to deliver an address on the pre-marital sex problem to the student body of a well-known co-educational New England college, to discover, with wonderment but not delight, posters and college paper deliberately announcing the topic as "International Relations." The question period, following an eight o'clock lecture, went on until two o'clock in the morning. When ten-thirty approached, all the girls had been required by college rules to return to their dormitories. Was this perhaps because of the naïve assumption, made years ago by some indiscriminating dean of women, that intercourse can be performed only between the hours of 10:30 P.M. and 2:00 A.M.?

What is needed is not restrictions which incite youth to outwit where they cannot defy, but an approach to morality and to sex which will become a vital force for improving marriage, and thus to increase human happiness. Young people are starved for sex information, authoritatively and fully given without self-consciousness or dogmatism. They are interested in sex not just because it is sex, but because sex is part of the business of living, and their business is learning how to live happily. This will require the presentation of *all* the facts, and a right emotional attitude in tendering them—not withholding them, not screening them, not forcing them into anyone's conscience in a narrow, dogmatic interpretation. The fact that sex is an acute problem is indicative of the kind of society we have built.

Can you think of any other area in all human activity where ignorance, or last minute instruction, is considered a good preparation? Would you want a nurse, a paperhanger, a clergyman, or a dentist who had acquired his professional attitude through smut sessions and dirty jokes, or via the naïve wonderings of complete ignorance? Would you maintain that after they had begun their life work was the appropriate time to share with them the lucid radiance of what their predecessors have learned? Ignorance answers no problems!

The problem is difficult because there are many alternatives. It is also difficult because of the time required. No one would think of trying to impart a knowledge of algebra in a few hours, yet we are constantly assuming that it can be done in the area of sex. Just before a person is about to be married is altogether too late to communicate information or to establish a healthy emotional attitude toward sex. This should be well under way by the time a child is six years old.

Information about sex is less important than a healthy attitude in giving it. *No matter how complete or authoritative the information, sex education is no better than the attitude it leaves behind.* Attitudes depend more on the way a question is answered than upon the content of the answer. An adult with distorted ideas cannot give a young person right ideas, nor can an adult with repressed emotions give a young person a wholesome attitude. Still, the people who lack normal, healthy, socially-approved sex outlets are often the very ones who tell us what our attitude toward sex should be. No wonder prudery, prejudice, superstition, intolerance have so dominated our beliefs and our emotions that an intelligent, normal approach is unusual. Do not fall into the error of thinking that what is average is also normal. Binding the feet of the high-class Chinese women was once average. Men without whiskers constitute the overwhelming majority in America, but it is not normal.

In our approach to sex we see again the interlocking and inseparable relationship between reason and emotion. When we believe many things not based on truth, we feel many things not based on reality, and vice versa. We think we are believing one thing, or experiencing one emotion, when actually we are believing and experiencing another. This is as easily true of intercourse as it is of love and hate. Copulation is often an unrecognized expression of direct or transferred contempt, as James Boswell demonstrated when he dashed off to a brothel on hearing of his mother's death. There is much apparently nonsexual behavior which has a sexual origin, and vice versa. A girl may become a prostitute as a revenge against an unfaithful lover, or against a domineering father. Often copulation is motivated by hate, feelings of inferiority, frustration, disappointment, anger. Intercourse can be, among other things, an outlet for:

(1) Rebellion against authority
(2) The attempt to prove one's self superior
(3) Reassurance as to one's masculinity or femininity
(4) Proof of one's social acceptability.

Much intercourse, both in and out of marriage, is due to feelings which are not the individual's true feelings. Our attempt to feel what we think someone else thinks we ought to feel, or not to feel what we think others think we should not feel, or even to be without feeling when feeling hurts too much, has already been discussed. "How do you feel about intercourse?" usually produces little verbal response. It produces a tremendous response as registered on that emotional seismograph commonly called a lie detector. We think we are shocked when our true natures tell us we ought not to be shocked; we behave as though we were insensitive to unnatural attitudes that should—and subconsciously do— make us angry.

After bloodshed and inquisition, we have at last become objective about chemistry and physics, with what splendid result even he who runs may read. Should we leave the sex relation to impulse, with the implication that this is all the preparation anyone needs? We have not done that with cooking, or with medicine, or with methods of sanitation. Why should we allow emotional cesspools, reeking with infection, when teaching and research could abolish them? Why go on making the mistakes of past generations? Good intentions are not enough. There has to be intelligent method. We want better plumbing, better automobiles, better food, better means of communication than our fathers had. Why not better sex education? And yet adults behave as though they were conspiring to keep youth ignorant of the sex relation. Do they not realize how difficult it is to endure something one does not understand? Is it possible to exercise intelligent control when one has only vague notions of what is to be controlled, and how, and most particularly why? *The only intelligent reason for restraint is that the long-run results are worth the effort.*

We confuse and confound sex with modesty to a point which has produced such emotional maladjustment that over two-thirds of our college-educated women are frigid. We leave the tough problems of adolescence and early maturity to chance. We punish little children for innocently undressing on a hot day, thereby teaching them, whether intentionally or not, that the naked body is nasty and that sex is sin.

Some sex, both in and out of wedlock, undoubtedly is sin—a different statement from the generalized idea that all sex is sinful, or that the naked body is nasty instead of beautiful. Do we blush that the cows are naked as God made them? Are we sexually stimulated by the sight of a beautiful herd of undraped Jerseys? We would be, quickly enough, if the farmers adopted the quaint custom of covering each cow with a brassière.

The desire for intercourse is a powerful impulse, but so is curiosity. To combine their immense capacities is to invite the thunderbolts. The mind should be filled with solid reality or it will be taken up with error, prejudice, and sentimentality. Ignorance is not innocence. Only out of a contempt for his children can a parent indulge in talk that is sexual humbug—the story about the stork bringing babies, for example.

So often the growing child is made to feel that his erotic impulses are degrading and wicked. Actually, they are part of normal emotional development—unless one wants the child to be a eunuch! It were as intelligent to teach him that inability to breathe under water is sinful, as to teach him that an erotic impulse is wrong. No honest emotion is ever wrong. Think what it implies about the God who created us, to say that a spontaneous feeling is sin. Not the emotion but the response is where morality comes in.

When a child has been taught to feel that his erotic impulses are degrading, he becomes divided against himself. He carries a constant load of guilt, and the more worthy his character the heavier the load. Every emotion is related to the satisfaction or dissatisfaction of other emotions, so his feelings of guilt result in a compulsion for social approval. His emotional center of gravity gets transferred from within him, where it ought to be, to the circle of people around him. Their approval will give him a temporary feeling of worth. This soon wears off, and the old load of guilt will make him compulsive again. If he fails to win approval, the result is devastation to his character because it seems to confirm the validity of his guilt.

The college-educated murderer, William Heirens of Chicago, who killed two women and a little girl in sex perversion, testified that his mother had warned him never to talk about sex because it was "dirty." The idea that intercourse is vulgar is nothing short of criminal. To be sure it can be made vulgar. The more inherently beautiful a thing is, the greater its possible degradation, but the abuse of a thing is no argument against its proper use. Sex desire is inborn. Rightly used it is spiritual and ennobling. It has the dual purpose of expressing love and of creating children. What a crime to give so large a percentage of the population—even at the college level—the idea that the ultimate embrace is little more than a few minutes of naughty pleasure, either to be completely repressed, or to be pursued with indiscriminate abandon.

"I'd just as soon be an old maid," was one college girl's reaction. "It's too much trouble doing all the things you have to do when you fall in love." Such ignorance was surely not her fault. The usual college boy's reaction to a girl is on the physical level. He does not see her as a person; he sees her as a sex machine. Such ignorance is not his fault either.

It is not true that sex begins at puberty. Every little child of two or three has already shown an active interest in his own genitals, and in those of other people. He soon wants to know where babies come from, why his mother's abdomen has grown big, what parents do to make a baby, why little sister has no penis. Eventually he will want to know something about the various positions in which intercourse can be performed, the incidence of desire, why it does not always result in pregnancy. When simply and sincerely answered at the time of normal appearance, questions fall naturally into their proper place. If the answer is accompanied by embarrassment or by anxiety on the part of the parent, the child senses it at once. He knows the emotional atmosphere is different than when he is buying a pair of sneakers or getting a haircut. After that he is likely to keep his questions to himself, while they ferment inside.

Too much emphasis on sex is a problem of adolescence. The mature person has a better sense of perspective. On the other hand, any boy of nineteen who is always more interested in quantum mechanics than in feminine pulchritude should be regarded with pity or suspicion.

Sex education is complicated by the fact that we do not always grade it for the child as we do his food. At age two the child should have two-year-old sex answers; at age six he should have six-year-old sex answers. Where a six-year-old gets entangled in the sex confusion of a twenty-six-year-old neurotic, there is subsequent trouble. Wretched people betray little children, the answer to whose questions should be emotionally balanced, specific, and appropriate. They should never, no matter what the circumstances, be self-conscious.

The proper place for sex education is in the home. The proper teachers are father and mother. But are they? Seventy-six percent of 5065 teen agers in thirty-five cities said they "never discuss the facts of life" with their parents.* They do not want to. Perhaps one reason is the fact that a third of these adolescents know one or both parents have lied to them. Then where do they get their information? There are multiple sources.

Conversation with friends	76%
Experience	36%
Books and magazines	20%
Parents	18%
School courses	8%

Naturally ignorance and unhappy misconceptions are widespread. When and by whom do these teen agers think sex education should be taught? Again, there are multiple sources.

	% Girls	% Boys	Average %
Before high school	48	42	45
High school	14	27	21
Parents	11	14	12
Before marriage by physician	8	5	6
Sunday school	2	4	3
Miscellaneous	39	19	28

* E. Gilbert: "We Don't Discuss Sex with Our Parents," *This Week*, December 11, 1955, p. 26-29.

Parents have brushed off questions about sex far too long. Still, it seems to many of us that father and mother ought to be the proper teachers. The proper time is when the child asks questions. "But Junior is not yet ready for this," someone protests. Why not? Refer me to the sociological study proving it! The proper content is determined by what he asks. Consider the thinking the child had to do before he could formulate his question. "I know you are mistaken. It gives my boy an erection to talk about these things," some parent says. What is wrong with having an erection? Do you want him to be a eunuch? It is only what is done about an erection that may be wrong. Perhaps if the boy had received an education sooner he would not have had an erection. Certainly to make him feel that an erection as such is something to be ashamed of is to interfere with his normal sexual development. I am personally acquainted with a case in which a man of unusually high intelligence experienced disturbing dreams directly concerned with his mother having told him, during his adolescence thirty-seven years before, that every time he had an erection he was less of a man.

Some kind of sex education is going on all the time in every child. Silence on the part of the parent does not keep the child in ignorance. It merely guarantees a poor psychological approach through questionable sources of information. Dr. William Healy has many times and in various books pointed out that the boy who has to bootleg his sex information also learns about stealing from his informant—or some close associate.* There is a dynamic relationship between stealing sex information and learning to steal other things.

No desire can be treated as isolated or discreet. Every desire is related to the state of satisfaction or dissatisfaction of other drives. Something concealed because of a sense of guilt will soon lead to the concealment of other things.

* W. Healy, *The Individual Delinquent* (Boston: Little, Brown, 1915); or W. Healy, *Mental Conflicts and Misconduct* (Boston: Little, Brown, 1917); or F. Alexander and W. Healy, *Roots of Crime* (New York: Knopf, 1935).

Denied information from his parents in a clean, intelligent, un-inhibited relationship, a child's interest in sex as sex grows out of all proportion to its actual importance because of the powerful stimulant contained in the mystery. Americans are the most seduced people on earth for just this reason. Why not become intellectually and emotionally honest with our children, instead of driving them to the gutter for their information, to the rhymes on public toilet walls, to nuzzling on the back seat of an auto-mobile in an ecstasy of animal affection, to laboratory experiments conducted in a canoe? Why leave the sex education of our most talented young people to the college bull session? The bull session is a powerful influence, and one in which there is probably no one who really knows what he is talking about.

Those who have had enough experience to know the boy and girl quarrels; the incongruous, wearing fear of a pregnancy out of wed-lock; the neuroses; the adultery; the divorce that might have been love, happiness, beauty, spiritual oneness—those who have had such experience never treat the problems of the sex relation as trivial. It is time we found and faced the truth, part of which seems to be that everything connected with sex has been under a ban for so long that rebellion has now swung to indulgence.

THE STATISTICAL STUDIES

Professor Alfred C. Kinsey of the University of Indiana has made what is undoubtedly the most extensive and reliable study of American sex behavior.* He has compiled over 12,000 individual case histories covering a variety of types and ages. He has increased the size of his sample groups until additional cases do not change the curve of data. He has even gone back and checked the original data two to eight years after it was given. It is possible for the subject individual to withhold information, but it is not possible for him to fake a case history. If, for example, he falsely claims

* A. C. Kinsey, *Sexual Behavior in the Human Male* (Philadelphia: W. B. Saunders, 1948). See also G. V. Ramsey, "The Sexual Development of Boys," *American Journal of Psychology*, Vol. LVI, No. 2 (April 1943), pp. 217-34.

promiscuity with twenty women, he will not know the right answers which tie in with this experience.

The unfortunate thing about the study is its obvious lack of concern with more than a fraction of a disturbing problem. Never in all history have marriages been happy on the basis of sex only; never in any race, or tribe, or on any level of society. In sixteen pages of double column, tightly packed index of the volume on men, and thirty-two similar pages in the volume on women, the word "love" does not even appear once. Where we most need light, these books are totally dark. To be sure, the researchers have counted accurately, but so can any bank clerk. As far as important insights are concerned the research is about like a study of football which paid exclusive attention to the number of feet the linesmen move, with no attention to what is happening out on the field. No sociological study has ever shown that pre-marital intercourse, or adultery, makes for happier marriage.

The most successful way of learning the truth, Professor Kinsey believes, is in an undisturbed, face-to-face interview in which the researcher is sincerely interested, without criticism, in how the interviewee feels and in what he does. By the questionnaire method 60 percent of the males admit masturbation. By the interview method 90 percent admit it. By the questionnaire method 2 percent will admit some homosexuality. Face-to-face, from 25 per cent to 50 per cent will admit it, depending upon the social group. Oral-genital contacts are admitted by 70 per cent; intercourse with a cow or sheep is admitted by 40 per cent of the farm boys. Kinsey concludes that 95 per cent of the male population have, at some time in their lives, indulged in sex behavior which could be grounds for sending them to a penal institution were it publicly known.

Parents and educators should pay particular attention to his conclusion that an individual's pattern of sex behavior is practically fixed by age sixteen. Few boys have not had some kind of an orgasm by that time. The median age for the first ejaculation is 13.8 years. In 75 per cent of the cases it occurred from masturbation; in 22 per cent of the cases it came as a nocturnal emission; in 3 per cent of the cases the method was either intercourse or homosexuality. In nine cases out of ten, if the pattern at sixteen is known, it can be accurately predicted for the rest of the person's life. Even great changes in social status do not alter the pattern of sexual outlet, as was demonstrated by the famous politician who never became mayor of Philadelphia because a newspaper reporter got a picture of him coming out of a brothel, silk-hatted and resplendent. Emotional background is extremely important in sexual matters.

Individuals vary greatly in their capacity to be aroused, the extremes observed by Professor Kinsey being from no sex experience of any kind in three years, to thirty ejaculations of semen every week for thirty years. Unmarried males average 3.2 ejaculations per week from age fifteen to age thirty, and thereafter drop on a gradual straight line to age sixty-five or thereabout. At age sixty the average is 0.9 ejaculations per week. For married males the figure is 4.8 ejaculations per week at age twenty, gradually diminishing along a fairly straight line, until the profile coincides with the unmarried male at the end.

The average male in our civilization has had a thousand orgasms before marriage, mostly from masturbation, but our changing morals are testified to by the Achilles study of 1923 which found 14 per cent of the boys of age eighteen had experience intercourse; the Hamilton study of 1929, which found the figure raised to 21 per cent; and the Ramsey* study of 1942 which reported 44 per cent.

Over 60 per cent of the females have never experienced an orgasm before marriage, and 90 per cent of those who ever have one reach age twenty-eight before it happens. Among the college girls who have cohabitated, only 33 per cent have reached an orgasm. This tremendous difference between the pre-marital sex experience of men and women is one factor in the difficulty of achieving a good sex adjustment. There seems to be no physical reason for

* G. V. Ramsey, *op. cit.*

supposing that the female does not develop as rapidly as the male, hence it must be the cultural, not the biological, factors which interfere—the repressions and the inhibitions received in so-called nice homes.

The frigidity of college women—which probably does not stem from the college, but from the home the girl comes from—is paralleled by the fact that practically 100 per cent of male impotence (again, practically always an emotional, not a physiological, difficulty), is to be found in college men. Masturbation among college men is about twice that of boys who do not go beyond high school. The latter group prefers fornication, and consequently has a far higher incidence of intercourse out of wedlock than the average college graduate. The latter cohabitates on the average not more than six times before marriage, but pets a great deal, sometimes to a climax. It does not often go all the way to the ultimate embrace. Two-thirds of the ejaculation-bringing sex experience of college males is solitary masturbation accompanied by an appropriate fantasy. Where the fantasy is lacking there is probably some abnormality.

By way of comparison with the 3.2 ejaculations per week Kinsey found for the average college man, the young male of the socially lowest segment of society, unencumbered by inhibitions, averages 6.8 ejaculations per week. For 15 per cent to 20 per cent of such males the figure would be higher. Professor Kinsey concludes that the emotional repressions of the upper levels of society reduce the natural frequency of their sex expressions. It seems equally logical to suppose that the restricted social outlets of the lower level of society channel emotional satisfaction into the available areas.

There are six sources of sexual stimulation:

(1) Masturbation
(2) Dreams or fantasies
(3) Physical contact not involving the genitals
(4) Actual intercouse
(5) Homosexuality
(6) Intercourse with animals.

The only legal outlets under American law are:

(1) Solitary masturbation

(2) Nocturnal emissions

(3) Intercourse between properly married people, method unspecified.

Let us now examine, as objectively as possible, the most common sources of pre-marital sex outlet, and discover what the body of competent psychological and medical opinion has to say regarding the alternatives and their probable consequences.

AUTOEROTICISM

This term is compounded from two Greek words, "auto," meaning "self" and "Eros," the Hellenic god of love. It has to do with self-love, more commonly called masturbation, which stems from repressed cravings denied a direct, normal outlet, and therefore creating an indirect outlet. Its importance depends upon its roots in conscious and subconscious motives, and almost everyone—men and women alike—has resorted to it without injury except for unwarranted feelings of guilt. All the available scientific evidence, free from cant or prejudice, shows this to be true. It also shows that stallions, elephants, and great apes masturbate under comparable conditions.

The infant finds by experiment that fondling his penis is a source of pleasure. The sexual exploration of the young child serves to confirm the finding. He has no ideas about intercourse, he has only discovered that stimulation of the sensitive nerve endings in the penis (or, in the females, the clitoris) is fun.

Sex interest is relatively dominant from age six or seven to the beginning of puberty at twelve or thirteen, at which time sex fantasies leading to self-discovered masturbation are a natural thing. By age fourteen two-thirds of the boys have had erotic play with girls, and 90 per cent of them masturbated.*

Much damage is done by well-intentioned parents who perpetrate the old poisonous untruths that masturbation will lead to insanity,

* G. V. Ramsey, *op. cit.*

or loss of virility, or inability to make a good sexual adjustment in marriage because of turning in on one's self emotionally and so short-circuiting intercourse.

The approach to this whole question of masturbation has been tainted with irrationality ever since Kraft-Ebbing tried to make a scientific investigation of sex about a century ago. He observed that the inmates of the insane asylum masturbated, and mistakenly publicized this as the cause of their insanity. He might as logically have said, "The mentally deranged eat, therefore eating is a cause of dementia." Fortunately Havelock Ellis and Sigmund Freud fell into no such insidious reasoning.

The well-adjusted child or adult will not practice autoeroticism to excess. The frequency among boys and young men varies between an average of one to four times a week, depending upon the individual's sexual vigor.

However, the practice does have distinct limitations. In the first place, there is no personality fulfillment, no sharing of enjoyment; only a spurious, imagined, interpersonal relationship, and a glandular release. Grace Loucks Elliott has compared the difference between masturbation and intercourse to the difference between the uninspired and trudging drill derived from a gymnasium class which exercises muscles but not emotions on the one hand, and on the other hand the jubilant awakening of fresh physical power which can come from a good game of tennis just because the game was played with an inspiring and treasured friend.

In the second place, as Mrs. Elliott's comparison implies, masturbation is more physically exhausting than intercourse, even though the actual ergs of energy expended may be less.

Finally, it has the limitation of being easily available and therefore may discourage worthwhile attempts to achieve something better. It pretends that a superficial act is a deep relationship because the pretense gives pleasure. Continued over a long period of time it may make difficult a good sex adjustment in marriage.

The only way to recover from unproductive fantasies is to find out what is actually going on in the emotions and why. As far as masturbation is concerned, the probable truth is that our civilization has postponed marriage beyond the biological normal age, but the postponement has left our biology unchanged. Hence the substitution.

Be that as it may, the overwhelming body of scientific evidence leads to the conclusion that any sense of guilt is far more injurious than the act itself. Absence of masturbation in a healthy youth is a matter of concern, not a matter of reassurance, to many intelligent parents. It probably indicates some frightening, early experience such as having seen an older boy masturbate behind the garage, and having repressed what was a shocking experience for fear of parental disapproval.

HOMOSEXUALITY

Values change from culture to culture in this world of confusion, instability, and fear. Among the artists and philosophers of the Golden Age of Greece were many homosexuals. In fact, the man who had no interest in such practices was considered something of a sissy by his contemporaries. The homosexual is now widely regarded with a shudder and a turning of the back.

About 3 per cent of our adult population are homosexuals in the narrow sense of the word. In the wide sense, anyone with an abnormally active, generalized interest in his own sex may be so classified. Sexual homosexuality may be due to a number of causes.

Hormones are the determinants of maleness and femaleness, which is why we have feminine women, women, masculine women, feminine men, men, and masculine men. An abnormal hormone difference may lead a feminine man to wish to play the woman, or a masculine woman to wish to play the man. This is physical deviation more than it is emotional perversion.

Perversion comes as the result of wrong social conditioning. A boy can be so terrified of his mother that he generalizes the fear into apprehension and dread of all women. He cannot live without the reassurance of an exchange of affection with someone. So he turns to his own sex for satisfaction, only to find that he is playing with loaded dice.

While we are undoubtedly mistaken in regarding the homosexual as criminal, nevertheless such a person is in great need of psychiatric or biochemical aid, and should not marry until he is cured.

The "crush" is a common form of adolescent semi-homosexuality. Often the real desire is only for sympathy and understanding. The cure is not opposition, but the removal of those pressures or restrictions which make necessary the search for sympathy. Sex standards can be, and often are, a mighty source of evil as well as of good. Society is honeycombed with minor perversions and mental upset because so many individuals are brought up in fear. This is a psychologically wrong foundation for any constructive self-expression, particularly where the expression should be cherished and beautiful.

A high school crush should be handled with care and understanding. Initial patterns are being formed, which fit and serve the final skill. Is the final skill to be sex satisfaction through abnormal channels, or through strong, deep-rooted, honestly felt affection?

HETEROSEXUALITY

Sex attraction between the male and female—not to be confused with affection—is merely a chemical phenomenon, and is no basis whatsoever for love. Love often expresses itself through the ultimate embrace, but animal passion is not love. Passion wants self-satisfaction, not the mutual development together of the self and the partner. The sex instinct has no interest in bringing about a happy marriage; only in at once propagating the race. The female animal in heat is attracted by any male of the species. Instinctively mankind probably is too, at least to some degree, but we have been conditioned into an immense capacity for self-deception in this matter.

Since 1890 there has been a consistent decrease in the percentage of both men and women who remained continent until marriage.

Terman and his associates made a study of this which showed the decrease to be so marked and so persistent, they concluded: "If the drop should continue at the average rate shown for those born since 1890, virginity at marriage will be close to the vanishing point for males born after 1930 and for females born after 1940."* This may be due to:

(1) Postponement of marriage beyond its natural time because of the demands of an industrial civilization

(2) The change in morals resulting from wars, depressions and the throwing off of old religious restrictions

(3) Increased knowledge of birth control

(4) The increased need for emotional reassurance due to the upsetting pressures of our civilization.

There is a wide variety of ways and degrees by which to express heterosexual attraction. Any young person needs to understand them and their implications.

Necking

One does not "make love" with his hands tied behind his back. Necking includes holding hands to be sure, but otherwise anything below the "Mason-Dixon Line" of the shoulders is out of bounds. In physical expression it comes down to holding hands, resting the head on each other's shoulder, and kissing.

Under the right circumstances there can be a lot of happiness in this. The important point is that it should have the same emotional significance to each partner, and that the emotional significance should be honest. If a kiss is to her a pledge and to him only a pastime, she is being exploited for his pleasure. Where both are engaged in mere pastime, and each accurately senses his own feelings and those of the other, the relationship is superficial, but it is not loaded with potential heartaches. Where either, or both, mistakenly suppose the feeling behind the kiss to be a pledge, their future relationship will be empty and full of shadows.

* L. M. Terman, *Psychological Factors in Marital Happiness* (New York: McGraw-Hill, 1938), p. 323.

When two individuals kiss they have definitely crossed one of the boundary lines of intimacy. This is easier to do now than it was in father's generation, but those of us who prefer to embrace only with cleansed and rejoicing heart regret the beauty which is lost by those who cheapen kissing to the level of a handshake, or those who employ its tingle as an impatient incentive to mate.

What happens is never as important as why it happens and how it happens.

Petting

In petting there is no Mason-Dixon Line below which one must not trespass. Fondling of the erogenous zones—that is, the sexually stimulating parts of the body*—even to the point of bringing about an orgasm, is within the rules of the relationship so long as actual intercourse is not attempted.

Such behavior is subject to the law of diminishing returns because it results in mutual arousal followed by mutual frustration. Petting is the correct approach to cohabitation, and a great many Americans make two mistakes regarding it: they indulge, to their frustration, in this preliminary before marriage; after marriage they omit it. Statistical studies lead one to conclude that the men who had the most pre-marital sex experience do the least petting after marriage. Is this a profitable exchange?

It is for each individual to decide what choices he wants to make, but if he or she decides to pet, the decision should be preceded by:

    (1) A realization that petting is the proper preliminary to intercourse. If an individual is not going to cohabitate, he is nevertheless acting as though he were

    (2) A resolve to be openly honest about the behavior, not furtive, secretive, and full of guilt feelings

    (3) An assurance that it means the same thing to the other person as it does to the individual, so one is not selfishly using the other for a thrill, a conquest, a cheap feeling of physical and emotional superiority.

* See Chapter 10 for a discussion of the physiology of sex.

Some young people will rationalize, saying, "Most girls pet and those who don't become wallflowers and old maids. Why shouldn't a girl pet? What does she have to lose?" Other young people feel that she loses the edge of her charm, as well as the joy of saving for the deep sweetness of real love something which becomes cheapened when lightly given. The superior person—boy or girl—will usually say, "Go slowly and search out the superior qualities in me, or try to go too far too fast, in which case I shall see how little integrity and emotional honesty there is in you."

For thousands of youngsters there is little conscious guilt because of petting, but guilt feelings are subconsciously present or they would not be secretive in their action.

At what stage in the thrill procession is a boy or a girl despoiled? At the exact point where integrity has been violated. This varies from individual to individual, but comes soonest in the most superior people. A boy's ideas depend greatly upon whether he is out with a girl whom he respects. If she will not participate in the petting, there is no fun in it for him. He may try, but will soon stop. One of the great differences between the sexes has been that a boy would never attempt venery with a girl unless he did not respect her, whereas a girl would cohabitate only with a boy she did respect.

Should a girl pet as a bid for popularity, or should she insist on being liked as a person, not just someone fondled for a thrill? If she seeks pay in popularity she is already half way to harlotry. The mathematics of human relations is different from the mathematics of arithmetic. In arithmetic something plus nothing is still equal to something. In human relations, sex plus nothing soon equals nothing—and often minus something. If two young people have no more resources on a date than petting they should ask themselves which to value most, the come-on of sex play out of wedlock, or a meaningful relationship which explores areas of mutual agreement, enjoyment, and dislike.

What if the boy is insistent? The time for the girl to say "No" is in the beginning, and the way to say it is, "I'm sure I am perfectly safe with someone like you, who would never be ungentlemanly." The wrong thing to do is to act shocked, for this is actually an attempt to prove how virtuous one is. The truly virtuous do not have to prove it, even to themselves.

If the girl feels that to refuse will be to lose her boy friend, she should dispatch him forthwith and congratulate herself. Would she care to be married to a man who had so little respect for others as to ignore her standards of value? Better think seriously about that. Certainly no girl is respected less by respectable people because she says "No."

The girl who does pet, often has no realization of the imperiousness of the impulses she arouses in the boy. If petting is revolting to her it may lead to frigidity, destroying years of later happiness. And there is always the danger of going the whole way, which could result in pregnancy.

I know no reason to suppose that petting itself is physically more harmful than frustration following stimulation. Emotionally the harm can be more serious. In any event, outside the precious relationships of marriage, it puts the accent in the wrong place because it not only ignores, it obscures the important long-run goals.

Prostitution

Here is the ultimate degradation of the sex relation; a purely physical thing, the only possible emotional satisfaction for the man being one of domination and conquest. It is merely getting close to someone's body without being close in mind or in emotion. I do not wish to deny nor to repudiate the physical enjoyment of intercourse, but merely to put it in proper perspective. There is a spiritual side, too, and the value of the experience is proportional to the depth of honest feeling that accompanies it.

Prostitution is being promiscuous for hire. This is no kind of preparation for marriage for either party. Such irresponsible degradation is far from an emotional adjustment, or even a physical one. The prostitute feels no joy, no fulfillment, no love. She merely goes through the motions of her trade. A gentleman is not only disgusted, he shudders.

All this is especially true now when marriage is becoming less of an economic arrangement and more of an emotional one, demanding understanding and response beyond anything ever experienced before in all history.

The prostitute solves no old problems, but may produce some serious new ones. Yet by age eighteen, so the Ramsey study* shows, approximately 20 per cent of American boys have had intercourse with a prostitute. A larger number have been visitors at a brothel.

Prostitution can be dismissed at once as impossible for any person of discernment. There may be a superficial novelty connected with it, but there is no deep understanding and no spiritual value.

Promiscuity

As already remarked, every man is sexually attracted to some degree by every woman. It may not be by much, but some attraction is there. This sex desire does not treat its object as a person in an interpersonal relationship, but merely as a means of satisfying sex desire.

Mature promiscuity is more an egotistical form of gratification than a sexual one. The real desire is for reassurance. Adolescent promiscuity probably arises from a combination of curiosity and the need for reassurance. Be that as it may, by age eighteen half of our boys have had intercourse with girls of their own social class.**

What happens is likely to follow some such sequence as this: the young man, perhaps a college freshman, hears a fraternity brother, or an upper classman down the dormitory corridor, boasting of his prowess in the mysterious and beautiful experience of sex. The freshman has no way of recognizing this boasting as a means of bolstering up feelings of inferiority. He was not taught that simple truth in school. Algebra, and French irregular verbs, and the exports of Argentina were considered more important

* G. V. Ramsey, *op. cit.*
** G. V. Ramsey, *op. cit.*

knowledge. Perhaps the freshman begins to feel a little inferior himself. He wants recognition. And besides, it all sounds so attractive. How can he know that the banjo eyes, the revealing glimpses of pretty curves, the invitation given by a little cough behind a screen, all have to do with a girl from the vegetable, not the flower garden?

So, out of curiosity, or the need for reassurance, or encouraged by some older girl—no doubt with the stimulating help of some cunning blend of C_2H_5OH—our freshman begins to pet. This now is not just a physiological urge, it is allied with powerful psychological ones. As a result, things may develop fast. He gets emotional, loses his ability to discriminate, goes into action, subsequently feels guilty. The honesty goes out of his eyes. He punishes himself and does not know it. He rationalizes a defense against conscience by adopting one or two attitudes toward the experience:

(1) It was wonderful! Actually it was probably only a shabby substitute for something wonderful. Certainly it could not be truly wonderful under conditions of fear and worry and feelings of guilt;

(2) It was absolved by love. Love? He does not yet know the meaning of the word! Here is only infatuation.

Thus does he deceive himself as to what he is actually feeling, and what his own real values are. The only safeguard against self-deception in the face of desire is emotional honesty.

For an act to be an honest value, the emotion behind it must be appropriate. Exactly as thoughts are true or false in terms of the accuracy with which they reflect the reality of the things to which they refer, so emotions are true or false in terms of the accuracy with which they reflect the reality of the relationship to which they refer. To act and to try to feel as though one were in love, when the relationship is selfish, is to be guilty of an emotional lie. As the intellectual liar soon comes to believe his own falsifications, until at last the truth is not in him—even for himself—so the emotional liar is soon entangled in a mendacious, evasive web of his own spinning. To cheat another person with regard to one's true feelings is soon to cheat one's self. Love cannot exist in the emotional liar any more than truth can exist in the intellectual liar.*

Thus, mutual sex desire can easily result in two persons pretending a loving relationship, but actually using each other as a means of selfish self-satisfaction; possessing each other, not in the effort to give as well as to receive pleasure, but merely to satisfy their own needs. Enjoying the self through the use of another individual's body is not love; it is lust. This, as Macmurray points out, is only a slave trade. Love could never survive such deceit.

It is a slave trade because the underlying emotion is one of conquest, domination, contempt, hate. Seduction followed by abandonment can leave no doubt of underlying hostility. Thus, promiscuity in either men or women is a symptom of an essential inability to find deep, emotional satisfaction anywhere.

Promiscuity and the inability to love go together. The promiscuous individual turns lightly from one person to another because he is incapable of giving himself in love.

What our hypothetical freshman needs to realize more than anything else is the old truth, emphasized in this book, that to tamper with the complete sincerity of his emotional life is to destroy the most precious possession he can ever have—his emotional integrity. Nothing is more destructive to all that is of value in human life. The tragedy is all the greater because one almost never realizes the enormity of his loss. It comes subconsciously.

As time goes by the freshman's casualness becomes hardness, not so much as a protection against other people as a protection against seeing how he feels about himself. Perhaps he marries. It probably ends in divorce. He thinks the reason is sexual incompatibility. He never knows the real reason.

If the objective is just a thrill, then one must perforce be promiscuous. There is a special kind of excitement to something new which never survives intimate knowledge. This is why a girl who feels unattractive and unloved can sometimes lure a boy with her

---

* For a superb treatment of this subject see J. Macmurray, *Reason and Emotion* (New York: Appleton Century, 1938), pp. 117-44.

body. It is also why the boy never stays lured. There are, as a result, thousands who believe it is far more satisfying to love one truly kindred spirit with fidelity than to be on a kissing, bed-sharing, physical level with twenty others. Then what about a mistress?

A Mistress

There are, if one is honest, undeniable instances in which a man and his mistress have developed a really beautiful relationship. There are situations in which a more truthful use of words would identify the mistress as the wife in all but the legal sense of the word, and the wife as the mistress. Napoleon, Lord Nelson, Alexander Hamilton, Wagner, Dickens, all had mistresses. In fact, Charles Dickens was buried in Westminster Abbey only because he was fortunate enough to escape public opprobrium by dying during the part of the week he spent at home.

A mistress is not physically harmful, is exciting, is pleasurable unless discovery creates a scandal; and she has no legal claims. She is entitled to neither divorce nor alimony. Then why not have a mistress? There are four and one-half arguments for it, and four arguments against it.

The first argument for a mistress—and indeed for promiscuity— is that "continence is unhealthy." This, according to the overwhelming body of competent biological opinion, is completely untrue. It is true that a good marriage enriches the personality, and that some old maids—of both sexes—are queer, but continence is only disagreeable. On the other hand, if continence is not to be emotionally destructive, there must be a good reason for it, including the feeling that it is worth while. If self-control becomes too disagreeable, the young man will find sitting on the opposite side of the room helpful, but this does not give him a feeling that his restraint is worth while.

The second argument is that "intercourse gives me pleasure." This is a more honest argument, but is it a true one in the long run? A few hours of worry over whether the relationship will be discovered, or whether a pregnancy must be faced, will turn the profit into a loss. Can anything on the pleasure side of pre-marital sex equal the suffering if the girl becomes pregnant? Of the four possible ways of handling pregnancy out of wedlock, none is a good solution, and at least one is illegal.

Anyone who has been the confidant of large numbers of young people knows the panic, the fear, the bleak unhappiness of the unmarried who have conceived a child. It is an evil thing for an unmarried girl to have a baby, not only because of what it does to her, but because the child has a right to a name, a father, and a home to welcome it. If the pregnancy results from a seduction, the judge may give the boy his choice between marriage or jail, and no subsequent court will annul the marriage as illegal because of duress.* Or suppose the girl tries to blackmail the boy into matrimony by deliberately becoming pregnant. Suppose the boy is not sure he is the father, but can prove nothing. Suppose there is no pregnancy, but worry has delayed her menstrual period for ten days of mutual torment. Even then, is it worth it?

In my observation it is not true that the primrose path is easy, the straight and narrow hard. The correct distinction is that the primrose path is an effortless way, but in the long run much the more demanding. Consider the following two letters. The first was in reply to the inquiry of a college girl who had attended a lecture on preparation for marriage. The second is hers of some years later.

Dearest Darling,

Tonight I am going to try to answer your question, "Why do I love you?" I know the answer as well as I know my name, but I can't seem to find the words to express that love. I will try, to the best of my ability, to answer truthfully and honestly.

Love, to my mind at least, is made up of several factors. Without these factors, which are sex, companionship, understanding, and mutual interests, true love cannot exist. One can love another for a part of them, for example love them for their beauty or intelligence, but it is not true love unless all the above things exist. It may not be clear to

* M. Ploscowe; *The Truth About Divorce* (New York: Hawthorne Books, 1955), p. 48.

you as to how I can love you because of the above facts, so I will explain.

I love you because of our mutual interest in sex. Our tastes in sex are very closely related, and our necessity for sex is the same. Without this close relationship I'm afraid a permanent love would be very difficult. I find a sex relation with anyone other than you does not interest me. A wise man once said that when one is in love he can hold no sex relations with anyone other than the one he loves, or if he does hold outside sex relations it is because of necessity, not because of any enjoyment or interest.

As for companionship, we are very close, my darling, whether you realize it or not. We are able to express our joys and sorrows to each other, and know that the other understands. I know, for my part at least, that when you are not around I feel that I am missing something. I feel as if my right arm has been taken away. I love you because we are so close, and because without you my life would not be worth living. Your ability to understand me and to make me understand is more than I had ever hoped to find in one person. You are my idol, my confessor, my queen.

Our biggest difficulty, my dear, is our various interests. Through your expert teaching you have made me enjoy and appreciate the things you are interested in, and I love you for it. Together, through the understanding we both have, we'll be able to appreciate each other's interests.

There are many other reasons why I love you. I love you for your beauty, your intelligence, and all your little tricks and habits. It would be almost impossible to tell you all the things I love you for, but I know that my love for you is a true love. When you get home, my dear, I will try to explain more clearly how very much I do love you.

Good night, my darling,

All my love,

Dear Professor:

Somewhere in my reading I gained knowledge of the fact that a different kind of love automatically takes place when passionate love begins to wane after marriage.

For my husband and me all the thrilling and exciting moments we had together in the beginning have disappeared. I mean I don't have that excited feeling any more when I hear his footsteps or when he kisses me. In fact, we don't even seem to need each other sexually any more, and consequently we are drifting apart.

Why do I not experience this closer bond which I thought would take place? I'm sure I love him just as much, but without any urges of any kind, one wonders at times whether it is worth living to be without feeling.

I'm in trouble. Can you help me?

Sincerely yours,

When a deep emotional communion is subconsciously sensed to be impossible, our inborn need for it says, "love and sex are identical." Unity in emotional maturity as the basic essence of love is abandoned for the reassurances of physical conquest. The trouble is not so much the fornication as the lack of character revealed by young people who think only about themselves, even when they talk of togetherness. If all marriages were like this marriage, loving homes and even society itself would crumble.

There are those who will call these platitudes. Certainly they are platitudes, and the reason is that so many countless generations have found them true and worth repeating. If morals are worth anything they should guarantee our happiness, not interefere with it. Morals ought to be morals only because experience shows them to be the surest way to happiness. If the surest way to sexual happiness is within the framework of marriage, then we should work for marriage. If it is not, then it is high time we worked for something else. In complete emotional honesty we should endeavor to support and to protect whatever offers the greatest happiness for the greatest number. The centuries and the millions say the answer is the home.

The third argument is that "pre-marital intercourse will make me a better husband." This is insincere and dishonest because it merely advances *the time when* the individual learns, with no guarantee whatever concerning the validity of *what* he learns. He may easily learn the wrong things. A good sex adjustment does not take place between male and female, but between a specific man and a specific woman. No two people are alike. The man-about-town never achieves a real adjustment with anyone. Moreover, as will be discussed more fully in the chapter on the period of engagement, introduction to the sex relation under conditions of fear, hurry, and guilt may ruin it. Even if it does not, Mary is not Alice, is not Elizabeth, is not Dorothy, and marriage to Mary may bring unjustified memories of ways in which Alice, or Elizabeth, or Dorothy were more sexually delicious. Does this make a man a better husband?

A good sex relation is not something to be tried for size. It is a relationship to be developed in beauty together. It were as sensible to take the attitude that the previous economic support of some woman (whose ideas about money would, of course, be individual) would make a man a better husband, as to argue that pre-marital sex experience has the same advantages. Marriage needs to be meaningful memories, experienced together. What more precious memory than the first intercourse, rightly entered into. Surely it is a wonderful and sacred boundary mark. Should it not be preciously shared in marriage?

The fourth argument is "for heaven's sake have intercourse before marriage to be sure you are well mated." The fallacy here is the incompetence of the two young people to arrive at a reliable conclusion. As far as genital differences are concerned, a gynecologist should be the judge. Great variations in physical size can be adjusted under the expert tutelage of a competent physician. As far as emotional differences are concerned, how can these be appraised when a real sexual adjustment often takes months under the most ideal conditions? More about this will be found in the chapters on the honeymoon and on the sex relation.

Sex alone is no adequate foundation for a happy marriage, though it may sometimes serve as an indicator of how the emotional relationships are developing.

And finally, there is the little half-argument of the engaged couple which says, "We're as good as married." This is not true. There is only a contract to be married; there is no legal responsibility, no moral sanction, no financial interdependence. Thus do we trim our facts to fit our desires. This is no search for truth, but only the attempt to rationalize an hypothesis because we want it. This lack of emotional-intellectual honesty is a good way to start to fail.

Because a girl can give no better reason than, "My mother would not approve," is no proof that society's reasons are not sound. Let us examine them, and discover how they stand up under attack. No one can hope to enrich his life by ignoring the experience of past generations.

The first argument against a mistress—as, indeed, against promiscuity—is fear of venereal* disease. "I don't go around with that kind of person, and even if I did, I would use a prophylactic," is the usual response. "Suppose I should become infected, there are sulfa drugs and penicillin." Very well, we will throw that argument out the window, with a tiny mental reservation due to the fact that between 3.8 per cent and 4.2 per cent of male college seniors, depending upon the location, have somehow contracted a venereal disease despite knowing so much. Ten million people in the United States now have, or have had, syphilis, and the figure for gonorrhea is about twice as large.

Merely as interesting detail, there is some evidence that syphilis was unknown in Europe until brought back from the Caribbean by Christopher Columbus.

The second argument—again in correspondence with one to be raised against promiscuity—is the danger of pregnancy. Is the supposed advantage of a mistress overbalanced by the risk? "Our knowledge of birth control will take care of that all right," somebody says. Very well. That argument goes out the window too, but again with a tiny mental reservation, because no method of birth control yet devised is wholly reliable except continence. In the United States 4 per cent of all births are illegitimate. Even doctors and nurses, who presumably have better information and better methods than the rest of us, are sometimes embarrassed to find themselves involved in an extra-marital pregnancy.

* The word "venereal" comes from Venus, the Roman goddess of love.

The third argument is that comparisons are odious, and sex experience with several individuals makes a person unhappy with but one. This is probably true, unless the person eventually marries someone who to him is the superlative sex partner, but it does not prove that the greatest happiness for the greatest number lies in monogamy. There still remains the argument, so far as this point is concerned, that variety is the spice of life, and why miss most of the flavors? Then perhaps we should discount this argument.

The last argument is one of such seriousness that it cannot be taken lightly: the effect on character and personality which results from fearing discovery, sneaking off together, nurturing a subconscious or perhaps painfully conscious sense of guilt. Self-respect is as necessary as bread and water and a roof. I have seen a girl paralyzed from the waist down as a subconscious self-punishment for her feeling of guilt at having harbored the blandishments of a designing male. She was saying in effect, "Legs, you have been very wicked, but you will never betray me again because I shall punish you by paralyzing you." When she came to understand this, she arose from her hospital bed and walked home.

This is an extreme case, but it conveys a truth: *every individual stands trial in the courtroom of his own conscience, and no guilty person is ever acquitted.*

Then there is the insecure dependence: the girl who is left a "college widow" after he graduates and moves away to marry someone else; the hysterical, "What can I do?" of the woman who has come to love her lover, but his fancy has now fled to the shelter of some other bosom. In a quarter century of counseling with students and others, I know of only two cases where apparently no one was hurt. Certainly there was the necessity to be secretive, to deceive, perhaps to lie for fear of being caught. Is this romance? It may have had suspense, adventure, possibly conquest on one side, or both, in finding out whether the other would cohabitate. Romance perhaps, but emphatically not love.

Almost always the lover-mistress relationship is inadequate in the long run. The two are only mated without the security of marriage. Sooner or later any relationship finds itself under a test load, and lacking the bonds of marriage it is likely to go to pieces. There are many available case histories: Goethe, Isadora Duncan, Bertrand Russell.

I am not so much concerned over whether or not an individual defiies convention or even law. Jesus Christ, Socrates, Galileo, Washington, Lincoln all went counter to some regulation of their time. The important thing is that they did so for the sake of some principle for which they were willing to give their lives, never for personal, selfish reasons.

Thus the acid test becomes whether the individual is concerned with extra-marital intercourse for his own pleasure, or whether, without any personal gain whatever, the individual is willing to fight openly for the right of some other man to have intercourse with his sister or the girl he may later marry. Sincerly held, this second position is one which commands respect no matter how vigorously one may disagree with it.

In any case, there is always a legal and social responsibility to any girl in terms of what her expectations are should she become pregnant.

The Problem of the Unmarried

It is absurd to suppose that the unmarried have no sex needs.

What then are young people to do whose circumstances of age, or finance, or opportunity do not permit marriage? What about the thirty-year-old widow? Sex desire is certainly active. How should it be handled?

Surely we cannot achieve improvement by throwing away all previous human experience. The premature acceptance of unwise ideas may hurt us, our children, and our children's children. It is desirable that the younger generation have some evidence of what the probabilities are in the light of what we now know.

The answer in the book, as far as the United States is concerned, has always been "physical exercise and continence." But physical exercise is no substitute for intercourse. Indeed, the sociological studies show that exercise increases sex desire. The farmers are more sexually active than the professional men. Then how about sex-releasing activities like square dances, where one goes from partner to partner with a rapidity which prevents specialized stimulation? How about amateur dramatics, or membership in a mountain climbing club, or a stag party? The truth seems to be that there is no adequate substitute for intercourse. Certainly the bull session, the movies, the hit parade songs, and the advertisements all subtly or openly imply that sex is a lot of fun and the answer in the book is mistaken. Impulse and a great deal of behavior agree with this interpretation.

Here is a dilemma, and a vicious trap for those who do not take the sex mores seriously, as well as for those who do. The first group finds that whereas society seemed to be only fooling in its declarations as to what conduct the community would tolerate, it becomes cruel, hypocritcal, and sadistic toward anyone who gets caught. The second group often tries to deny the existence of the sex impulse. This does not destroy it, but only drives it under cover where it takes a fearful vengeance in emotional tensions. John McPartland has expressed this two-valued attitude:

". . . at one level of our social existence we are the most sensual and profligate of peoples, worshipers of breast and thigh, separating the fun and frolic of sex from any bindings of family and child. At the other level of our social existence we are the prissiest of prudes, a monogamous and chaste people to whom virginity is so sacred that it cannot be mentioned on our radios."*

What a maze of inconsistencies in which to rear the young or with which to confront the unmarried! How much better to point out the alternatives and their probable consequences, and then allow people to choose for themselves instead of giving them judgments that are sharp, unyielding, and dictatorial.

Free and Uninhibited Sex Expression

For the Eskimo and the Patagonian a much freer sex activity for the unmarried works happily because children are welcomed and

* J. McPartland, "Footnote on Sex," *Harper's Magazine*, Vol. 192, No. 1150 (March 1946), p. 212.

loved by the tribe without regard for legitimacy or parental economic responsibility. If a girl has given birth to a child out of wedlock, she is now more desirable as a wife than before because of her proven fecundity.

Our society has a different approach to these questions, with the result that no matter what the ultimate cosmic truth may be, certainly the one sure, absolutely safe procedure for the individual in our culture is to limit intercourse to experience with one's spouse. Despite this, the socioliogical studies, as previously mentioned, show that we in America are rapidly approaching a time when no one, male or female, will be virginal at marriage.

Sex Repression

Most clergy, the dean of woman, Aunt Hannah, and the textbooks on marriage all imply or openly declare that intercourse is not for the unmarried. They could never agree that infidelity is by no means the most serious offense against marriage. They are only embarrassed by a reminder that Christ condoned the woman taken in the act of adultery. They do not differentiate between adultery and fornication, but twist the wording of the seventh commandment to bolster their position. They behave as though the content of one's conscience were one's own inborn sense of truth, instead of the result of one's desire to feel approved and safe in one's environment. Thus does civilization distort what should be our true conscience into a false conscience. What we ourselves, independent of any outside influence, feel to be wrong is our true conscience. What someone else has impressed upon us as conduct we must embrace or we shall be ostracized, gives rise to our false conscience. This falseness is what leads us to self-hatred, to false emphasis on our unworthiness, and to repressions.

The harm done by repression is being more and more widely recognized. Certainly repression is not virtue, if for no other reason than because it is not emotionally honest. How can anyone be frightened into virtue? To attempt it is criminally wrong, cruelly false, and deceptively ineffective because the result is fear, not the discriminating judgment which alone is in virtue. It results in the need for a glorified and a degraded image, both of which are idealized and despised as discussed in an earlier chapter. It squeezes, and twists, and warps until the goodness has gone out of us. It destroys with fear that eats below the level of consciousness, leaving only a discontented, cancerous shell of what should have been healthy emotions.

A Long-run View with Short-run Substitutions

Trying to compel the individual to conform to the conventions of society is not always possible, and has not succeeded. We do not tell men that they must not contract tuberculosis; we try to remove the conditions that cause it. By the same reasoning, we must either revise our professed sex conventions, or find real values beyond mere obedience in observing the old conventions.

Every thought will express itself in action unless inhibited by some other thought. The thought which finally remains is the one which determines behavior. The only power of restraint worth talking about is seeing what is most worth while over the long-run, and working for it.

Sacrifices? Of course. This is a universal experience. All behavior is a matter of what one wants to have, and what he is willing to give up in order to possess it. There is no procedure by which to gain everything and to lose nothing. What are the things which must be given up in order "to make holy" what remains? What are the things which must be given up in order that a marriage shall not be unhappy, or just commonplace? The test of marriage is not passion, but character.

The pre-marital sex problem is to find emotional outlets which in no way conflict with the interests of others, which are not accompanied by feelings of guilt for anyone because they in no way damage anyone. For different individuals in different environments the behavior which fulfills these requirements will be different.

Each of us should find what are for him the real values, and then work for them. This is not to be done superficially, or by following an impulse. It requires the difficult effort of achieving emotional honesty. Ask the happily married people what their real values are. Ask the man-about-town what his real values are. Better still, do not listen just to what they say, but watch what they do. Then compare the results.

The sociological studies throw some light on the problem. Terman found only a negligible effect on happiness when intercourse took place with the future spouse only. He says, however:

"One's chances of marital happiness are at present favored by the selection of a mate who has not had intercourse with any other person."*

And also:

"It is not true that the happiness of a marriage is less adversely affected by lax sex practices on the part of the future husband than it is by lax sex practices on the part of the future wife." If this is true, then is it not worth a few years of self-control to improve the chances of many years of happiness? Terman believes, however—and the overwhelming preponderance of competent professional opinion agrees—that many other factors are far more important than virginity in the achieving of a successful marriage. Nevertheless, it is not to be dismissed as a stone age relic.

Mistaken Ideas

There are four mistakes young people are likely to make about the sexual side of marriage. In the first place they so often think the problem of intercourse is solved by marriage. So it is, in a good marriage, but this does not mean the necessity for self-control has gone. Is a wife a barometer to her husband's sexual weather? Just because he comes home from a successful day, quivering with expectancy, will she be dry tinder to his spark? She may very much want to be left alone, in which case, if he is a good husband, her desire will not only be respected but will be graciously respected.

Much of our lives must be intelligently controlled if we are to

---

* L. M. Terman, *Psychological Factors in Marital Happiness, op. cit.,* pp. 327-29.

be happy. Perhaps one of the advantages of being virginal at marriage is the practice it has afforded for considerate self-control after marriage. As in school the ability to do algebra does not mean no more problems, but rather the capacity to go on to the calculus, so in life the ability to handle wisely the pre-marital sex problem does not mean no more problems, but rather the capacity to go on to marriage.

The second mistake is the idea that sex is a short-run value. So many young people think "eat, drink, and have intercourse, for tomorrow we shall be incapable of it." Actually sexual vigor goes on for at least thirty years, followed then by a gradual tapering off. Numerous are the grandparents who still find indescribable ecstacy in expressing their deep and abiding love through the ultimate embrace.

The third mistake is the idea that intercourse, as our vulgar expressions imply, is something one person does to another. This is not true, even on the barnyard level. It is a beautiful experience two people enter into *together*, always preceded by a meeting of minds. The only exception is rape, of which no animal except man is ever guilty.

This implies the answer to the fourth mistake: namely, that intercourse is only a meeting of bodies. On the level of the prostitute this is almost true. Between husband and wife it should be a meeting of minds and of personalities on a spiritual plane, then and only then, physically expressed in a complete reciprocity of affection.

In Conclusion

One final necessity remains: to examine what one's feelings should be to make intercourse proper in the light of the fact that it is a physical and emotional expression of love. If love is taking delight in the existence of the other person for her sake; if it is being completely and delicately aware of her feelings and her needs; if it is chershing her above all else for what she *is*, and never as an instrument for feeling pleased with one's self, then intercourse will be undertaken even more for the enjoyment it conveys than for the enjoyment it gives.

By this criterion there is surely as much sexual immorality among married people as among the unmarried, for as Macmurray says,* the fact of legal marriage cannot make chaste what is already unchaste. "Chastity is emotional sincerity."

Virtue is not a means. It is the end result of good method applied with discriminating judgment. The power of restraint ought never to stem from fear, but from a sincere feeling that the restraint is worth while over the long run. Otherwise, the feeling that the fruit is ripe and it is foolish not to eat it will lead many young people to find ways to outwit any restrictions.

The sociologists say that no society has yet existed without placing some restrictions on the sex urge.** If these are worth while, they should be obeyed. If they are not, they should be abandoned. Let us find the rational restrictions and gladly follow them for the sake of our own happiness, remembering that there is no procedure by which to gain everything and to lose nothing. Value depends upon what a person uses a thing for and what it is worth to him.

* Macmurray, *op. cit.*, p. 133.
** The idea that primitive societies have unregulated sex expression will be dispelled by reading any text such as G. May, *Social Control of Sex Expression* (New York: Wm. Morrow, 1931).

6

Criteria for Choosing a Mate

BECAUSE we know so little about bringing up children, many young people look to marrige as the Utopia which will furnish them the intellectual soil and emotional climate they so yearned to have in childhood. They want something harmonious, sustained, and time-proof as the eternal, but often fail to realize that such a marriage must find, create together, and maintain a mature relationship with sufficient factors of safety neither to break under overload nor to develop cracks due to repeated pressures.

Marriage is, to be sure, a calculated risk, but there had better be some thoroughgoing, intelligent calculation, based on reasonable assumptions.

Among many so-called savage tribes no young man or young woman is allowed to go courting without first having demonstrated sufficient skill and maturity to convince the elders of the tribe that the responsibilities of marriage can be successfully discharged. Boys must know how to provide food; girls must be able to prepare and to serve it.

Similarly, in our culture, certain requirements should be objectively considered before courtship is undertaken. To begin with, referring back to the pyramid of desires discussed in Chapter 2, self-realization through creative self-expression should precede love. How can a person know what he wants until he has found out what he is? The average young person needs to know a great deal more about himself before he can accurately sense whether he is in love, or is only infatuated.

A wife who complains that her husband is weak and without courage is often sickened by her own misdeed. The weakness and the lack of courage is probably the very reason she married him. A more self-reliant man would never have suffered the domination she was determined, perhaps unknowingly, to exercise. The woman who first marries a chronic alcoholic, then a gambler, and finally ends up with someone who is physically abusive, does not realize that what she is seeking is sympathy and attention, not love. Because of ignorance of herself she sacrifices her happiness.

Until a person fully understands the emotional forces within him, he will be betrayed by his own subconscious fears and desires. There is no field where ignorance is so calamitous. Sometimes it is not the calamity of ignorance but the evil of false knowledge that betrays us. By the amount one fails to know the truth about himself, by exactly so much will he misunderstand what he is looking for in a partner and why. What does he need? What does he have to offer? *If the kind of person who can give what he needs would not be happy with what he has to offer, then some character changes are necessary.* Trouble always rises from incompatible things.

Understanding one's self must include an accurate perception of why marriage is being contemplated. To escape from an unhappy home? Because she is beautiful, or he is handsome, or either has money? For revenge of the "I'll show her!" variety? As a way of defying parents with an, "I'll marry Joe if I want to!" To escape being an old maid? Because other women will envy her, or because she will give him more social prestige? No one of these is in any way concerned with creating together an intellectual soil and an emotional climate in which each can flourish, far superior to what either could achieve alone.

Almost invariably the approach to courting is, "What sort of a girl is she?" "Good dancer, pretty, able to entertain, nice disposition, good housekeeper, etc." Sometimes we are intelligent enough to look beyond the showcase to what is in the warehouse; to perceive the difference between the dazzling beauty of an ornamental hussy and the less obvious but more important beauty of character, intelligence, and emotional maturity. What an individual pays attention to is an important part of wisdom, because what reaches an individual in any situation is a function of what he pays attention to.

Almost never is the approach to courting an honest, searching, "What sort of person am I?" Without knowing this, it is so easy to marry someone who possesses a characteristic the individual admires, but lacks: energy, ideas, good looks, money, contentment. This is no basis for lasting happiness. Philip is not Ruth. Annoyed and envious, he may be unhappy with her bye and bye.

The great need is for less romance and more analysis before marriage, by which to bring about more love and less analysis after marriage. Benefits stem from right action. Good intentions are not enough. Nothing short of right method leading to the truth will do, and few men in the world seek truth at the expense of all else. A scientific approach—providing that it really is scientific —is far better than a romantic one. No man would pick out a cow by moonlight or without some knowledge of dairying.

How then, can one be reasonably sure of making a right choice? Certainly the answers that one gets are always in terms of the questions which one asks. There must be truth to the question before there can be truth to the answer, and only right questions lead to right answers. Too often we accept answers before we know what the questions ought to be.

It is not possible to postulate rules in answer to, "How shall I know when I am in love?" To establish a set of requirements like health, intelligence, sense of humor, emotional maturity, etc., is like offering honesty, loyalty, industriousness, reliability, promptness as the reason for deserving a raise. These are the reasons a person is not fired. Everyone is expected to fulfill these qualifications.

There are, however, general observations which deserve attention. Intelligent people are more likely to be happy together than ignorant ones. Girls who are popular with other women, and men who are admired by other men, more often have happy marriages than those who are not. One does marry the other person's family, if for no other reason than that it contributes half the heredity of the children. The family tree should be examined for good health, sound minds, and sound emotions. Here again we are unearthing reasons without which no marriage should be considered, instead of reasons for the probable success of a specific marriage.

When a man acts wisely, he proceeds on facts that reasonably assure the result he wants, and he is motivated by an intention based on his really wanting that result over the long run. Consequently, despite the jeers of the romanticists, the wise young person will approach courtship by first writing down his long-run objective. He should not be discouraged if the resulting analysis leaves a good deal to be desired. This very fact will help him to realize how his thinking is befogged by the confusing vapors of sentimentality, lack of self-understanding, ignorance of purpose. What are the objectives? What are his genuine values in life:

Competion with other men?
The creation of something beautiful?
A home in which to be made physically comfortable?
Legitimate sex outlets?
Getting drunk?
Love, according to the definition in Chapter 1?

What are the feelings, attitudes, hopes, fears behind the answers? Reliable answers depend upon the reality of one's standards of value in relation to his real self and his true environment. A value judgment that is sound, both subjectively and objectively, can be depended upon. On the other hand, the sure way of never arriving at a reliable answer is not knowing what one really wants. Failure follows impulsive starts, lack of good method, and even too much emphasis on intellectual response, as though reasoning instead of feeling were basic. An intellectual conclusion, reached before feelings are understood, often results in a stalemate on the intellectual level. This leads to differences in what we say and what we subsequently do.

There are four areas which deserve careful, penetrating examination, and objective proof of correct fulfillment, if a marriage is to have a good prognosis. Some marriages may be happy despite seeming to violate these principles, but they represent rare exceptions.

Mutual Emotional Maturity

Emotional maturity has already been discussed at length in Chapter 4, but is of such importance as to merit renewed consideration here. The personal observation of many competent authorities and the evidence of every sociological study has shown it to be not only the first but the most fundamental requirement for happiness. With mutual emotional maturity a husband and wife can channel their vexations, not just spill them. Lack of emotional maturity is a fatal disqualification.

We are shocked when some hillbilly marries a twelve-year-old girl. She will outgrow her physical immaturity. Emotional immaturity is far more serious and is not remedied by the mere passage of time. The childhood pattern for meeting disappointment or for trying to get what one wants is to cry. This is to be expected at age six. It is out of place at age twenty-six.

Many Americans have the idea that emotional maturity consists of not showing what one feels and not caring what others feel. I disagree. A person has achieved emotional maturity when he can handle his own inner emotional experiences without loss of equilibrium. He is not upset by outside emotional pressures because he does not recognize the authority of outside emotional pressures. Hence, he can listen to and profit from constructive criticism without resentment or rationalizing. He can accept responsibility for himself; be subordinate to good leadership, though never allowing himself to be enticed or coerced by any-one; give attention to what needs to be done now, without trou-bling over the past or worrying about the future save as they relate to what ought to be done now, and how, and why; make in-telligent decisions without dawdling; realize and react in terms of the fact that other people are involved in every situation; main-tain an open mind that is willing to "wait and see"; be free from foolish fears or anxieties; approach religion and sex with a whole-some attitude; refrain from trying to dominate other people, or interfere with their lives; perceive both good and evil in himself, and know how to react to both; absorb an attack without fight-ing back, at least until he has thought through what he wants to do and why. The emotionally mature person possesses self-con-fidence, serenity, forthrightness. He cannot be lured into an argument. He refuses to be beguiled into doing anything he feels incompetent to do, or has a good reason for not wanting to do. He has a sound approach to life because he has a sound method of self-evaluation. And he is capable of creative self-expression without needing much reward beside his own satisfaction in the achievement.

Some signs of emotional maturity are:
(1) Confidence in and respect for one's own integrity:
    (a) believing one's self to be important without taking one's self too seriously
    (b) recognizing and evaluating
        pressures from other persons
        pressures from outside events
(2) Ability to face reality honestly, no matter how disagree-able
(3) Self-control, even in upsetting situations
(4) The desire to serve instead of the desire to shine
(5) Well-developed discrimination.

In a good marriage, both husband and wife will grow in emotional maturity, although it is first necessary that they each have reasonable emotional maturity to start with.

Two emotionally mature people, once married, almost always remain husband and wife. They do this not only in the legal sense, but also in the emotional sense. She will not later find it necessary to try to get from her children the emotional satisfactions she should experience with her husband. He will not later transfer his affection to the accumulation of a bank account.

Some signs of emotional immaturity are:

(1) Overdependence on others
    (a) inability to be a self-governing person
    (b) desire to be babied
(2) Inability to face unpleasant reality (failure to face a fact makes it none the less a fact)
(3) More emotion than the apparent situation warrants
    (a) oversensitive to praise or blame
    (b) too much "in love" to eat, sleep, work
    (c) groping from thrill to thrill
(4) Desire to dominate
    (a) wanting to shine instead of to serve
    (b) bluster, boasting, bravado
    (c) demanding special consideration
(5) Poor sense of proportion
    (a) overemphasis on sex
    (b) thinking personal problems will be solved by marriage
    (c) assuming a pretty face is a wife, or a handsome physique is a husband
    (d) believing being in love with feeling loved *is* love
    (e) supposing one has a right to be loved without earning it.

An emotionally immature woman may marry a man because subconsciously she desires to mother him. This is a source of happiness for a while, but the wet footprints of her immaturity become apparent when the children come along and she finds it is more gratifying to mother them. The husband is now ignored. If he too is emotionally immature, he will respond in hurt anger at no longer being babied, by establishing a tyranny over the family finances, or some such reprisal.

The "clinging vine" is an emotionally immature person. A man feels greatly flattered by such a girl during courtship because she feeds his ego by making him feel so strong and superior. But marriage is a partnership, not a dependency. He soon gets annoyed by her inability to row her weight in the boat, or to make a bilateral approach to their problems. She responds by pouting, crying, refusing to talk, spending money they do not have, or exploding in unfounded jealousy. Every night he comes home to quarrels that begin again, but for years they both hope for a miracle which will turn the crucifixion of their marriage into a resurrection of what they experienced while courting. Neither one makes any attempt to grow up.

Jealousy and overpossessiveness are signs of emotional immaturity. Will a husband, imprisoned by a wife, be happy just because the rounds of his custodian are accompanied by the rustle of a pretty skirt?

Oversensitivity to criticism, the desire to dominate or to be babied, overemphasis on sex, are all dangerous emotions. So are attempts to appear radiant, delighted, superior. Happy people are spontaneous and natural. They never pretend.

Emotionally immature people lack dependability; are unwilling to help others, but want to command others; exaggerate; show off; cannot keep a secret; feel inferior, and reveal it through sarcasm and ridicule, especially behind the backs of their victims. Every one of these characteristics is due to lack of self-respect, and consequently wanting revenge on other people because of being afraid of other people. Such individuals build barriers of prejudice, suspicion, and hate because they can never see another person as a potenial friend.

Emotional maturity is most likely to be found in a person who had:

(1) Happily married parents
(2) A happy childhood, devoid of anxieties
(3) Love from his parents in the sense discussed in Chapter 1
(4) No severe punishments as a child, and therefore, no repressed hates
(5) Discipline that was a kind but firm education instead of punishment, and therefore resulted in self-control instead of in rebellion.

The superior happiness of the parents is of great importance.

Those who grow up on a battlefield know best the technique of fighting. Better methods can be learned, but only with determination stemming from wholehearted desire. The domestic battlefield is as much a place of emotional fear as the Waterloos and the Gettysburgs are places of physical fear. He who is afraid dares not expose his real self (physical or emotional); he who is not sincere cannot love or be lovable.

The necessity of having been loved as a child has been emphasized in previous chapters—perhaps overemphasized, but I think not. Remember how we tend throughout our lives to recreate the situations we could not solve as children? If a boy was not loved by his mother, he will be ill at ease with girls, subconsciously always suspecting that he is in the mother situation all over again. The girl will sense his suspicion and resent it. He senses the resentment, and so the snowball grows. Only by a miracle will he discover his trouble is emotional immaturity, and remedy it.

How these emotional relationships operate has been illustrated in Figure 6. A child is dependent upon other people. An adult should be able to take care of himself. But exactly as a child who is not allowed to learn to walk, will never get above a toddling dependence on someone else to support him, so a child who is not allowed to take responsibility for himself will suffer from the arrested emotional development we call suspended adolescence. Given the opportunity, a child will learn good judgment by making mistakes exactly as he will learn to walk by bumping his nose.

If now, an emotionally mature person marries someone whose emotional development was arrested, the result is incompatibilty. The mature individual will resent the other's childish dependence (or the overcompensations he uses in the attempt to convince himself of his independence), and the suspended adolescent, despite his compensations will be panic-stricken by feelings of rejection.

If both husband and wife are emotionally immature, the result

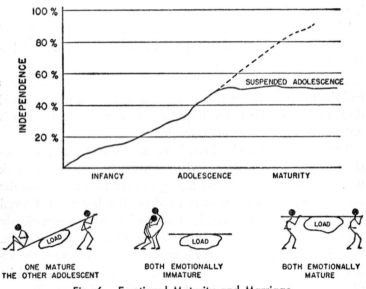

Fig. 6.   Emotional Maturity and Marriage

is even worse. Because of the conscious desire for support they cannot have, and of the subconscious anger at not being able to take care of themselves, there will be hostility in each of them. The result will be two frightened individuals, each trying to be held up emotionally by the other. They will fall together in weakness as they fight to cling to each other for support. Each will hate himself for his weakness.

If two emotionally mature individuals live and work together, each will take the responsibility for his share of the load, and in an emergency, each will be strong enough to help the other without the feeling of being threatened or imposed upon. But I know of no presently availabe way by which the layman can determine quickly how emotionally mature a person is.

MUTUAL BACKGROUND AND OUTLOOK

One does not attempt to team up a Percheron and a race horse, although only an aristocratic prejudice would assert that the latter is more valuable to mankind. Similarly, without implication as to the value of either as a person, a man is not sufficiently versatile to hold a $10,000 job during the day and come home to a $3,500 wife at night.

Let no one make the mistake of thinking this is equivalent to saying a high school graduate is somehow a lesser intellectual breed than a college graduate. It is the intelligence, not the schooling, that counts. Brains are not a matter of classroom credits. If a doctor of philosophy persuades a girl to leave college to marry him, he will not outstrip her intellectually just for that reason.

It is not the characteristic itself which makes a marriage succeed or fail, but *how the partner feels* about the characteristic. The sources of harmony or of discord are the congruence or the conflict of the concepts of value which husband and wife hold, and these are all basically emotional. Marriages succeed or fail because the behavior patterns involved complement or frustrate each other. Frustration is due to a collision of desires, and desires are a function of background.

Pretense here is no good. Of all the times in a person's life when he should lay all the cards on the table as honestly as he knows how, none is more important than courtship. Not to do so is always hazardous. It is often ruinous.

"I like," "I detest," "I want," "I resent," are all evaluations which depend upon the background of one's bringing up. The fundamental desire for food becomes the specific longing for roast beef, or whale blubber, or rice, or macaroni, or chili con carne, depending upon where eating habits were established.

This is a world of values in which all values are relative, but in which we live by our own particular evaluations. The shadow of an untouchable means nothing to an American, cows are not sacred, and divorce is not unthinkable. On the other hand, population control by infanticide instead of contraception does not

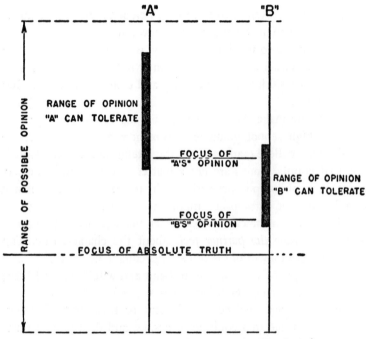

Fig. 7.   Opinion Relationships Between Two People

shock the Hindu. Nor does a million people starving each year because of overpopulation.

Mutuality of background and outlook is important in order that there shall not be too great differences in judgment. Each one of us has a range of opinion he can tolerate (Figure 7). This not only depends upon emotional maturity, intelligence, and information, but also upon background. Reality is always in terms of individual conclusions. Whether or not man will ever find absolute truth—and know it—is one of the last, stark questions of the human mind.

There are situations in which "A" can tolerate "B's" opinion but "B" cannot tolerate "A's" opinion. They may both agree on a position which is a long way from reality, or one may be close to the truth and not know it, supporting a correct opinion with wrong reasoning. If the focus of "B's" opinion were close to the truth, and backed up by adequate reasoning, would this narrow the range of opinion which "B" can tolerate because his attitude would now be, "I know the truth and you are missing the boat completely!" or would it widen the range with an attitude of, "Because I feel I know the truth, any other opinion does not threaten mine?" The answer is a matter of individual personality.

One thing is certain: as long as there are two people in the world there will be differences of opinion—some of them serious. One man's honesty is another man's lie. Marriage itself does not mean the same thing to all peoples. The Frenchman has his wife and his mistress (who is customarily of lower social standing than himself and thus no rival to his wife); the women of Tibet have several husbands; the Eskimo shares his wife with his guests. Here are great differences in evaluation.

Marriage was not so hazardous years ago when things were simpler. The kind of co-operation needed between a farmer and his wife was clearly understood. Their shared economic activity and shared homemaking were not much different from the circumstances under which they had lived and seen each other before marriage. Modern young people can go together, sometimes for years, and yet never see each other under natural, homemaking conditions. Real circumstances are what count.

A "Cavalier" bride may marry a "Puritan" and be distressed because her husband knows more about literature than she. Actually, she should be concerned over the collision of their cultures. Suppose she wants to stack the dirty dishes, sit down, and watch the world go by. Suppose he wants to do things when they are ready to be done. She decides that seven-thirty in the morning is the proper time to leave on their trip. To him this is an agreement; to her it is only an approximation. At seven-thirty he is booted and spurred, and eager to be off. Sometime after eight, wholly unconcerned over what to him is failure to live up to an arrangement of her own making, she is ready to depart. Punctuality to him is a necessary virtue in a schedule-filled world. To her, punctuality is an invention of the devil in a world where the great virtue is continuous relaxation—most particularly in the face of any disagreeable task. "What difference does it make whether we start at seven-thirty or at eight?" she asks. In ten years she will find out that the difference in evaluation makes a great deal of difference.

The point here is not that one way of life is right and the other mistaken, but that the difference in tempo and in standards is discordant. *It is not the behavior itself so much as the difference in how husband and wife feel about behavior, from which unhappiness is compounded.* With the same feeling as to the flexibility or rigidity of starting the trip at seven-thirty, there can be disagreements without conflict. The reason is easy to perceive. Where there is no basic difference in feeling, husband and wife are already the same kind of individual. But a basic difference in feeling results in each wanting to change the other into his kind of person. "I can change him," says the little bride. Fear on her part that it cannot be done, and resentment on his part of the offense against his personality lead to fighting.

Cinderella, of the famous glass slipper, is an excellent example of similarity despite apparent difference. Her story is not so much a saga of rags to royalty, as it is one of agreement on values. What the prince wanted was character, not clothes. She, and not her step-sisters, felt about the values of life as he did. This is why being the wife of a banker—with a cook, butler, maid and chauffeur to manage—requires different kinds of desires and abilities, from being the wife of an impoverished artist who has just as much intelligence as the banker.

In the foundation for a good marriage are to be found the

things which hubsand and wife want to do together. They should respond to life in about the same way. A pampered girl will find it difficult to realize that a tired man needs a prompt, hot, attractively served meal. She cannot sense what he is feeling.

With about the same background and outlook husband and wife can stand side by side, look out at the world together, see approximately the same things, want to engage in about the same reactions as a result, and meet many disappointments without bitterness because they have each other. For this they need a community of tastes and standards that appeal to both with about equal force, mutual respect, and pride in each other. They will be in love because they care about so many things together.

The cactus and the fern are both valuable and respectable members of the plant family, but they cannot survive in the same soil and the same climate. They could not possibly create together conditions in which each can flourish, superior to what either could find alone. Different plants require different conditions. So do different people. All living things have individual, minimal conditions for:

(1) Remaining alive
(2) Sustaining growth
(3) Achieving self-realization.

Two young people while courting need to learn more and more of what conditions each needs in order to attain personality fulfillment. No individual can successfully learn what he needs without experience with a variety of others and an analysis of the responses they call out from him. These responses will vary, and so will his happiness. This is not only a question of background, but also one of outlook and the road ahead.

Suppose a dull, passive man marries an active, intellectually keen woman. We are not at the moment concerned with why they married, but only with what happens afterward. Even if they are going down parallel tracks, they can be half a world apart, and going at different speeds. Her self-fulfillment needs will be frustrated. His limitations will probably provide little outlet for her potentialities. Even if he does not reject or block her ideas, he certainly will fail to stimulate her intellectually. She must have some satisfactions, so she seeks them outside the home by getting a job, becoming active in club work, or even by leaving him.

This is intellectual incompatibility. It could also be social, or sexual, or financial, or religious, or endless combinations thereof. It is not necessary that husband and wife both be interested in history, or mathematics, or philosophy, or the theater. It may easily be that his study of philosophy and her interest in the theater are individual outlets for the same desire to understand and to express a love of people (as well as individual ways of expressing aptitudes and attitudes). His interest in philosophy has to do with human nature in the abstract, her interest in the theater has to do with human nature in the specific case. Their marriage may produce conditions under which each can stimulate and develop the other in such a way that both can use their gifts to the optimum.

On the other hand, husband and wife could both be interested in the theater in different ways: he because of the drama; she because of the philosophy expressed by what the characters say and do. It is now improbable that they will stimulate and develop each other. Their feeling about values is not the same. He will want the children to be little show-offs; she will want them to have serious thoughts.

Opposites attract? Perhaps—until the temporary romance of differences wears off. Then they will as surely repel each other as the two little pith balls, with opposite charges of static electricity, repel each other in the physics experiment once they have touched. Because curiosity, novelty, mystery may cause temporary attraction, do not be misled into thinking attraction will last. Like tends to mate with like, providing the similarity is real, in personality, religion, interests, and even in height or color of eyes. Should an honest person marry a dishonest one? We naturally seek and are happiest with personalities who are most like ourselves. Then there can be complete reciprocity of affection without sacrificing either person's right to self-development.

Baber made an interesting study of 325 mixed marriages, representing differences in race, religion, and nationality. These factors play such a fundamental part in determining our evaluations and our responses to life that a mixed marriage is a distinct hazard. Baber concluded that, ". . . comparing all three groups—interfaith, inter-nationality, inter-racial—*the degree of happiness varied inversely with the degree of difference in culture or color.*"* [Italics his.]

AGREEMENT ON METHOD

Unity of purpose is what holds people together. This is not nearly so much in terms of goals as it is in terms of method, for we differ far more in methods than we do in goals. Consider how Protestants, Catholics, Jews, Hindus, Mohammedans, Buddhists all regard each other with suspicion because of the inflexibility of the respective theologies, but all are presumably pursuing the same goal: the good life.

It is, therefore, easy to realize the importance to husband and wife of agreement on method in four areas:

Religion

It is dangerous to marry across religious lines. In the first place, religious training is far more important and unshakable than most young people realize. It involves more than mere theological views, because religion is a way of life. Let us consider for a moment the two great branches of the Christian church.

"You must accept and believe what you are told by the Church," says the Catholic.

"Oh no, or at least not quite," says the Protestant parent. "You must think things through for yourself according to a pattern I will give you. Blind acceptance is idolatry."

---

* R. Baber, "A Study of 325 Mixed Marriages," *American Sociological Review*, Vol. 2, No. 5 (October 1937), pp. 705-16.

"Not so fast," says the Catholic. "Do you try to determine for yourself the manner in which your infected appendix is to be removed, or do you put yourself into the hands of a qualified expert?"

"Now you have changed the argument," counters the Protestant. "Surgery is an objective science; religion is a subjective philosophy."

"What difference does that make?" the Catholic answers, and so the argument goes on concerning the concentration of authority in the clergy in one church, and in the individual in the other.

Even though both husband and wife may have little active interest in religion, or may feel tolerant toward the other's beliefs, nevertheless, the children will have four grandparents who are likely to create barriers and even threats.

Of the three great religions in America it appears that the best prognosis for an interfaith marriage is to be expected between Protestant and Jew, and the poorest prognosis between Catholic and Protestant, this being a slightly greater risk than that between Catholic and Jew.*

Burgess and Cottrell found that other things being equal, the chances of happiness are eleven times greater where husband and wife agree on all religious matters than where they disagree.** Rigid adherence to dogma on the part of either spouse, no matter what the religion, tends to increase the hazards to happiness, which is why the people who "usually" go to church are happier as a group than those who "always" go.

Money

Money has a prominent place in American culture. To many it seems the key to happiness. Thus, instead of developing our real selves to perceive accurately, to feel deeply, to love enduringly, we

* R. E. Baber, *Marriage and the Family* (New York: McGraw-Hill, 1939), pp. 167-73.
** E. W. Burgess, and L. S. Cottrell, *Predicting Success or Failure in Marriage* (New York: Prentice-Hall, 1939), p. 63.

struggle to snag a spouse with plenty of money, to drive a big car, to excel in the rat-race values, and then wonder why we are so unaccountably uneasy. What we all want are loving relationships which are therefore trustworthy, joyous, and creative.

The attitude a couple has toward each other's ideas of money is more significant than the amount of money they have. It is important that he be prepared to earn a reasonable amount. It is important that both be able to save a little and to spend the rest wisely without quarreling.

Each person brings to the marriage a pattern of past habits concerning the meaning, value, and use of money. If these are not in agreement there will be much to unlearn, or there will be continuous trouble. No area of married life is more likely to be a battleground. Few topics are more difficult for husband and wife to discuss frankly than how they spend their money.

Since money is a demand on the efforts of other people it is only good for whatever it will buy. This is the goal, but the method of ariving at that goal can vary all the way from "spend every cent the minute it is earned for fear of inflation" to "hoard every penny for fear of depression."

John may be a practical, realistic, person who counts things. He knows how many B.T.U.'s there are in a pound of coal; he can reproduce the arrangement of chemical elements in the periodic table; he reads the meter in the subway turnstile to see how many coins have been deposited since yesterday; he budgets his resources, keeps an exact count of every nickel he spends, and never spends money he does not have. Mary may be an artistic dreamer. To her life is a series of inspired follies. It matters little whether or not vitamins have ears, but to refer to a street sweeper as "one of the city's housecleaners" gives her pleasure. When she has money, she spends it according to her whims. When it is gone, she sometimes buys things anyway. What was credit invented for?

Think how this difference in method will baffle and annoy these two. Here again is the cactus and the fern. If they marry, having wrongly interpreted as love a mutual interest in good music—he because of its mathematical construction, she because of its ability to express deep feeling—if they marry, her flights of fancy will seem to him "mush, rot, nonsense"; his methodical budgeting will seem to her "so boring and inconsequential." Some day when she orders a Frigidaire without consultation as to the state of the family exchequer or the merits of this investment as compared to other expenditures, he will have a look in his eye that means look out.

The hard efficiency which is the price of money, and the moments of extravagance which bring satisfaction to the dreamer, are so great a difference in method—not just of spending money but of living itself—as to constitute an almost insuperable obstacle to happiness. Husband and wife need to agree genuinely and without submission or coercion on the part of either, as to the method of dividing the family income, the financial responsibilities of each, and under what circumstances either may properly invade the financial category of the other.

A wife's experience in business before marriage is often helpful in making a good financial adjustment. She has a better idea of how many hours' effort it requires to pay for a muskrat coat, and how money is handled beyond the confines of her own home.

Children

Here is the point about which the philosophy of the home is most likely to revolve. Is home to be a family circle around the hearth side, or merely a place to sleep? Some people adore children. To other individuals they are just little brats from whom to seek deliverance. For the first time in history children are no longer universally looked on as the ultimate fulfillment of marriage. This is another area in which there should be agreement before seriously considering the question of establishing a home. Do both want children? How many? How spaced? How disciplined? How educated?

Only those homes with unwanted children are statistically

more unhappy than those homes with no children, but *unwanted* should be emphasized and thought through to the end. No one but a sadistic person could deliberately impose upon a child the curse of being brought up by a parent who did not want him— no one except the other parent who wanted him very much indeed. What a tangled source of satisfaction, of quarreling, and of guilt!

Recreation

Back in the days of an agricultural civilization when husband and wife ate three meals together every day—continually met and co-operated in the garden, in the buttery, in the orchard, in the root cellar—it was not so important that they enjoy the same recreations. If grandfather's idea of relaxation was to pit his intelligence against that of a trout by dropping a dry fly into the clear, clean water of the pool just below the waterfall; if grandmother's idea of an afternoon's entertainment was attendance at the Ladies' Sewing Circle—partly out of the knowledge that they would talk about her if she were not there—it made little difference to their marriage. These two worked together all the time. But in our industrial civilization, where father catches the 8:17 commuters' train, and neither mother nor children see him again until dinner, recreational time is important. Thus has come about the saying that the family which plays together, stays together.

Burgess and Cottrell found* fifteen times the probable chance of happiness for a husband and wife who shared and enjoyed all their outside activities together, as for those who shared only a few. If the wife's idea of relaxation and enjoyment is the Browning Society, a symphony concert, discussion of the Hundred Great Books, or a few hours in an art gallery, and the husband's idea is a stag party, a strip tease act, or betting at the races, how can the two want to be together? They are continuously going by each other without touching, to say nothing of traveling down

* E. W. Burgess and L. S. Cottrell, *op. cit.*, p. 62.

the same track, toward the same objective, while enjoying each other's enjoyment.

Agreement on method in what constitutes recreation has become of great importance to the family. As has already been pointed out, enjoying the same thing from entirely alien points of view is not enough. His enjoying swimming for the water-cooled exercise is not the same as her regard for it as a method of showing off her figure. His enthusiasm for bridge as a game of concentration and skill is not the same as her delight in its potentialities as a background for ragged remnants of gossip. His discussion of politics from the point of view of personalities is not the same thing as her examination of politics from the point of view of ideas. In neither case is the couple responding to life with the same feeling, or even the same activity.

MUTUAL, LONG-RUN SEX ATTRACTION

In any honestly drawn up set of criteria for choosing a mate probably the majority of the population would place sex attraction as number one on the list. Actually, it belongs last because it is the corollary of, not the antecedent of, the other three.

Sex is, to be sure, the area where rifts in the lute of happiness often appear first, but this is because the sex relation is of such delicacy as to be unable to withstand the impact of quarreling in other areas. Two people cannot long wrangle over money in the early evening, and achieve a spiritual unity three hours later. Contrariwise, a man and woman who are both emotionally mature; who both have similar background and outlook; who both agree on method concerning religion, money, children, and recreation, usually cannot long live together in marriage without building such bonds of affection that sexual attraction results.

Physical attraction, plus nothing else, plus time, quickly equals nothing, despite the poisonous falsity of much modern advertising. On the other hand, liking many things together so strengthens and renews physical attraction, as to make it almost life-long. Not perceiving the distinction, many middle-aged women make frantic efforts to preserve the showcase rather than to develop more in-terpersonal relationships. Victims of the same confusion, many middle-aged men fight for money, power, or fame.

The Statistical Studies

There have been many research projects on marriage carried out by the social scientists, the two most important American ones being the one by L. M. Terman and associates (792 married couples, 1938); and the one by Burgess and Cottrell (526 couples, 1939). Statistics are not a substitute for sense, but the results of a dozen people working six or seven years on the scientific classi-fication and interpretation of 600,000 separate bits of related information—as was the case in the Terman study—are not to be ignored. However, in evaluating a statistical study one should always remember:

(1) It is only part of the story. Because more people die in bed than anywhere else does not make bed the most dangerous place

(2) There are no statistics for the individual

(3) Apparent correlations are not always real

(4) A fact may be true, but that does not always make it a truth. First, it must be understood in its context, as a whole.

My impression is that where emotions are involved, only a psychiatric study could produce anything better than superficial answers. At present the psychiatrists are concerned almost ex-clusively with maladjusted people, and in addition the method would be prohibitively expensive.

Terman* believes many people are psychologically incapable of married happiness because of a predisposition to unhappiness. He also believes that others will make the best of it no matter what. Happy people tend to ignore the imperfections; unhappy people

* L. M. Terman, *Psychological Factors in Marital Happiness* (New York: McGraw-Hill, 1938), p. 110.

tend to demand perfection, which, of course, no human being can offer. And they magnify the imperfections.

No one of these researchers has found any correlation between happiness and the amount of income, although the Burgess and Cottrell* study of happiness as related to occupations does imply a correlation between happiness and the security of a regular, assured income. Chemical engineers, ministers, and professors were among the happiest; laborers, traveling salesman and mechanics the least happy.

Himes** points out that the first group are more subject to the surveillance of the community as regards conduct than the second. He also points out that although physicians, bankers, and lawyers usually earn more than engineers, professors, or ministers, their lower happiness rating may be due to uncertain fluctuations in income. Absence of emotionally upsetting experiences and marital happiness seem to be closely associated.

Terman (p. 33) found "no consistent relationship" between happiness and the amount of schooling, although he was convinced that education did not unfit a woman for succesful marriage. Burgess and Cottrell (p. 121) concluded that the more education, the greater the chances of happiness for both men and women, particularly for those who did graduate work. Education, they said (p. 122) after studying their statistical results, makes a person "more objective and intelligent in his social relationships, more tolerant in attitude, and better equipped with reliable information about the sexual and other adjustments of married life." They also point out what Hamilton and others had already concluded; education postpones marriage and there are "increased chances of success in marriage with increasing age at the time of marriage."

The sociologists have found no positive correlations between children and happy marriage. Lang concluded that it was better

* E. W. Burgess and L. S. Cottrell, *op. cit.*, p. 140.
** N. E. Himes, *Your Marriage* (New York: Farrar and Rinehart, 1940), p. 290.

not to have a child until two years after marriage. Adjust to being a husband or wife before adjusting to being a parent. But homes with unwanted children are the least happy.

Every research which has touched on the problem agrees that the chance for happiness is reduced by a self-conscious or unhealthy attitude toward the sex relation. The usual sources of such attitudes are:

(1) Victorian parents
(2) Information via the "gutter school"
(3) Information from a person whose own sex experiences were unhappy.

Burgess and Cottrell concluded that the probability of success was greater where the marriage began with a church wedding. This may have something to do with the kind of people who are church members. It probably also has to do with the fact that church weddings are rare unless the family approves the match. In any case, a secret civil ceremony is far more likely to precede disaster. Secret weddings are usually for the purpose of making a physical relation also a legal one.

It was further concluded that the bride's successfully holding a job before marriage contributes to success. Similarly, a man who has held a position for some time seems a better risk than one who flits from job to job.

Prognosis

According to Terman (p. 372), the factors contributing to a happy marriage, arranged in the order of their importance, are:

(1) Superior happiness of parents
(2) Childhood happiness
(3) Absence of conflict with mother
(4) Home discipline firm but not harsh
(5) Strong attachment to mother
(6) Strong attachment to father
(7) Absence of conflict with father
(8) Parent frank about sex matters

(9) Infrequency and mildness of childhood punishment

(10) Pre-marital attitude toward sex free from disgust or aversion.

According to Burgess and Cottrell, the factors, again arranged in the order of their importance, are:

(1) Parents happily married

(2) Affection for parents and siblings (best prognosis if four or more children; hardest for youngest child to adjust)

(3) Parental approval of the marriage

(4) College education (particularly in a co-educational college)

(5) Ability to save money wisely

(6) Long acquaintance

(7) Sound health

(8) Participation in several social organizations

(9) Belonging to the same church.

Burgess and Cottrell believed the prognosis to be poor where bride or groom were:

(1) Raised by unhappy parents

(2) Married without parental approval

(3) Brought together in a romantic courtship

(4) From different backgrounds of religion, education, money.

Both studies base their prognosis essentially on:

(1) Happy parents providing a happy childhood

(2) Good parental discipline developing good self-discipline (it is essential to differentiate between discipline and punishment)

(3) Childhood security.

Burgess and Cottrell devised an elaborate list of questions resulting in a score by which to predict success or failure in marriage. The result stems essentially from a measurement of value judgment distribution, and the final answer is a single number like 441 or 588. I prefer a technique developed by Bishop Richard T. Loring of Illinois, and his brother, John C. G. Loring of Boston, who have used a comparison of the profiles obtained with Allport and Vernon's

Study of Values. To an expert observer these profiles—one made out by the prospective bride and one by the prospective groom—not only reveal the distribution of value judgments within the individual, and between the individuals, but shows also their dynamic relationships. Thus the areas of probable strife, whether over ideas, things, aesthetic concepts, social values, personal influence, or religion can be spotted and investigated.

A composite picture of the characteristics possessed by happy and unhappy married people, as determined by the sociological researches, would look something like this:

Happy Husbands and Wives:
    emotionally stable
    co-operative
      (willing to be subordinate but not subservient)
    considerate to inferiors
    self-confident
    optimistic
    willing to take advice
    prudent with money
      (intelligent thrift is money-planning, not money-pinching)
    doing things methodically and also choosing friends who do
    attention to details
    good disciplinarian
      (do not confuse discipline and punishment)
    conservative in:
      politics, religion, morals

Unhappy Husbands and Wives:
    vacillating moods
      (easily affected by praise or blame; lose temper easily)
    domineering and contentious
      (rebellious against discipline)
    little interest in inferiors
    make excuses when wrong
    critical of others
      (express dislikes instead of conquering them)
    selfish over money or clothes

fitful, impatient workers
neglectful of details
poor disciplinarian
more radical in:
    politics, religion, morals

Age

What is the proper time to marry? Actually, of course, when one is physically, mentally, and emotionally ready for marriage . . . not before: physically old enough, and properly developed; mentally educated and capable of earning a living; emotionally wanting to marry, and sufficiently mature to undertake it with prospects of happy success. Hamilton and MacGowan concluded that a man's chance of marrying the wrong girl is 40 per cent to 50 per cent greater at age 22 than at age 27, despite which 64 per cent of the men are married by their 25th birthday. The table is as follows:

> 33 per cent of men married by age 20
> 64 per cent of men married by age 25
> 79 per cent of men married by age 30
> 86 per cent of men married by age 35
> 89 per cent of men married by age 40

According to the 1940 census, the median age at which first marriages take place is 24.3 years for the husbands, and 21.6 years for the wives. The usual age differential between man and wife in the United States is about three years, the man being the older. Most investigators believe there is little correlation between age difference and happiness. The average age at which the women marry is 22.4 whereas the figure is 25.6 for the men. These have changed little in the last half century.

Early marriage is usually due to strong sex attraction. The drawbacks include a limited field to choose from and a limited background with which to make the choice. Unless there is parental economic help, or an inheritance to fall back on, the very young couple are likely to have a hard financial struggle.

Late marriage has its drawbacks. The most eligible people, particularly among the women, are already married. Habits have become deeply set, making adjustments more difficult. It is harder both to have and to bring up children, as well as harder on the children. Then too, much of the zest the ordinary couple has for making their way in the world together is missed.

The older a man is when he marries, the more likely he is to marry someone substantially younger. At age 25 he chooses a bride who is 22. When he is 40, she is probably no more than 32, or perhaps still just a radiant girl. Big differences in age usually bring extensive problems. By and large a person's friends approximate his age group. One or the other will have dilemmas to face in this area. When she has reached her prime, he will be a doddering old man with internal complaints. Since the average male expectancy of life is six to seven years less than the female, she must face an unusually long widowhood. If there are children, they had a father who should have been a grandfather. Still, some of these marriages are unusually happy.

IN CONCLUSION

All this has to do with the plea for less romance and more analysis before marriage, bringing about more love and less analysis after marriage. *Where analysis spoils romance it is also preventing catastrophe,* even including the situations where it is being subconsciously used as an excuse for escaping a relationship which the individual is afraid to face. Romance alone is an oversimplification, used in the attempt to fit reality into an ideal. Analysis makes the ideal face the reality. Does one daydream the structural members of a bridge? Is the joy of watching a locomotive ruined by knowing with what care the strength of the boiler was calculated to prevent explosion? Does the scientist go on combining oxygen and hydrogen in the presence of a flame, hoping that someday the result will not be an explosion?

Then why gamble on the success of a marriage? The laws of physics and chemistry do not argue. They operate. Jump off the roof of a building and the law of gravity will not argue. It will break your bones. Similarly the laws of human nature do not argue; they produce the appropriate result. If a person must have castles in the air he should first build a solid foundation under them. Otherwise the structure will fall, and there will be a rude awakening, saddening to his spirit.

7

Courtship

THE SEARCH FOR LOVE

COURTING basically implies an endeavor to win the affection of a person by wooing. Folsom says, "Mate selection involves a competitive interaction process similar to that found in the operation of other markets, exchanges, and clearing houses."* Maybe so, but it certainly should involve a great deal more than persuading a person he needs something, making him want it now, and convincing him you have the goods which will best fulfill that need. During intelligent mate selection each is buying as well as selling, and for the purpose of giving as well as of getting.

Courting is among life's important activities. People who give a knowing wink behind the backs of courting youngsters are making light of a serious thing. Much depends upon how seriously it is undertaken, for poor judgment here leads to failure in marriage. As in many other human activities, the damage gets done a long time before the result begins to show.

The sales approach concentrates on parties, excitement, and thrills, overlooking the relentless round of daily responsibilities

* J. K. Folsom: *The Family and Democratic Society* (New York: Wiley, 1943), p. 538.

which marriage demands. It can hardly see beyond the next prom date. To penetrate beneath the superficial persuasions and seek to examine the quality of the factors involved in a courtship, it is necessary to do more than dance. Careful analysis may result in painful insights, but refusal to face a fact makes it none the less a fact. For a good marriage, one needs a clear awareness of himself and of the natural direction of his capacities. How else can he estimate the extent to which he and the prospective partner's life will be influenced, enriched, or thwarted by the other?

The first requirement of intelligent courting is to find and to know one's self; to understand the kind of person one most naturally can and should be. Anyone lacking knowledge of his real self, or alienated from himself by the bewilderments and anxiety of a wrong bringing up, will be incapable of appraising the the quality of his emotions.

Chemicals just unite. Some of the lower animals do not even do that, but among the higher animals mating is always preceded by courtship. Primitive man was simple and direct. Modern youth gives courting a large and important place.

Love-making divides itself into four different periods, each with its own particular functions and conventions:

(1) Exploration—friendly with several, serious with none. This is far more to be desired than a series of emotional affairs from which one never learns much

(2) Courtship—"going steady" with serious intentions;

(3) Engagement—a period of final testing leading into a period of final preparation for marriage

(4) Marriage—serving and being served, loving and being loved, blessing and being blessed.

Courting is the search for and presumably the discovery of a mate one can love. Sometimes it is an exciting adventure; sometimes it takes place quietly and calmly. Beware the courtship which proceeds as though either individual were trying to entrap the other. This can only be a variation of seduction, and seduction— like all conquest—is based on hostility and contempt. Beware the romantic courtship that slogs through emotional ooze. This is infatuation, and infatuation does not last. On the contrary, it leads to the most bitter disappointment of our civilization, an unhappy marriage. The trouble was either:

(1) Courting the wrong person, or

(2) Marrying before emotionally mature.

Courting is all too often an eruption of feelings. If a graph of the demonstrative affection received were plotted against time for the ordinary life span, there would be two peaks in it; one during infancy, and one reaching from courtship to early marriage. No individual should marry or even become engaged on the crest of an untested emotional wave. Violent things are usually short-lived, like an earthquake, a tornado, or an infatuation. Successful marriage must rest on the solid ground of congeniality. A spiritual loveliness that enriches every day with understanding can only be built between two people who have chosen each other wisely. This is not a matter of chance; it is a matter of deliberate discrimination based on sound observation, penetrating comparison, logical analysis, and valid judgment as to one's real feelings. Romance, as Webster says, is "a dreamy, imaginative, habit of mind."

OUTGROWING DEPENDENT LOVE

The first step before one can be successful in love is the growing out of dependent love for one's parents. When this is badly handled, serious and perhaps permanent damage results. Unless this step has been successfully negotiated, those that follow will be faltering indeed. For the neurotic, whose still active, dependent love prevents him from facing the responsibilities of marriage, courting becomes an end in itself instead of the means to an end.

This fear of loving on a mature level because the emotional umbilical cord to the parent has never been cut, may express itself in various ways:

(1) Flitting lightly from one affair to another, always quitting as soon as the conquest has been made

(2) Apparently never giving love a thought.

The first individual, particularly if it is a man, is often thought of as a great lover. Actually, he is afraid of responsibility and wants to be babied. This dependence on mama leads to disguised fear and hate. Observe how cruel he is to the girls he courts and leaves. Consider also the girl of superior intelligence, good health, naturally affectionate nature, who nevertheless manages to have a disruptive quarrel with every man who courts her seriously. Such inconsistency is a symptom of internal conflict. She seems to be destroying the very thing she desires most, but also she is rejecting something she is as yet emotionally unprepared to accept.

Individuals who are attractive and who go out on numerous dates but never marry are people who do not want to marry. They enjoy attention and a good time, but marriage is more than that, and there is something about the responsibility of making a home which they, at least subconsciously, fear and reject. Afraid to love, they first temporize, and then flee the threat of being hurt. In essence this is saying, "I'm going to stop before he (she) breaks my heart, as he surely will when he sees me as I am." This reaction is seldom analyzed by the people such individuals go out with, but it is felt by them.

The individual, incapable of working with another person to produce a soil and a climate in which each can flourish and spontaneously express his real self, has to kill the love that is offered him. He knows he does not deserve it and he dare not become indebted for something he is completely unable to repay. Consequently he has no alternative but to rebuff and to reject the very thing he apparently most wants.

Both boys and girls often work hard to become wallflowers. The little girl, glowering from the side lines as she hurls hate at the boys who do not ask her to dance, is doing just that. She wastes hours in mulling over the humiliation of the last affair, and hours in dreading the times to come, but she does nothing constructive about growing up or learning how to be her real self.

The unattractive girl—not to be confused with the merely homely—comforts herself by saying, "I'm not interested in boys."

Inveigled or coerced by a parent into accepting a date, she will start the evening by baring her teeth in ice-cold geniality, and then come home full of criticism and resentment, as though everything had been wrong with the evening but herself. The truth probably is that the poisonous emotions are only excuses for staying home with mama from whom she has not yet been emotionally separated.

Or perhaps she is merely shy. Being shy is the result of unhappy experiences with the significant persons in one's childhood. In adolescence it results in mobilizing the previous fear of people in one disheartening surge of apprehension. It may be irrational, but it is perfectly logical and terribly real.

Meeting Eligible People

The second step is getting acquainted with eligible people. Not one but several.

Burgess and Cottrell report that 50 per cent of the unhappily married men had almost no women friends before marriage.* With both men and women the best prognosis occurs where the individual has had at least several good friends of the opposite sex before beginning a courtship.

It is wise to confine friendship to people who, quite coldly and analytically, are eligible, for the only time one can think objectively is before the emotions take over—or after they have burned out. To meet eligible individuals is difficult for anyone who is afraid of people. Relations that should be normal and friendly, now become strained and unnatural.

Building up a circle of friends is usually considered easier for a young man than for a young woman because there are more ways in which our conventions allow him to take the initiative. Opportunity is influenced both by occupation and by place of residence. Propinquity is the father of Dan Cupid. In separate investigations, Hart and Popenoe both found that New England was a difficult place for a girl to marry, and correspondingly, one

* E. W. Burgess and L. S. Cottrell, *Predicting Success or Failure in Marriage* (New York: Prentice-Hall, 1939), pp. 128-32.

which offered the men an unusually large choice. As for occupations, nurses, social workers, and librarians are much less likely to marry than stenographers. Their conditions of employment produce fewer fruitful contacts with eligible men.

Most men assume that they can find a suitable wife when the time comes. Many women, particularly after a war, feel that they will have to take their chances. This naturally produces emotional pressures in girls who would prefer a good marriage to being single. They become competitive in their attitude toward other women, and being denied the privilege of actively hunting a mate, embark on what might be described as wishful luring. There is no reason why a girl should not take delicate initiative in courting. Women, so Terman* found, can size up a man in a year as accurately as a man can size up woman in three years. If they are better judges of character, is there any valid reason for their not using that judgment? Indirectly, they always do.

To develop good contacts, go where the right kind of people are. This may be a church group, a mountain climbing club, a dancing class, a summer resort, an adult education course. Do not just sit and wait for something to happen. Go out and make a friend. One will do as a beginning. For the intelligent young person the best place is probably the college campus, particularly the co-educational college campus where boys and girls not only meet at the parties, but see each other in class the next morning minus the fancy wrappings! Attractive packaging is definitely a part of the merchandiser's art, but what matters most is the quality of the goods inside. The unusual person, or the person of exceptional qualities, will need to realize that another unusual person is required to appreciate and be attracted by him. It may be that a precocious man cannot be seen for his real values except by a mature girl of twenty-three or twenty-four.

A woman needs three things to be beautiful: an erect, graceful carriage; a beautiful voice; and the charm of being spontaneously

* L. M. Terman, *Psychological Factors in Marital Happiness* (New York: McGraw-Hill, 1938), p. 198.

natural. No one can be more attractive than by being his or her sincere, best self. All three of these requirements come from right attitudes and healthy emotions, not from inheritance, and they can outshine a pretty face any day. The basic principle of establishing good friendships is not some quivering romanticism, but a sincere informality. Sheer zest for life is a tremendous asset if it is real.

There is much to be said in favor of a frank and honest shopping around during this period of finding eligible individuals. A choice is involved and two is the smallest possible number from which a choice can be made. The romantic idea that in all the world there is but a single person with whom one can be happily married, has no foundation in fact. To forsake all others after having reached a satisfactory agreement with one congenial person is something else again. Hamilton* found that the average individual has seven love affairs during his life.

Many a girl has lost the friendship of a boy because she became possessive before he was ready to specialize. The lassoes in her eyes were probably the result of little confidence in herself. If she sincerely likes other people, she will have no qualms about other people liking her. On the other hand, a girl with too many suitors is only trying to reassure herself. Doubtless she only further confuses herself.

Mistakes

Before specializing, in addition to a complete understanding of the criteria discussed in the previous chapter, resolve to avoid a number of tragic and common mistakes.

Do not make the mistake of overlooking the fact that during courtship both parties put their best foot forward, and therefore it is often difficult to know each other as each really is. Courting was much simpler years ago. People met under natural conditions. Alonzo and Elizabeth knew each other's family history from way back when. She observed how he handled an ox team, heard stories

* G. V. Hamilton and K. MacGowan, *What is Wrong with Marriage?* (New York: Boni, 1929), p. 251.

of how much cord wood he could cut in a day, saw the condition of a field after he had planted it. He knew her reputation as a butter maker, saw the results of her activity over a wash tub, could watch from afar the way a Sunday school class responded to her leadership.

All this has mostly gone. In its place we have few fixed roots; are not always acquainted with each other's families; sometimes never see each other except at a party or alone in the living room, until after the clergyman has pronounced us man and wife. Life is not lived at a party. The way to evaluate a person is to see him in his family background. It is then possible to appraise the feeling and the meaning various circumstances have for him in terms of his heredity and his previous experience.

The automobile has not greatly changed a man's tendency to marry a girl from his own neighborhood. The Bossard* study of 5,000 consecutive marriage licenses issued in Philadelphia, and the Kennedy** study of licenses issued in New Haven, both showed that over 50 per cent of the couples who married lived within twenty blocks of each other. In New Haven it was 76 per cent for the year 1940. But modern living conditions seldom result in people knowing each other as they did when we were largely rural and agricultural instead of largely urban and industrial.

Do not make the mistake of thinking that courtship is a relationship in which a young woman is to be persuaded that she is in love. Courting ought not to be a conquest, but a mutual search by two people to discover together what they have in common. Are they compatible? Can they provide together a soil and climate in which each will flourish, far superior to what either could achieve alone? Courting ought to be recognized as something more than a buyer-seller relationship both ways; each individual endeavoring to offer himself in the truest possible light, and attempting to appraise the real value of togetherness in a lifelong relationship. All too often

---

* J. H. S. Bossard, "Residential Propinquity as a Factor in Marriage Selection," *American Journal of Sociology*, Vol. 38 (September 1932), pp. 219-24.
** R. J. R. Kennedy, "Premarital Residential Propinquity and Ethnic Endogamy," *American Journal of Sociology*, Vol. 48 (March 1943), pp. 580-84.

it is merely two people trying to sell each other a bill of goods. What is needed is relentlessly finding and facing the facts.

The old idea of a contest between the immovable man and the irresistible girl is nonsense. If either existed, the other would be impossible!

Do not make the mistake of avoiding disagreements. To do so is to make a prediction of future relationships which is based on inadequate information. Each needs to evaluate what the attitudes and faults of the other will mean to their mutual happiness in so intense a togetherness as marriage. The hope for a happy relationship is not enough. There should be faith based on experience.

Do not make the mistake of trying to be loved. It is only necessary to be lovable. This is difficult for an emotionally damaged individual to achieve, but the way to do it can be easily expressed. First, sincerely try to be your own best self according to your own lights. Second, treat everyone else as though he were in fact his best self because you feel in your heart that within the limits of his opportunities each of us really is trying to be his best self, and, because you feel this, do everything to nourish that best self. Third, never try to make an impression. The most attractive people live with effortless ease. They are simply their natural selves. They never try to take on the mannerisms of someone else. They do not smoke because so-and-so does, or stop smoking because someone else has. They are themselves and consequently have no need to try to sell themselves.

"I will be loved even if I have to fight for it," is a fairly common attitude, and a tragic one. Such a statement has little to do with love.

An illustration of the fight to be loved is found where a man inadvertently pays attention to a girl, only because of his longing for companionship, and she deliberately transforms it into a love affair. She can get her friends to ask leading questions so that he commits himself in public. Or indirect emotional pressure comes through her father who greets the young man with, "Mary speaks very well of you." Or perhaps the two just drift along together until the expectations of other people begin to exert pressure. On the other hand, the young man may pretend that he owns a car, when the truth is he has only made one payment on it.

To try to ingratiate one's self with others is often an attempt to hide from one's self a lack of any feeling of real affection. Hence the attempt to snare someone else to love one, as though that were possible. Such an individual is not eager; he or she is only anxious. What colossal self-deception!

The need for conquest is always based on a feeling of inadequacy. Thus do lovers quarrel when they feel insecure, and persistent quarreling should be regarded as a symptom of some basic disharmony.

Beware daydreaming. This is, to be sure, the quickest and easiest way of making a silk purse out of the traditional material, but the accomplishment is only imagined. It is wishful thinking by which to achieve a spurious satisfaction which has no basis in reality. Real work is thrown out the window in an attempt to get something for nothing. When daydreaming becomes repetitive and wholly absorbing it is a dangerous procedure, as many a girl has demonstrated by reiterative and engrossing reveries to the effect that some day her prince would come. Believing something because one likes it, is usually followed by discovering it is not true. The wise young lady does not daydream. She faces reality and does something sensible. Thinking about ends with no regard to means is silly sentimentalism.

Do not make the mistake of marrying an inferior person because of the desire to feel superior. In such a situation one will soon have nothing but loneliness. The big word in marriage is *together*. Only when a man's sick ego gets the best of his intelligence will he want his wife to be inferior to him. It is not true that intelligent men shun intelligent women, "therefore, girls, act dumb." What men shun is a good brain used as a verbal scalpel, or an independent pose which is really no more than a masculine protest. Men who achieve distinction usually marry intelligent women who meet them as equals. Even if this were not so, all great men have unusual mothers. Gentlemen, give your children a chance!

Do not make the mistake of thinking that because a girl did not go to college she is inferior. College does not confer intelligence, it only *trains* intelligence. Even the most outstanding universities have gratified the desire of more than one fool to have some letters to put after his name. How did she stand in high school? Does she have an alert mind? Is she interested in gossip or in events or in ideas?

Do not make the mistake of thinking that all women are like your mother; or all men like your father. Because mother was a college graduate and a meticulous housekeeper is no reason for thinking that all college women are the same. Because the peas are green and the pod is green, does not mean that the whole world is green.

Do not make the mistake of thinking "This is love, and happiness is therefore inevitable." Assumptions of inevitability are usually dangerous.

Do not expect everything you want except in the area of decent behavior. Expecting too much is as fatal as accepting too little. Human beings are not perfect, and neither are human institutions, of which marriage is one. Radiant disposition, distinguished ancestry, inherited wealth, physical perfection, outstanding beauty, unusual intellect, devoted affection, are rarely to be found all in the same individual. Are *you* able to offer all these things?

Finally, do not drift into a selection. Use good method with intelligence. Quality is never an accident. It depends, for one thing, on careful selection. In the beginning, be friendly with a dozen, intimate with none. Study their characteristics and how these synchronize with your own personality. Then if the lightning strikes there is less danger of subsequent tragedy.

Going Steady

The third step is deciding on someone with whom to go steady. Specializing too soon is a great mistake because it:

    (1) Cuts down the area of choice

    (2) Offers no standards for comparison

(3) Takes the girl (particularly) out of circulation at a time when she should be widening her contacts.

"Going steady" does not necessarily mean a serious, long-run relationship of intended permanence. The enterprising young lady from Baltimore who "went steady" with eight boys during the first seven months of 1955 was not exactly out of circulation. Three months to a year is the average length for "steadies" to last in high school.

The trouble with this adolescent, unsteady steadiness is its romantic quality. Its objective is possessive reassurance. The force behind it is fear of unworthiness. The real need is to grow up emotionally. Then the person can face doubts about the outcome of any courtship, for he will know he is lovable. Then he can reach out, explore, find a satisfying relationship based on a rich togetherness of real selves.

For most of us the best time really to go steady is toward the end of college, or later. The intelligent time is not measured by years but by how well the individual knows himself, and how accurately he can appraise others.

Emotional Dishonesties

To our subsequent disillusionment and unhappiness, in most courtships a great deal is based on misrepresentation and deceit. In any human relationship the time always comes when people see each other as they really are. Every deception comes home to roost, and the deceiver is always in the henhouse when the chickens arrive. The reason we do not learn this early in life is that the deceit is often on the conscious level, but the resulting punishment is often unrecognized or unconnected with its root cause. Nevertheless, deceptions in courting can quickly change what once seemed beautiful and full of hope into a dead, empty, cold-war marriage.

Deceit and bribery are so commonplace in courtship, their accomplishment so thoughtlessly undertaken, and their results so disastrous that before the emotional seismographs begin to record tremors, both the boy and the girl ought to be sure they are not being duped. Many an unhappy marriage has resulted when pretense made a selfish, vindictive person appear generous, thoughtful, and kind. Women are much more likely to warn each other against being victimized than men, and the women are probably right, even though speaking out sometimes loses a friend. The subject is so important that it deserves a section of its own.

Courting ought to be a relatively slow process, not only in order to allow honest people to discover the truth about themselves and about each other, but also to allow time to expose the pretenders. The girl who pretends to adore babies, or to love housekeeping, or to be a sweet dispositioned person, will find it impossible to maintain the pretense for a year without some revealing slip. The man who pretends to be generous with his money, or thoughtful toward his mother, or innocent of any dishonorable intent, will show his true colors if given time. Sooner or later he will descend to caveman tactics and behave as though the only way to make a woman love him was to make her suffer.

The girl who fails to be ready on time, and keeps her escort waiting downstairs until the moment when she can make a grand entry, is motivated by a desire to dominate, not a desire to love. The boy who is impressed by such behavior is also a superficial person who cannot feel honestly, or he would identify so cheap a technique as exactly what it is: the attempt on the part of the girl to feel powerful and important because she can make him subservient. His reaction is likely to be, "Shall I be bowled over, or shall I be masterful? Which will get me further with her?" It ought to be, "What is my motive in having dates with this girl, and what is her motive in having dates with me?"

The man who keeps a girl upset and uncertain by alternately paying her pointed attention and then transferring his extravagant forays to other girls, is equally sadistic. To be sure, no girl wants a husband whom no one else appreciates, but does she want a man more intent on triumph than on cherishing her? What chance has she of his loving her for forty years? With him it is likely to be:

L'Amour fait passe le temps
Le temps fait passeé l'amour

Beware feeling it is smart to provide a rival in order to produce an atmosphere of competition. This is to introduce befogging emotions and an element of deceit which may lead to trouble. A permanently satisfactory marriage must be an honest marriage. If this be true, then the real thing will take care of itself. Even if this were not so, conquest is not intelligent selection.

Deception and conquest may be romantic fun, but they most emphatically are not love, and they cannot lead to years of married happiness. It is legitimate to tell a girl she has the most beautiful eyes in the world if this is a sincere, considered opinion, but it will be fatal to deceive her as to what the financial situation is: present earnings, indebtedness, future expectations, in-laws to be supported. It will be equally fatal to deceive him, for example, as to what her homemaking and cooking abilities are.

Letting down the moral standard in high elation over the power it apparently releases to attract another person is sheer enticement to bolster a faltering self-esteem. As first the thrill of feeling loved grows, defenses are demolished: old value standards are replaced with, "I don't have to be unappreciated any more. Now I can belong." Alas, this soon requires restatement in some such words as, "If I am going to be liked, either I must fool people, or I must sacrifice myself for someone else's advantage." This is a bribe, and a bribe is always dishonest.

But suppose he does not call again unless the bars go down? Clearly it was not love that he wanted. *Probably no one ever lost anything of value by being honestly and sincerely herself.* In the long run it is the fraud who loses.

Is the glamorous girl, who dreams dreams and hears voices, discriminating in whom she attracts? Are her emotions honest? Or is she sidetracking her real values for the superficial ones of seeming admired and appearing powerful? Is the emphasis on producing together the conditions in which each can be and spontaneously express his real self, or is the emphasis on cardiac-respiratory responses? Will the girl who works to attract the sort of man who wants only a pretty face and a sleek figure be able to hold him in fifteen years when her physical charms fade? Or will she lose him to some younger girl with a pretty face and a sleek figure?

Many gifts are no more than bribes used as power over someone; an investment, subconsciously intended to arouse feelings of guilt in the receiver should she have hostile thoughts toward the giver. It may be books, candy, and theater tickets; or it may be orchids, a mink coat, and pearls; or it may even be some achievement intended to impress the impressionable. This is not to say that gifts cannot be given in emotional honesty. It is to say that *love cannot be bought.* The only real gift is one's self, and using munificence as a substitute is hypocrisy.

If a young man and a young woman are sharing the expense of a date, let it be done inconspicuously but without emotional dishonesty. No passing of money under the table. The girl should ascertain her share of the dinner check and give her escort the amount, quietly but straightforwardly, before he goes to the cashier. Only people who are frightened or ashamed try to pretend.

He who seeks to marry the boss's daughter needs to be particularly sure that what he is seeking is not mere protection for his job. Fear cannot be the basis for love.

Another form of emotional dishonesty is the attempted suicide of the disappointed lover. Suicides undertaken because of ill health almost always succeed. Suicides undertaken because of the unhappy ending of what is but ought not to be called a love affair, seldom succeed. They were not intended to succeed. The real effort was not self-destruction but an indirect expression of self-pity, aimed at the unresponding object of an infatuation.

In courting, a person should be completely himself without

pretense. He should drop with all speed any acquaintance who turns out to be pretending to be what he is not.* The counterfeit may look all right for a while, but eventually what seemed love will always be recognized for what it really is—FEAR.

If two people have been emotionally dishonest with each other, they will have some indication of this in a moment of uncertainty or of embarrassment the next time they meet. Why? Because in the meantime their subconscious minds have had time to evaluate what happened. Despite all our conscious obtuseness and lack of understanding, the weight of evidence seems to be that subconscious understands subconscious with incredible rapidity. Perhaps this is why we can stand tragedy and sorrow far better than we can endure deceit.

Good Manners

Many so-called manners—like rising when an elder comes into the room—were devised by people who wanted others to show their subservience. All good manners are based on kindness and consideration; a feeling for the ideas, interests, enthusiasms, shortcomings of other people. Whenever we meet good manners all of us are pleased.

Kindness in courting will show itself in being on time; in being careful not to wrinkle the back of her dress at a dance (girls like to dress up, so go formal once in a while); in being as concerned that the other person is having a good time as that one is enjoying one's self; in being careful with other people's property, (cigarette burns damage furniture); in being honest in the little ways which show whether one is serious, still uncertain, or only trifling. It is true that the girl is strong enough to put her coat on by herself, or to handle her own chair at the table, but holding her coat or pushing in her chair will, by tacit convention, symbolize thoughtfulness to her.

---

* This should not be confused with the person who is sincerely trying to improve himself. Self-improvement is among the highest manifestations of the human personality.

Show courtesy to her or his parents. Time should be spent talking with them so they can see the kind of person with whom their daughter or son is keeping company. They have a right to know. Also, since one does marry the other's family, it is the part of wisdom to find out what the family is like, as will be discussed more fully later. "It is not good to marry a maiden who is the only good maiden in her family."

A kind person will be embarrassed by attentions which cannot be reciprocated. This not only applies to material gifts, but even more to affection itself. A kind girl will be distressed by the necessity of refusing a proposal; a kind man will never ask her to marry him until he is reasonably sure that her answer is going to be "yes."

Courting can be an expensive process: taxi, tea dance, theater, dinner, corsage. There are just as many ways to enjoy each other without spending money: a walk through the park or along the riverbank, a game of tennis; talking philosophy in the long winter evening. The ingredients of a happy date do *not* depend on money.

The superior girl will not want to go out with a boy who has no more resources within himself, and no more consideration for what might give her pleasure, than to want to spend the evening petting. Anyone can pet if he has two arms. It takes only sexual stimulus, and that is all it gives. If two people can do no more worthwhile courting than to neck and pet, they will be thoroughly bored in marriage. It takes brains and personality to keep a marriage interesting, exactly as it takes brains and personality to have a thrilling time together that is not physical.

If a boy (or girl) suggests that one is "slow" or "inhibited" because one does not neck or pet, the proper reply is, "Why not just say I'm choosy?" If a philanderer approaches a girl with undue optimism, unless her actions belie her words, she can easily restore his good manners by simply saying, "I know I don't have to worry with you, because a man like you would always protect a girl." He will, because he has been treated as though he were, in fact, his best self.

It may be that the undue optimism was based on some little thing he has seen or heard. Harriet may go over to Joe's to see his new television set, but it would be better manners not to invite her at midnight. Whatever a person does always gets talked about. Sometimes society is mistaken, but if a person does certain unconventional things he, or she, is going to be talked about in socially predetermined ways.

One thing much resented—and rightly—is the man who dishonestly pays pointed attention to two girls at the same time. This is unethical for either sex. How a boy treats a girl, or vice versa, will always be talked about.

Politeness evolves from insight which affords emotional and intellectual comprehension at the same time. When a young man invites a girl to a dance, concert, picnic, football game, dinner, or whatever it may be, and she politely declines, he must be able to interpret what she means. There are several possibilities:

(1) "Slow up a little. Let's not go too fast."
(2) "I have something else I'd rather do."
(3) "I am uncertain as to what I think."
(4) "I do not care to go out with you."

A series of polite refusals almost invariably add up to an attempt to say in a kind way, "Please leave me alone."

How long may a young man monopolize a marriageable girl's dates without making up his mind as to his intentions? Her stock in trade in the matrimonial market is her youth, which makes it unkind to keep occupying her time indefinitely without making clear whether the affair is serious to him or only of passing interest. Perhaps a year would be reasonable.

Penetrating Analysis

As has already been remarked, the answers one gets are always in terms of the questions one asks. "Is Mary prettier than Eleanor?" or "Does Dick have more money to spend than Ted?" are superficial. Intelligent inquiry does not follow a chain of unrelated questions. By careful reflection it explores whole areas. It looks for circumstantial evidence which is far more convincing than direct evidence. It concentrates not so much on what a person says as on what he shows. It sees the answers as a whole, in detail, dynamically related, and thought through to the end without distortion. This is a time for prospective lovers to undertake calm, analytical thinking when they are apart; not just to have a good time when they are together.

Happiness in shared activities that are superficial, like dances or parties, is not enough to show whether two people have the necessary common denominators to flourish in the same kind of domestic soil and atmosphere. The temptation is to go into action. What is needed is delay in order that there may be time for comparisons, evaluations, thinking beyond the thrill of an engagement.

Anything done before a person has had time to find out what he is subconsciously feeling, is false and therefore suspect. Many a boy, without knowing it, is more interested in discovering whether a girl will let him kiss her, than he is in kissing her.

In trying to analyze what one is actually feeling, there is advantage in using Korzybski's technique of particularizing instead of generalizing.* An individual, believing himself to be in love, should never say, "I feel this way about her." The accurate statement is, "On such and such a date at such and such a time, I experienced these conscious emotions about her, probably as a result of the following influences." To say, "Ralph is a wonderful person," is a meaningless generality. "Ralph was wonderful in 1948," is still only a fiction. Ralph, on June 20, 1948, doing a given thing for a specific—even though subconscious—reason, and producing certain results, may be a fact.

During courtship two people should see each other under as many and varied conditions as possible: in a group, alone, summer, winter, early, late, happy, angry, tired, full of *elan vital*, under the

* A. Korzybski, *Science and Sanity* (Lancaster, Pa.: Science Press Printing Company, 1933), pp. 371-451.

bright lights, in the quiet of the commonplace, and particularly in each other's homes. No person can be truly understood except in terms of his family background. Here are to be found the conditions which gave him his responses to life. This is where he learned his standards of value, about which so many people learn so little during courtship, but which determine how any one of us feels in any given situation. These are the real circumstances of his life; not the parties, the dances, or the automobile rides. One can often learn more about a person in three days at his home than in three years of superficial contacts. What is his attitude toward his mother and sisters? This may not correspond with how he treats his sweetheart, but it will be the foundation of how he treats his wife. What is her attitude toward her father and brothers? When there are dishes to be done does the family co-operate or try to escape work?

It is necessary to project one's thinking beyond the surface look of things. Some of the most superficially charming people are the most unkind and selfish underneath. Understood, the circumstantial evidence will expose them. Analyze the little acts. These are important because they show the essence of a person. Diogenes is not known to us as the most famous of the cynic philosophers, but for asking Alexander the Great to stand out of his sunlight. In that one unresponsive instant, the man's lifetime of thinking as to the value of pomp and power flowed from him. Ordinary circumstances are symbols of our attitudes. When a person says, "You're crazy," his attitude is different from when he says, "That's a crazy idea." The second statement has nothing to do with looking down on the originator of the idea. Thus do little things betray tremendous things.

An individual's style of courting is a subconscious index of the kind of affection he desires. It demonstrates a man's concept of the nature of love. Does the young man treat his sweetheart like a tawdry trinket, or like a personality to be respected and cherished? What does a girl do in response to what the boy does? If he says, "I think you're wonderful!" does she say, "Tell me more," or does she say, "Thank you," and immediately go on to some other topic? Does the girl spend the evening talking about other people? What she says will convey far more information about herself than about anyone else.

Serious courting is a time for questions, which should be continuously propounded, and penetratingly answered. People are usually expected to be dreamy and romantic during courtship. If they are not, we think them queer. Stupid of us, is it not? They should be analytical, not romantic. They should remember that throughout life a husband and wife always subject each other to comparison with other people. Will the individual being courted be able to stand up under such comparison?

Why are the two young people happy together at the moment? What need is their togetherness now answering in each of them, and how will this fit into the rest of their lives? What they conclude to be the answer is not as important as why they think it the answer. Is it wishful thinking? Are they caught in the thermal updraft of an infatuation which can soar to dizzy heights on the basis of a few expressions of mutual interest? Mixed with sex attraction it becomes easy to conclude they have at last found eternal love. Then comes the sudden downdrafts of disagreement and rejection. What then?

How soundly has each developed his true self? Do they want to be influenced by each other? How much? Why? What do they have to gain from each other? How will they frustrate and impede each other? Would each be gladly willing to be the child of the other if ages were appropriately changed? What are the tendencies in each at present? Will they result in parallel or conflicting development? How far? How fast? Is this a person whose thoughts and feelings and action will be forever interesting? Is he valuable and forgivable? Would there still be interest in her if he were blind? If he were a eunuch? If the honest answer is "Yes," then it is so wonderful not to be blind, and not to be a eunuch.

Aside from sex, how broad and how deep is the relation from the point of view of each individual? On what scale of values does the relationship rest? Trust, patience, consideration? The recognition of a suitor's internal concepts concerning the relationship is an important discovery in any courtship.

Has there been at least one serious, mutually important difference of opinion? Has sufficient time elapsed to evaluate how it was handled? Because it was important were the reactions defensive and domineering, or was there a mutually emotional mature attempt to devise a constructive solution together?

If the affair breaks up what emotions resulted? Anger? A sense of worthlessness? Desire for revenge? An attempt to understand what happened and why? Effort to learn from the experience?

Men and women would still be married if they correctly answered these questions, but often married to different individuals from those they now choose. They would know themselves better and have more competent judgment as to whether they were in love, or only enjoying an adventure, enamored by a pretty face.

George and Alice failed to do this. It was, as a matter of fact, some years after they were married before they began to see each other as they really were. He was interested in ideas and cared little for the accumulation of things. She had grown up in a moderately well-off home, surrounded by wealthy estates. All her girlhood the subconscious emotional pressures in her life had been on money. Other people had two cars, other people had a butler, other people had European travel.

So George and Alice started off together; he wanting to add something to the sum total of human knowledge; she daydreaming about the romance of beginning at the bottom, but soon living in a larger house further up the hill and covered with whiter paint than any of the other houses. After that the retinue of servants, and the European travel.

Time went by. They still lived in the same little house while George carried on his research and let the world go by. It was the friends across the street who moved into the big white house on the hill. At first Alice was annoyed. Then she realized that the future was already here but the servants were not. That led to rebellion. Meanwhile, she spent money he had not yet earned, and both realized the marriage was a failure.

Each of these young people was a respectable, desirable citizen. The trouble was the different kind of domestic soil and climate they needed. He was a thinker. She was a social climber. The time to have found this out was before they were married, not afterward.

The only reason marriages fail is incompatibility. All else— cruelty, adultery, drunkeness—is merely how rebellion against the frustration of incompatibility expresses itself. Divorce is the result, not the cause of failure. When a husband and wife expect conflicting things of a marriage, without being able to work out a satisfactory pattern for interweaving their interests and their sacrifices, they will be continually frustrating each other. This will lead to continual acts of retaliation. Thus does basic disharmony widen a chasm which nothing can bridge.

The time to realize this is early in the courtship. The problem is not to prevent people from being divorced, but to prevent its tragic necessity because of unwise marriages. Whenever a suspicion arises, it should be pursued until the facts either substantiate or disprove it. Love must have a reservoir of confidence. To suppress a suspicion with, "He wouldn't do that," does not resolve it. A suspicion or a quarrel is a symbol of something wrong. Bring it out into the open. To stifle it produces misunderstanding, develops barriers, conceals truth.

If one is, for the rest of his life, to be principally dependent upon a single other person for companionship, the choice needs to be made with eyes open, not just with hearts aflame. Here, as in other areas, the capacity to be analytical is directly proportional to one's freedom from any dominating influence.

THE BEGINNING OF LOVE

The final step is actually beginning to be in love. The kind of person one selects is greatly influenced by the kind of children one played with as a youngster. We also tend to court not only someone on the same economical and social level—because that is where our contacts usually are—but to court someone having similar characteristics of stature, intelligence, complexion, vivacity, etc. Inevitably a boy expects in a wife the things he admired in his mother, and hopes for the things which he felt she lacked. Inevitably, a girl does the same by seeking father substitutions in her husband.

When courting has become completely serious, wise young people will seek corroborative, objective judgments. Listen to what mature people do and do not say about the match. Observe how each likes the other's parents and siblings, the other's friends. In courting, "two's company, three's a crowd," but four are an excellent idea. The value of a double date is the evidence it gives through the mutual reactions of the other couple to the person one is courting. It also gives an opportunity to make comparisons, and to see whether there is pleasure in being together with other people —which is a healthy sign—or whether the two are unhappy unless they are alone—which is a sign of danger.

Occasionally a young person will seek advice because he (she) believes himself in love with two girls and does not know which to choose. It is true we can be genuinely in love with more than one person. However, when such a dilemma arises during courtship, a reasonable assumption is infatuation, not love. Among the best things Bobby Burns ever wrote are the following lines from *Mary Morison*:

> I sat, but neither heard nor saw:
> Though this was fair and that was braw
> And yon the toast of a' the town,
> I sighed, and said among them a',
> "Ye arena Mary Morison."

When in doubt don't, or at least get some good advice. Postpone. Get more experience, more evidence, take more time to reach a conviction. Never marry until you have an unshakable conviction.

Even then you may be wrong. If your convictions are always shaky, the real problem is emotional immaturity.

There is increasing reliability in the judgments of the marriage counseling centers. At Los Angeles, for example, where 50 per cent of the people who get married are divorced, only five or six traceable couples who have undergone preparation for marriage at the American Institute of Family Relations and to whom marriage was recommended, have been divorced in the last ten years.

Once the validity of one's love has been objectively established and tested, the time has at last come to allow the imagination full reign. Presents of flowers, candy, books, theater tickets, are all evidence of attraction. The evidence of love and affection goes much deeper, and requires a greater involvement of self-expression. Almost anyone in love can produce one good piece of verse. The imaginative person will perhaps produce a whole series of alphabet verses, mailing them one at a time beginning with:

> A is for alphabet, Angel,
> Ardently authored for thee;
> Authored in hope that some change'll
> Find who in whose arms before Z?

and following through each letter all the way down to:

> Z is for zest over zero,
> The signs of the zodiac too;
> Zounds! now that you say, "My hero,"
> My answer must be, "I love you."

Or perhaps there will be a series of little letter-page magazines, called *The Gay Gazette*, dealing with ideas as to what a home should be like. Here, the emphasis is on the end to be fulfilled. We do not want things for themselves so much as for what can be accomplished with them. Or perhaps the imagination goes no further than getting a ten-yard piece of narrow paper on which ribbon is packaged, and writing a letter that unrolls and unrolls and unrolls.

Many a young man has agonized over what to say in making his proposal. This is usually a danger sign, for when one knows who one loves and where one stands, the business of making a declaration is easy.

Not Every Arrow Hits

Courting is a problem in research, and much good research ends in failure. Also, it will not be undertaken unless the investigator is convinced there is an answer, and that he can find it. Often when the right answer is discovered it seems so simple.

Courting is a little like going fishing, with faith that the fish are there, that the bait is adequate, and that unacceptable fish can be thrown back into the pond without excessive damage to them.

There is, however, no Aristotelian logic to courtship. If A is attracted to B, B may or may not be attracted to A. If A is attracted to B, and B is attracted to C, A may or may not be attracted to C. The relation between people is like the relation between atoms: some attract, some do not. Thus, there are nine possible emotional relationships between a young man and a young woman.*

A attracted B attracted	A indifferent B attracted	A repelled B attracted
A attracted B indifferent	A indifferent B indifferent	A repelled B indifferent
A attracted B repelled	A indifferent B repelled	A repelled B repelled

Six of these relationships are unbalanced because there is not agreement between A and B. The other three may become un-

* This was worked out with Suresh Nanavati during an hour of counseling.

balanced because agreement may not last. With time, by an emotional equivalent of Newton's first law, dynamic equilibrium will be arrived at because A and B will change under the influence of the unbalanced forces acting upon them. People are flexible. They adapt themselves to circumstances.

This has been expressed graphically in Figure 8. The distance B is above the axis of indifference, or the distance A is below it, represents the amount of attraction each feels for the other. Thus,

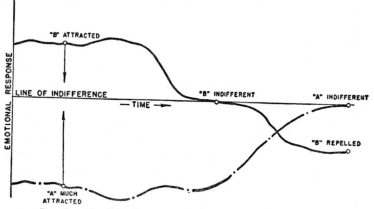

Fig. 8.   Possible Emotional Responses During Courtship

A is pictured as more attracted to B than B is to A. As time goes by the situation alters still further. There are many degrees of attraction, indifference, or dislike. Whereas A maintains a reasonably constant attitude of attraction, B first becomes indifferent, and is finally repelled. What happens now is not a matter of certainty. Both may become indifferent. B may once more feel attracted, or A may be repelled as B softens to indifference. Adjustments will eventually be arrived at by the more flexible person making the greater change. This, indeed, is the law of all adjustment. There are, however, only three possibilities of mutually satisfactory balance: both are honestly attracted; both are honestly indifferent; both are honestly repelled.

This does not mean that equilibrium cannot be achieved in any other way. An emotionally mature person will not become hateful just because someone reacts by disliking him. Attraction may never get beyond wanting to love and to be loved, with a slow adjustment toward indifference. Nevertheless, in this world of emotional dishonesty, thousands of people who have been disappointed in love think their reaction is affection, or at least indifference, when actually the true feeling is closer to hate. If A can love long enough without resentment, must B adjust by hating less? Perhaps. It all depends upon the strength and direction of *all* the emotional forces acting on him.

The situation is even more complicated, because we have subconscious as well as conscious reactions, and because our estimates of another individual's feelings are sometimes mistaken, having been deceived by an emotion which prevented judgment from corresponding with reality.

Thus A may believe his feeling to be "I am attracted" whereas his true motivation may be, "This will give me a good revenge on Mother." He may also mistakenly believe that B's response is indifference. Meanwhile B may feel that her emotion toward A is dislike, although the real truth may be she fears to admit the degree to which she is attracted.

In short, any evaluation of the relationship between A and B is always made by both, and always on a subconscious as well as a conscious level. The result may be complete harmony, or an almost endless diversity of conflicts.

Love is not love unless it is reciprocal. There is no sense in allowing life to be bitter because someone else does not see a relationship as you do. Pick yourself up and go on to other things. Many upset youngsters hide their narrow selfishness behind a false idea of loyalty to the person who jilted them. The real truth is they fear no one else will love them. How silly!

In courting, if a mistake has been made, start over. The right to learn implies the right to make mistakes, but an intelligent person does not keep making the same mistakes. Try again, and use what you learned.

Not every arrow hits. During the war a student came into my office, heartbroken because his fiancee had eloped with another man. He was almost in tears as I congratulated him on his deliverance from danger. That it was deliverance would be apparent as soon as what he thought a breaking heart could be recognized as only bleeding vanity. Beside me is a letter from him.

"This note is about four months too early, but I feel a compulsion to write it. You told me that in two years I would send you a letter saying, 'I'm glad it happened. She wasn't the right girl for me anyway.' I'll never forget the time I came to you with the sad story of how I had been jilted, and you leaned across the desk to congratulate me. Thanks. You were right."

No one can pull a deep emotion up by the roots and instantly banish it to the land of forgetfulness. There is a gnawing at one's heart. The first reaction, due to hurt pride, is for revenge. But bitterness is a potent source of self-poisoning. Nothing ever happens to anyone of us that we are not at least partially responsible for. We build our own destiny. Perhaps what happened was the only sensible thing. Find some new friends. Feed the hunger for affection by discovering something to serve, bigger than yourself, that gives you emotional satisfaction, and then lose yourself in serving it. Time will wash away all tears, leaving memories and the wisdom of experience.

The Time Factor

Burgess and Cottrell concluded, "It is evident that the longer the period of intimate association before marriage, the greater are the probabilities of harmonious marital adjustment. Companionship tested by time appears, therefore, to be a better basis for successful marriage than the emotional feeling of certainty inspired by short-lived romantic love."*

The two things that contribute most to a successful courtship are sincerity and time, for both help make it possible to see facts as facts without distortion.

* Burgess and Cottrell, *op. cit.*, p. 168.

Just because two young people are mutually attracted is no reason for them to rush to the altar. They need to explore the relationship intelligently, in a searching courtship, taking into account the areas and degree of their attraction and its potentialities for growth. It is perfectly possible to love and yet not to love enough or in the right ways to sustain a happy marriage.

Friendship, courting, engagement, marriage, constitute a series of steps in a process. Love is not a feeling of oneness at the beginning of courtship. That emotion is largely joy over the affirmation of the excellence of one's self; an emotion which may deepen into love over a long period of marriage. Love is cumulative. No one should expect to maintain the atmosphere of romance, the exultation, the stardust that usually encompasses the last stages of an ardent courtship. This is produced by the miracle of discovering a new love. It does not last, which may be why most novels end with the accomplishment of the courtship. But it can be replaced by a deeper, closer, more precious relationship. Courting usually takes place during planned recreational time. Marriage is giving one's self in complete affection on the level of "every day's most quiet need, by sun or candlelight."

8

The Period of Engagement

AN ENGAGEMENT is a happy situation because it is one of the few in which both sides feel they have won something. Sociologically it is a period of final testing and of transition; a "wait and see" as well as a "now get ready" sort of arrangement, which may explain why there is no poetry about it in the anthologies. Man is the only animal to provide such a period. All the other animals follow courtship with immediate mating.

Thus, the period of engagement is basically for the purpose of providing two things:

(1) A period of testing (a claim has been staked, but some degree of doubt still remains)

(2) A period of transition (time must be allowed for the necessary social, economic, and emotional readjustments).

A PERIOD OF TESTING

The value of this "chance to check" which an engagement provides is proven by the sociological studies. A five-day license law stops 6 percent of all marriages—at least the license is never used. In a study of engagements lasting up to two years and over, Burgess and Cottrell found a consistent increase in the percentage of happy marriage with lengthening engagement. "It is apparent that duration of engagement is positively associated with probabilities of good adjustment in marriage."* They admit that too long an engagement is probably undesirable, but were unable to determine what constitutes "too long." Under the usual circumstances a year seems to be a reasonable length of time.

Much depends upon how long and how valid a courtship has preceded the engagement. Long acquaintance, a reasonable length of engagement, and lasting happiness can be expected to go together. The hazard of the short engagement, not preceded by long acquaintance, is that the prospective bride and groom are too much in a hurry to learn much about each other. The hazard of the long engagement is that under continued stimulation without outlet the lovers get on each other's nerves and the engagement is broken.

It is not just the length of the engagement, but the length of the entire relationship that is important. Even after long acquaintance, the engagement should be long enough to make a final check on the validity of the choice, and to provide a successful transition between courtship and marriage.

Of the unhappily married people, Burgess and Cottrell found that 40 per cent had practically no period of engagement, whereas only 11 per cent of those with enough emotional maturity to stand an engagement of over two years were unhappy. Terman concluded that an engagement of less than six months was dangerous. Less than three months was particularly dangerous. There is eight times the probability of unhappy marriage following a few days of engagement as there is following two years of courting plus a year's engagement.

An engagement is a contract to marry, and should not be entered into impulsively. It brings public recognition of this contract, as well as of a special relationship of testing and transition. An engaged person is off the eligibility list, and must behave with

* E. W. Burgess and L. S. Cottrell, *Predicting Success or Failure in Marriage* (New York: Prentice-Hall, 1939), p. 168.

appropriate discretion. There should be security and exclusiveness to the relationship, while still recognizing the possibility of doubt as to whether the two individuals respond to life in the same way.

A Period of Transition

An engagement is recognized as a time for:
(1) Family acceptance and readjustment
(2) Recognition from friends (showers for the bride; bachelor dinners for the groom)
(3) Acquiring needed skills (she learns to cook; he learns to carve)
(4) Making economic readjustments (it is not true that two can live as cheaply as one. If both are good managers, they can live as cheaply as 1.6)
(5) Finding and preparing a place to live.

Here is a gradual reorientation from the emotions of acquaintance to the emotions of intimacy. Properly entered into as a period of transition, the engagement should go as far in the accomplishment of pre-marital mutual adjustment as is genuinely helpful in the long run. Personalities should be adapted more unreservedly than is wise during courtship, but with no attempt to pound them into alterations. Love is not the itch to alter. That is wanting to destroy, not to affirm, the reality of the other individual. *The only person one ever has the right to try to change is one's self.* Immaturity often manifests itself in an attempt to reform the betrothed. A mature person sees faults, balances them against virtues, and accepts another individual for what he is.

Inevitably there will be areas where complete agreement cannot be reached. Inevitably there will be things for each to unlearn as well as to learn for the sake of the partnership. *Two people seldom really love each other until they discover that there are a few places where mutual understanding is impossible, until they accept this, and until it does not seem calamitous.*

In making the transition from courtship to marriage it is well to discuss freely and completely any questions which will come up after marriage. These areas were doubtless touched on many times during the courtship. They should now be examined more intimately. For example:

(1) The man's present and probable future earnings
(2) How it is to be divided
(3) Whether the wife wants a career
(4) Relatives who may prove difficult
(5) Attitudes toward sex and children
(6) Ultimate values in life.

In any event, disagreements should not be detoured. "Let's not talk about that now. It makes us unhappy," sees but ignores the point. The engagement is the time to get such things identified and understood. The engagement is the time to find out whether disagreements can be handled with an emotional maturity which guarantees a bilateral approach and an interweaving of interests, or whether answers are to be arrived at on the battlefield.

Do not retreat before a misunderstanding. Failure to face a variance of viewpoint makes it none the less a variance of viewpoint. A quarrel sometimes clears the air because it helps to determine relative positions. Between well-balanced people the end result need not be domination. Inability to solve most differences of opinion without upset emotion indicates lack of sufficient maturity to be ready for marriage.

Frankly discuss personality differences, areas of self-doubt, even criticize each other and discover whether it can be done with no trace of an attempt to humiliate. Is there a struggle for domination? How are frustrations and disappointments handled? Share a wide range of activity, particularly on the level of everyday living, and observe whether the resulting feeling is one of growing confidence. Do the betrothed consult each other's opinions before making decisions? Do they say "I" when they mean and should mean "I," and "We" when they mean and should mean "We"?

An engaged couple should be together in a group as much as possible to be sure they have more in common than mere physical attraction. If they are happy only when they are alone, their prognosis is probably poor.

Nevertheless, the question of sex now begins to become important. A gradual reorientation of behavior patterns from those of acquaintance to those of real intimacy is proper, providing it does not go so far as to become harmful. Engaged couples should neither be afraid to face sex frankly, nor be misled by its glamour.

If either the boy or the girl has been brought up in ignorance, it is of importance that this be corrected without delay. If either acquired a background of knowledge through the gutter school it is important that this be replaced by adequate information from an authoritative source, in order, if possible, to correct wrong attitudes. The sociological studies show that people make better husbands and wives when frankly and naturally told about pregnancy and birth before age six. To wait until young people are engaged to give them sex information is inexcusable. New habits of thinking are not acquired that easily.

The more purely physical the transition, the less likely the engagement is to last, or the marriage to be happy. "We're just as good as married," is not true. There are as many reasons why a marriage contract should be formalized and witnessed by society as there are that a will be properly drawn and witnessed.

It is possible to endanger the future success of the marriage by:

(1) Psychic fears due to a clandestine relationship which forfeited security, aesthetic values, and leisurely time

(2) Frigidity developed in the woman due to the emotional shock of having been seduced by the man she loved

(3) Suspicion of infidelity and recrimination. (Groves* says, "It is the man rather oftener than the woman who in retrospect reacts to excessive freedom during the engagement with antagonisms or regret or even with a deep-seated suspicion of his life partner, which makes affection difficult.")

* E. R. Groves, *Marriage* (Rev. ed., New York: Henry Holt, 1941), p. 153.

(4) Unexpected pregnancy; (The question of a child's status at birth is a concern of the state because it involves the right to a name, to support, to inheritance, and sometimes to citizenship.)

(5) An adjustment narrowed to sex. Marriage requires an adjustment in all areas of living.

It is true that there is a drift toward greater sex freedom during the engagement. It is also true that many young people feel, "It took the edge off our marriage. We should have been told that it often requires months under the most auspicious circumstances to make a successful sex adjustment. We needed security, perfect conditions, plenty of time. All we had was haste, worry, and a feeling of guilt. As a result we thought we were poorly mated when the truth was that a proper adjustment was made difficult by our impatience." It often takes three months, or perhaps a year, to achieve a real sex adjustment. Under proper conditions it can be done by almost anyone. Under poor conditions people come to think they are wrongly mated when the truth is they mated under wrong conditions.

It is equally true that a few young people go into an engagement unbelievably ignorant in the area of sex. I have personally known two girls who believed that pregnancy resulted from a kiss. No one can be suddenly freed from such misunderstanding by a marriage ceremony. This is why some thoughtful and respectable people believe that fornication should be countenanced, if not indeed approved. Probably it is preferable to the happiness-destroying congelations of frigidity, but there are other alternatives.

During the last weeks of the engagement there is value in the couple freely discussing their sexual anxieties. Will he be considerate of her? Will she turn out to be frigid? Suppose the union proves to be childless? What can be done if there is a wide variance in their sexual appetites? How about the difficulties each has experienced in the exercise of self-control? This is an excellent method of improving the understanding and rapport between them, particularly if it can be done impersonally (at least in the initial stages), after the manner of a psychiatrist who says, "Perhaps a case I had some years ago will be of interest here. The man was in such and such trouble (almost identical with the patient's). The difficulty was caused by this and this. What he did about it was so and so."

Such an approach should give each individual an insight into his own experiences. It should strengthen the bonds of understanding—or show where there are not but should be such bonds.

Need for a Physical Examination

By any standard that makes sense, an engaged couple—even before the engagement is announced—should each have a thorough physical examination in order to forestall later emotional shock. The usual routine examination is not enough. The blood test for venereal disease, required since 1940 by twenty states, is not enough. It is only fair that each partner should find out for himself, and for his betrothed, what conditions they may be required to face. The results may make them unhappy, but if this is to happen the time for it to happen is during the engagement.

The man should be examined for:

(1) Inheritable diseases, especially venereal. If found, what steps are now needed?

(2) Malformations of the penis, like a foreskin adhering to the glans

(3) Congruence of the size of genital organs with those of the betrothed

(4) Sterility

(5) Emotional interferences with intercourse or normal potency.

The woman should be examined for:

(1) Inheritable diseases, especially venereal. If found, what steps are now needed?

(2) A leathery hymen which should be surgically ruptured (a simple matter)

(3) Congruence of the size of genital organs

(4) Sterility (much more difficult and less certain of correct diagnosis than with the male)

(5) The clitoris free from adhesions to the prepuce which covers it

(6) The uterus in correct position and without malformation or adhesions

(7) Bad pelvic measurements which make normal child-birth difficult

(8) Any emotional interference with intercourse.

An additional reason for each having a competent physical examination early in the engagement is the possibility of an Rh factor in the blood. The name comes from the Rhesus monkey in which the blood substance involved was first identified. If the father is Rh+ and the mother Rh−, the baby will be Rh+. Any leakage of the baby's blood into the mother's circulatory system will result in antibodies being produced there. Once the mother has developed enough antibodies any subsequent fetus will be affected. Mothers who are Rh− lose about one baby in fifty-six.

Among educated Americans one marriage in five is permanently childless. Of these about a third are believed to be actually steril. Even so, a competent physician is able to cure the sterility in something like one-quarter of the cases. Contrary to popular opinion, the barrenness is as often due to the husband as to the wife. It is possible to count the number of spermatozoa per cubic centimeter and from this to draw conclusions concerning a man's virility. Available techniques lead to no comparable information concerning the ova. Little can be done beyond determining whether a woman's fallopian tubes are open, or choked off.

Just previous to the marriage it is desirable for the girl to consult a gynecologist concerning the simple but helpful procedure of self-dilation by which to rupture the hymen and to expand the vagina before the honeymoon. However, as Himes, after explaining the process in detail, says, "Custom will lag behind the best medical opinion in this regard for some time."*

* N. E. Himes, *Your Marriage* (New York: Farrar and Rinehart, 1940), p. 317.

Where there is lack of congruence in the size of sexual organs of the prospective bride and groom, a gynecologist can effect amazing adjustments, not only because the vagina itself is an extremely distensible part of the body, but because of what can be done through the variety of bodily positions possible in intercourse.

What to Confess

In some instances, "What shall I confess?" is an important consideration. If a not too serious mistake was made years ago with no recent breach, the answer is, "Say nothing." The important thing is to convey the truth, which is not always accomplished by a recitation of the actual facts. A confession may wrongly arouse later suspicion. But if it is not just a mistake or two made years ago, the obligation is still to convey the truth, which probably means, "Tell everything." The underlying principles are to divulge:
  (1) Information that helps the betrothed to realize and to appraise the problems of adjustment that must be faced
  (2) Information that would justify questioning the advisability of the marriage. Tell whatever would be detrimental to the marriage if found out, and rest assured it is far better to confess than to be caught after a denial made even by implication.

It is well to realize that the impulse to confess is often a piece of self-inflicted punishment which relieves one of his feeling of guilt. But by so doing the betrothed is asked to carry part of the burden. In case of doubt, as a matter of happiness insurance, consult:
  (1) A reliable marriage counselor
  (2) A psychiatrist.

Broken Engagements

If, during the engagement, doubt arises as to the wisdom of choice, it is foolish to go through with the marriage because of an exaggerated sense of loyalty, or because of false pride. No one can successfully live a lie. No one can play the martyr and be happy. It is not even possible to make the other person happy, for the happiness of the second cannot long survive the unhappiness of the first. Break the engagement wherever:

(1) Persistent doubt arises (almost everyone has a fleeting doubt or two)

(2) New and unfavorable conditions arise such as serious physical or emotional injury.

Pride often mistakenly impels two people to go through with the marriage, but it is far better for the relationship to go on the rocks as an engagement than for it to do so later as a marriage. To think that any spirit of self-sacrifice or Spartan "grin and bear it" can be the basis of a successful marriage is foolish, because it is futile.

In our culture, convention decrees that the girl be the one who breaks, or at least seems to break, the engagement. This is logical because the man, having more opportunity to take the initiative in courting, suffers least.

Whenever an engagement is to be broken it should be done with firmness and finality. Except where there is an excessive dependency, nothing is to be gained for anyone by "cutting the dog's tail off an inch at a time." Do it in one clean slash. Where there is an excessive dependency, it should be made perfectly clear to the individual that the engagement is off, but since it has been such an important experience in his life it may be kind to give him time to transfer his feelings to other people. If the two young people could have made a successful adjustment by dint of much effort, all is not lost. They will still have other chances. If a questionable adjustment is attempted and fails, the result is sure misery. It is to prevent exactly this that the period of engagement exists.

Parental Disapproval

Parents have a great deal to do with the emotional forces which bring about the choices their children make. A parent who has been an excellent parent will, I think, seldom have reason to disapprove a prospective son- or daughter-in-law.

It is a hard task to express disapproval in a form which will permit the child to feel cherished as an individual and whole-heartedly united with the parent. "Don't marry her!" expresses a father's longer experience, greater wisdom, and love for his son. For *him*, that is! The son may see it as, "You want to continue to dominate me," or "Your judgment is no good," or "You continue to ruin my happiness."

It is not enough for father to be right, he must also be accepta-ble. He may have to choose between being wholly right and com-pletely ineffective, or partly right and partially helpful. Certainly the boy's reluctance to heed his father's counsel is a reflection of their previous relationship.

Children are too often made to see things as an either-or situa-tion. "Either I must submit to the pressures of my parent and violate my own integrity by calling the engagement off, or I must stand up for my rights and in spite of all the objections go ahead with the marriage." The problem is to get the child to examine the parent's advice instead of feeling he must submit to it. This will be impossible if the parent has cause to fear his own ineffectiveness, for the more he fears (up to a point) the more domineering he will become, and the more any child whose personality has not been badly destroyed will resist. This is a long way from calmly weighing evidence on either side.

Surely this makes clear why some young people go ahead with the wedding anyway; why some elope; why some are torn to pieces by inner conflict; why a few get pregnant as they seek in despera-tion to feel loved after all; why a few break with their parents, to remain forever hostile; why still fewer give up in pathetic resigna-tion, never marrying; and why a very few commit suicide.

Attention to breaking up the engagement is focused in the wrong place. What is the son (daughter) feeling, and what is the present meaning of the situation from his point of view. For the parent to think intelligent ends without regard to intelligent means is fatal. Not, "Why can't he see the truth?" but "What emotions are causing him to hold the opinions he does? What are his present emotional needs? How can he be helped to find more adequate satisfaction for them?"

Such questions should be wholly for the parent's guidance. To use the answers to expose the son's (daughter's) motives may easily tear him down further instead of helping him grow toward a more healthy orientation. He now not only feels isolated from the parent, but the flimsy character of his own position is flouted in his face. What has he left to cling to but his infatuation? If he does change under this pressure it will be a compulsive, not a genuine change. He is now even more a man against himself. The probability is he will soon become involved with another unsuitable girl.

On the other hand, if an adequate emotional maturing can be fostered, the unwise engagement (or courtship) will effortlessly shrivel away, not only so far as the present choice is concerned, but permanently. Therefore work with the boy, not against him. Try to grow up yourself. Emotionally mature parents rarely have these troubles. Possessive parents find a way to object to any marriage.

Try to expand the scope, not just lengthen the time of the couple's experience together, so they can make better comparisons, so they can run into disagreements to be faced and find them easy or difficult to cope with. Perhaps the parent is wrong. A camping trip with emotionally mature young people might help.

Subconsciously at least, and in occasional moments of awareness, the boy knows the engagement is no good (if it is). It is a union of real selves he wants, and knows he is incapable of in his present condition. His basic decency would prevent a relationship where he is a fraud and the other person is real. Respect his present feelings. Deserve his trust. Perhaps then he will ask questions, objectively analyze facts, come to wise conclusions for himself. These will not always be father's conclusions, but they should be closer to reality than compulsively defiant ones.

In Conclusion

An engagement has been completely successful when it provides:
  (1) An adequate period for testing whether or not the two individuals respond to life in the same way
  (2) An adequate transition from the formalities of courting to the intimacies of marriage.

Must we repeat that quality is never an accident? It is the product of intelligent thinking, good method, and hard work.

9

The Honeymoon

Value of a Honeymoon

The purpose of a honeymoon is to allow a bride and groom to make the most significant transition of their lives under the best circumstances. By marrying they have established an exclusive relationship, promising to forsake all others, to cherish each other despite neither being perfect, and to do it under all manner of circumstances.

The wedding is predominantly—and rightly so—the bride's event. Hers is the greater transition. She changes her name, her social status, her legal rights, her responsibilities, and often the town she lives in. The groom changes some of these things, but to a lesser degree.

By all means have a real wedding, not a cold ceremony in the city clerk's office. The clergyman's parlor will do; the bride's home is still better. The church is probably best of all. Here, if the clergyman is a sincere man of God, one is surrounded by an atmopsere of peace and hope and exaltation which makes the marriage ceremony a sacrament and a holy thing. Here all the sacred forces of mankind combine to recognize and to approve the togetherness of husband and wife, including especially the sex relation. "Now," the church says in effect, "this man and this woman belong to each other fully, completely, and with our blessing. In the sanctity of marriage, intercourse should be for both of you the ultimate ecstasy, because you have now accepted and fulfilled the conditions under which the church welcomes and approves this fundamental urge."

It is not possible for marriage to be a sacrament and yet for the resulting children to be conceived in sin. The two ideas are incompatible—that is unless the husband is a brute, or the wife adulterous, or both depraved.

Secret marriages—and they are more common than is usually supposed—are almost always evidence that some important factor in the espousal is amiss: parental disapproval, legalizing an intimacy, illegitimate pregnancy, doubt of the legal or moral right to marry. As would be expected, secret marriages are less likely to succeed, church weddings more likely to succeed, not because they are held in church but because of the kind of people who usually have church weddings.

To contract a marriage and to consummate a marriage are not one and the same thing. The marriage has been contracted when the clergyman says, "I pronounce you man and wife." It has not been legally consummated until the first intercourse. When it is emotionally consummated is something else again. It is not uncommon for two people to contract a marriage, to have physical union, and never to be emotionally or intellectually married at all. The marriage ceremony is not an end in itself. It is intended as a beginning. The throwing of rice is an old symbol of fertility, and the tying of tin cans to the bridal automobile is what remains of an old procedure intended to frighten away all evil spirits.

Some sociologists condemn the idea of a honeymoon on the grounds that it constitutes an unreal inroduction to life together. They maintain that a honeymoon is artificial; that it implies a perennial extension of romance, with sex privileges added.

My own feeling is that marriage involves a definite break with the past, and that the transition should be made under the best possible conditions. To be sure, marriages sometimes do start to fail on the honeymoon, but the honeymoon is not the root cause. The purpose of the honeymoon is to provide the bride and groom with an opportunity to begin their many new personal adjustments under the most favorable conditions. This means privacy in quiet, relaxing surroundings. It will be time enough later to undertake the last steps in their adaptation to each other's families.

The honeymoon should make it possible for the newlyweds to approach physical union:

(1) As a beautiful experience mutually entered into
(2) At a suitable time and place
(3) Without domination or resistance
(4) Secure from meddling by outsiders
(5) Not as sensual gluttony, but as an apprenticeship for both in developing skill in their interrelationships.

Here is a period of transition of great importance. Both bride and groom should know what to expect, what to avoid, and good method in starting toward their ultimate goal—a happy marriage. Otherwise, how can they be willing to make the transition, able to make the transition, and successful in accomplishing the transition?

There is no place for ignorant blundering, no place for self-assertion, vulgarity, fear, feelings of guilt, or mere acquiescence. There is need for intelligence, mutual forebearance, security, leisure, loveliness. These are hardly possible in the clandestine relationship.

The public part of the marriage is elaborately planned. The private part is much more important and usually much less carefully thought out. *It is possible to ruin a marriage in the process of learning how to be married.* Leave good bedroom manners to instinct? As well leave good table manners to instinct! Most of man's rise from savagery to culture has been due to a better understanding of wholesome ways for meeting basic, biological needs. Good method is no more inborn than a knowledge of cooking or the ability to sing a duet. The superior quality of artistic performance does not just happen; it rests upon being able to appreciate and to apply the best results of previous knowledge.

ADJUSTING SEXUALLY

In a study of the factors affecting the success or failure of a honeymoon, Brav* found that "adjusting sexually" was the principal source of difficulty, and "lack of adequate sex education" considered the reason for the trouble. As already pointed out elsewhere, my own opinion is that a difficult sex adjustment is usually caused by lack of good emotional adjustment, to which ignorance of sex is contributory. Only 10 per cent of the women involved in the study felt that pre-marital sex experience was helpful during a honeymoon. Over 80 per cent were sure that it was not. At the same time, 70 per cent felt that "book knowledge" was to be desired. Half the women claimed to have possessed such knowledge; 70 per cent said their husbands possessed such knowledge. By inference it can be concluded that 50 per cent of the women and 30 per cent of the men have little or no authoritative sex education prior to marriage.

Both bride and groom should have been given enough instruction since childhood to enable each to enter the relationship without fear of hurting or being hurt, either physically or emotionally. Both bride and groom need to understand each other's emotions bilaterally. How can this be possible if either is emotionally dishonest with himself? The groom should be sensitive to every minute signal that betrays the feelings of his bride. Approaching the marriage bed with the passionate proficiency of a man who has been romantic about love, yet rakish about women, is shortsighted in the extreme.

The individual situation needs to be carefully studied by *both* participants, without assumptions or the careless following of what may be old habit patterns. The bride's reaction may be one of prudery due to wrong bringing-up. She may say in effect, "If I

* S. R. Brav, "Note on Honeymoons," *Marriage and Family Living,* Vol. IX, No. 3 (Summer 1947), p. 60.

must submit to your lust, I suppose I must. But you may as well know right now that I shall loathe the experience, and despise you for wanting it." Such an attitude should have been discovered during the engagement in order that there be no upsetting surprises on the honeymoon. Such an attitude requires the most carefully thought out and skillfully applied remedial measures. The young husband will probably experience a sleepless night and a painful, unrelieved erection. He will probably conclude that his bride's attitude can be overcome only by patient education which never threatens her security, and which—perhaps months, or even years later—wins, because it deserves, her participation in the thrilling discovery that she is radiant, human, and in need of expressing and finding satisfaction in her love.

A right frame of mind cannot be maintained by a girl who has been brought up in fear or in ignorance. A sense of shame about sex is often felt by improperly educated people who have never violated the moral law. In a perfectly normal intercourse such people sometimes feel guilty. The only intelligent response here is patience . . . probably a great deal of patience combined with complete re-education, which is always a slow process.

What a price for parental mistakes! It will take a long time to break down the stupid tradition that the human body is something to be despised, subjugated, mortified. Such false evaluations make a mockery of marriage. If God had felt that a body was sinful instead of beautiful, He would have made us differently. We should accept our true natures as God made them.

On the other hand, it may be the groom who reacts with uncertainty and fear. Sometimes a bride, who wants to be hurried into a sexual response, finds the cadenzas of adoration with which her husband courted her have now been hushed by painfully self-searching emotions not at all in tune with her own eagerness. She may behave distantly because she wants him to be more seductive and is afraid to say so. Or perhaps the groom's caveman tactics threaten her safety needs and produce a feeling of fear and revulsion. No real unity is possible where the underlying motivation is conquest. Nevertheless, this is exactly what some men have done with their sweethearts as an initial preparation for what they will do with their wives.

Any of these experiences can be grim and lonely, ending with secret resentments boiling underneath what should have been the indescribable ecstasy and incommunicable beauty of the sex relation when rightly entered into. Gifts, holding hands, an embrace, a kiss, are all evidence of attraction, perhaps of affection, possibly of love. The perfect fulfillment reaches end perfection in the ultimate embrace of intercourse . . . there is no fulfillment in inexpressible longing. How tragic to allow a young person to grow up believing intercourse in wedlock is to endure submission, or to violate modesty, or to complete a conquest. Are we like the spiders who conclude their nuptials by the bride eating the groom?

The honeymoon will not be marred by either physical or emotional difficulties if the bride and groom are adequately prepared. Nevertheless, they need to be ready for any surprise. The emotions of shame and guilt, false modesty, prudery, conquest, expectation of pain, fear of pregnancy, may influence and all too often do mar the honeymoon. The assumption that two respectable people, because they are physically capable of intercourse, possess whatever knowledge is necessary for a satisfactory sex life, is absurd. We need correct and honest answers to sincere and intelligent questions. The urge is biological. How it is expressed is cultural. Why let each new generation learn by repeating the same old mistakes? Why not pass on experience from generation to generation with cumulative results? Van de Velde, the great Dutch gynecologist, says, "We will only repeat, with all possible seriousness and emphasis, that much marital unhappiness, attributed to the apparent sexual frigidity of the wife, could be avoided and prevented if the medical profession had not allowed themselves to be deterred from explaining the many technicalities of a normal married life. . . ."*

Mental inhibitions cannot be overcome in a short time. Right

* Van de Velde, *Ideal Marriage*, American translation (New York: Random House, 1930), p. 168.

attitude cannot be acquired in a short time. Prudery, false modesty, force, resistance, blundering, submission, all lead to spiritual degradation. In an earnest, reverent attitude desirous of using good method lies the road to happiness.

Good Method

When should the marriage be consummated? Only when both bride and groom are ready, which usually means when the bride is ready. This often depends on the skill of the groom as a lover, never on his capacities as a caveman. Skillful seduction on a honeymoon is entirely proper.

The bride is likely to be nervously tired by all the sweet delirium of preparing for the wedding. She is likely to be tense because of uncertainty as to whether her husband understands the situation well enough to avoid hurting her either emotionally or physically. This is not a situation where selfishness or impatience will suffice. It needs mutual exertion which, like a beautiful duet, comes at last to perfection as a result of continued artistic effort together.

The virgin usually offers both emotional and bodily resistance. Few girls who have not had previous intercourse have a large enough vagina to cohabitate without discomfort. The resistance may be emotionally subconscious, but it is there. This does not mean that the groom should become inactive. It certainly does mean that he should be considerate, gentle, patient, and reassuring. Many a marriage is ruined right here by what is little less than legalized rape.

The first step in overcoming fear is to offer convincing evidence of acceptable behavior. In human relations it is not what one says that matters, but what the other person senses. The most reassuring evidence is the evidence of action.

Between two people really in love, the action of each intercourse covers the entire range from courtship to marriage:

(I) *Mutual thoughtfulness in preliminary courting, beginning with words, then followed by caresses.*

This begins by a meeting of minds which is a genuinely shared interest. It carries on to perfection when husband and wife:

(1) Maintain a right frame of mind

(2) Understand the significance of their behavior.

Sex can be a continuing relation of beauty only between emotionally mature lovers uninhibited by disturbing psychological factors.

The most serious difficulties are due more to gross inconsiderateness than to faulty technique. A right frame of mind cannot be maintained by one who approaches a virtuous and sensitive bride in terms of what he has learned from promiscuous girls.

Throughout the marriage, but particularly during the honeymoon, a woman's modesty should be respected. It is difficult for men, who have legitimate reason for handling their genitals from earliest boyhood and who have always undressed together without self-consciousness, to realize how different is a woman's attitude. Young women are only beginning to disrobe among themselves, and they have much less reason for handling their genitals. Consequently, to expect that a bride will yield her body immediately to her husband's inspection is unreasonable. This precious privilege should be approached gradually. Contrariwise, to display the phallus to an emotionally unprepared bride often frightens and may disgust her. It can be a terrifying thing to discover that concepts of size acquired in the Art Museum were misleading.

The bride should try to understand that nature gave most men a powerful sex instinct because of which, throughout their late adolescent and adult lives, they recurrently experience the urge to mate. This desire is not vague, as a woman's sometimes is, but demanding, imperious, and specific.

Any mental incompatibility is serious. If the bride is afraid . . . wait. Half a century of happiness is worth waiting a few days or even weeks to guarantee. If after three months as a maximum, there are not definite signs of achieving a satisfactory adjustment, the situation should not be allowed to drift. The help of a competent marriage counselor is indicated, such as will be found at the American Institute of Family Relations in Los Angeles, or the

Marriage Counsel in Philadelphia, or the nearest reliable person recommended by the American Association of Marriage Counselors, 270 Park Ave., New York. Failing this, find a good psychiatrist.

(II) *Before proceeding with the physical union the groom should wait till he knows his bride is ready.*

It is sometimes difficult to know exactly when assent has been achieved. She may be desirous, but embarrassed and inhibited. There may be emotional resistance of which she is unaware. She may submit, but she cannot participate until her mind is ready. When all fear has disappeared, her confidence will allow the sphincter muscles around the vagina to relax. If contracted due to apprehension, unnecessary pain will result if intercourse is attempted.

An objective test of her readiness is the presence of a mucous secretion around the vulva. This is a lubricating substance produced by Skenes' and by Bartholin's glands. The corresponding mucous is manufactured in the man by Cowper's glands.* In both male and female the secretion results from psychic sex excitement. Its function is similar to that of the lubricating oil in the cylinder of an engine.

Petting is both proper and important here. Exactly as it should not be indulged in before marriage, it should not be omitted after marriage. It is frustration to go halfway and stop; it is unintelligent to begin in the middle and rush on. Petting is an art husbands and wives should cultivate. A look of tenderness; an expression of affection; a kiss; a caress, beginning perhaps with the breast and progressing to the clitoris—all these are part of good method in love making.

The groom should take the initiative, always being cautious and watchful of his bride's reactions. Trifles now become matters of great significance. Presently, in successful marriages, the wife will gradually express herself. From the very beginning she should be encouraged to do so.

* See Chapter 10 on "The Sex Relation."

(III) *The actual physical union should be accomplished with patience and in such a way that the bride retains the underlying power of decision.*

When the woman is asked to participate without sharing, she is first bewildered, then disillusioned, then resentful. When she is tenderly handled, she begins to love abidingly. If not previously ruptured surgically, or with the fingers, the hymen should be slowly and gently stretched, not forcibly broken. In rare instances the hymen is tough and should be surgically incised—a simple procedure. And such necessity ought to have been discovered during the engagement in order to avoid unexpected shock. Again we see the value of a thorough medical examination at that time.

To an increasing degree, as suggested in the previous chapter, the matter of stretching the hymen and the vagina is being attended to by the bride herself, previous to the wedding, under the direction of a gynecologist. This makes for a much easier adjustment.

(IV) *Using patience and affection, the groom should strive to insure his wife's achieving an orgasm.*

Most women rouse sexually much more slowly than men. The man practically always reaches his climax, but unless he learns how to adjust his tempo to hers, holding back until she is completely awakened, it often happens that she is denied an orgasm (throbbing of the vagina and the pelvic floor corresponding to the male sensation of ejaculating the semen). It may take weeks of conscientious effort to achieve success. Responsibility for it does not rest exclusively on the husband, but the consensus of competent opinion is that he must contribute by far the larger share of effort. His self-control can best be achieved by pausing and remaining quiet for a few moments, or by thinking about some entirely unrelated subject—like grandmother's goiter.

(V) *Remember that intercourse is not just a meeting of bodies; it is even more a meeting of minds.*

Sexual response is a delicately adjusted affair. Some trivial thing may spoil the whole experience. For example, as women rouse more slowly than men, so also they recede more slowly. They enjoy the preliminary petting; they prize the subsequent communion. Many a man has ruined the possibility of achieving a good sex adjustment by not realizing this. He did not intend to be crude. The trouble was no one ever told him that when he immediately rolls over and goes to sleep, his wife is left stark alone, craving a few moments of affection, and filling the vacuum of her disappointment with such thoughts as, "So that's all he wanted me for!"

A satisfactory intercourse must fulfill all the erotic demands of both body and soul. It must focus upon the spiritual loveliness of the beloved. It must concentrate not only on the joy received, but on the delight given. It must be bilateral; not an active man proceeding with a passive woman, but two people fused together in a glorious unity. She has a need for consideration. He has a need for response. Both husband and wife are accountable. Often they just muddle along hoping for a miracle.

Achieving a good sex adjustment is not easy. Certainly at least 50 per cent of us fail to achieve complete sexual harmony during the honeymoon. But between people who are psychologically well mated it is no more difficult than many much less worth-while things. Nothing else in all human experience remotely approaches the indescribable ecstacy of the sex relation, rightly entered into. Here is a delicate, intimate sense of oneness which is truly perfect. It is worth working for, and the purpose of the honeymoon is to provide the right conditions for establishing the initial pattern.

In Conclusion

What makes a honeymoon a honeymoon is not expensive hotels, or a shiny new roadster, or a breath-taking trousseau. What makes a honeymoon is a deep feeling of love in the hearts of two people who swim, read, hear the wood thrush at dusk, walk down a country road as they establish a more intimate pattern of togetherness. The gift of love is a precious and delicate thing.

On the honeymoon the bride and groom will surely discover new things about each other. Some will be cause for joy. Be glad because of this, and say so. A person always expands in the presence of individuals who believe in him. Other qualities will be sources of disappointment. This is inevitable. The wise individual will not set about trying to change his mate; he will set about making an adjustment which causes neither to suffer any indignity. The first year of married life ought to be the hardest because it is the year during which these adjustments should be made. It usually is not the hardest, simply because so many people coast through it on the momentum of a glamorous adventure. Subsequently the marriage will decelerate, and finally relapse into inertia.

If the miracle of the honeymoon is to be maintained there must be a never-ending renewal of its joy in togetherness, and no taking each other for granted. Problems must be met together, solved together, remembered together. The honeymoon, as indeed every day in life, soon becomes only an unalterable memory. The walk down the country road and the wood thrush at dusk are soon replaced by washing dishes and going on with the job at the office. The tender devotion need not be replaced. Perhaps after she has learned to make the coffee his way, he just drinks it without a word of appreciation. Then some morning when she is in the kitchen in curlers and an apron, streaked with absent-minded cooking, he will tell her how beautiful he thinks she is. If she has a good sense of proportion the two experiences will add up to devotion.

To have is passive, and is usually consummated on their wedding day, but to hold is active, and can never be finished so long as they both shall live.

10

The Sex Relation

THE Puritans pretended there was no such thing as intercourse. Many modern young people make the opposite error of behaving as though there were little else to marriage. The truth lies somewhere in the middle. Sex is indeed an important part of wedlock, which should promote both unity and happiness, but it is by no means the "be all and the end all" which the present rebellion against previous repression would lead one to suppose.

On the other hand, if a man from Mars were to visit our industrial civilization he would exclaim, "What? So much education on how to build machinery and so little education on how to produce people!"

The biological function of intercourse is the perpetuation of the human race. Its emotional function is not only the ultimate expression of affection in bodily communion; it is also the relieving of nervous tensions, the heightening of vitality, the evolving of better balance, the hope of clearer thinking, the achievement of greater beauty. Passion, not to be confused with sensuality, is a worthy part of marriage; a glorious, sensitive, and creative personality fulfillment. Here is a means of expressing the unity between husband

252

and wife: not only their right to the recreation of life, but the recreating of themselves and of each other.

Thus, there is a close relation between married love and intercourse, because of which the establishment and maintenance of a healthy sex relation is as important as food, health, or financial solvency. Marriage is now a far more complicated and emotionally demanding thing than it was in great-grandfather's day. He could go out behind the barn and work off his peevishness by chopping wood. Our comradeship is more closely confined. We live intimately, crowded into apartments amid the uncertainty of people and human institutions, instead of the uncertainty of weather, crops, or animal fecundity.

Moreover, sex itself is a complex phenomenon which we are gradually coming to understand. Long before the Greeks and the Romans, it was realized that there was a relationship between intercourse and pregnancy, but not until the seventeenth century did Swammerdam demonstrate the necessity of semen being deposited within the vagina in order for conception to take place. In the seventeenth century it was widely believed that fertilization by the male was unnecessary. Male germ cells were identified during the eighteenth century, and only in the last century has the uniting of the spermatozoon with the ovum been demonstrated to be the origin of reproduction.

The sex relation involves all five senses. In most instances the first impressions come through the eye, although as time goes by physical beauty becomes less important. Hearing begins as and remains a major factor, for personal vanity plays an important part. The one thing in all of life which does not become monotonous with repetition is, "I love you." Everyone knows that the sense of smell is sexually important to the animals. The male butterfly can locate a female in heat a mile away by the sense of smell. The male rabbit, despite his great reputation as a progenitor, becomes impotent if his olfactory nerve is cut. Van de Velde believes odors important to mankind, thus giving indirect support to the claims of the soap and perfume manufacturers. Most important of all is the sense of touch, which includes touch in general as well as touch for the erogenous (sexually stimulating) zones.

"Complete sexual intercourse," says Van de Velde, "comprises: the prelude, or love-play; the sexual union; and the after-play or epilogue. Its summit and its purpose alike blend in the *third stage*."* [Italics his.] The great gynecologist is talking about a mental and bodily communion which merges the melodious mutuality of interaction and response. This "implies *equal rights* and *equal joys* in sexual union." [Again italics his.] The wife should not be a passive receiver but an active coparticipant.

Surely there is little which could be considered vulgar in love making between husband and wife, providing it is welcomed by both without frustration, interference with normal sex relations, or guilt feelings. On the other hand, terrible destruction to the affections of one spouse inevitably follows the offensiveness of some procedure both unwelcome and unnatural.

Terman concluded that only two sexual factors can be considered with statistical certainty of significance in marital happiness: similarity of desire, and the capacity of the wife to achieve an orgasm.**

In order for this to happen, among other things, husband and wife need to understand what their reproductive organs are like, and how they function.

THE MALE SEX ORGANS

The Penis

A diagrammatic representation of the male sex organs will be found in Figure 9. The penis is shown in the relaxed position under which circumstances it is usually from 3½" to 4" long outside the body. Except for the tube, called the urethra, located near the under side, through which urine as well as seminal fluid leaves the body, it consists of a spongy network of blood vessels which, when stimulated by the brain or by manual titillation, fill with blood

---

* Van de Velde, *Ideal Marriage, op. cit.,* p. 145.
** L. M. Terman, *Psychological Factors in Marital Happiness* (New York: McGraw-Hill, 1938), p. 374.

under pressure, thus causing the penis to enlarge, to become elastically rigid, and to assume a vertical position. It now will average 5″ to 6½″ long, and 1½″ in diameter. So great is the variation in reproductive organs—which have no correlation whatever with the size of the individual—examples have been found of genitals twice this size. But size has no relation to the capacity for intercourse, or to the ability to become a father.

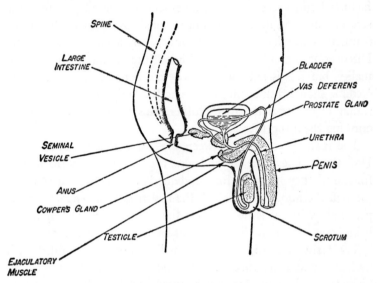

Fig. 9. The Male Sex Organs

In the erect position the penis curves slightly toward the body, and thus corresponds somewhat to the curve of the vagina. Like the feet and the skull, it never develops any layers of fat as other parts of the body may do. The most sexually sensitive part of the penis is the ridge, near its tip, which contains a cluster of nerves and is called the glans. This is normally covered by the foreskin.

Cowpers' Gland

Located inside the body at the base of the penis lies Cowper's gland. This is about the size of a pea, and produces an alkaline, slippery fluid which serves as a lubricant during intercourse. It is thought by some to have, in addition, a stimulating effect upon the motor activity of the sperm. This fluid may appear even before the erection, particularly if the sexual stimulation takes place slowly. Occasionally it is mistaken for the semen itself.

The Testicles

The male is born with a two-unit, biological factory which manufactures human seed. These testicles, enclosed in a sack called the scrotum, are oval in shape and of unequal size. The left hand one is usually somewhat larger and hangs slightly lower in the scrotum. Discovering this, a boy may feel himself the victim of some abnormality, but this is not the case. These differences are nature's incredible thoughtfulness in so building the body as to facilitate the sliding of one testicle past the other, thus preventing the pain of crushing them together.

The mature testicle is between 1½″ to 1¾″ long, and ¾″ to 1⅛″ thick. The testicles—and also the ovaries—perform a dual function: they provide for reproduction and they determine, through the hormones secreted, the maleness or femaleness of the personality. But it is not true, as the ancients thought, that boy babies come from one testis and girl babies from the other.

The testicles consist of many small compartments filled with multitudinous little tubes about two-thousandths of an inch in diameter, and totaling several hundred feet long. These are convoluted and intertwined into new systems which at last collect at the side and empty into a single duct at the bottom of the testicles. The tubes are lined with cuboidal cells which appear to be the raw material from which the spermatozoa are made. (Figure 10.)

Until he reaches puberty sometime between age ten and sixteen, a boy has no ability to produce sperm. The changes leading to puberty are believed to be due to the production of sex hormones by the testicles (or ovaries), under the influence of the anterior pituitary gland. This is located at the base of the brain, and controls the sex hormones as well as others, such as those determining growth.

Because the normal production of sperm takes place at a lower temperature than that of the body, the scrotum is entirely outside the body. On a cold day the muscles suspending the scrotum contract, thus bringing the testicles closer to the bodily source of heat. On a hot day the muscles slacken, increasing the distance and therefore the rate of cooling. Fear will also cause the muscles to contract, bringing the scrotum closer to the body to reduce the vulnerability of the testicles to injury.

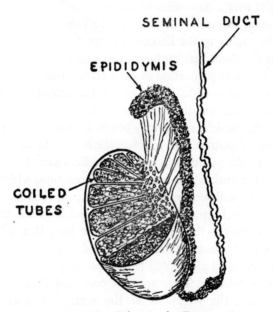

Fig. 10. Tubes in the Testes

The prodigality of nature is amazing. Unless a man is over-exerting himself, between four and eight cubic centimeters (something like a teaspoonful) of seminal fluid is delivered during an intercourse. Since there should be 60,000,000 or more spermatozoa per cubic centimeter, this means that a healthy male implants within the female between 250 million and 500 million individual seeds in a single copulation, the union of only one of which with a live ovum is necessary to produce pregnancy. Thus, as Dr. Alan F. Guttmacher of Johns Hopkins has said, "The baby that the germ cell engenders has a far greater chance of becoming President than the cell ever had of becoming a baby."

The spermatozoa itself is shaped like a tadpole with a long tail. It is about two ten-thousandths of an inch in length, and when released, by lashing its tail, swims upstream at a speed comparable to the best Olympic records: namely, its own length per second. This is just over a hundredth of an inch a minute. The sperm are such vigorous swimmers they can travel all the way from the outer lips of the vagina to the Fallopian tubes, thus making possible a conception without first rupturing the hymen.

Following their production in the testicles, the sperm are stored in the epididymis—coiled tubes, one in the rear of each testicle— and in the vasa deferentia (again two of them), but apparently not in the seminal vesicles as formerly believed. (See Figures 9 and 10.)

A nocturnal emission occurs when the storage capacity has been overtaxed by the productivity of the testicles. Once these reservoirs have been emptied, which two or three ejaculations within a space of a few hours will accomplish, the man cannot then have another orgasm—although an erection may be possible—until the glands have had sufficient time to recover. How long this will require depends upon the sexual vitality of the individual.

The sperm travel a long way before reaching the the end of the penis for ejaculation. They are also conveyed in a liquid compounded from the secretions of the seminal vesicles and the prostate gland. How long the sperm are capable of producing life after being deposited in the vagina nobody knows. Educated guesses range from a few hours to several days.

Seminal Vesicles

Leading from the testicles into the abdominal cavity are two tubes called the vasa deferentia, through which the sperm travel between the testicles and the penis. Between the bladder and the rectum each one of these tubes is attached to an elongated chamber called a seminal vesicle. Each vesicle is about two inches long, and contains a coiled up tube with short lateral branches. The vesicles secrete a special yellowish ingredient which makes the ejaculation less liquid and more gelatinous. Its grains give the seminal fluid a sticky consistency, but they soon dissolve and leave the solution wholly liquid.

Normally the outlets from the seminal vesicles are closed by muscles in the prostate gland. During an orgasm these outlets are opened, allowing the secretion to escape into the urethra.

Prostate Gland

Resembling a horse-chestnut in size and shape, the prostate gland lies between the bladder and the bodily end of the penis. The vasa deferentia pass through it separately, after their union at the lower ends of the seminal vesicles, and rejoin on reaching the urethra. The prostate gland secretes a thin, milky, alkaline fluid which gives the seminal discharge its characteristic odor and preserves the sperm from destruction by any residue of acid from urine which has previously passed through the urethra. Together with the fluid from the seminal vesicles, this liquid serves as a carrier for the sperm and a stimulant to their mobility.

By muscular contraction at the moment of orgasm the prostate gland forces its secretions into the urethra, thus producing part of the propulsive force which sends the resultant seminal fluid to the end of the penis, where it emerges in the pulsating spurts characteristic of ejaculation. At the same time, the contraction of the prostate gland cuts off the portion of the urethra leading to the bladder, and thus both insures the delivery of all the seminal fluid at the end of the penis and prevents any destructive leakage of urine from destroying the semen.

The Female Sex Organs

The feminine sex organs (see Figure 11) are larger, more numerous, and more widely distributed than the masculine ones.

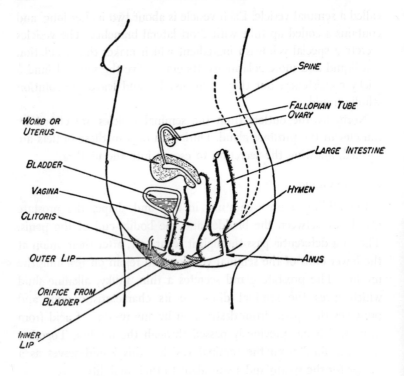

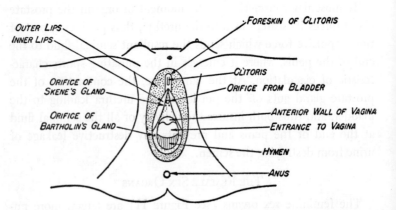

Fig. 11. The Female Sex Organs

With the exception of the breasts and those organs covered by the outer and inner lips of the vagina, they lie within her body. The breasts perform three functions: they suckle a child during his early life; they give the wife pleasure and sexual stimulation when skillfully fondled; and the accomplishment of this fondling does the same for the husband.

The Clitoris

As a man has vestigial breasts, so a woman has a vestigial penis called the clitoris, the outer portion of which is about the size of a small bean. In the newly married woman it is usually the most sexually stimulating zone in her entire body, although as time goes by the inner recesses of the vagina should become even more so.

Unlike the penis, the clitoris is normally covered from sight by the outer lips of the vagina. Like the penis, it grows from roots further within the body, and has a delicate fold of foreskin tissue, which however, in the female, cannot be drawn back. It too is tipped with a cluster of nerves which are involved in the enlargement of erection and in subsequent delightful sensations when gently titillated. It will also become erect as the result of emotional stimulation.

The Skene and the Bartholin Glands

Below the clitoris and on either side of the exit from the urinary duct (which has but one function in the female), are two small openings no larger than a pin head, connected by tiny tubes about ½" long leading to a gland named for its discoverer: Dr. Skene. The function of this gland is not definitely known, but it is believed to secrete a colorless, viscous substance which is lubricatory.

On each side of the opening of the vagina, and again only a short distance from the surface, are Bartholin's glands. (Also named for their discoverer.) The tiny orifices of their ducts open through the inner lips of the vagina, and deliver the mucous secretion which prevents intercourse from irritating tender membranes because of excessive friction. As with Cowper's gland in the male, these glands become active with psychic stimulation like petting, and should always be aroused to activity before actual intercourse is undertaken. Otherwise inadequate lubrication will result in unpleasantness for both husband and wife.

The Vagina and the Hymen

The vagina is the female organ of intercourse, as well as the passage, connecting the uterus (or womb) with the external genitalia, through which an unfertilized egg or a baby travels into the world, and through which the menstrual discharge does the same thing. It is closed by double lips, the outer of which are much broader than the lips of the mouth.

Behind these, the opening is partially obstructed in a virgin by a diaphragm called the hymen. This varies enormously in size, shape, and thickness; sometimes being so small as to present almost no obstruction; sometimes almost completely covering the opening; sometimes being so thin as to have been ruptured by a childhood fall; sometimes being so tough and leathery as to require surgical incision before intercourse is possible. Usually it is about one-sixteenth of an inch thick. As a woman grows older, like the other parts of the body, the hymen grows tougher.

The failure of a hymen to rupture during the first intercourse is no proof of lost virginity. It may have been ruptured during childhood as already explained, or it may, in exceptional cases, be so distensible as to survive undamaged the birth of a child.

The vagina itself is an elastic tube whose walls ordinarily practically touch. It is smallest in diameter at its opening, and between 3″ and 4″ long. During sexual intercourse it will easily stretch back into the abdominal cavity until it is 6″ long or more. Although the size of genitals varies from woman to woman, exactly as it does from man to man, in the virgin the orifice of the vagina is about ¾″ in diameter. In the married woman who has had some months of sexual activity it has stretched to 1¼″ in diameter. During childbirth, by the skill of cellular changes which we do not fully understand, it will stretch to 5″ or 6″ in diameter, and then return almost to its previous size.

Rarely is a penis too long for a vagina, especially if the husband will realize it takes longer to arouse the vagina than it does to arouse the penis, and will thoughtfully behave accordingly.

The Womb, or Uterus, and Menstruation

Extending a half-inch or so into the upper end of the vaginal tube is the mouth of the womb, or uterus. Normally, its outside dimensions are 3″ by 1″. It hangs above and behind the bladder, suspended almost at right angles to the vagina by muscular ligaments. It is pear-shaped, composed of muscles (which can stretch) supported on a framework of connective tissue, and its hollow inside is lined with mucous membrane filled with blood vessels.

Every twenty-eight days or so it is prepared to receive a fertilized egg. If none arrives, the preparation is discarded in the process called menstruation, and new preparations begun with the most undiscouragable hospitality known to science. Menstruation usually begins about fourteen days after an egg or eggs explode from their encompassing follicles in the ovaries, and find their way into the Fallopian tubes (ovulation)—irrespective of when the last period ended. If fertilized, an egg (or eggs) will remain in the womb where the baby matures, and the womb stretches from an organ the size of a woman's fist to one a foot long and eight inches in diameter. Finally the child is expelled by muscular contraction of the womb, which requires six weeks to return to its previous size. Unfertilized, the egg passes through the womb, into the vagina, and out of the body.

Menstruation usually lasts three or four days, but may be longer or shorter. The amount of blood lost (as it carries out the endometrium) may be as little as a teaspoonful, but the average is two or three fluid ounces. With some women, this process is merely one of life's minor annoyances. Others suffer from abdominal pains preceding or during the early stages of the flow.

Girls begin to menstruate usually between the ages of twelve and fifteen. As the trees which bud first in the spring lose their leaves last in the fall, so the earlier menstruation begins, the more years it will probably go on—normally somewhere between thirty and thirty-eight.

Ten per cent of the women vary one to three days in the timing of their periods. Many will vary by a week now and then, perhaps longer, especially if ill or fatigued.

Few animals, but all that are primates, menstruate. One other amazing thing about it is that menstrual blood does not clot. It flows freely even in its slow journey out of the body.

The Fallopian Tubes and the Ovaries

Leading from the further end of the womb, up to and around an ovary on one side of the body and the other, are the two Fallopian tubes. These are lovers' lanes, for it is here that spermatozoon meets and fertilizes ovum. Nobody knows why the sperm go into the Fallopian tubes. Perhaps it is pure chance. Each tube is between 4″ and 6″ long, with a wide funnel-shaped mouth ½″ to ¾″ in diameter turned toward its respective ovary, but not directly connected to it. As they approach the womb, the tubes decrease in diameter until they are scarcely a hundreth of an inch across at the uterine end.

Since the ovum cannot move by itself, hairlike projections inside the tubes, called *cilia*, wave back and forth to propel it toward the womb until the tubes have become small enough in diameter for peristaltic action, similar to that which takes place in the bowels, to accomplish the propulsion. The journey from ovary to womb probably takes about a week. Nobody knows. How long the egg itself is viable (capable of sustaining life) is not definitely known; some think during the entire week.

The ovaries themselves are almond-shaped, and approximately 1¼″ x ¾″ x ½″ in size. Each ovary is attached by one edge to the pelvic tissues, but otherwise is free. Unlike the testicle, which is a factory, the ovary is a warehouse. Within the baby girl at birth are present all the eggs she will ever have: physicians are uncertain as to exactly how many, but a total of 300,000 to 400,000 is now considered probable. The unripe ovum is encased in a layer of cells called a follicle. Beginning with puberty, and every menstrual month thereafter, lasting until the menopause, one or more eggs ripen, burst out of the follicles like seeds from the blossom of a flower, and find their way, by chemical attraction we do not fully comprehend, across the intervening abdominal cavity and into the open funnel at the end of the Fallopian tubes. The egg is now a little less than a hundredth of an inch in diameter, or about as visible to the naked eye as the point of a sharp pin.

It would be possible to put 3 million of them into an ordinary thimble. Still, the ovum is the largest single cell in the human body and many times large than the spermatazoon.

It is currently believed that one egg at a time, from alternate ovaries, usually ripens each month. Obviously this cannot always be so or there would be no such thing as fraternal twins. (See page 288.)

After the ripened egg leaves the follicle, the latter fills with cells called *corpus luteum*, (Latin for "yellow body"). These cells, by some marvelous biochemical process, produce hormones which cause a new lining to form on the soft walls of the uterus in preparation for receiving a fertilized egg. This, in turn, requires an increased blood supply. If no fertilized egg attaches itself to the wall of the uterus, menstruation discards the preparation which was made to receive it. Thus, the time of menstruation seems to be determined by the time of ovulation.

The Menopause

The idea is widespread that the menopause takes place when all the eggs are used up, but this is not the case. The ovaries contain eggs enough to last for perhaps two thousand years, but under the influence of the endocrine glands, eggs and ovaries gradually atrophy, after which a woman ceases to menstruate and cannot be impregnated, since no egg ripens and leaves the ovaries to be fertilized. The sooner a girl begins to menstruate, the older she usually is before reaching the menopause.

26 per cent reach the menopause between ages 40-45.

40 per cent reach the menopause between ages 45-50.

15 per cent reach the menopause between ages 50-55.

19 per cent reach the menopause earlier or later.

Many women dread this period in their lives, mistakenly fearing they will no longer be able to enjoy intercourse themselves or to give enjoyment to their husbands. Any such consequence is wholly emotional. The menopause is a normal experience, not one for apprehension. Sexual desire is not destroyed. Indeed, a new freedom may follow.

Emotional upsets sometimes do accompany the chemical changes which are taking place in the body, but this is only because the menopause serves as the trigger which sets off an emotional explosion, the powder train for which was laid long before. It might equally well have been ignited by a death in the family, or a bad accident.

INTERCOURSE

Between two people in love, the sensations of copulation are extremely pleasurable. Intercourse in wedlock, for reasons other than reproduction, is as valid as eating cakes and ice cream at a party when someone is not hungry. Happiness which harms no one, most particularly if it reaches appropriate enjoyment with someone, is a proper end in itself.

Most husbands and wives do not get enough out of sexual intercourse, not only because of ignorance of good sex technique but even more because they are not in love. Cohabitation ought not to be mutual satisfaction; it should be mutual satisfaction *together*. To lust together is not to love together. To enjoy one's spouse is not necessarily also to enjoy giving enjoyment to one's spouse. It is not just going to bed together that matters; it is going as the expression of a shared emotional unity.

The physical sex impulse comes from hormones produced by

the male and female sex glands. This is much modified by the electrocolloidal influence of emotions. There is far more here than in the response of the lower animals. The male fish never sees his mate, but discovers the eggs she has laid on the top of the water and appends the necessary sperm. The higher one goes in the evolution of the animal kingdom, the more complicated and the more beautiful the foreplay preceding intercouse, and the more careful the provision that the sperm and the eggs will meet and have a favorable environment. The rooster has no penis, but merely sprays his semen onto the hen. In the ascending scale of development an erect penis occurs first in the crocodile and the turtle. With them intercourse is an act of immobility, broken by moments of sheer violence. The thoroughbred stallion, on the other hand, will precede serving a mare with behavior of unforgettable beauty; arching his neck, pawing the air, leaping with lyric motions, shaking his mane. He may then become violent.

Intercourse, as an expression of domination and even of cruelty, has a long history in the evolutionary process. Tenderness has developed comparatively late in the story. Even now men and women sometimes undertake intercourse as an outlet for aggression or an escape from boredom.

The sex act at its best is like a great novel, beginning with an introductory section which states the situation and the narrative question, building up through the various ramifications of this question to the climax, and receding to the denouement which ties up whatever loose strings need attention following the climax. It should have the ascending emotion and the final peace of the Bach-Gounod "Ave Maria."

The more cultured and refined the wife, the more likely she is to need and to appreciate the preliminary courting which should precede every intercourse. There should be assured privacy without interruption—including that most impertinent of modern inventions, the telephone. There should be physical comfort, quiet, and plenty of time.

The first erogenous zone, though not usually listed as such, is the mind. The tenderness, the affection, and the complete giving of one's self has been beautifully expressed by Rebecca West.

"I will pour myself in devotion to you, I will empty myself without hoping for return, and I can do this serenely, for I know that as I empty myself I shall be filled again." Human beings cannot remind themselves too often that they are capable of performing this miracle, the existence of which cannot be proved by logic.*

An unshaven cheek, a dirty body, rough handling, careless words can quickly change what should be a sweet and jubilant thing into bewilderment and fear. Compare the above with this excerpt from the letter of a brilliant college woman, married less than a year to an equally brilliant and even more "educated" man.

"He doesn't seem to be able to excite me any more. He tries to act like a caveman, and I don't like it. I don't think he realizes that he is so rough. I have asked him to be more gentle, but he still pulls my hair by leaning his arm on it when he kisses me, and is likely to crush my stomach with his unsupported weight, or event to brandish an elbow in my face. Sometimes he crumples me against the mattress in what resembles a clutch far more than an embrace, and scours my cheek with his unshaven stubble."

Intercourse is often an unburdening process, but such a performance is a sensuous attack; probably an attack due to transferring to the wife anger felt years before against the mother.

The second erogenous area, to be approached after there has been a meeting of minds and a unifying of personalities, is the surface of the body: holding hands, kissing, fondling the breasts or the clitoris or the penis. As soon as self-consciousness has worn off, this foreplay should be entered into by the wife as well as the husband. She should recognize it as both a privilege and a responsibility. It is not enough for a wife to acquiesce passively. She should first be aroused beyond mere consent. Then she should participate eagerly and actively.

* R. West, *Black Lamb and Grey Falcon* (New York: Viking Press, 1941), p. 825.

Grandma's ideas were not always right. Biologically there is no significant difference between men and women in the strength of the sex urge. Any seeming difference is due to our mistaken conventions. Result: the wife is often unable to achieve the fullest enjoyment because of inhibitions which impede her and prevent a perfect union. The Victorian idea that a lady submitted but did not enjoy intercourse was an evil thing.

The final erogenous zone, which crowns the whole sequence with perfection, is stimulated by the gentle insertion of the erect penis into the vagina, followed by a thrilling series of forward and backward movements which may be brought about by husband, or wife, or both. Like a piston in a cylinder, this creates a contact between the most sensitive parts of the genital organs of husband and wife: the clitoris is touched by the base of the penis at the end of each thrust, and the vaginal walls are stimulated by the top of the penis, while they in turn stimulate it.

During the latter stages of the intercourse a woman who is not frigid will contract the vaginal muscles greatly to her husband's and to her own delight. Although I cannot subscribe to Kinsey's criterion that sexual activity is to be measured solely by the counting of orgasms, this ability to contract the vagina and subsequently to experience an orgasm is one of the "natural" reasons for believing there is nothing indecent and unclean about intercourse deliberately entered into merely for the mutual ecstasy of husband and wife. Women are the only females in the entire animal kingdom capable of experiencing an orgasm.

Reaching an orgasm together is the ultimate goal. For this a woman needs "extensive and intensive preparation" because her biological make-up requires a longer continuance and a wider range of stimuli than a man's. It may take the bride and groom several months to understand each other's particular needs and specific behavior signals so that each can have a reasonable expectation of the highest possible enjoyment.

The husband can usually reach an orgasm in a few minutes, perhaps less. For him, an orgasm consists of the contractions of the prostate gland and the ejaculatory muscle which, as already described, propel the various conveying fluids and the sperm from the seminal vesicles through the urethra in a series of spurts.

The wife may require half an hour to reach an orgasm. (Wrongly handled she will be entirely incapable of it. Certainly she can never experience an orgasm with a man she does not respect.) For her, there is no discharge of secretion. The vaginal muscles will contract, there will be a throbbing of the pelvic floor, quick breathing, and the most exquisite tingling sensations for a few seconds. She is also likely to express her ecstasy of delight. Some women are capable of several orgasms while the husband has one.

Failure to reach an orgasm may leave a woman with upset emotions, unnatural bodily fatigue from internal rebellion, headaches, backache, and over a long period of time perhaps a nervous breakdown.

One impediment here is premature ejaculation by some 15 per cent of the men. Early in the marriage premature ejaculation is a frequent condition. Should it persist for a year, it may be a symptom of serious difficulty. After a few weeks or months of marriage, the bodily union of a perfectly carried out intercourse should last long enough to insure the wife's orgasm. The husband who has no regard for his wife can reach his orgasm in two or three minutes after entry. This leaves the woman wanting to achieve her orgasm, but wholly unsatisfied. When the husband gratifies his passion without attention to the emotional needs or satisfactions of the wife, she sustains a real emotional injury. Her mate is either ignorant of proper techniques or else selfish. As she approaches her moment of maximum anticipation there is a sudden change in her chance for satisfaction. For her, the energy of a compulsive "must" has been blocked by the utter finality of "can't." Or, if the stimulation has not gone so far, she is left in a state of suspended gratification. She anticipates an orgasm and there is none (see Figure 12).

The thoughtful husband gradually achieves insight into his wife's behavior signals, until he knows without a word from her, just when she is close to her climax, and makes no attempt to reach his own until then. If his ejaculation is premature, he may either complete the experience for her by titillating the clitoris with his finger, or wait an hour and begin all over. Self-control in these matters is much easier for him than for her.

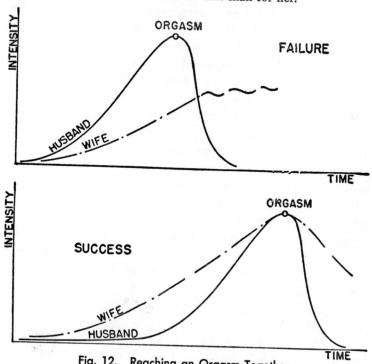

Fig. 12. Reaching an Orgasm Together

Premature ejaculation is due to a variety of causes:
(1) Wrong emotional conditions
(2) Tremendous stimulation before the union, inevitable early in the marriage
(3) Failure of the husband to think about the wife's needs, and to conduct himself accordingly—perhaps by no more than lying still for a few minutes. (Even so, if her vaginal muscles contract, he may ejaculate.)

(4) Some unusual physical condition needing correction.

Terman found* that in a group of 1133 wives, one-third of them had "never" had an orgasm or "only sometimes" achieved one. Naturally they were less happy than the wives who "usually" or "almost always" experienced an orgasm. R. L. Dickinson, most distinguished of American gynecologists, collaborating with Dr. Beam in a book called A *Thousand Marriages*, reports that in more than one-quarter of the cases where data is available, the wife never experienced an orgasm with her husband. Terman concluded that women with low vitality, colorless personalities, and neurasthenic tendencies were incapable of an orgasm.

While it is probably true that the possibility of pregnancy is increased by a mutual orgasm, many women go through their whole married lives, including the bearing of several children, without experiencing any orgasm whatsoever. This is as much the fault of our bringing-up as it is of our bedroom manners.

The after-play of intercourse is as often neglected or ignored as the preliminary petting. Here is a time for peaceful relaxation together, ending in refreshing sleep. Where the man ignores this transition and goes to sleep at once, he leaves his wife to experience alone the slow ebb of sexual excitement and to wonder how much he really does love her after all.

Loving is an art. Carelessly entered into it can do serious psychological damage. Rightly entered into it provides:

(1) Emotional preparation, resulting in
(2) Mutual sexual stimulation, at last expressed by
(3) Gentle introduction of the penis into the vagina, which begins
(4) Intercourse itself, leading to a mutually achieved
(5) Orgasm, after which should come the
(6) After-play of affection; appreciation for the joy of mutual self-fulfillment, unspoiled by fear or inhibitions, as the emotions slow down and disappear.

* L. M. Terman, *op. cit.*, p. 375.

VARIATIONS IN POSTURE

There are five basic positions in which copulation may be accomplished, and sound reasons for knowing about them. Psychologically, as Van de Velde says,*

". . . Monotony can only be relieved by variations, and, to the uninstructed man, the only possible variation seems to be in the *object* of his efforts; and the rift in the lute is there, and widens.

"The thought that the defect and the failure might be on *his* side, that he himself might have prevented the alienation which he truly deplores—this enlightening and humbling truth never dawns on him!

"For he does not know that there are numberless delicate differentiations and modifications of sexual pleasure, all lying strictly within the bounds of normality, which can banish the mechanical monotony of the too well-known from the marriage bed, and give new attractions to conjugal intercourse. . . . He thinks his wife is 'far above that sort of thing', leaves her more and more to herself, seeks the diversity of stimulation he needs outside his home, and often ends in *real* debauchery in consequence."

Observe that the real trouble is not monotony but lack of togetherness. If husband and wife are bored by an unvaried approach to intercourse, this is probably a sign of some more fundamental difficulty. If they want to experiment with new techniques this should be done simply because of renewed enjoyment. Physiologically there are also good reasons for knowing which position is most advisable during pregnancy, after an illness, or where there are great differences in height or weight.

It is natural for mankind to seek satisfaction in wholesome ways. When we are embarrassed by experiments which decrease the monotony of intercourse, we are insulting the intelligence of our instincts. Between husband and wife, probably no sex practice is

* Van de Velde, *op. cit.*, p. 7.

vulgar which is mutually acceptable. Not every position and not every method of fore-play is equally welcomed by all couples.

Husband Prone and the Wife Supine

This is the most common arrangement in our culture, although it is considered immoral by some savage tribes. The husband should support his weight on his elbows and knees as he lies above the wife, who has spread her legs to receive him. In this position he can contribute all the motion. Also he can remain quiet while she moves up and down or in a small circle below him, thus contributing more to her stimulation than to his, and helping to bring about a simultaneous orgasm.

A pillow under the wife's hips to increase the pelvic inclination may help to accomplish a pregnancy as well as to increase her satisfaction.

Wife Prone and the Husband Supine

This is a variant which sometimes helps the emotional attitude of a woman who feels it to be a man's world. She should kneel astride the husband, and after the penis has been inserted, can lie down upon him in a position which makes her the more active partner. Where the husband is a large man and the wife diminutive, it has the advantage of protecting her from any chance of a crushing load.

Lateral Posture

Here husband and wife lie on their sides facing each other. This has advantage if either has been ill or is physically weak, for there can be no weight on either. This is by far the best position when two people desire to be passively in and of each other, without activity.

Lying on their sides and facing the same way, with the husband approaching from the rear as the wife draws up her knees, is advantageous after a pregnancy is a few months along, for it guarantees that no pressure whatsoever will be exerted on the wife's abdominal cavity. This position will not prove satisfactory if the wife is obese and the husband has a short penis.

With some combinations of bodily proportions, another pleasant lateral variation is for the man to lie on his left side, left leg drawn up and knee bent; while the wife lies on her right side, her right hip below his thigh, her left leg—which will be uppermost—over his right leg. This, too, will not be satisfactory for corpulent individuals.

Sitting Posture

This requires a strong, armless chair upon which the husband sits with legs together, holding the wife facing and astride him with legs apart. A low chair or hassock is best, so her feet can easily reach the floor, for she must undertake most of the action. To many people this is a delightful variant, but none of these less standard positions should be tried unless and until both husband and wife are ready to experiment.

A combination of the man supine and the sitting position can be accomplished by the husband lying on his back while the wife sits astride him, after the penis is inserted, perhaps resting her back against his drawn up knees (if the bodily dimensions are not too heavy).

Standing Posture

Most fatiguing of all is the standing position. This is not recommended for a tall husband and a short wife, or vice versa. The intercourse must be accomplished face to face, for if both partners face in the same direction with the husband behind, the penis will curve in a direction opposite to the curve of the vagina, with unsatisfactory results.

Times for Particular Consideration

There are four circumstances in which the husband should be particularly considerate of his wife's sexual wishes:

(1) On the honeymoon

(2) During her menstrual periods

(3) At the menopause

(4) During pregnancy.

The most difficult of these is usually restraint before and during menstruation, because it is recurrent over so long a period of time. Many women want to be let completely alone before and during the menstrual flow, but are eager and responsive a few days later. Instead of saying, "I just can't understand a woman. I tried to be affectionate to my wife last week and she rebuffed me. Now I'm leaving her alone, and she doesn't like that either. There just isn't any rhyme or reason to the creatures," . . . instead of saying that, a husband should understand her cyclical nature and realize that her conduct is completely logical. He should even keep track of when her next period is due, and plan accordingly.

Areas of Adjustment

A good sex adjustment is more a psychological than a physiological problem, and there will be reprisals in the form of unreasonableness and revenge where adjustments are not made.

Although this chapter is concerned specifically with sex adjustment, it should be pointed out again that the various departments of a marriage cannot be separated any more than the functions of the body can be treated as isolated variables. Everything affects, and is affected by, everything else. To treat intercourse as an independent thing is a purely artificial subdivision. The nervous system acts as a whole, and every part of our lives acts on every other part. "Sexual attitudes and behaviors are directed by the basic motivations which the human being acquires in the process of being socialized."[*]

This view is the exact opposite of the position taken by Freud, who believed that sexual desire was the source of character formation. Most modern authorities agree that character determines the particular way in which our inborn sex urge finds expression. The emotionally honest person will not endeavor to coerce or to

---

[*] J. J. Honigmann, "Cultural Dynamics of Sex," *Psychiatry*, Vol. 10, No. 1 (February 1947), p. 47.

entice as the emotionally dishonest individual will. The sadistic husband, who only feels safe when he exercises power over someone else, will completely disregard the needs of his wife. He may even find a perverted delight through inflicting physical or emotional pain in his sexual demands. The masochistic wife may subconsciously so wish to punish herself as to be frigid. The masochistic man may become impotent.

Sexual intercourse is always an intimate expression of the interrelatedness between two people. A good adjustment must be rooted in self-respect, rooted in a mutual desire to create *together* the best conditions under which to develop *together*. In short, it must be rooted in love.

Genital Differences

As has already been pointed out, there is no correlation, either for men or for women, between stature and genital dimensions. There is much variation, exactly as there is variation in the size of mouths. However, where two normal people have access to expert medical advice there is probably no such thing as permanent physical incompatibility. Usually there is no difficulty after the first few unions, if at all.

Tempo Differences

Neither the sex appetite, nor the optimum technique of satisfying it, can be expected to be exactly the same in husband and wife. There will inevitably be a need for mutual adaptation. If no mutually acceptable balance of activity can be found, the result will be unhappy. It may be that an ardent husband and a passive wife can solve their differences happily through her pleasure in giving him enjoyment during her periods of indifference. If, however, she is sexually vigorous and he passive, no good solution is possible. It is probable that the sex relation is most intense between a vigorous masculine man and a vigorous feminine woman.

Doctors do not agree as to when women are the most ardent. They do agree that women go in cycles with crests and hollows as the tide of their sex desire ebbs and flows. Men have no such cycles. Dickinson believes that wives most welcome intercourse just before and just after the menstrual period. Since there is not always equality of sexual urge, each husband should study the particular nature of his wife and plan his activities so that she has a maximum chance to participate. Each wife should study the particular needs of her husband and endeavor to co-operate with them so long as he does not insist on something that is distasteful to her, and so long as her requirements are not ignored.

The one rule for frequency of intercourse is that it should not be undertaken unless acceptable to both husband and wife, nor should it be carried on to the point of exhaustion. Sex gluttony is sensuality. The variations in interim are great, covering a range from almost daily to but a few times a year. A number of physicians, including my brother, have reported to me cases in which a couple has had one or more intercourses every day, practically without exception, for twenty years or so. On the other hand, some husbands and wives cohabitate only a few times a year. The average for young married people is three or four times a week, gradually diminishing after age thirty to about once a week at age sixty. But no convincing, objective proof has been found in any scientific investigation of a correlation between happiness and the frequency of copulation.

The idea that the woman alone should decide when to cohabitate is as unwarranted as the assumption that the man possesses rights and the woman only faces duties. The most important word in marriage is "together." A good approach is to remember that sex has reached excess whenever an individual is worn out or cross next day as a result, or has feelings of guilt and regret, or when the partner has been imposed on.

Variations in Mood

In love, and all other activities, as Solomon intimates, there is "a time to weep, and a time to laugh; a time to mourn, and a time to dance."

Traditionally, intercourse was for procreation only. The most competent modern opinion is that it embraces many other values, including the highest fulfillment of love. Usually the sex relation is preceded by a meeting of minds and a meeting of personalities on a spiritual plane. Nevertheless, among the universal, inborn, and ineradicable fundamental desires of mankind is the need for new experience. We must have variations or monotony will result. Consequently, intercourse is by no means a continually spiritual thing. Often it is purely pleasurable, the approach changing as the meeting of minds varies from mood to mood.

It can be close, affectionate, tender passion. It can be a wholly frivolous, giggling, and jocular event, even to the point of pretending the relation to be illicit. It can be completely routine. It can be a little rough, for in our culture intercourse is sometimes used as a compensation for business frustrations.

Complaints

The things men complain of in their sex relations are that the wife is not yielding enough, that she is too frigid, that she only submits, that her reaction is too slow, that she is too fat, and in some instances that she is too amorous. Or—of all things—that she is no lady because she enjoys intercourse.

Wives complain about lack of adequate petting as a preparation, no orgasm, too much sensuality or lack of sufficient potency on the part of the husband, too much intercourse, not enough intercourse, brutality, their own feelings of guilt in what should be a beautiful experience mutually entered into, prudery on the part of the husband, and fear that he is unfaithful.

Frigidity

Frigidity is not, as many people think, a conscious reluctance on the part of a wife to cohabitate; it is the inability to contract the vaginal muscles so as to seize the penis with a pulsating grip. This inability is entirely subconscious. A woman who is frigid by nature, say the psychoanalysts,* is a rare exception. She becomes frigid as a result of psychic difficulties acquired in childhood or later. Being taught, either directly or by implication, that sex is nasty (many sexually unsatisfied wives take revenge on humanity by making sex seem loathsome to their children); being seduced or attacked; unexpectedly coming upon two people in the act of cohabitating, and experiencing fear or revulsion as a result; disgust and bewilderment caused by watching someone masturbate—any one of these could be the root cause. Or it might be a subconscious revenge against parents for wrong sex education, saying, in effect, "Look what you've done to me! I'd rather stay as I am so people will see how awful you were, then to straighten myself out and be happy." It might be a conscious revenge against the husband for disappointment over his behavior as a lover. Sometimes it is no more than fear of pregnancy, and the many conflicts concerning intercourse which such a fear arouses. This point is well demonstrated by the women who find an heretofore unexperienced exaltation in intercourse after the menopause.

The man or woman who cannot be physically responsive ought to have help. Frigidity can ruin wedlock. It can be overcome only with great patience and skill—usually professional skill—and the long time required in any unlearning process where an individual is "emotionally fixed" within the narrow limits of an unrealistic childhood.

Consider the man who said, "I've heard of frigid women, but my wife is frozen stone. Imagine what she put me through on our honeymoon. She had been brought up to believe that decent people never have intercourse until they've been married at least three months. The bride might become pregnant and have a premature baby. Then what would people think!" What a vicious distortion.

To give joyfully of one's self with gentleness and warmth, and to be met by passive receptiveness, or worse still by pretended re-

---

* E. Hitschmann and E. Bergler. *Frigidity in Women* (New York, Nervous and Mental Disease Publishing Co., 1936), p. 2.

sponse, is a painful rejection to anyone—man or woman—who feels a deep and delicate love. Our self-expression here is not complete unless it has an equally sincere response from the person loved. If the husband tries to give his wife an orgasm through the exercise of prolonged self-control and has no response, the result on him is soon no response! *No response!* NO RESPONSE!!

The trouble can equally well be the other way around.

STERILITY

An individual's ability to have intercouse is no guarantee of fertility. Because a man can deliver semen does not mean that he is capable of becoming a father. There is a connection, not yet much understood, between emotions and bodily chemistry.

Frigidity, or fear of having a baby before there has been opportunity to get adjusted to each other or financially prepared, may lead to childlessness, for the sympathetic nervous system controls the sex functions. A woman's emotions have a great deal to do with her impregnation. Her nervous system affects the pituitary and hypothalamus glands which control the production of sex hormones, and these influence fecundity. On the husband's side, deep or prolonged anxiety will sometimes result in the manufacture of sperm with no life in them.

A husband and wife want children. None come. The prospective parents first worry a little and then become anxious. At last they accept the situation and adopt a child. The anxiety disappears as they pour out their affection. In many instances they soon discover that a child of their own is on the way.

How much better it would have been had these two people known in the first place that it may require months to impregnate a woman of twenty, and longer for a woman of forty. No conclusion of sterility should be drawn short of two or three years of unimpaired intercourse.

Sometimes the use of contraceptives early in the marriage is blamed for subsequent childlessness. The question of proof at once arises. What is there to show that this couple was fertile in the first place? Even though it could be shown that neither was sterile, there still remains the question of whether conception is possible between them.

One-seventh of all married couples in the United States are childless, half of them are deliberately so. Of the remainder, perhaps a third to a half can be helped through medical science.

PREGNANCY

The general consensus of competent opinion is that the first child should be born about two years after the marriage. This gives the husband and wife a chance to become adjusted to each other. It is probably better not to wait longer than three years.

Desire to become pregnant will greatly heighten the anticipation and joy of intercourse. Pregnancy results from the union of a single spermatozoon from the male testicles with a single ovum in the fallopian tubes, and must take place at a time when both the egg and the spermatozoon are viable. No woman is so pregnable that she will always conceive whenever intercourse takes place during the time the ovum is viable. The reason for this is clear when the factors are considered which must be fufilled in order for pregnancy to result:

(1) The testicles must produce healthy spermatozoa

(2) The spermatozoa must have free and successful passage from the testicles to the seminal vesicle

(3) The secretions of the seminal vesicle and the prostate gland must effectively protect and stimulate the spermatozoa

(4) The ejaculation must successfully traverse the urethra to the end of the penis and be delivered at least within the vagina, and preferably at the mouth of the womb

(5) There must be no secretions or other substances in the vagina destructive to the spermatozoa

(6) The womb must contain no destructive substances, and also must permit the successful passage (this is some-

thing more than just permitting free passage) of the spermatozoa to the fallopian tubes

(7) The fallopian tubes, in turn, must allow the successful passage of the spermatozoa upward, and of the ripe ova downward

(8) At least one ripe ovum must escape its follicle, find its way into the fallopian tubes, and be there—alive—at the time when the live spermatozoa is there

(9) The ovaries must have produced a healthy ovum;

(10) A live spermatozoa must find and penetrate the ovum at a time when it too is still alive.

As the head of the spermatozoon penetrates the outer membrane of the ovum, a change takes place in the membrane, and no other spermatozoon can now enter. The neck and long tail drop off outside the ovum, and in the course of three or four days the fertilized egg travels from the fallopian tubes into the womb (a distance of about four inches), where it attaches itself to the wall, and a new life has begun.

Most of the cells in the human body contain forty-eight chromosomes. This, however, is not true of the ova or of the spermatozoa. The female sex cell contains twenty-three chromosomes plus a funny little one called "X" by the biologists. The male sex cells occur in two numerically equal varieties: one having twenty-three chromosomes plus a funny little one called "X," as in the female; the other having the characteristic twenty-three chromosomes plus a funnier and an even smaller one called "Y." There are thus two possible final combinations: the forty-six, plus "X," plus "X" summation which results in a girl; or the forty-six, plus "X," plus "Y" summation which results in a boy.

Consequently, in spite of all the sputterings of disappointed fathers, the wife contributes nothing toward the determination of the sex of a baby.

From the moment of fertilization, the egg begins to grow. At the outset it is less than a hundredth of an inch in diameter, and weighs about .000004 gram. In eight weeks it has grown 275,000 times heavier. In forty weeks (the length of a normal pregnancy) it has increased 851,250,000 times. But between birth and maturity the ordinary individual grows only 23 times heavier. What amazing control!

The development of a fetus is one of nature's greatest miracles. At the end of a month the single tiny cell from which it started has multiplied into a shapeless little thing, ¼″ long, already with a circulatory system of its own, which can hardly be distinguished from the young embryo of any other animal. It has already

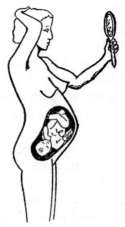

Fig. 13.   The Fetus in the Womb

increased 8,000 times in weight. In two months it is about an inch long and looks like a little monkey. In three months it is three inches long, has arms, legs, fingers, toes, and recognizable sex which, however, there is no present way of determining until the baby has left its mother. In six months it is a foot long and able to move now and then in the womb. In nine months it is about nineteen inches long, but of course curled up into a compact little bundle until it is born (see Figure 13).

As soon as the wife is reasonably sure she is pregnant, she should promptly select and consult a physician. He ought to be someone not only professionally competent, but someone she likes, for their relationship will be both an important and a somewhat intimate one. If it has been five or six weeks since her last period, by means of certain tests carried out with mice, he can usually determine with accuracy whether or not she is pregnant. Later, of course, no such test is necessary. If she is pregnant he will undertake a number of important things:

(1) Vaginal examination

(2) Pelvic measurements to be sure there is room between the bones for a normal birth (this should have been done before the marriage)

(3) Examination of the urine for general health conditions. Urinanalysis will be repeated during the pregnancy as one means of identifying the presence of any serious complications

(4) Blood test for pressure, anaemia, and venereal disease

(5) Weight. This, too, will be watched, with the expectancy that the mother's weight will increase a total of twenty to thirty pounds for a seven-and-a-half pound baby. Some of this will be fat, but beside the baby there is the weight of the placenta and of the amniotic fluid in which the baby floats. The size of the baby's skeleton is a matter of heredity and the length of the pregnancy

(6) Advice as to diet (probably milk, vegetables, and fruit for vitamins and minerals)

(7) When the pregnancy is further along, the physician will check the fetal heart beat, the position of the baby in the womb, etc.

There is no direct transference of blood from the mother to the fetus, as many people believe. The umbilical cord, which connects the wall of the sac (or placenta) to the baby, contains two arteries and one vein. Blood circulates through these as a closed system, pulsating with the fetal heart, which supplies the power. Nourishment for the fetus and waste products from it pass between the placenta and the walls of the womb by the chemical process called osmosis. Thus, the mother breathes, eats, digests, and eliminates waste products for her unborn baby. There are no waste products from the baby's intestine because he is fed through his blood stream.

The closer to the full period of gestation (forty weeks) the baby remains in the womb, the better chance he has of living. Modern equipment makes possible the saving of many prematurely born babies, even some who are only seven months along.

Whether to go to a hospital or remain at home for the delivery is a question which requires consideration. There are advantages and disadvantages both ways. The hospital is easier for the doctor, which often settles the question. It is desirable from every point of view when serious complications arise. If she cannot have rest at home, it may be better for the mother. It probably deprives the baby of the immediate love and affection it should have and would be more likely to receive at home. Also, the hospital is expensive.

The beginning of labor may be heralded by the rupturing of the membranes and the escape of the fluid encompassing the baby; by a bloody discharge called the "show"; or by regularly recurring pains of gradually increasing intensity. These are caused by the contraction and dilation of the cervix. With the first child, the various stages of labor add up to about eighteen hours. Subsequent children are born more easily, with labor lasting perhaps twelve hours. There are wide variations. At the end of her first pregnancy a woman may eat breakfast with the family, and be a mother before noon.

The normal position for the child in the womb is head down (see Figure 13). Thus, once the slow process of expanding the vagina, stretching the baby's head, and getting the skull through the bottle neck of the pelvis is complete, the rest of the little body slips out quickly and easily. About 95 per cent of babies are born head first. If the feet come first the umbilical cord gets squeezed between the bones of the pelvis and the child's skull before his head is out, and he may die as a result. The buttocks presentation, in which the baby is doubled up, is still more difficult and danger-ous. Then the doctor tries to push the baby back into the womb, and to deliver him feet first. A good obstetrician can determine the position of the fetus prior to the onset of labor, and if neces-sary, turn it around by exterior manipulation.

Sometimes the mother is unable to deliver the child unaided. If this is due to a pelvis so small the baby's head cannot pass through, delivery should be by the Caesarian operation (so called because Julius Caesar is supposed to have been the first child to be born in this way). This is a dangerous operation once labor has begun because the powerful muscular contractions of the walls of the uterus may tear apart what should not be torn apart where incisions have weakened the body structure. Correctly performed, a woman may have four or five children by Caesarian section.

Another way of helping to expel the fetus is by catching hold of its head with forceps and pulling. This has the disadvantage of possible damage to the child—serious damage. My physician brother believes that the increasing use of drugs to speed up labor, and forceps to expedite the process still farther, has injured the brains of thousands of babies.

As soon as the child can breathe he usually cries. Many people believe he cries in order that he can breathe. This seems mistaken to me, for baby has just taken a worse beating than his mother, and a sensitive ear will identify his crying as unrestrained rage.

The attending physician, carefully using sterilized materials, ties the umbilical cord in two places when pulsation through it stops, and cuts between his knots. There is no pain involved for there are no nerves. Neither mother nor child feel anything. The cord itself is in the order of half an inch in diameter and two feet long.

At the beginning of this century, baby's chances of not surviving birth were approximately one in two hundred. They are now in the order of one in fifteen hundred.

Pregnancy and childbirth are perfectly normal experiences; not something to be feared. Trouble comes from little girls hearing stories; suppressing anxiety, expecting the worst, and subconsciously making their own difficulties greater. Hypnotic suggestion, which reduces fear and relaxes tension, is an excellent way of combating this.

Intercourse following fertilization should be avoided at the time when the second and third menstruation would have ordinarily occurred. These are the times when the danger of miscarriage is greatest. In order to avoid any possible infection or irritation, intercourse should be completely interrupted during the last six weeks of pregnancy and for a month after the baby is born.

Menstruation usually does not begin again while the baby is nursing, although with some women its reappearance takes place in two or three months.

Sometimes two ova become fertilized at the same time. The result is *fraternal* twins. They need not be of the same sex, and they will not look alike. Each will have his own separate placenta to develop in. The twin occupying the lower position in the womb (and therefore being born first) usually has advantages which are apparent later in somewhat better intelligence and a greater physical size—allowances being made for differences between male and female body structure.

Where, in the process of cell multiplication, a single fertilized ovum separates completely into two, the result is *identical* twins. These must always be of the same sex and must always look alike because their inheritance is exactly the same. They develop within the covering of a single placenta. But again, the lower position in the womb is preferable.

Sometimes a single cell will separate into three, or four, or five, producing triplets, or quadruplets, or quintuplets. It is even possible to draw a diagram of how the single cell which produced the Dionne quintuplets split up in its process of multiplication.

Most multiple births are somewhat premature because, even though the fetuses are less than normal size, the amount of room needed for a full-time pregnancy is in excess of the amount available.

The chance of a multiple birth decreases rapidly with the number involved, as will be seen from the following table:

twins	1 in 90
triplets	1 in 8000
quadruplets	1 in 500,000
quintuplets	1 in 40,000,000

There have been forty-eight recorded cases of quintuplets since medical records were kept, four of them in the United States. Usually they all die at birth.

About 105 boy babies will be born to every 100 girl babies. But because they are more susceptible to disease, enter more dangerous activities, and are sometimes destroyed in large numbers by war, when it comes time to marry there are more women than men.

Birth Control

Contraception has been a controversial topic for thousands of years, and probably will remain so for some time to come. Of the many possibilities in any situation, each of us tends to select as the whole truth that aspect which most nearly mirrors what has been going on emotionally inside himself. Reality is always in terms of personal interpretations.

If it be assumed that intercourse is only for the purpose of recreating life, then clearly any type of contraceptive is sin. So too, if we are to be logical, is intercourse with an already pregnant woman. Few people are willing to accept such a doctrine, for despite twenty centuries and more of effort by church and state to wipe out the practice of birth control, it has increased enormously.

There are many reasons for this in addition to the fact that intercourse is the ultimate expression of affection. Principal among these is the advance of medical science. As recently as the Civil War half our population was under twenty-one years of age and only one person in eleven lived to be fifty. Now two-thirds of the population is over twenty-one, and over three-quarters of them reach the half-century mark. In 1847 the average expectancy of life was exactly forty years. A century later it was sixty-seven years. If the annual birth rate in Massachusetts were allowed to reach the biological normal of 45 per 1000, and the present death rate of 12 per 1000 were maintained, in a single century the population of this Commonwealth would be over 145,000,000—almost the present population of the United States. In two hundred years it would exceed 4,000,000,000 people, which is nearly twice the present world population.*

In October 1947 Secretary General D. A. Fitzgerald of the International Emergency Food Council estimated that despite the 15,000,000 military personnel killed or missing in World War II, and the 20,000,000 civilians murdered, starved, or blown up by bombs, the population of the earth had increased by almost 200,000,000 since 1937. This is comparable to adding "Another North America" to the people who must be fed.

Without some form of contraception, pregnancy is theoretically possible as the result of any intercourse between two healthy, mature individuals. Normal intercourse without contraceptive methods would, in our civilization where the ravages of disease have been so reduced, result in one of several major catastrophes:

(1) War to reduce the population pressure. Is medical science to overcome disease only to have us die violently by each other's hands?

(2) Famine (as in China and India)

(3) Infanticide** (as in India)

(4) Abortion, of which we already have at least 700,000 cases annually, largely performed on married women. The number of abortions is about 30 per cent of the live births, and 10,000 to 14,000 women die in the United

* Karl Sax, Boston *Herald*, March 29, 1948, p. 14.

** Himes believes that infanticide and abortion were the "chief primitive substitutes for conception control." See N. E. Himes *Medical History of Contraception* (Baltimore: Williams & Wilkins, 1936), p. 53.

States each year as a result. Once the egg has been fertilized, to destroy it is to destroy a life, even though legally it is not considered murder until the fetus is capable of movement

(5) Greatly restricted intercourse unless at least one partner is sterile, the husband and wife are mutually unfertile, or where—for one reason or another—the fecundity of the wife is limited. Continence before marriage has much to recommend it, but "self-control instead of birth-control" in wedlock seems, to the great body of medical and psychiatric opinion, an attack upon the instincts God gave us, a source of nervous breakdown, and an unnecessary suffering that often leads to hate.

A survey among 15,000 physicians in America, conducted by Dr. Alan F. Guttmacher* of Johns Hopkins Medical School, showed that 97.8 per cent of the physicians favor birth control for health reasons and 79.4 per cent favor it for economic reasons. The American Institute of Public Opinion found that 11 per cent of the population would express no opinion about birth control, 68.5 per cent approved and 20.5 per cent disapproved the idea of birth control clinics run by the government.** Currently there are 584 child spacing centers in the United States, 238 of which are sponsored by state public health departments.

Quality in conceiving human beings ought to be as important as quality in breeding hogs. Can the child have a good inheritance if the mother is rundown? Is planned parenthood wrong for humans but advantageous for horses? The average mother of six children in East Boston is twenty-eight years old. It is not uncommon to find a fourteen-year-old the eldest of ten children—not all living. In February 1940 an acquaintance of mine delivered a Boston woman of her sixth child in two years and fifteen days— three sets of premature twins, all now dead.

* A. F. Guttmacher, "Conception Control and the Medical Profession," *Human Fertility*, Vol. 12, No. 1 (March 1947), pp. 1-10.
** N. E. Himes, *Your Marriage* (New York: Farrar & Rinehart, 1940), p. 336.

The theory that contraception is sin because it is unnatural, has a number of amazing implications. Celibacy is unnatural too. So is cooking, or stainless steel, or an appendicitis operation, or a wheel. Most of man's rise in civilization has come about by his doing things that did not occur in nature.

The principle of birth control is merely that spermatozoon never meets ovum. This is no more murder than it is murder never to have intercourse which, incidentally, is the only absolutely reliable method of contraception yet known to man. Many of the other methods, besides being useless, are emotionally objectionable or physically harmful. Every one of them has some aesthetic drawback.

It is from my point of view a matter of profound regret that a discussion of the relative merits of the common methods of birth control is not possible here because of legislative prohibition. The law is, indeed, somewhat incongruous, since any one of these methods is used in the United States well over a million times every day. Silence on the part of responsible sources does not keep people in ignorance. It merely guarantees garbled information and poisonous feelings of underhandedness which so often turn into quarrels, adultery, and divorce what should have been happiness, beauty, and spiritual oneness. My own observation is that those who consider it indecent to be forthright about matters of sex— when treated with dignity and reverence—are those who were brought up in ignorance, in prudery, or worse still, in the belief that life itself is a rather unseemly affair.

The open consideration of this subject, including the fact that chemicals may be injurious and the method of rhythm is of doubtful efficacy, is prevented by an atmosphere of concealment and hyprocrisy which is hard to understand and still harder to defend. Planned parenthood has been accepted and practised by intelligent people for hundreds of years. Indeed, the Greeks and Romans knew almost as much about birth control as we do.* But where

* C. C. Zimmerman, *The Family of Tomorrow* (New York: Harper, 1949), Chapter 3.

they were open and honest about it, we are secretive and hypocritical. Advice, even given by a physician to save a woman's life,
is, for example, illegal in Massachusetts, although the sale and
subsequent use of any form of contraceptive is perfectly legal. In
Connecticut it is legal to sell a contraceptive, but against the law
to use it.

An interesting sidelight on this situation is the fact that the
birthrates in these two states are, as proven by the statistics for the
years 1935-40, the third lowest in the entire United States, lower
even than in France before World War II, and only a third of
the physiological maximum. According to the U. S. Census of
Religious Bodies, made in 1936, the seven most Catholic cities in
Massachusetts were Salem, Holyoke, Fall River, Lowell, Lawrence,
Revere, and Fitchburg, with an average of 62 per cent Catholics.
The seven most non-Catholic cities were Quincy, Medford, Brook-
line, Newton, Arlington, Brockton and Somerville, which averaged
25 per cent Catholic. For the years 1935-40, the average annual
birthrate of the predominantly Catholic cities was 14.0 per thousand, whereas in the cities having the smallest Catholic population
the average annual birthrate for the same period was 13.9 per
thousand. The annual birthrate in New England in the year 1800
has been estimated at 55 per thousand.

It is a matter of surprise to many people to learn that the Catholic Church was the first of the Christian denominations to sanction
birth control. The widely held idea that the Catholic Church
is opposed to the dissemination of birth control information for
religious reasons is not true. It only opposes certain methods of
contraception. It has long sanctioned continence as a means of
birth control. In his encyclical on *Christian Marriage*, Pope Pius
XI approved the method called rhythm on the ground that it
was co-operation with rather than interference with nature. At
the same time he vigorously condemned all other methods. The
translation of his words reads as follows:

"Any use whatsoever of matrimony exercised in such a way that
the act is deliberately frustrated in its natural power to generate

life is an offense against the law of God and of nature and those who indulge in such are branded with the guilt of a grave sin. . . . Nor are those considered as acting against nature who in the married state use their right in the proper manner, although on account of natural reasons either of time or of certain defects, new life cannot be brought forth."*

PHILANDERING

"Cleave ye only unto her so long as ye both shall live," is a beautiful way of swearing lifelong sex attraction and fidelity. Mental infidelity is frequent, universal, and a general source of guilt feelings in our culture because of the way we are brought up. Nevertheless, fight as we will against admitting it, every man is attracted by every woman, and vice versa, to some degree.

Some women, without knowing it, practically ask their husbands to be unfaithful. This may be a subconscious method of imposing on another woman some of the physical and emotional responsibilities the wife does not care to assume, and at the same time of leaving the wife in a position to blame the husband instead of herself. Or infidelity may be a flight from the anxiety aroused by an intense interpersonal relationship for which an emotionally immature individual is not yet ready.

The middle-aged man who is beginning to have to face the unpleasant truth that he is not as important or successful as he had hoped to become, is particularly likely to get involved in an errant sex attraction as a means of reassuring himself. Because he feels weak he wants the feeling of conquest. He is unable to distinguish between love and the inflation of his ego. He tells the counselor to whom he goes that he "cannot give her up" when what he means is, "I am so confused I do not know what I am feeling." The probability is that of all married Americans as of the present time, at least half the men and a quarter of the women have been physically unfaithful at least once or twice.

* Encyclical of Pope Pius XI, *Casti Connubii, Christian Marriage* (New York: The American Press, 1936), pp. 17-18.

The cure for infidelity is not to be found in an attempt to out sex the philanderer, but rather in a reappraisal of the quality of one's total love relationship which leads to effective efforts to clarify and to enrich it. "Perhaps nothing has such a high potential for causing a married man to fall in love with another woman than that woman's real or pretended interest in the things he highly values but cannot induce his wife to value."*

In Conclusion

Just as happiness is a by-product and cannot be achieved directly by itself alone, so also a good sex adjustment is a by-product of right relationships in marriage, of which mental attitude is the most important. It is because it is based on a meeting of minds that intercourse is so often the place where incompatibilities first show themselves seriously. People quarrel over money, children, social situations, but they blame divorce on sexual incompatibility. The truth may be that the sex relation cannot survive the ignorant way in which it has been handled, but the probability is it cannot surmount the other incompatibilities. A mere meeting of bodies soon degenerates into no meeting at all.

Intercourse is an emotional pressure gauge. If the other relationships in a marriage are right, wide sex differences can be happily integrated. If they are wrong, the personality clash may show in sexual incompatibility even before it can be detected elsewhere.

A good sex adjustment contributes immensely to lasting values, and lasting values contribute immensely to a good sex adjustment. Husband and wife can become fused together in noble unity only when each has ceased to be merely an individual and the two have become united in mind, in personality, and in body. Intercourse is a means of closer union—mental, emotional, and physical—in a world of much uncertainty, bewilderment, and loneliness.

* J. K. Folsom: *Plan For Marriage* (New York: Harper, 1938), p. 94.

11

Emotional Adjustments

COURTSHIP is the discovery of love; happy marriage its perpetuation. Discovery is an adventure, perpetuation the reward of following good method. Yet many young people, without thinking a step beyond the engagement, regard marriage as a perennial holiday in which happiness is presented as a gift of the gods. It should be thought of as an honest partnership to which both husband and wife contribute an honest share of effort and adjustment. The wedding is the beginning of the undertaking, not the end. We are willing to work to become competent in the office or the factory. We must do the same in the home, especially since for most of us emotional adjustment is something we know little about. Success in marriage depends principally on the ability to make fruitful adjustments. Between the cactus and the fern this is impossible because they cannot flourish in the same soil and the same climate.

Edith thinks she has married Prince Charming; Bill thought she was an angel. There was no expectation of an anticlimax when they faced the task of learning to live together. Then someday they wake up to the fact that each is a human being with the

296

limitations of his humanity. They begin to see faults without having expected them. Marriage inevitably comes to some level of interaction between husband and wife, without glamour, for no relationship can be lived on a continuously dizzy level. Any transition from effortless dreaming to laborious doing may be a change in the expectation of satisfaction, which can lead to trouble.

This is one of the real advantages resulting from the marriage customs of other cultures, outnumbering our own, in which marriages are based on parental choice. There is no heart-throbbing romance to obscure the need for emotional adjustments. Bride and groom know from the outset that if they are to be happy together they must set about producing the conditions which are prerequisite to happiness. There is no chance to coast through the first year on the bliss of an infatuation which has few, if any, foundations in fact. Actually, happiness as a criterion for marriage is recent in the history of the family, and even today would be looked upon as strange by most of the people in the world.

All success comes at a price. The more worthwhile the achievement, the more one usually has to pay for it in effort. When it is possible to acquire something of value for a small down payment, look out for the installments! A marriage license costs $2.00. That is the down payment.

Any new occupation requires adjustments. The wise man finds out what these are likely to be and plans accordingly. Marriage usually means:

(1) Readjustment to the family one comes from
(2) Adjustment to the family of one's spouse
(3) Readjustment to each other.

Thus the bride and groom should set about understanding each other and their family backgrounds as though their very lives depended upon it—for they do. This is more important than any college degree, may be more difficult to achieve, and is much more rewarding. Deep and abiding love is not something a young couple starts out with, it is something they may succeed in build-

ing over the years. It should be reiterated that the first year ought
to be the hardest because conscientiously devoted to readjustments.
It is infatuation that is blind, not love. Love sees the faults that
must be met and gladly makes whatever adjustments are needed
for the sake of the greater values of the marriage. Infatuation, being
alternately blind in one eye, first sees only sentimentalized virtues,
but soon sees nothing but the faults. Naturally there are no readjustments where there is no:

(1) Realization of need

(2) Desire to readjust

(3) Understanding of what to do and how.

Naturally there is little happiness where all the emphasis is on
rights, and little attention on responsibilities. The usual idea of
accomplishing an adjustment is trying to make the other person
change. This pretense of possessing the superior personality is
an indication of a subconscious feeling of inferiority. The truly
superior person says, "What changes ought I to undertake in myself
in order to bring about a better intellectual soil and emotional
climate in which we can each be and spontaneously express our
real selves?"

Nor is it just hard work that brings success. It is intelligent work
that counts. *Each one of us has many opportunities to be happy
everywhere, and many opportunities to be unhappy everywhere.*
Whether we are happy or unhappy depends largely upon ourselves.
We make our own destinies. Things do not just happen to us.
They always take place, to some degree, through us.

The kind of readjustments each person will attempt—both as
to nature and to manner—will depend on the kind of upbringing
he has had. They fall into many areas:

legal	psychological
sociological	aesthetic
economic	recreational
religious	geographical
philosophical	dietary

A husband must expect that his wife will not make an apple-sauce cake the way his mother did. Perhaps she can do it better. A girl from New England going to live in the Great Plains States must expect to miss the clear streams, the hills, and the little surprises of driving along a winding, wooded road.

There is an endless complexity of variables in environment and in each other which must be faced and assimilated. Any event of the magnitude of marriage always changes life unpredictably. We must allow for change, no matter who we are or where we are. For husband and wife, the important thing is to meet change and adjust to it together.

Is the wife to be merely a housekeeper and concubine? When the glamour wears off she is likely to think so for a while, and to question the wisdom of her marriage. Both husband and wife should expect this, and make provision for the development of a deeper, more abiding love between them. Otherwise, they will begin to concentrate on each other's faults.

Happy people tend to overlook shortcomings; unhappy people to overemphasize or to imagine them. Misery continually asks questions about one's intimates. Happiness has no need to. Nothing on earth is perfect; why expect marriage to be? We all have faults. The wrong mate discovers them and attacks them in such a way that one never tries to improve. The right mate discovers them and goes about adjusting to them so skillfully that resistances disappear and one is not even aware of it until an old friend says, "Your wife has done a lot to develop you, hasn't she!"

Certainly they cannot expect always to agree, and they must learn how to function satisfactorily when they do not agree. Any organization which can perform its duties only when there is unanimity of opinion is unreliable and of little value, for insistance or unanimity ends either in frustration and paralysis (as is the case with the veto power in the United Nations), or in tyranny (as has been the case in all one party governments.) Good adjustment means the possibility of vigorous differences of opinion without any loss of emotional unity.

Every marriage is marred by some disagreements over money, or relatives, or religion, or food, or how to spend a vacation. A young couple's uncritical assumption of mutual understanding because they have used the word love—each with his own private meanings—soon proves to have been pure poetry. Whether the discovery leads to battle fatigue, or the precious knowledge of how deeply each cares for their togetherness, depends upon whether they are in love.

There are no rules for emotional adjustments, but there definitely are principles. When one partner says, "We never disagree," the specialist in human relations wants to ask, "And which one of you is sacrificing his integrity on the altar of the other's demands?" No one-sided attempt can ever solve an inescapably two-sided problem. "We each go half-way," is another fallacy which suggests the defining of limits and the setting up of defenses. "We try to go together," is the real thing.

Gertrude and Harry sometimes disagreed vigorously, but they made up just as vigorously—and soon. Neither allowed their differences to last long enough for the blight which follows going to bed angry. Grace and Will never disagreed vigorously and never made up vigorously either. They just held it all inside and lived mutually frustrated lives under the same roof.

There can be virtue to battle, for it may lead to sound adjustments which lessen emotional tensions. Battle may bring about:

(1) New values pounded out together and acceptable to both

(2) The best compromise they can make

(3) The acknowledged right of each to differ with the other and to go his separate way on this particular issue.

Certainly husband and wife should not be afraid to express their disagreements . . . to each other, that is, never to an outsider in the hope of gaining a sympathetic ally. To suppress honest anger is to express it destructively in some subconscious way. A young bridegroom, cloudy with embarrassment, apologized for flinging an arm across the bed as he awoke, for it struck his bride a smart blow across the face. He thought the trouble was the break in his long habit of sleeping alone. How he misled himself with this disguised aggression. Two years later they were divorced.

As pointed out in the chapter on "Criteria for Choosing a Mate," differences of opinion are inevitable—some of them serious. There are a number of alternatives:

(A) Agreement because:

    (1) Husband and wife hold practically identical positions, the focus of each one's opinion being not only within the range of the other's tolerance, but close to his focus (see Figure 7, Page 178)

    (2) Their differences are within the tolerance range

(B) Disagreement resolved because:

    (1) Husband or wife makes a genuine change to a new opinion because of new information brought out by the other, or discovered together

    (2) With respect for mutual individuality within a togetherness, each allows the other to go his own way. This is not always a possible solution, for often the problem is inescapably two-sided

    (3) One, or perhaps each, makes a false change because coerced, thus eventually bringing about hidden or overt rebellion

(C) Disagreement:

    (1) Husband and wife endeavor to adjust to opinions which lie outside their tolerance range, but are unable to do so. The resources which can be drawn from the generalized emotional security reservoir of each now become vitally important

    (2) Unresolved conflict. This becomes almost inevitable where there is

        (a) no attempt to get better information

        (b) a fixed, unyielding personality

        (c) no desire to preserve the marriage.

Suppose the wife, plumey with desire, has seen a fur coat in a store window which her friend urges her to buy. This she is unwilling to do without consulting her husband because it breaks the budget. He points out the life insurance premiums and the installment on the car now almost due. She knows he tries hard to be a good provider, and willingly gives up the coat. Or perhaps he says, "Let's stay home this year when my vacation comes. That coat means a lot to you and if we stay home we could afford it." Or they decide together the coat would be an unwarranted extravagance, but how about a new hat (shoes, handbag, dress) instead.

Suppose he feels the expenditure unwise, but she wants the fur so much she is willing to borrow from the bank and to pay for the garment out of her allowance for the next two years. To him this is silly, but he does not say so. After all, it is her allowance. She did not tease him to buy it for her anyway. Each sees and respects how the other feels. The wife is accepting the consequences of her own decision. (The procedure is a corroding deception if she does not.) Each retains a self-respecting status in a togetherness despite their difference of opinion.

This is how happy marriages operate. More than one reality is seen in a given situation. There is a whole table of perceptions to consider. Each must think about them all.

	My perceptions include	Your perceptions include
I	My values' *assumed* significance to me	My values' *apparent* significance to you
YOU	Your values' *apparent* significance to you	Your values' *assumed* significance to me
WE	The interaction of my values' *apparent* significance to you and your values' *assumed* significance to me	The interaction of my values' *assumed* significance to you and your values' *apparent* significance to me

Observe that the understandings represented by the two columns may not coincide at all. Furthermore, either individual (or both) may lack, or be wrong, about some perceptions, including his own. And, of course, the table applies to past or to predicted relationships, as well as to present ones.

Once the husband (wife) recognizes that the wife's behavior may have a different reality for her than for him, he can begin to try to understand her point of view. Is her wanting the fur coat spontaneous; or a coldly calculated attempt to take advantage of him; or a compulsive submission to inner demands that she live a life of "I ought because people expect it of me whether I want to or not;" or an anxious attempt to escape someone's domination by anticipating the demands and building counterdefenses. Just asking her is nonsense. She may not even know the why of her behavior.

The situation is actually more complicated than either the above or Figure 7 indicates, because the husband may consciously fight and subconsciously agree with the wife, whereas she may consciously agree but subconsciously want to fight the husband.

IRRATIONAL BEHAVIOR

In any relationship with other people, even a loving one, it is important to realize that *a certain amount of irrational behavior is inevitable and must be expected.* It is equally important to realize that:

(1) No matter how irrational the behavior may be, it always seems and *is* logical to the perpetrator in terms of his interpretation of his situation at the time

(2) Motive is more important than specific action. Anger or resentment in response to such behavior is warranted only when the individual *intended* to hurt. But most of us react in terms of our own frustrations, not in terms of the other person's intent. This can easily become a whole cycle of mutual restimulation

(3) We are all, as Rabbi Liebman said, part saint, part sinner, and wholly human

(4) Mutually to forgive and to overlook makes life easy; to harbor grudges and to want revenge makes life hard.

Behavior is often irrational, but it is always logical in terms of the particular person in the particular environment at the particular time.

Perhaps if dinner is not ready on the dot, the husband is intolerant and unsympathetic to the point of active malice. When dinner is on time he wants to finish what he is doing, and refuses to eat a bite. From the point of view of scheduling meals this is entirely irrational. From the point of view of his emotions at the time, it is completely logical, or he would not do it. Perhaps what he really wants is merely to be annoying.

When the psychologists say that behavior is adapted to the conditioning action of the environment, they need to add that life is lived in an infinite series of environments, because of which every individual interprets the present surroundings in terms of past experience. It is the individual's own interpretation of the environment, not someone else's, that is the basis of behavior. Evaluations are personal, and it is the husband's evaluation of "dinner is ready"—nobody else's—which is operating.

Situations always affect emotional reactions in completely logical ways, had we the wit to see it. Every act has a motive, and all motives are emotional. The wrappings of politeness may disguise a complaint in words like, "Why did you have to say that?" when what we are feeling—doubtless unknowingly—is "Damn You!" Politeness is often self-deception as well as appeasement, but the underneath feeling will get expressed in some recognizably logical way could we but see all the steps.

Jealousy

Jealousy shows there is something wrong with an interpersonal relationship. Where there is love, there is no room for a rival, and both partners feel this. Life with a jealous person can be a living hell. Jealousy is caused by fearing the loss of something because of being unworthy to possess it. The excessive struggle to possess another person completely and without sharing is an indication of how desperately the loss is feared, and how pathetically it is believed to be inevitable if the truth about the would-be possessor were known.

The feeling may be irrational in the light of the objective facts; it is logical in the light of the felt facts. The jealous person is one whose self-confidence was perhaps destroyed by an overcritical parent, by being compelled to wear the outgrown clothes of an older child, or by suffering disparaging comparisons with siblings and playmates. The emotional sequence usually is:

(1) Fearing the loss of some desired thing because of feeling considered inferior

(2) Wanting revenge

(3) Feeling guilty because of desiring revenge

(4) Hence, fearing the inevitability of losing the desired thing because of deserving to lose it as a punishment

(5) And so on around until the jealous person cannot stand on his own self-respect, but must be externally supported.

This explains why we are so ashamed of jealousy, and so clever in attempting to conceal it. This is why it only makes matters worse to accuse a jealous person of being jealous. He should feel his emotions through to the end. He should take time to know what he is feeling, why he is feeling it, and what he wants to do about such feelings. Few people are willing to do this.

Jealousy is felt largely by those people who assumed they were in love instead of endeavoring, in an emotionally mature way, to establish a loving relationship. Feelings which are not grounded in experience make it easy to switch from being "insanely in love" to being "insanely jealous." In other words, the light sense of worthiness and being lovable which come to the individual from someone outside himself, proves to be the superficial bubbles atop an unsavory brew as soon as the continued reassurance is withdrawn. He feels isolated again, as he subconsciously knew all the time was the case.

What a sad testimony to the inadequacy of our thinking, that the usual advice for dealing with jealousy puts the emphasis on somehow managing the other person instead of on healing one's self.

Sometimes an adolescent, or a young married person for that matter, thinks arousing someone's jealousy is a proof of his affection. How superficial! Jealousy kills love. It is a symptom of weakness and of selfishness. Wanting a suitor, or a wife, or a husband to pay exclusive attention to one has nothing in common with real devotion.

The spectre at the domestic feast is often an old sweetheart. He or she is not physically present, but a ghost is there to allow the inventions of new endings to an unfinished story, which should have been (and very likely was) finished long ago. Of course the old sweetheart is there in the husband's (or the wife's) heart— ineradicably and forever part of the individual's subconscious, because part of his past experience. The influence should be dormant, not active, but the best way to give it new life is to be jealous.

Is it not clear that a jealous person is deliberately attempting self-punishment by behavior subconsciously recognized as the way to guarantee the loss of the very thing consciously sought? What he does seems so irrational until his subconscious motives are understood.

INTEGRATED, ADAPTIVE BEHAVIOR

The two most important factors of permanence and emotional stability in marriage are integration of effort and adaptability of behavior. With these, it is possible to weather a crisis. If successfully integrated, adaptive behavior toward each other is to be achieved, we must foresee the consequences of our own acts, not only on other people but on ourselves, and be able to make the right adjustment without disturbing either person's sense of emotional security. "What do I really want to do?" must be answered in terms of the total situation, including most particularly the emotional reactions of all the significant persons in it.

"What do I really want to do?" is vastly different from, "I'm going to have my way!" which never stops to ask, "Where does this lead and how fast, and will it be the sort of relationship I am going to want in the long run?" The idea that it is possible to get more and more for one's self merely by taking it from someone else has been a form of psychological stupidity and emotional illness with the human race ever since the days of Cain and Abel. Can the husband's happiness long survive the unhappiness of the wife? The reality of both individual's reactions must be penetrated, understood, accepted . . . *and adjusted to* in a way which is neither submission nor domination.

When no opinion but one's own matters, one is, of course, right about everything, and being right, is without conscious imperfection. When Alfred says, "It's all Ellen's fault because she does not give me what I want," there is no room for inquiry into Ellen's ability to give the desired thing. A loving relationship is not an all-or-none-affair. One loving person alone cannot make a marriage succeed. To attempt it is to become submissive at the cost of integrity and self-respect. Again, the big word in marriage is *together*. There needs to be communion of emotions between husband and wife (and children) because each is part of the environment of the other, and gladly takes account, for his own sake, of the needs and the rights of the other.

This is an entirely different thing from a balance of power which, as history has amply shown, is an underlying clash of forces which do not stay balanced. It is an entirely different thing from compromise where each side reluctantly yields something in order that the situation may temporarily go forward, only at long last to abandon expedient appearances and to fight. It is wanting to co-operate, and trying to co-operate, no matter what difficulties arise.

Suppose that early in the marriage husband and wife find that, despite the reassuring discussions they had during the engagement, a difference exists in their ideas concerning sex, or how the furniture is to be arranged, or who will pay what bills. This may bring about a spectacular fight for domination, with all its sad consequences. It may result in a temporary stalemate because there is a balance of power. For a time it may appear to be solved by some compromise arrangement. Or there may be a sincere desire to work out an intelligent solution together. If the latter is true, in a few months the bride may say, "I was a little worried about intercourse, but soon found we could work out a very happy relation together." Or the groom may say, "It was hard for me to let my wife take care of the household expenses, but I know now she can do it better than I." Here are no spectacular behavior pyrotechniques, no subconscious efforts to slay each other emotionally by nagging at each other's weaknesses, no withdrawals of affection now that the honeymoon is over. Here are two people giving evidence of good emotional adjustment.

It is not what one says but what is meant by what one says and the feeling it conveys that matters. It is not the act itself but the at-present-felt meaning of the act which is emotionally significant. Bob can say, "Yes, dear, I let the dog in," and be either criticizing or reassuring Jane. He cannot be emotionally honest until he knows which he is doing and why. Nevertheless, Jane will sense, though perhaps only subconsciously, what he is really feeling, and will be influenced by it in her own feeling and subsequent action toward him.

Two people in love will disagree when to do so is to learn something from each other. The disagreement may not be resolved, but there will be no attempt at victory on the emotional battlefield. Where personality clashes do occur, it will be because the motivational purpose of husband, or wife, (or both) is wrong, bringing about wrong emotional relationships. What usually happens is that one expects something from the other which the other does not give. The original "I want" changes first to a more or less frightened "Am I going to get?" When the answer seems to be, "You certainly are not going to get," what was "I want" usually turns into "I hate," although it takes a long time, and a great deal of repetition, to realize the actuality of the "I hate."

As R. C. Nyman said in discussing this with me, when a desire is frustrated, it becomes perverted. An unusually mature individual may find a sublimation, or substitute some new desire (as almost all of us do when we are balked by nature). So many of us, frustrated by a person with whom we live intimately—particularly when it is someone we want to love—will seek to coerce or entice until the frustrating individual is in our power. This is love being perverted into a desire to dominate. How hard it is to realize this, or to realize that the perversion is always accompanied by feelings of guilt.

Despite the old adage that experience is the best teacher, on the adult level most of us learn little wisdom by experience. Two people, unhappy at the beginning of their marriage, are likely to be even more unhappy twenty-five years later. They have failed to learn anything about the forces behind various types of behavior, or about adapting their behavior to each other. They try to manage each other as though human relations are to be conducted successfully by pulling the strings attached to a marionette.

Types of Behavior

Emotional energy flows down the love stream or the hate stream, depending upon whether there is confidence or fear. (See Figure 4.) Confidence will result in co-operative behavior. Fear will result in an attempt at self-protection either by fighting, giving in, or running away. Thus human behavior falls basically into two emotional causes and four classes, which are capable of endless combinations of degree and kind. People:

(1) Dominate and fight because of fear
(2) Become subservient and give in because of fear
(3) Avoid by running away because of fear
(4) Co-operate in confidence.

When husband and wife have poor interpersonal relationships, one of three things happens:

(1) They try to dominate each other in quarreling, which snowballs the trouble into even greater dissatisfaction

(2) One or the other becomes subservient. Or perhaps this is only apparently so. By contracting some chronic illness a person may seem to give in, but actually attack

(3) They separate in spirit, or perhaps go all the way to a divorce.

Successful marriage, like any other successful partnership, is based on right relationships which bring about co-operative, willing hearts. Let us now examine each one of these types of behavior.

DOMINATION

As long as there are two people in the world, there will be disagreements, some of them serious. Emotionally mature people can discuss a disagreement without loss of emotional unity. Others simply explode in anger, or engage in heated debate. A discussion is entered into for the purpose of exchanging ideas. In a debate each side is trying to win.

When husband and wife try to dominate each other, the root cause goes far deeper than dinner not being ready on time, or leaving the cap off the toothpaste, or spending too much money for a hat, or lounging unshaven in bathrobe and slippers while systematically discarding the various sections of the Sunday paper all over the living room floor. For some reason, husband and wife want to fight, the usual underlying reason being the attempt to prove to one's self that one is not as weak as he believes himself to be. Perhaps the husband is angry at himself for stupid behavior he cannot face, and so projects the guilt onto the wife; perhaps the wife is transferring to the husband rage she was never allowed to express against her father. Projection and transference are going on all the time. This is why some individuals get on well with almost everyone (they were loved as children), and others hate almost everyone (they were not loved as children and spend most of their lives in perpetual rebellion against that fact).

It is so natural for us to think the other person entirely in the wrong because *this was the truth* in the beginning of each individual's experience in human relations. The baby is incapable of being at fault, but parents and parent substitutes can be cruelly at fault in the way they treat him. Our subconscious remembers this. On the adult level, on the other hand, it is almost impossible for anyone to be completely blameless.

The intelligent individual will not waste time in trying to fix blame. His effort will be expended in trying to set the situation right. If this is to be achieved, it is first necessary to be able to identify his feelings and to understand their significance. Even a little candlelight is helpful in an immensity of darkness.

Self-pity

Of all the indirect expressions of anger, self-pity is the most subtle. That it is an indirect request for help is fairly obvious. Not so its content of anger.

In an unsatisfactory situation, the emotionally mature person will say, "See what you've done to me. Now this is what I propose to do as a result." Here is an honest, direct approach, devoid of fear or vindictiveness, and carried out on a man-to-man basis. The self-pitying individual, on the other hand, is saying in effect, "See what you've done to me! I hate you for it, and I am afraid to tell you so, or to express my anger directly. But I shall get even with you. I'll pity myself. Then other people will see what a brute you are. They'll dislike you, they'll get even with you for me. Poor me."

Defiance

Defiance is the other extreme. Here is the person who opens up his defenses at full throttle when only confronted with the preliminaries of what may become a conflict. The conflict is now assured, unless the other individual involved has great emotional maturity, for we react as readily to the signals of conflict as to conflict itself.

Again we see the tragedy of pre-conditioning which has destroyed the capacity for delayed reaction, discrimination, intel-

ligent solution. Again the individual fears his attacker and wants
to destroy him—or at least to destroy his power. Feeling too weak
to undertake it openly, he accomplishes it figuratively by behavior
which implies that the other person's wishes do not exist as far as he
is concerned. He is subconsciously terrified by what he thinks
would happen if the other individual found out his true feeling
(wanting to destroy), so he rationalizes his attitude by saying,
"This is a matter of principle with me." Thus he hides, even from
himself, the destructive emotions which are controlling him. The
whole behavior mechanism comes full circle when he subconsciously punishes himself for his feelings of guilt because of the
destructive attitude, by using the defiance as a means of guarantee-
ing that his behavior will fail. A co-operative approach would have
succeeded.

The "Martyr" Pose

A "martyr" is a person with intense feelings of inferiority, who
wants to be credited with qualities he does not possess. He thinks
he is sacrificing for others, whereas what he really wants is power
over them by making them beholden to him. He will do almost
anything for a person whom he respects and considers to be important, if only the person will recognize him as a competent
individual in return.

Such individuals imagine that their martyrdom makes them
loved. Actually it cannot but take the edge of any true affection.
"Though I speak with the tongues of men and of angels, and have
not love . . ."—*without asking for it.*

Chip on the Shoulder

The individual with a chip on his shoulder is feeling exactly the
opposite thing from what he is trying to show. He attempts to
appear self-sufficient, powerful, independent, unconcerned. Actually, he desperately wants to be made to feel that he belongs, that
he will be accepted, wanted, loved. He fears but expects rejection,

and so comes in with his emotional defenses up, on the theory that offense is the best defense.

This represents a common sequence:

(1) Anger, with recurring stimulation
(2) Fear of expressing it, and therefore suppressing it
(3) Panic
(4) Attack in desperation to keep one's self from seeing how frightened one is.

Unfortunately most people interpret such an individual's actions at their face value, and respond by trying to crush the apparent attack. What they should do is to disarm the person's fears with kindness, realizing that the impulse with which a person will fight is inversely proportional to how solid he believes the ground to be on which his security depends.

Revenge

Wanting retaliation against another person is a character-searing procedure, but it is not just "cussedness." The object is to prove to one's self and to the other person—which is why a revenge is unsatisfactory unless the other person is aware of it—that one is not subservient. If an individual already knows that he is not subservient, there is no need to prove it to himself, and what the other person thinks does not matter. To him revenge is a degrading thing.

Wanting Power Over Others

The desire to dominate another person is due to some feeling of weakness. It is the same old story. To want to seem superior is unknowingly to confess an inner conviction of inferiority. Wanting to dominate is wanting to destroy the other personality instead of wanting to give it the chance to grow. Domination is always destruction of some sort. Even the effort to help or to influence other people is often tainted with an unrecognized desire to dominate.

"My husband makes me sick!" is emotionally saying, "I do not want to change, but I do want to change him." An insight that, "I react to this particular behavior of my husband by feeling sick," may make adjustment possible.

If he says, "Bye and bye you'll see I'm right!" her self-respect has been attacked, for he has claimed to represent an assumed future attitude of hers, in conflict with her presently functioning attitude.

All too often marriage turns out to be two unhappy people trying to force a system of behavior on each other. Of course they are unhappy. Wanting the world to bow to one's wishes always leads to despair. This trying to work together by imposing narrow restrictions does not succeed anywhere in human relations.

Nevertheless, everybody has power and exerts it in one way or another. The question is, how? Using power for the achievement of an end result which has nothing to do with making someone subservient, is the proper function of power. But using power to get power over others, makes power the end instead of the means. We need to be able to use power without wanting power for itself alone. "I have responsibilities to perform—or to get someone else to perform," is all right. "I have power to make him do," bespeaks a person who is afraid.

Often the way a person tries to exert power over someone else is not by open warfare but by indirection. Wives who are slovenly, or lazy, or habitually late in keeping appointments, are expressing aggression against other people. (The husband may only be the victim, not the root cause.) A man may have arthritis as a means, among other things, of compelling his wife to tend the furnace.

Sometimes a person will try to make impotent the efforts of his spouse, no matter what the consequences to himself. A compulsive desire to destroy another individual's power can only be hate. It is necessary to despise someone before wanting power over him, which is why the struggle for domination seldom lifts its ugly head on the honeymoon.

How stupid to expect someone to love you even though you try to destroy his personality—and do destroy it as far as his influence on you is concerned. Nevertheless, this is the great, natural test we all use: "If you will love me despite the fact that I am mean to you, then I can trust your love. If you love me only when I am good to you, then how can I know that it isn't just a lure? I know about these efforts at domination and these bribes used as means for getting power over someone, because that is what I experienced with my parents."

Stubbornness

Stubbornness is caused by repressed anger. It is one of the last ways (the last being suicide) by which a person who feels in a weak position, can fight to preserve his personality. When we dare not express anger openly, we become sullen and stubborn.

Quarreling

The superficial thinker says, "Don't take seriously what happens in a quarrel. Some conflict is normal in all human relations, particularly marriage. The bleak words of hot anger don't reflect the real relationship." Perhaps not, but they may reflect forces behind the quarrel which need attention. "Forget it," is another wrong attitude. Examine it. Understand it. Remedy it.

A quarrel is always rooted in the conditions that produced the quarrel. The precipitating cause is often only the symbol of the underlying trouble. A man who loses his temper because the coffee is cold or the dinner is late is not revealing, and probably is not conscious of the real trouble. The explosion is a symptom of his dissatisfaction with something else: perhaps his home life in general; possibly the unwillingness of his parents to allow him to express honest anger as a boy; it could even be a way of saying he married the wrong woman. The cold coffee or the late dinner is only the precipitating cause. There is also an underlying cause. The husband loses his temper because the precipitating cause triggered off something deep and emotionally important to him. An unreasonable person is someone who feels too weak to adjust satisfactorily to something of importance, and who does not know how else to express his anger.

The attitude subconsciously is, "I don't know how to handle this, and therefore I'm going to dominate because if I don't I'm afraid you will, and then I would be lost. I must nail my supremacy down or my whole position will fall."

People cannot habitually quarrel without developing hate. A fight seldom settles anything, except that each person intensifies the defense of his position. The only way to solve a disagreement is to find out how to love. After a woman has been wrong at the top of her voice for fifteen minutes she may suddenly realize that she cares more about her marriage than she does about winning a fight. She may sense, for a moment, that the way to solve the disagreement is to find out how to love. "Good Lord, what have I done?" she will feel. Her husband at once feels this change in her attitude. "Now I've got her on the run!" he thinks, "This is the time to put on the pressure." So he renews the attack, she is restimulated with a feeling of desperation, and away goes the chance to think out the validity of her insight concerning the ineffectiveness of fighting. She is hurt, and wants to hurt back. People withstand misfortune better than they withstand intended injury. Then the husband begins to feel, "Gee, look what I've done now."

Even if they should come to see at the same time that quarreling is destructive to both of them, there still remains the problem of finding the root cause instead of merely retiring to lick their wounds. It is of no use to try to do away with the harmful results of their quarreling without changing anything in the underlying causative situation. It would be beneficial if they understood the meaning of their behavior, for repeated failures lead to violent attempts at solution.

They should realize the difference between the way each interprets his own responsibility for the quarrel in terms of the literal meaning of his own words, and the way he interprets the other's responsibility in terms of the subtle inflection, the facial expressions, the suspected intentions which can turn an otherwise harmless utterance into an insult. Each of them probably takes advantage of these weapons, and responds with offended innocence if his own responsibility for the fight is assessed beyond the face value of his words. He may even have a spell of self-pity over it.

Indirect expressions of anger, like self-pity and stubbornness, are always an indication of feelings of weakness. Direct anger may be strength. There are occasions when a quarrel can be more productive than a calm discussion. We need emotional baths as much as we need skin baths. Going to church should be cleansing to the spirit. So may direct, honest anger. Just as dirt is matter out of place, so indirect anger is an emotion out of place. Direct, honest anger is no more dirty in itself than direct, honest love, although the reason for the anger may be disgraceful.

The value of anger is not so much in the emotional catharsis which it brings, as in what can be learned about what is going on inside the personality. Thus direct, honest anger should:

(1) Relieve the tension
(2) Indicate something is wrong
(3) Serve as a means of locating the difficulty by bringing out some disagreeable truth otherwise overlooked
(4) Lead to a better understanding of each other, and of each other's needs. A man does not achieve this with a mistress, which is one of the ways in which that relationship fails.

Direct, honest anger will be expressed in a pitched battle, never in a long siege. After the battle, peace negotiations will be undertaken promptly. Where the cessation of hostilities comes about through victory by husband or wife, the result is likely to be the downfall of both. If a quarrel settles nothing except who is to be top dog, it settles nothing for long. If the only aim of war is to win in order to dictate the peace, then peace remains undeclared war in which feelings of bitterness do not wear off. One does not need to know much history to realize that.

Honest anger will sometimes bring about an adjustment which would not have been achieved in any other way.

There is a vast difference between mere anger and the ruinous emotion of revenge. Everybody is angry at times; vengeance is self-defeating. Trying to repress anger as many of us have been taught to do, does not destroy it, but drives it into the subconscious where it becomes stronger, disguised, indirect in its expression. Nor is the trouble corrected by doing whatever the feeling of the moment dictates. Impulse is not the answer either. The wise man does not try to avoid anger; he determines what, for him, is worth being angry about, then is angry at the right person, in the right way, at the right time. *He expresses the anger in a constructive way*, and he gets over being angry as soon as this is accomplished. Honestly understood feelings, plus honestly considered alternatives, plus an honest choice of what he wants over the long-run is the only right procedure.

What we feel and how we feel is far more important than what we think or how we think. The inevitable result of pulling apart, so far as husband and wife are concerned, is eventually banging together.

Fighting is a relatively simple business which substitutes an attempt to use force for the application of thought in the solution of a conflict of interests. It is a symptom that more intelligent and legitimate channels are lacking. It produces misunderstanding, stiffens resentment, and develops barriers.

What causes a quarrel?

(1) Some motive for wanting a readjustment of the situation because
   (a) the person is wrongly adjusted to it
   (b) it is wrongly adjusted to him

(2) An attempt to work out a plan to accomplish the readjustment.

(3) Failure of the plan due to the interference, real or imagined, of
   (a) forces outside the personality
   (b) forces inside the personality

(4) Overflow of the emotional energy into anger.

In the beginning, some wrong outside stimulus produced wrong inner response. Real trouble comes when this has happened enough times to generalize the inner response to the point where right outside stimulus also produces wrong inner response because only through wrong inner response has there been any sense of security. When this happens, the individual gets satisfaction out of the emotional response itself. This is doubly true if he also apparently solves his problem by the outburst. But it is not possible to set a situation right until one stops behaving like a child.

The frequency of disputes is by no means as important as the seriousness with which they are intended or received. Where an important source of irritation continues, the trouble is almost never what it seems to be. Instead of tinkering with consequences, find the cause even though it requires the professional assistance of a marriage counselor or a psychiatrist. What matters is one's real attitude; not what he thinks he thinks.

The sociological studies give as the cause of quarrels such items as insufficient income, nagging, lack of affection, jealousy, selfishness. These reasons are usually superficial. They are but the last car on the train of events. Anyone with a knowledge of psychiatry knows that the real reasons are far deeper: the lack of feeling genuinely loved as a child; subconscious hatred of the mother being transferred to the wife; compensation for the frustrations of competitive business being worked off through aggressive behavior at home.

Absence of quarreling may only indicate indifference to each other. Husband and wife can become adjusted to a manner of living together that is not a real adjustment to each other. An upset to their manner of living, such as the wreckage caused by a depression, may unmask such counterfeits.

SUBSERVIENCY

Wise people know that many things are not worth fighting for. On the other hand, where the issue is of fundamental importance, only the weak give in.

Whenever husband or wife gives in, it should never be in a

surrendering way. Being a pacifist through fear achieves nothing. It only leaves unresolved conflicts which persist. When a serious disagreement is shelved without satisfactory feelings on the part of both husband and wife, it will break out again and cause increased trouble.

Surrender does not settle anything, for there is no togetherness in it. Strange as it seems, even the dominator is frightened and angered by it. Slavery also enslaves the master by making him dependent, insecure, and apprehensive. There is much to be feared from the dispossessed. It is not "my values instead of yours" people want, but the mutual discovery and adoption of "our values."

"Clever Wife Submissive in the Home," says a newspaper headline. How can human relationships based on dishonesty or pretense succeed? They must be sincere or they will fail. Pretense might change the form of discontent, but it cannot change the discontent. "Always Put the Welfare of Your Family First." The family will hardly flourish unless this is done, but how can it be done unless the individual flourishes doing it? Can the fern pretend to be a cactus and live?

Occasionally a wife will act as though she wanted to be imposed upon. Perhaps it reasserts her childhood feeling of inferiority and therefore her right to be babied and protected. Be that as it may, one thing is sure: *no one ever has more authority over an individual than the individual is willing to accept.* He may be liquidated, but to liquidate is not to compel subservience.

AVOIDANCE

When faced with a difficult problem, if he does not quit in discouragement the immature person tends to behave as though it were not there, or if that is impossible, to run to someone else for advice. What someone else thinks is not as important as the facts. Yet many of us act as though we wanted to be made to feel important by getting sympathy, more than we wanted to face and to solve our problems. We feel weak, so we tell mama, tell the clergyman, tell the neighbors. The more Eleanor tells her intimates that she finds Harry difficult to get along with, the more she avoids facing the problem honestly. The more she convinces her friends of her own righteousness, the more she establishes a position which she must maintain.

The first step ought to have been to get the right facts and to face them, no matter how disagreeable. No one can turn from hopelessness to right relatedness by trying to avoid either the situation or doing honest work on himself. "How can I escape whatever is disagreeable?" is an attitude far removed from, "How can I set the situation right?"

There are situations where the intelligent thing to do is to elude, to keep away, to escape whatever threatens. In this sense of avoid, one keeps away from being burned by the stove or being involved with a dishonest tradesman, but these are different from failure to face the facts.

CO-OPERATION

The desire for a happy home is often nothing more than a desire for the benefits of a happy home—not for the discovery and establishment of the factors which are a prerequisite. Husbands and wives must be brought to see that the benefits of a happy home stem from right value standards and right emotional relationships.

If husband and wife are seeking to function independently, the result must be disintegration of the family exactly as explosion results when the elements of an atom decide to be rid of each other's influences. Trying to be free from each other is contrary to the very purpose for which the marriage was undertaken.

Basically everyone wants to be part of a co-operative effort. "I can't co-operate" is the emotional equivalent of, "I am in pain." Lacking good method, people try ineffective methods, such as:
   (1) I'm no good, please help me
   (2) Please treat me as an equal although I feel inferior and afraid. I want to co-operate
   (3) You do as I say. Then we can co-operate.

What, then, is good method? This is a matter so widely neglected in our education and yet of such vital importance as to deserve detailed analysis.

PSYCHOLOGICAL REQUIREMENTS FOR CO-OPERATION[*]

(I) *Both husband and wife must have a self-respecting status.*
In order to be self-respecting one needs:
- (A) To be self-governing
    - (1) When a person is not self-governing he feels weak, expects attacks, and so builds unnecessary defenses which compel others to erect counterdefenses
    - (2) A person cannot be self-governing unless and until he himself can make choices which conform to the recognized standards of the group to which he belongs (or consciously repudiates these standards), and unless he has the character to live up to his decisions
    - (3) Nevertheless, we are all subject to emotional pressures. These pressures come from the circumstances around us, and they affect our choices
- (B) Opportunities for self-fulfillment
    - (1) Unused abilities beg to be given outlets. When denied outlets, they make for uneasiness if not unhappiness
    - (2) With opportunity for self-fulfillment a person can lose himself in something bigger than himself because he has found himself
- (C) Recognition as belonging and being wanted
    - (1) The team is the thing, and although one may sometimes be subordinate, there is no requirement to be subservient

(II) *Both husband and wife must have a continuing and healthy understanding of how the desires and the performance of each are*

---

[*] The basic idea for this was worked out in collaboration with the late R. C. Nyman, Personnel Director of Yale University.

affecting and are affected by the performance and desires of the other in every situation as it occurs. This can be accomplished by:

    (A) Open channels of communication by which to recognize each other's legitimate needs, and no refusal to negotiate

        (1) People cannot isolate themselves from one another and still have mutual understanding. But physical nearness is no guarantee of emotional togetherness

    (B) Proper adjustment between one's selfish impulses and the community of needs arising from the partnership

        (1) As far as possible, adjustments should be made in terms of each person's background and aptitudes

        (2) Adjustments usually have to do with methods, not with goals, and it takes intelligence to see what is the best way in the long-run

        (3) Both husband and wife must realize that no matter what happens, something is gained and something is lost

        (4) The greatest single hindrance to co-operation is power in the hands of someone who wants to be domineering

    (C) The sure feeling that each person's legitimate wants will be satisfied without the necessity of fighting for them

        (1) Whenever either partner does not attend to his share in making the home, the other will punish that failure by resistance and non-co-operation.

(III) *Both husband and wife must have confidence in the availability of and the effectiveness of adequate good method in working out acceptable solutions for the inevitable disagreements which arise.* Adequate good method requires:

    (A) A constructive rather than a destructive approach to conflict. Constructive differences result when both sides (most particularly the one with responsibility to make the decision) are trying to discover the truth. This leads to solution together. Destructive differences result when husband and wife are merely trying to defeat each other

(1) Differences of opinion are of value only insofar as they stimulate new thinking. They result in loss of unity when they are allowed to prevent the working out of a shared plan

(2) Where there are unresolved differences of opinion, the situation can go forward only when one of three things happens

(a) both husband and wife make adjustments to equalize the emotional pressures

(b) the stronger personality overpowers the weaker, and thus sows the seeds of a new quarrel, because to the conquered a war is never over

(c) husband and wife are held together by force. This cannot persist for long

(B) Not only an attempt at "solution with" but an intelligent, realistic approach

(1) Husband and wife should each search for an understanding of the true nature of the situation, both as to each other's character and the character of the other people or things involved

(2) Logical thinking tends to forestall emotion because it increases the chances of solution. Every successful solution helps to build a background of experience which says, "This is the way to behave adequately." It is of great importance that both husband and wife have a conviction that disagreements can be worked out together. Such a conviction is empty when it is merely intellectual. It must be *felt* because it has been developed through experiences in solving disagreement. Here, perhaps, is the *most essential ingredient of a happy marriage*

(C) Effective solutions, honestly arrived at

(1) Begin with an analysis of the emotional past

(a) only the baby can start from scratch. Grownups must always begin with where the situation is now. This was inescapably determined by the past

(b) in any situation involving human relations the root of the trouble often occurred a long time before the harm becomes evident

(2) Proceed constructively to talk the situation out, thus producing mutual cross-education

(3) Look for the key log in the jam. Never mind the superficial logs

(4) Worry and emotion are most likely to occur when
    (a) no previous similar case has been met
    (b) a previous similar case was badly handled

(5) Whenever the problem is family-wide, the solution must be family-wide

(D) A minimum of self-assertion

(1) Never work for the mere surface control of force. Work for the fundamental control of respect and confidence

(2) Always remember it is not what a person says that matters as much as what the other individual senses

(3) After the funeral, bury the corpse. When a difference of opinion is settled, that by no means establishes peace unless bygones become bygones.

(IV) *Both husband and wife must accept mutual responsibility for results, and yet recognize clear-cut lines of authority so that their activities do not conflict. This requires:*

(A) A satisfactory division of labor

(1) The manner of the division is less important than that it be divided, with separate responsibilities that are respected co-operatively

(2) To share all decisions is to share all mistakes, which is unfair because of differences in responsibility.

Mutuality of responsibility does not mean identity of responsibility

(B) Efforts that fit together

(1) Using the family budget as an example, husband and wife may have a joint checking account but keep separate stubs, the pay envelope being divided by mutual consent into amounts suitable for the financial responsibilities of each. Then no cross-interference should be attempted except in serious emergencies. The wife should never have to ask for money. If she is a good wife she earns her half of the husband's salary. If she is not, she will surely think she does.

Co-operation is the result of right emotional relationships, produced and nurtured by fulfilling the psychological requirements discussed at length above. If the husband so engrosses himself in making money that he gives little time to helping make a home and treats his wife like a legalized mistress, he should expect his marriage to fail. If a woman keeps her house by slipshod methods, using her husband for a meal ticket, she deserves to be unhappy. Neither person may be to blame for what he is, but each has the inescapable responsibility to straighten himself out.

Assuming responsibility that does not belong to one is not co-operation. Dave wanted to be co-operative but Dave overdid his part. He not only arose early to make the calls on his sales route, he got his own breakfast and breakfast for Bertha too. He waited on her like a devoted slave. Eventually she despised him for contributing to her loss of self-respect, and he resented her for exploiting him.

FACE TROUBLES SQUARELY AND USE GOOD METHOD

Trouble should be faced squarely. It cannot be escaped by ignoring its existence, or by blaming someone else, or by relying on others to correct it, or by pretending that somehow it will solve itself. Stubborn defense of one's self is of no use. Many people grow old, never getting beyond the emotions of childhood because they never took responsibility for their own acts; never discriminated between reality and rationalization.

After a quarrel—better still beforehand if that is possible—when emotions have had a chance to cool, ask the other individual to state his issues. Then try to listen creatively.

Listening creatively can be a powerful thing. It is often much more effective than glib talk because it relaxes the other person's defenses. I am not referring to the impatient listening of someone in an argument, acidly awaiting an opportunity to reassert his own ideas with renewed vigor. I am not referring to the inquisitive listening of the gossip, eager to acquire some new bit of information to be whispered with relish, nor to the critical listening of one who waits to pounce on some misstatement of fact or flaw in logic. I am not talking about the empty listening of someone who merely keeps quiet but hears nothing, nor about the sapless and mechanical listening of someone who wants only to be analytical. All of these create emotional distance. They separate because they threaten.

Creative listening is something else again. With no flaw of impatience, no insincerity, no stupidity, no mere mechanics, no attempt at imposing one's own ideas, it sets about honestly trying to find what the other person is feeling. With quiet comprehending it attempts to discover the real nature of the intellectual soil and the emotional climate which the other requires in order to flourish; it tries to sense his underlying motives, his standards of value, his emotional hungers.

So an individual listens. At first all that comes may be superficial, obvious, even rebellious. But by being skillful enough, sincere enough, patient enough; by asking the right questions in the right way; by avoiding any attempt to impress by being brilliant, or witty, or superior; by encouraging the other person to talk, it is possible to create the conditions in which he can express his real self. At first he may be suspicious, uneasy, self-conscious. But wait. Soon he will demobilize his emotions, cast off his personality armor, crawl out of the dust bowl of despair, and allow his inner self to come alive. He will analyze his own feelings as he pours them out, discriminate between what he has done and what he more honestly would have wanted to do. Through the miracle of someone else listening creatively, he will at last listen to himself.

Perhaps neither person has ever thought the situation through. Try to explain it. Explanation requires analysis, and gives each a chance to feel out what he believes to be right. Talking things over is an important part of arriving at integrated, adaptive be-havior. Indeed, Menninger* believes that the high divorce rate among Anglo-Saxons as compared to Latins is due to the repression of emotional differences instead of the catharsis of differences "freely expressed, and discussed, and readjusted to."

We have to feel out our differences. The important factor in the solution of conflict is the emotional relationship between the parties. Great difficulties are readily solved by men of good will. But words are of no use unless people listen. Otherwise only acts count.

There is strength in quietness. There is great strength in gentle-ness. There is no strength in mere words, unless it be in talking loudly enough to keep from hearing one's own thoughts about one's self. Even when a sentence hits one in the jaw, it is not the words but the feelings behind them that cause him to see stars. Discussion can winnow wisdom out of experience, but again it is not the words that count. We talk about not being able to trust another person's word, whereas the important thing is being able to trust his nature.

"How am I going to change my wife?" Certainly not by talking. Continued discussion may even become an excuse for not doing anything constructive. Indeed, "How am I going to change her?" is probably the wrong question. Possibly something can be done by leading a more loving life one's self. The more fundamental

* K. Menninger, *Love Against Hate* (New York: Harcourt, Brace, 1942), p. 274.

question may be, "What is there in me that makes me want to change her, or to see her change?" Any effort at forcing change surely produces some sort of resistance.

The degree to which we can adjust our behavior in terms of other people is a function of our knowledge of the nature of other people. When knowledge is lacking or mistaken, we may act subjectively and on impulse. The cerebral cortex, or outer layer of the brain, makes man capable of delayed responses. If the individual habitually uses good method in approaching a problem, he will always use this delay to recognize that:

(1) There are many possibilities. The ones that occur to him may not be correct

(2) Failure in human relations always means that behavior did not conform with the reality of the environment or with the inner reality of the personalities involved

(3) Conflicts cannot be solved until the real values of each person are discovered and some workable integration devised

(4) Behavior is not the conflict, but only the attempt to solve it. In examining the nature of behavior, always examine the consequences to which it leads. Inability or unwillingness to discover the basis of the trouble is as harmful as the original problem. There must be insight before there can be foresight

(5) Whenever a person blows up emotionally, he should try to discover what he is afraid of. Does something make him feel guilty and fearful of punishment, or humiliated and fearful of exploitation or ridicule?

Emotional outbursts are often due to fear arising from incomplete understanding of a situation. After a calm appraisal, the anger or humiliation will often disappear. What leads away from a situation may be more important than what leads up to it. Certainly adjustments will not come by uncontrolled evolution. There must be an analysis, a plan, action based on that plan, and then an evaluation of results.

It is not so much the actual events as what is done about them that matters. Get the key emotional facts, not the superficial facts. Then try to interpret them accurately. When the same problem is incorrectly analyzed and wrongly handled over and over again, trouble inevitably results because of the failure to locate it and to correct it in action.

In a troublesome situation where an adjustment needs to be made, but where a quarrel seems to be coming on:

(1) First, recognize that you are now getting angry. Go off by yourself (take a walk, sit in the park, or in an empty church)

(2) Wait until your fantasies have stopped imagining what you would like to do, or say, to the other person

(3) Ask yourself what is going on inside you and inside the other person. What is the disagreement really about? Her changing the furniture around, or a struggle for domination? Most of us perceive only an expurgated edition of what goes on in our minds

(4) Carefully distinguish between your interpretation of the situation and the actual situation. Each of us must realize and accept his lack of complete knowledge in every situation. Any good mind knows that all ideas are relative and only partial truth is possible for anyone. Then why make personal opinions a matter to be defended against attack? How much better to endeavor to see the other person's facts, and how the reality of the situation appears to him? When you say, "The cause of all this trouble is . . ." the statement is incomplete. There are undoubtedly other causes

(5) Seek an explanation for your feelings in your childhood experiences

(6) Figure out the requirements of what you want to do, and never underestimate the difficulties

(7) Formulate several possible solutions, and study these alternatives. What is inevitable? What is possible? What

will you gain? What will you lose? Is the result worth a quarrel? What do you want to do about it? Never overestimate your abilities. Beware of hope pretending to be judgment

(8) Put your plan into action at the right time
(9) Evaluate the results after the issues are clarified and passions have cooled
(10) Think through what further to expect in future as a result of what has happened. Where is this going, and how fast?

If, after all this, a person still wants to fight, then fight, but do it wisely and openly; eye-to-eye and toe-to-toe, not by indirect sniping. Be careful to feel, "I don't think the facts support your conclusion," instead of, "You're a liar." Stick to the point at issue. Raking up all the mistakes of the past can only result from feeling weak, wanting to dominate, and so grasping for any weapon, no matter how inappropriate.

An individual has acted intelligently when he finds good solutions to his problems. As long as he feels equal to his problems, he will have no apprehensions about the future. On the other hand, when he feels inadequate and afraid, he will endeavor to escape in one of several ways:

(1) Unintelligent fighting
(2) Refusal to recognize the facts
(3) Feverish activity
(4) Becoming subservient
(5) Drunkenness, drugs, infidelity
(6) Divorce.

Brooding over a mistake is common and silly. People should not be afraid to make mistakes. There is nothing to fear in failure. Not only is experience largely a matter of learning from mistakes; we do not tell the truth about mistakes. Everybody knows that Babe Ruth made 851 home runs. They should also know that he struck out more times than any other ball player in the history of the game—1330 times. One should not be afraid to fail. Try again.

"In the light of what we know now, this is what I think," should be the attitude. Grow from experience to experience.

Evidence of successfully assimilating a disagreement will include:

(1) Catharsis of the emotional tensions between husband and wife

(2) The home functioning once again in its normal way without domination, enticement, self-pity, repression, defiance, jealousy, or self-deception on the part of either husband or wife

(3) Acceptance by both husband and wife of the elements in the situation which cannot be changed

(4) Reappraisal of the relationship between them and reorientation in the light of the new experience

(5) Increased confidence, and refilling of each individual's emotional security reservoir.

Never try to solve all the troubles at once. One thing at a time is good method. Never concentrate on the negatives to the exclusion of the positives. Nothing is completely bad, exactly as nothing is completely good.

PROBLEM AREAS

There are a number of areas where problems will almost inevitably arise.

In-Laws

Before the marriage, and perhaps even during courtship, the prospective in-laws complicate the situation. In this respect the Montagues and the Capulets were not so different from the Martins and the McCoys.

While he is courting, during the engagement, or even when he goes home for a visit after he is married, Walter's mother may say, "Betty is such a lovely girl, but she's—well, I don't know just how to tell you." Actually what mother wants to do is to destroy Betty.

In-laws, too, have responsibility for the success or failure of a marriage. They should realize that the children's choices are not their choices. They should try to love without interference. They should allow the husband and wife to make and to correct their own mistakes. There was wisdom as well as affection in what my own father-in-law said to me many years ago, "I could give you advice perhaps, but it would not be of any use to you unless you understood it, and if you understood it you wouldn't need it."

In-laws often want to ask personal questions, interfere with finances, help in ways which are not welcomed as helpful, criticize, dictate how the grandchildren are to be raised, and in general treat the husband and wife as though they were still children. They should not be allowed to do any of these things.

Everyone concerned needs to remember that adjustments have to be made all around, and adjustments take time. Father and mother have to adjust to daughter-in-law exactly as she has to adjust to them. And the process is probably more difficult for them than for her because they are older. Parents cannot quickly alter affection to include someone new, particularly someone with different values. They have bestowed effort and hope and money as well as love in bringing up their child. They cannot change their relationship to him at once. The young couple will be aware of their problems with the in-laws. They should also realize that the in-laws have problems with them.

It is particularly important that the husband and wife should start out alone. For any in-law to move in with them is dangerous, because it complicates the relationships and interferes with the successful readjustment of husband and wife to each other. For one thing, an in-law constitutes a reinforcement to one, thus outnumbering the other party to the marriage. Naturally any parent is prejudiced in favor of his own flesh and blood.

Money

No relation between money and happiness has ever been scientifically shown, but because money is so important in our civilization some mutually agreeable financial division is essential. To be fair it must recognize that each earns part of the income, and each has a right to spend some of it as he chooses. If the husband thinks the wife earns nothing while running the home, let him try hiring a housekeeper.

One excellent plan is for the couple to make out and to agree on a budget together, then to divide the responsibilities and the money accordingly. Perhaps he will be answerable for the rent, taxes, insurance premiums, fuel, automobile, savings, and his own clothes. She may pay for food, utilities, entertainment, clothes for herself and the children, doctor, dentist, charities, and household equipment. From time to time, as both income and expenses vary, revisions will be necessary.

Criticism

Sooner or later husband and wife will inevitably make some criticism of each other. Criticism is actually only another person's ideas, but to so many of us "critical" means "hostile" because it did so in fact during our childhood.

Where criticism is used to crush another person in the old struggle for domination, it serves as the missile with which husband and wife take pot shots at each other. People will listen eagerly to a suggestion given in an acceptable way. They resent criticism because it is wrong in method. It hurts the other person and prevents the criticizer from learning how to adjust, for all he is trying to do is to enforce his will. Part of the art of love is to be uncritical, to suspend judgment, to find out first what one is feeling.

When criticized, the issue at stake is not so much the fault under discussion as it is a person's sense of personal worth. Criticism hurts because it touches a sore spot in a hostile way. The pang it causes is in itself the symptom that something is wrong and needs to be corrected. Putting a finger on sound flesh does not hurt. Thus, the quicker a person rushes to self-defense as the result of a criticism, the more he is already subconsciously criticizing himself. An honest facing of himself would have made unnecessary the defense by which he is trying to conceal truth from himself far more than he is trying to convince someone else.

There is a difference between the critical and the questioning or investigatory. The two should not be confused, for the motives behind them are entirely different.

Occasionally something intended as kindness will be interpreted as criticism. With delight and anticipation Arthur came home carrying a dozen shiny new tumblers to replace the jelly glasses which had served so long. He had expected Margaret to be happy over his lavish purchase. Instead she looked at the unwrapped package with tears. "I've tried so hard to be economical and you didn't appreciate it," she sobbed.

Obviously the substitution of tumblers for jelly glasses was not the real trouble. Perhaps Margaret found this a moment in which to improvise a reprisal for something he had done to her days before. Perhaps it was indirectly expressed anger that he had been so long in seeing her need for tumblers. The tendency is to blame Margaret. The truth must be that Arthur was merely reaping what he or someone else had sometime sown.

In considering incidents of this kind the husband ought always to remember that a woman is more likely to say something contrary to what she feels than a man is. She may be cross to him when what she wants is affection. Convention did not allow her to say so as a girl. Now pride will not let her.

Nagging

One of the most deadly dangers in marriage is that chronic criticism which we call nagging. No good ever came of it except an outlet for dishonest emotions. Nagging is a symptom, not a cause. To say, "You simply must stop this infernal nagging," is the equivalent of saying, "You just must cease and desist from having that fever." In both instances the problem is to find the cause of sickness, and to correct it. "He never remembers our anniversary or my birthday," may be because she is selfish or nags all the time, but that answer does not examine why she nags.

It is seldom possible to fix the blame. Does the wife nag because he philanders, or does he philander because she nags? What about the influence of the parents, and of the grandparents, and of generations back to Adam and Eve? Certainly it is not a situation of all praise on one side and all blame on the other, with no in-between degrees. Who is to blame does not matter. The problem is to set the situation right.

Reassurances of Self-Importance

One of the deepest urges in human nature, as conditioned in our civilization, is the desire to feel important. Just as the monkeys try to excite the admiration and astonishment of the other monkeys by swinging further out on a limb, just as Cheops built the pyramid to outdo all pyramids, so on a smaller scale each one of us attempts to impress other people. Actually we may be only trying to impress ourselves. The way to make an impression on people is not to try. It is done by spontaneously being one's natural self without pretense.

To say that a person wants attention because he exaggerates the severity of an injury, talks all the time, wears conspicuous clothes, is not to examine or explain why he does these things. Most of us have subconsciously a poor opinion of ourselves, which is why we fight so hard for self-esteem. The more uncertain we are, deep in our hearts, of our own worth, the more easily our self-esteem is offended, and the more quickly we resort to aggression as a response. We may realize how much we want to be considered superior. We are unaware of how desperately we want to prove to ourselves that we are superior, or how people dislike us for it. We should stop wondering how to impress someone else and discover how we impress ourselves. Never mind what anyone else is saying about us; what is our subconscious saying? Are we dogmatically insisting to someone else that we are right because of our unrecognized conviction that we are already wrong? Need one repeat that any good mind knows all ideas are relative? No one has the complete truth.

Tears may be an indirect way of asking for attention. Self-assertion is almost always the reaction to injured self-esteem. Headaches, high blood pressure, heart attacks and numerous other forms of chronic invalidism are often indirect ways of demanding attention. Punishing one's self with what appears to be hard luck is another such hoax. Women (or men) gossip only because they feel inferior and strive to raise their own self-esteem by pulling someone else down. An adequate, self-respecting person has no interest in gossip.

Husbands and wives need to understand these things, particularly about themselves. A wife who is making a tragic failure of her marriage will say in effect, "See all the important things I do out-side my home: Garden Club, Girl Scouts, Church, Parent-Teacher Association." It makes her feel important and prevents her from facing herself as she really is: a tragic failure as a wife.

When a wife says, "Don't you think Marjorie is beautiful?" her husband should recognize the indirect request for reassurance. His sincere reply should be, "Of course Marjorie is beautiful, but to me she is not as lovely as you." If he does not mean it, the words will be sand in her ears and pennies on her eyes.

"If I don't ask her what she's been doing during the day, she thinks I'm not interested in her any more. If I do ask her, she tells about going over to Mrs. So-and-So's for the Red Cross, or washing the windows, or trying out a new recipe."

Why not? All these things represent accomplishment to her, and are as important as who is ahead in the National League, or how many points the stock market fell, or what the boss said when his secretary eloped.

If the husband lowers his newspaper, like the quivering and rumbling of a drawbridge coming down after a siege, to say, "I've read that last paragraph five times. Now just what is it you want!" the humiliation experienced by his wife will soon ferment into resentment, rebellion, and at last, revenge. The worst treatment a husband can give his wife is to ignore her—or to make her feel he wants to.

Up to the time the first baby is born, the wife often gives her husband a great deal of attention. If then she concentrates on the baby with a concurrent withdrawal of affection from the husband, he is almost sure to take revenge, perhaps through companionship with another woman.

Worry

Worry is concentrating all one's attention on one's self in a situation requiring action but in which one does not know what to do. Worry is partly due to a refusal to face reality, which, in turn, comes from a feeling of helplessness in coping with life. It is expecting—one could almost say anticipating—future trouble without concern over present conditions or future action (in the sense of carefully planned action based on sound judgments).

Instead of wasting energy in useless worry it is far better to make a plan—any plan no matter how impossible. Once some kind of a plan has been made, revise it. Then revise it some more. Eventually something workable may evolve.

Worry should be faced as a form of weakness and fear, and probably a form of self-punishment. Fear is a bully who loves to dominate weak people. But like other cowards, fear will flee once a person shows enough courage to face the situation. The best remedy is a carefully thought out plan, and the best way to overcome worry is to act in accordance with the plan. If a person must worry, he should follow Guy Keeler's suggestion: bow his head at the breakfast table, worry for five minutes, and let that suffice for the rest of the day!

Self-punishment

We punish ourselves more often and more cruelly than we would ever punish anyone else, but alas, we are seldom aware of it, because the emotions take place below the level of consciousness.

There are many ways in which we punish ourselves. Some common ones are:

    (1) Conscious or subconscious feelings of guilt which make us unknowingly want to fail because we have transgressed our moral code. (Sometimes it is not our own code at all,

but one which has been imposed upon us.) As long as the individual suffers the feeling of guilt, he may

(a) feel virtuous because he can see his act as evil—there are delusions of grandeur, even in sin

(b) feel justified in continuing the forbidden but pleasurable activity because "it is being paid for." This only adds more sense of guilt and makes a cancer of conscience

(2) Fear: fear of inferiority, fear of disease, fear of insanity. Fear to the point of being afraid of fear, and blindly becoming one's own enemy through such indirect (because frightened) expressions of emotion as self-pity, stubbornness, jealousy, revenge. I sometimes feel that fear is the most evil force in the world

(3) Insomnia: an inability to sleep, which is really an inability to relax. During the day one can drug his mind with activity, but when he tries to sleep he is alone with his unhappy self

(4) Unnatural fatigue which results from inner conflict because of rage against the self for frustration of the self by the self: as in the case of the man who stays in the wrong job, afraid to find the right one; or the person who does not possess the ability to work out a satisfactory marriage, and lacks the courage to do something constructive about it. The individual who is always tired, is trying to avoid some intolerable situation

(5) Physical impairment through psychosomatic illness or what looks like an accident but was subconsciously deliberate.

A person gets satisfaction out of self-punishment; otherwise he would not do it. We enjoy feeling lonely, unloved, abused. We enjoy wallowing in self-pity because it allows us to put the blame on someone else instead of where it belongs.

And sometimes we punish ourselves in utter stupidity because we think we ought to be able to do what no one can do. Everyone has ignoble thoughts. That is inevitable. Most of us are able to handle them satisfactorily. But to be attacked by a wrongly educated conscience for being human to the point of having occasional evil thoughts is one of the great tragedies of humanity.

People who are punishing themselves are not happy people, and they are completely incapable of making others happy. They understand little about why they crucify themselves, why they hurt most the individuals they love most, why they give their enemies so much power over them. Their inability to understand or to face their real emotions results from fear that their true selves will be discovered *by themselves*. The cocoons of their personalities have been wound so tightly by over-strict parents that they cannot break free. Revolt, even in order to love and to be loved, is almost impossible. This has so profound an effect on emotional adjustments in marriage as to merit a section on the fundamental necessity of being one's real self.

Being One's Real Self

When an individual has used his time and his abilities to achieve ends he was intended to pursue, he is cheerful and stable. To think he has succeeded in doing this is not enough. To fail, or even to believe that he has failed, will bring unhappiness, frustration, and maladjustment. But as long as we live we must go on building—honestly or dishonestly—the unfinished structure of our lives.

A frustrated person will tend to "regress"; that is, to go back to some former, more childish form of behavior in which he feels more secure, not because it *is* safer, but because he *felt* safer during the period of his development when the particular behavior was appropriate. Like a child, he will have emotional responses out of proportion to the actuality of a situation. This gives him relief, but does not solve his problems. Stone walls are not washed away by tears; doors are not opened by angry words; problem situations are not corrected by sulking.

An individual in this condition may realize something is wrong with him. He will not know what is wrong, because he never knows what he is really feeling. Self-realization and personality growth depend on:

(1) Knowing what one feels in order to evaluate accurately what is happening in a conflict between
    (a) value standards
    (b) attempts at creative self-expression
    (c) reality
    Otherwise it is so easy to transfer a repressed hatred of mother into a conscious hatred of wife

(2) Intelligent personality defenses. All of us have personality defense in depth exactly as an army does. We use:
    (a) sense of humor as an exploratory patrol
    (b) superior knowledge at the skirmish line
    (c) a variety of ways of fighting when the battle is joined
    Misuse of one's talents in defense is a prostitution.

(3) Ability to adjust to new situations because they are successfully integrated emotionally. The intellectual level alone is totally inadequate. An unfelt idea is impotent.

For such a person, only self-understanding can lead to self-transformation and self-realization. Solitary self-realization is practically impossible. It is through loving relationships with other people that we achieve happiness. Often our struggle for self-realization defeats itself because of wrong method. Fighting for power over other people can only bring about counterattacks, and the more bitter the fighting the less self-realization is possible. The end result is mutual frustration. Wrong method makes success practically impossible. Wrong intention always does.

But the admonition to stop quarrelling, give up self-pity, cast out fear, is of no use. The individual must first see what he is doing to himself, and what it is costing him in happiness. His behavior does not come primarily from the encompassing forces of his environment any more than an engine gets its thrust from the guides and bearings which hold the connecting rod and the crankshaft. The source of power is inside the cylinder—and the brain.

We all have purposes and intentions of our own; what kind of purpose determines the source of power behind behavior?

Unfortunately it is not just honest purpose that acts. As was pointed out in a previous chapter, again and again we try to feel what we think someone else thinks we ought to feel. This includes the idea that self-control by will power is morality. Actually, it is only self-frustration, without freedom to think out discriminatory judgments. When a person fills his conscious mind with, "I'm determined to make myself do this!" it leaves no room in consciousness for him to see how frightened he is that he cannot do it, or how confused he is over what he ought to do.

Following emotions which have not been thought through to the end is behaving by blind impulse. Emotions, frustrated by thought, vary in intensity from stoicism to suicide. But when the emotions of desire and the discriminating judgments of wisdom are united in agreement, the result is purpose, not will power.

Feeling becomes action unless some other stronger feeling replaces it, either because of changed conditions, or because of thoughtful examination. "Why should I feel like this?" or "What do I really want to do in the light of how I may feel about this in a year?" can change action. Thus, emotion will result in action unless:

    (1) The desire was reconsidered because
        (a) considered unrealistic or unworthy
        (b) fear of the consequences prevented
    (2) Wrong habits have produced unrecognized spurious feelings.

Inner conflicts come from the struggle between honest purpose and externally imposed standards, which has developed into a contradictory set of values and contradictory attitudes toward the self. The intensity of the resulting emotional struggle is evidence of the effort we will exert in order to make ourselves fit the mold selected by our parents, and of our resistance to being anything except our real selves. Such strong influences necessarily result in trouble when they conflict. They are most often handled by:

    (1) Suppression and repression

(2) Avoiding other people

(3) Substituting a glorified image for the truth

(4) Blaming troubles on other people.

There is a vast difference between suppressing a thing by will power until it has been repressed into the subconscious, and understanding which leads to intelligent control. If suppression were only the equivalent of destroying, or even of really forgetting, it might be worth while. Instead, the result is forcing the emotion underground, where it lurks to burst out in some disguised, indirect form, defeating as well as betraying the very mind that repressed it.

When a person is emotionally ill, the key to the problem is always loss of emotional integrity. A husband trying to give up quarreling for the sake of the wife, or so she will like him more, is not acting from honest purpose. The only valid reason is because it makes him happier. To say, "Why do I hate myself?" is not an honest question because it implies either that there is nothing to be hated, or that someone else is exclusively responsible. As Izette de Forest expresses it, the honest question is, "What are the hateful things in me, and what does my heart say I want to do about them?"

For the emotionally ill, the discovery of the truth is a painful process of disillusionment, doubly disagreeable because we all dislike being disillusioned and because no one enjoys thinking of himself as mean or underhanded or vindictive. Yet each one of us must understand the interplay of forces acting in his personality, for their resultant represents our basic attitude toward ourselves, and therefore, toward other people. The man in conflict with himself is the enemy of anyone who opposes him. He will have confidence in himself, and in other people, only when he is emotionally honest with himself.

Sometime during every day each one of us should lay aside all activity and be still. The deep resources of our personalities are not in the whirlwind, nor in the earthquake, nor in the fire, but in the still small voice. What does your heart say? Why did someone else's action get on your nerves? Obviously because you were unwilling to have him do what he was doing. Why? Because it somehow was a threat to your emotional security? Why? Because it indicated that you are not completely the boss in your own home? Why do you want to be? Is there a feeling that, "Because I have failed in this important human relation, therefore I shall fail in every other one"? Is that intelligent?

Unhappiness for any length of time is a symptom of something emotionally wrong in the way life is being lived. Concentrate on it as you would concentrate on an infected appendix or a cancer. When an appendix is about to rupture, of what use is it to point out that the stomach and lungs and heart are perfectly healthy? Peritonitis, caused by the ruptured appendix, threatens the very life of every other organ in the body. Similarly, the cancer of lost emotional integrity can wreck a marriage, and all the children who issue from the marriage. Concentrate on the trouble and correct it.

It is almost literally true that on the adult level no one in all the world can harm you but yourself. Socrates demonstrated that when he drank the hemlock. Did his enemies really harm him? There was a carpenter who demonstrated it too.

The Problem of the Wife Working

Should wives work? In 1920 of all American wives, 9.0 per cent were employed outside the home. In 1930 it was 11.7 per cent. In 1940 it was 16.7 per cent.* This is one of our perplexing modern problems. How will the wife's having a job affect the husband or the children? We do not yet know. Many initial failures are evident, but who can say that the trouble resulted from the wife working? Perhaps working is merely her way of reacting to the real trouble.

The calamity of modern homemaking is not the greater attractiveness of a career. Few men and even fewer women have a career; most of us just work. If a woman teaches college girls we call it a career. If she teaches her own children, we call it housework. If she designs dresses, or provides a balanced diet for the

---

* Figures furnished by U. S. Department of Labor, Women's Bureau, Washington, D. C.

public, is it a career, but only a job if she does it for her own family? A scientifically-run home can be as great a career as an office job. The difficulty is the isolation of the modern home. For a young bride it often amounts to solitary confinement most of the day.

Woman's place is in the home only if she can do work there which is emotionally satisfying to her. Some women simply are not domestic, and a frustrated wife will surely leave her mark on husband and on children. When a woman says, "Housework may be all right, but there's no future in it, and twenty years is too long to work where there's no possibility for promotion," it is the wrong job for her, either because of her aptitudes, her standards of value, or the man she married. No one can be happy in the wrong job. If the family interferes too much with the spontaneous self-expression of its members, the frustration will result in explosion. Because the sociological studies show that happiness is greater in families where the wife does not work outside the home, does not prove that happiness comes as a *result* of her staying at home.

When two young people do not have enough money to live unless the wife also works, the problem is no longer marriage versus a career, but "Shall we marry and both work, or both of us work and stay single?" The answer usually is marry and both work, but beware the long-run results. It is easy for the husband to expect the wife to work, or for both to become accustomed to an income which cannot be maintained should she become pregnant, or for them to postpone too long having children.

The wife may ask, "How will my working affect my husband? My children? How will it affect my husband's pride? If I have an outside job will he also help to run the house?" The answers must be in terms of the particular case. It may not be the fact that she works which makes trouble, but her attitude. What kind of attention a husband or the children get is perhaps even more important than the amount. A little "healthy neglect" is often an excellent thing for children. On the other hand, when both parents continue working, the big money they make is often expensive money as far as the children are concerned. The neglect they suffer is far from healthy.

SUPPORTING RELATIONSHIPS

Some marriages are sheer hell. Most marriages are pretty mediocre. A few marriages are positively delicious. These are usually the ones in which husband and wife were wise enough to establish supporting relationships.

If an inventory at stated intervals is good for business, why is it not equally good for home-making? Surely to go to the dentist twice a year or to have the automobile greased every thousand miles is no more important than a periodic check concerning what goes on in a marriage. The "Goodnight for Husbands and Wives" printed at the front of this volume is one such check. No human relation ever stands still. Either it starves or it grows.

Periodically, particularly in the early days, a husband and wife should stop to ask, "How is our marriage developing, and how fast?" They should endeavor to enlarge existing areas of agreement and to develop new ones. It is useless for the wife to pretend enthusiasm for the husband's fishing trips unless she genuinely feels it, but unless there are many things they can love together they will not love each other long.

It helps if they try:

(1) Never to get tired at the same time. Fatigue is the optimum condition for peevishness because a tired person rebels against additional demands, and to him a disappointment often seems like some intended injury

(2) To make each other laugh at least once a day. The oil of humor has reduced a great deal of emotional friction in this world

(3) To discover each other's needs in emotional vitamins and see that they are fulfilled. Obviously there are limits to the amount of emotional starvation a person can endure.

Understanding is the only thing which keeps us from hurting each other. This does not imply that husbands and wives always feel the same way about the same things. That would be impossible for the inescapable reason that they are different people with differing backgrounds. But gnawing unhappiness is no true part of real marriage.

The value of a sense of humor is that it keeps things in true proportion. Be sure it is real humor (laughing with), not wit (laughing at). Nothing hurts more than an oblique attack under the guise of make-believe fun. Again, it is not the words that matter but the feeling behind them.

"You're going to be upset about this. Go ahead, sputter. Let's see some of your best fussing. Huh! (She imitates.) You can't sputter!" This could be cutting sarcasm or delightful humor that has him in a gale of laughter at himself—all depending upon the emotion behind the words.

A true sense of humor requires confidence in one's self; confidence enough to be able to laugh at one's self without feeling humiliated. For example:

"Won't you drink your coffee, dear?"

"No. I'm mad now."

"Why don't you try to see my side of this?"

"That's just the trouble. I've seen your side and now I'm mad at me."

Healthy self-criticism is indispensable to happiness. Refusing to recognize or to admit one's faults is fatal. But faults cannot be faced unless an individual possesses, or has hope of acquiring, adequate ways of dealing with them in his interpersonal relationships and particularly within himself.

There is great advantage in having established some household jest, at a time when there is no emotional tension, which can be used to blow up emotional blockings. An excellent one is related by McEvoy* concerning the Chinese who, traveling in America, was annoyed by the clerk in the checkroom being unable to locate his suitcase as train time approached.

"Pretty damn seldom where my bag go," exclaimed the Oriental.

* J. P. McEvoy, "That's All I Hope," *Reader's Digest*, January 1947, p. 49.

"She no fly. You no more fit run station than Godsake. That's all I hope!"

As McEvoy suggests, if the husband says, "Pretty damn seldom where my papers go. They no fly," there may be laughter instead of a quarrel. This is capable of innumerable variations. "You no more fit run my kitchen . . . typewriter . . . checkbook . . . furnace . . . automobile . . . radio . . . dishpan . . ." or whatever it may be. The most intelligent people often find outlets in pure nonsense. Have fun together. The thing that makes people lose their zest for life is not having fun any more.

Happiness comes from loving, and the consciousness of being loved. Unhappiness comes from concentration on the past and its mistakes, or the future and its dangers. Both of these have a place in our thinking, but to concentrate on them is mostly futile. Sometimes we have to go through a great deal of unhappiness to find out what real happiness is.

Understand, and therefore effectively eliminate suspicion and resentment. Such emotions can decrease a person's happiness by half, and accomplish nothing. By all means learn to forgive and forget. *Forgiving is not enough. There must also be forgetting. Basically this means coming to understand.* One does not forget until he does understand, for only then does the problem seem solved. Human relations on a workable level are difficult for anyone who harbors grudges. Everyone has personality quirks. Accept it in yourself and expect it in others. We need to realize that nothing is absolutely white or absolutely black. There is only a great variety of shades of grey. This is not a one-value world, or a two-value world, but a many-value world. To grasp that is to make understanding other people more easy. A person is never identically the same person he was yesterday. For one thing he is older.

In working out adjustments, be patient. There is always a time lag. People change slowly. We write a book one word at a time, swim a mile one stroke at a time, eat tons of food in a life-time, bite by bite. We live one day at a time. Yet impatience—because of fear of failure—is such a human characteristic. *Failure, like success, never lasts long unless one works to make it last.*

Professional life cuts across married life. What happened in the office will be reflected at the dinner table, exactly as what happened in the kitchen will be. Fear and insecurity due to war, depression, unemployment, serious illness also make people irritable and impatient.

When a marriage is not going well, it is as important for husband and wife to procure wise advice as it is for labor and management to employ a mediator in a wage dispute. The husband going to a business associate and the wife to her mother or a neighbor will usually only restimulate the trouble. What is needed is competent, professional help sought by husband and wife together.

Finally, it might be well for husbands and wives to remember the fundamental principle of wild animal training: never put the animal into a position where he thinks he has to defend himself against you. It is not just the animal and the trainer reacting on each other. The situation always is the animal, plus how the trainer has made him feel, reacting to the trainer, plus how the animal has made him feel.

In Conclusion

Quality is never an accident. It is the result of discriminating judgments brought to skillful execution through sincere effort. Quality is the final result of intelligent analysis and less romance before marriage, resulting in less fault-finding and more affection after marriage. Marriage is serving as well as being served, loving as well as being loved, blessing as well as being blessed. It is a relationship of giving as well as of getting. It raises religious, social, economic, emotional, and sexual problems which should be faced squarely without prudery, grossness, fear, or evasion.

It takes honest effort to make a success of marriage. Each partner must be able to meet both triumph and disaster without being emotionally upset or losing his inner consistency. Neither can be emotionally dependent upon the other. Together they face and readjust to frustration, disappointment, change, good fortune—in short, to whatever life brings, and do it in a way which never sacrifices integrity, but allows each to be and to express his spontaneous self in an intellectual soil and an emotional climate far superior to that he could create alone. Many people say this requires a high order of persuasion, showing the other person the benefits which will result for him if he follows the procedure suggested. Their argument is that the only way to influence anyone is through what he wants; that this is even true of force, for it too operates on what is wanted in the situation as it exists.

A far more fundamental approach is to recognize that the only legitimate compulsion is the compulsion of unalterable fact. Any other compulsion, be it iron-fisted or velvet-gloved, begets resentment and resistance. It is far better to analyze the situation together as two physicians diagnose a case. Then prescribe a sound course of action, and implement what is to be done. For husband or wife merely to persuade acceptably is comparable to the doctor who has no more competence to recommend him than a pleasing bedside manner. They must diagnose accurately and follow a prescription which brings happiness to each because it gives significance and fulfillment to their life together.

Let them talk out their differences frankly, keeping their quarrels private. Let them continuously remind themselves of the human tendency to try to transfer blame onto someone else. Let them help each other to save face in a disagreement. Above all, let them never forget that they are going to go on living together after a quarrel is over. One good way to get a quarrel over is for whoever calms down first to say, "I think we've been going at this unreasonably. Now, can't we begin all over at the beginning? Let's try again." The sincere manifestation of loving behavior will almost always stop a quarrel.

We cannot expect always to be able to satisfy each other's needs. But if they are to be happy in their emotional adjustments, neither husband nor wife can ever forget that when we are emotionally tangled up—and all of us are at times—we demand that other people understand us without our explaining anything to them. As we said before, the art of love is patience.

12

Parents and Children

THE SUPERLATIVE SATISFACTION

THE achievement of a deep and abiding love between a husband and wife normally results in the growing desire to share, as well as to perpetuate, their happiness. The natural way to do this is by raising a family of happy, intelligent, healthy, emotionally mature children. The result is probably life's superlative satisfaction.

UNWANTED CHILDREN

But for the first time in history, children are no longer universally looked upon as the ultimate fulfillment of marriage. Most of us still believe that they are the strongest emotional link between husband and wife. A few of us act as though the bearing and raising of children were a task for peasant women or milch cows, with worthwhile feminine careers only to be found in the arts, business, or the unrecognized concubinage of a wife who endeavors to escape everything except pleasure. Pleasure and happiness are not the same. Pleasure is only diversion.

Nevertheless, a family with no children is much to be preferred over one having unwanted children. When a father or mother does not want a child, one of two things happens: either the child is rejected by loading him with feelings of humiliation, inferiority, helplessness, stupidity, unattractiveness, guilt, fear; or the parent becomes oversolicitous, hating the child with all his "love." The falseness of such affection will betray itself in a series of inconsistencies, such as exaggerated statements of affection, followed by acts like forgetting the little one's birthday. *Children are not spoiled by too much love; they are spoiled by false love.*

An unloved child has an urgent need for reassurance, and a compulsive need for revenge upon a world which neglected him because it did not want him. His life is likely to become a perpetual rebellion against what happened to him in childhood. His revenge can find many outlets: tyranny over his playmates, business associates, wife, children; intolerance of ideas other than his own; sadistic delight in bringing about wars—domestic, industrial, or international; behavior motivated by that fear of other people which results in selfishness. As Ernest M. Ligon has somewhere said, it is possible that the most costly conflicts in society are not the wars among nations but the conflicts between parents and their children.

On the other hand, a child who has been truly cherished, who has known peace and happiness in his home surroundings, will grow up to work for similar conditions in every situation he experiences.

The family is the new baby's whole world. His parents are his first gods and his first devils. He has no alternative but to accept their creative or destructive conduct, and to adapt himself to it as though this were the only pattern of behavior for all the world. He interacts with his parents because he is part of his parents, physically, emotionally, and environmentally.

Thus does the chain go from generation to generation.

ADJUSTMENTS

Parenthood always requires adjustments. Husband and wife are no longer children with parents; they have now progressed all the way to being parents with children. The husband-wife relationship has now come full circle to the father-mother relationship. This is entirely new. Children:

(1) Hold the parents together because they are a common responsibility and a common interest

(2) Sometimes—particularly when they are small—separate the parents. The old freedom of going out together may be gone; a new source of disagreement has been introduced, such as, "Which doctor?" "What school?" The husband may become jealous of attention the wife gives to the baby. The wife may use the child to replace the husband in her affections. When a mother gives affection to the children which the father should receive, he often nurses a grudge and becomes over-severe with the children. Parents should never allow their progeny to come between them. Even to the children, the emotional unity of the parents is as important as the fulfillment of physical needs

(3) Bring the deepest satisfactions, not only as the objective reality of creative love, not only as a claim to racial immortality, but as a rewarding source of comfort and companionship.

Profound physiological and psychological changes take place in a woman while she is pregnant. The adjustments demanded of the wife are usually greater than those required of the husband. The devoted husband will sense this and share insofar as possible the burden of uncertainties, discomforts, and fear as well as the moments of ecstasy. Some men are reluctant to be seen publicly with a wife during the last months of her pregnancy. What strange psychological twist changes the honest delicacy of an expectant mother carrying on her usual activities into something unwholesome and grotesque? Is the crispy sleekness of a bride as significant and marvelous as the promise of a new life?

Husband and wife will need to plan and to provide together for the welcome of their baby: the layette, a crib, toilet articles, arrangements for bathing, and a carriage, among other things.

As the pregnancy progresses the mother will be more and more conscious that she is the instrument through which a new personality it being born. Her relation to the baby is probably the strongest bond on earth, for the little one is flesh of her own flesh, blood of her own blood, as well as part of her spirit too. It is easy to love a baby. When the child begins to become self-assertive it is not so easy.

Wise parents will make a diligent study of the best available material on the rearing of children. This means fathers as well as mothers. It is a tragic commentary on our educational system that we train young men in bookkeeping, or romance languages, or bridge design, or quantum mechanics, or how to raise a hog, but not in how to be a good father. There are courses on how to be a good mother, but is responsibility for the happiness of the home and the rearing of the children exclusively the mother's? Father is equally accountable and equally necessary. He will find equal satisfaction in fulfilling his responsibility. The primary reason for being a male is to be a father, giving the children companionship, understanding, sympathy, and counsel as well as life. Sending Junior off to summer camp, leaving him to the comic strips, paying his bills, scolding him, is no substitute for doing things *with* him.

A real father will clean the cellar, rake the leaves, go for a walk, read a book, wash the dishes with his children, showing them as well as telling them that it is much more fun doing things together as a family than doing them alone.

A few days before these words were written, the plant manager of a factory for which I am a consultant arrived at his office with laggard step and tired eye. The previous day his wife and their fifth baby had come home from the hospital. This was, for the child, a new and probably frightening transition. It was, for the father, an opportunity to which he gave adequate response by making every effort to assure the child of its welcome, even though this involved arising several times in the night, including occasions when all the baby wanted was a little reassuring sociability.

A child needs a sense of "belongingness" from the moment of his birth.

We know that a sudden physical discontinuity—like a loud noise, a bright flash of light, or loss of stability—is frightening to a baby. A sudden emotional discontinuity must be just as frightening. This can be brought about by a change in who cares for the baby, by an angry parent, or even by an outburst of anger within the baby himself. If this is true, the faster the reaction the greater the fear.

What a frightening experience birth must be to the baby. Here is a sudden change brought about suddenly (as well as with violence). He may be alarmed and frustrated again when he is weaned. Baby cannot prepare for the change by saying to himself, "Mother starts to wean me next Tuesday, damn it!" How important that the process take place gradually through the progressive introduction of new ways of nourishment beside the nursing. Otherwise, what the baby knows is true is no longer true, and his understanding of the environment is shattered.

We emphasize the need for making a good first impression on a new friend, at a new job, with a new employee. How about a new baby? Has a baby less rights than an adult? Initial impacts will influence him for life. His attitudes toward people are deeply set by age two. Here is the time when he most needs to dare to love because he feels securely loved himself. Too often little children are loved only to the extent that they satisfy their parents. They should be loved for themselves alone . . . and *loved unconditionally*.

In every parent should be implanted a profound respect for human beings as human beings. This must be rooted in experience, clearly perceived, which teaches that respect for others builds love, whereas contempt for them nurtures hate. The baby is no more a chattel possession of its parents than a wife is the property of her husband. Children belong to life itself—that mysterious torch which never dies, but has been handed on from generation to generation for millions of years. The parents are only the instruments through which the miracle takes place. Each child is an end in himself, a personality to be nourished and allowed to grow; not a possession to be shaped or molded according to the whim or the emotional need of the parent. It is an unforgivable sin to smother the growth of another personality. "True motherhood (and fatherhood) is denied to those who fail to recognize that the child's own developing personality is the only acceptable goal of intelligent parenthood."*

Types of Homes

The task of growing up can be one of the most difficult things a person ever does. It can also be one of the most delightful. Some children experience criticism, punishment, broken promises, unrealized hopes, interference with self-development, the need to accept everything the parents believe or else to feel guilty.

Such children resort to defiance, disobedience, and the destruction of property as a defense against the bitter disappointment of so hostile an environment. Or they are broken by it, becoming emotionally damaged children who are often mistaken for model children merely because they are subservient children.** In either case, the child abandons his emotional integrity. He must do so, unless he runs away, for he has discovered that in order to survive he must allow himself to be forced into some mold of the parents' choosing. He cannot now learn from his own mistakes, because all his effort is concentrated on defending himself. (See the story about Bobby beginning on page 98.)

Other children experience encouragement, tolerance, carefully fulfilled promises, anticipations that often come true, the oppor-

* A. G. Truxal, and F. E. Merrill; *The Family in American Culture* (New York: Prentice-Hall, 1947), p. 554.

** Scientific observations show that the sullen or deeply inhibited child is more seriously maladjusted than the openly aggressive child. In each case the harm was done by trying to compel the child to be submissive. The Child's behavior should be allowed to remain appropriate for his age, mental and emotional as well as physical, and some children develop more slowly than others. Whereas the neighbor may say of the deeply inhibited child, "How well behaved Johnny is!" the psychologist would add, "—and receiving such tragic preparation for living." Anyone who thinks this means that the child should be allowed to do as he pleases, should reread page 99.

tunity to be and to express their spontaneous selves, parental respect for their ambitions and their standards of value. Such children become happy, co-operative adolescents and adults because they have been encouraged in an honest, emotional growth. They have not been preached at or pushed into a mold. They have been taught to think through their own emotions for themselves. Consequently, there is no attempt to keep from seeing the disagreeable things about themselves which make trouble for themselves. They have emotional health because their emotions are real, not spurious and counterfeit. To such children the whole process of growing up is a natural training in true humility, for the more they understand the more free they become of pride, self-assertiveness, or outward show.

The duty of any parent, as all animals know instinctively, is to make himself unnecessary to the well-being of the child as fast as possible at the child's rate of speed. On the human level this does not destroy love; this creates love because it sets the child free. It is a mistake to think that freedom consists of being out from under the domination of someone else. That is, of course, one aspect of freedom, but an even more fundamental one is being willing and able to take full responsibility for one's self. Freedom is always limited by the extent to which an individual can fulfill his own needs through effective action.

The problems which parents have in bringing up children are always a reflection of their own personal problems. The inadequate parent may be oversevere, demanding perfection of the child as a compensation for the inability to accept his own imperfections. The emotionally dishonest parent will have emotionally dishonest children. But as with artillerymen, there will be no neurological effect on the parent because he does not see the consequences of his acts. The consequences are sometimes years and years away. If he could realize what he has done, as the infantryman who has experienced bayonet fighting does, he would be as terribly upset. The result might be a colossal increase in human happiness, because to correct a source of trouble it must first be perceived.

What is the matter with children? Parents, of course. But it is not fair to stop there. What is the matter with parents? Grandparents. And so on back to Adam and Eve. Trying to place the blame achieves nothing. Causes go too far back, and their tentacles spread out in too many directions. The need is rather for parents to discover and to understand their own motives. Ends cannot be separated from means, for means produce ends of their own.

In many instances parents are seeking revenge on grandparents by releasing against the children the consequences of what the parents suffered from the grandparents. Tyranny engenders the desire to be a tyrant, and for most of us the only time when we can be dictatorial without fear of retaliation is when our children are small. Subconscious hatred of parents becomes subconscious tyranny over children. Anthropologists like Abram Kardiner* have reported that in primitive societies parents are affectionate where they were loved as children, and indifferent where they were unloved in childhood.

Parents cannot be real parents until they have felt out their mistakes, and felt out how to set the situation right. Just blaming parents achieves nothing. Merely to point out what the child needs achieves little. It confers no capacity to distinguish real emotion from insincerity. It gives the parent no feeling—as distinct from mere intellectual acceptance—of the fact that one emotionally unhealthy thing may ruin many healthy ones. Parents cannot be real parents until they recognize that what they do to and with their children is a result of *what they feel toward the child at the moment of action.* The only way to choose the right moments to act is to know what one is really feeling.

Most of us understand our emotions so superficially. Father scolds Junior for not taking adequate care of little sister, when the reason Junior resents sister may be that father loves her more. Junior has no opportunity to appraise the rightness of his feelings. He is forced, protesting fitfully, into a sense of guilt and shame. He flees to the shelter of his room, with a look in his eye akin to

* A. Kardiner, *The Psychological Frontiers of Society* (New York: Columbia University Press, 1945).

that of a kicking mule. Father considers this flight a sign of the triumph of severity. Then when Junior lies, steals, and fights in an attempt to throw the emotional infection out of his system, father either says, "He gets it from his mother's side of the family," or quoting the Bible in cold sacrilege, he says, "Lord, my son is at fault. Am I my brother's keeper?"

All the scientific studies of child development lead to the conclusion that the first five or six years of a person's life are the most important for the formation of his character, his attitudes toward other people, his behavior techniques, his fears, his goals, his standards, or his ways of feeling secure. What then, are the basic types of home environment which are possible, and what are the probable consequences of each?

TYRANNY

As was pointed out in Chapter 2, the only way to make a complicated thing like human relations seem simple is to employ domination. Thus comes about the autocracy of the elders in those homes where authority is mistaken for knowledge; power on the part of the parents, and fear on the part of the children in a household divided into those who can order and those who must obey.

With a mixture of ignorance, prejudice, and self-righteousness covering subconscious feelings of weakness, such parents seek methods by which to control their children, rather than wisdom by which to understand them. They want only to manipulate power more effectively, not realizing that the exercise of power over another person is always self-defeating because it produces some sort of defense creating a vicious circle which grows at last into actual conflict.

These are the parents who continually check up on their children, never really trusting them; who expect immediate and unquestioning acceptance of orders; who will take advantage of ignorance or weakness; who destroy self-respect; who lie about facts; and yet who consider themselves right about everything. The result is submission in early childhood, leading in later life to rebellion, open hatred, and sometimes the refusal to take responsibility or to use the aptitudes one was born with—all this as the result of a destitute and unloved childhood. In such a household there can be no co-operation because there is no confidence. There will be fighting among the children, no sense of security, no possibility of a child sensing or becoming his real self. The more intelligent the child, the more he will be damaged; the more inner strength he possesses, the more he will fight back.

Carol was compelled to eat whatever food was one her plate, father being the sole judge as to both amount and variety. One day after complying with an order to devour a generous portion of turnip, which she particularly disliked, Carol regurgitated in a long, besmearing arc across the corner of the dining table into her father's lap. He spanked her, saying, "This is for your own good." Probably no sentence is capable of being more emotionally dishonest, with the possible exception of "I love you."

Where the child has exceptional inner strength, such tyranny may result in complete estrangement. At the public telephone in the corridor of a college dormitory, another tragic story was told in a short, one-sided conversation. "Hello. Yes, this is Mr.—. Long distance? Oh, hello, mother. What? He dropped dead this morning. The funeral Thursday. No, mother, I'm not coming. No, mother! As far as I am concerned my father died fifteen years ago when he forced me to . . . I tell you, I'm not coming."

How terrible, you say, for him to desert his mother in her hour of need. Where was she in the hour of his little boy need?

Coerced behavior is always a threat to a child. At first he will fight with all his available resources. But unless the parent has the sense to see the method is wrong, or the child is not yet ready to learn the matter in hand, the child will usually be overpowered. After a few repetitions he will have learned three things:

(1) Those I am dependent on can dominate me and they do not love me as I need to be loved

(2) I cannot love in an unloving environment

(3) I get hurt if I resist.

What he cannot cope with, he tries to avoid, especially if it is severe punishment. Suppose mother wants her four-year-old to come into the house. He wants to stay out and play. Here is an interpersonal conflict. An emotionally mature mother will handle it in accordance with the various perceptions of value found in the table on page 302. Otherwise she may carry him in by bodily force when he refuses. The child now feels an increasing inconsistency between his environment and his values. Next time perhaps he receives a severe spanking. After that his attitude is, "If I give in you will not threaten me more than I can bear. Therefore, I still have some control here." The spanking is a more severe conflict than whether mother will allow him to go on with his play. Frustrated and angry he comes when she calls, but he wants revenge. Sooner or later he will have it.

If he has a strong personality he will begin to make compulsive demands on others. His will be a frightened intolerance of anyone who questions his exteriorly imposed convictions. He is subconsciously saying, "If everybody I rub elbows with thinks and does as I do, I'll never have to recognize I don't believe all this. I'm safe from myself as long as no comparisons are forced on me. But something in me rebels. My parents talk love, but they don't live lovingly."

The children of domineering parents become frightened people who go through life as though everyone were either *for* them, or *against* them; never *with* them. To be sure they rebel, but we are always frightened when we rebel. The rebel wants to beat down his antagonist; the coward gives in but wants to destroy; the cooperator seeks neither to conquer not to appease, but listens to the arguments of the other side in a united effort to find the truth.

Where there is no respect for a child's personality what can he do but give in or become defiant? The compulsive need to fight comes from feeling unloved, and from the fear that only by fighting can one preserve his personality from being trapped and destroyed. The defiant child:

(1) Is terrified by the power of his parents, and almost lit-

erally would like to be rid of the threat to his emotional security by killing them

(2) Figuratively accomplishes the riddance by ignoring their wishes and acting as though, for him, the parents do not exist

(3) Hides his real feelings, even from himself, by some rationalization

(4) Feels subconsciously guilty because of his feelings, and is subconsciously frightened at what would happen if his feelings were discovered

(5) Soon completes the personality destruction by subconsciously punishing himself for his murderous thoughts by making his interpersonal relations fail because of defiant behavior in situations where co-operation would have succeeded. A frightened person does many foolish things which only make matters worse.

Every parent should continuously ask himself, "What kind of person am I making of my child?" When a father realizes that defiance is simply one way of expressing fear, he will not punish. Fear never produces good results. More punishment will only turn a rebellious child into a deceptive chid. So will forcing the child into a parentally-chosen mold.

Insisting that the child go to bed at an unreasonably early hour —as though if left alone* he would not know what was right for him—will bring about evasive action. A frequent form of deceptive rebellion is reading by flashlight under the bed clothes. This is damaging to the eyes, to the emotions, and to the parent-child relationship.

A four-year-old, given too large a serving and subsequently told that he must finish his left-over breakfast oatmeal before he can

---

* Obviously, to suddenly remove restraint from a dominated child will produce an explosion of rebellion. He will be slow in learning discriminating judgments of his own because his emotional growth has been retarded, if not warped. Most of the unwise behavior of college students, living away from home for the first time, can be explained in this way.

have any dinner,* is justified in slyly giving it to the dog, and then piously claiming that he ate it all by himself like a good boy. No one lies until he fears personal suffering from telling the truth. The necessity for the lie is more tragic than the lie itself.

Children are made to feel that they must be deceptive for self-protection, exactly as an adult population feels this when invaded by a hostile army. Think of the great relief with which a conquered people witness the withdrawal of an enemy. This is not to say that they want anarchy. Nor do children. Without individual, personal independence developed from childhood on, a strong nation is impossible. The alternative is a nation of unthinking followers who soon become exploited as the pawns of clever and usually evil men. History offers many examples. The ability to make discriminating judgments is always directly proportional to one's freedom from domination.

What is important to the child is the right to be his spontaneous self at all times. This includes the right to express anger against his parents, to feel safe while expressing it, and to be loved right through the anger and the subsequent analysis of its results. It is natural for children to experience anger against their parents because it is inevitable that parents frustrate them. Emotionally immature fathers and mothers consider the attack of a child as impertinent, disrespectful, and impudent. Tyrannical parents fight back instead of trying to understand themselves, or to help the child to think through his behavior. All adults are superior in power to a child. Because he has learned to be afraid of that power, the child holds in his anger, to take it out later on some innocent bystander like baby sister or the cat.

Children should not be forced to stop fighting unless serious bodily harm is involved. Let them work it through. Then, when the emotions have burned out, help them to analyze the results of their behavior by asking honest questions. In the process of ques-

---

* Where the child has determined the amount of the serving there is some reason for saying, "You took it, Honey. Now you must eat it, because it is wrong to waste food."

tioning, it is appropriate to remember once more that the fundamental principle of wild animal training is never to put the
animal into a position where he thinks he has to defend himself
against you. It is difficult for a child to be angry, feel safe, examine
the cause of his anger, and know that he is loved—all at the same
time.

This feeling cannot be created by an emotionally immature
parent. Such an individual will want action in punishment or
argument which he hopes will somehow give him power over the
child. He will be seeking mechanisms of conquest, not emotions
of co-operation, little realizing how much he strives for power,
nor how little he actually wants it. In common with all mankind,
what he really seeks is self-fulfillment.

Perhaps father has asked Junior to cut the grass. On returning
from the office he finds Junior on the front porch reading, the
grass untouched. If he is emotionally immature, he may grumble
to his wife about the boy, put on his old clothes, and begin to
mow the grass himself. When Junior says, "Dad, did you . . ."
he says, "Go into the house! I don't want to talk to you!" This
is an attempt to humiliate Junior.

Or father may storm up the front walk in a thundercloud of
wrath, bellowing, "What the Sam Hill is the matter! I thought
I asked you to mow that lawn!" What this means is, "I (God)
told you (an insignificant worm) to mow that lawn!!!"

Neither of these approaches recognizes that there may be valid
reasons why Junior could not mow the lawn. An emotionally
mature parent will not consider failure to cut the grass as a threat
to his personality, and will not form an opinion until he has the
facts. There is no reason to scold Junior until it is established that
he has been intentionally remiss. It is the significance of the act
that matters, not the act itself. Even then, father will do nothing to threaten the boy's self-respect, but will encourage him to
state his case in man-to-man fashion, and will treat him as he
would treat an adult for whom he had respect. Treating the boy
as though he were a miscreant, will cause him to retreat into him-

self with smouldering resentment. Between parents and children, upset emotions are a contagious disease.

What a shame that emotionally mature parents do not have a monopoly on the bringing up of children! But we have already come a long way. Only three hundred years ago an unruly child was legally punishable in Massachusetts by death.* The idea that children must honor their parents, regardless of whether respect is deserved or not, has done great damage to the human race.

SUGAR-COATED DOMINATION

Probably the most demoralizing atmosphere is to be found in a home run by alternate threats and bribes: threats to make the children completely dependent, and bribes to buy affection with calculated rewards. Such parents consider themselves as kind, superior individuals, who have a happy family because they know all the answers.

Actually there is only a false feeling of happiness, a false co-operation, a false security; all as a sort of sugar-coating over the subconscious hatred. The children are ambivalent toward the parents, feeling that they ought to be grateful for all the gifts, and not knowing why they feel uneasy, self-conscious, entangled. The parent thinks the child ungrateful, and cannot understand the ingratitude.

Sometimes the child perceives more clearly than the parent. Leon was promised a trip to New York if he made the honor roll at school. At first there were frantic efforts, both direct and indirect, on Leon's part to bribe the teacher. When it became apparent that the honor roll was not within his grasp, mother said, "I'll still take you to New York if you have only one C on your report card." To his playmates Leon said, "Aw, that's only a threat. She'll take me anyway."

The sugar-coating on this particular pill is greater than the core of domination, but the result can still be demoralizing, particularly

* W. Goodsell, *A History of Marriage and the Family* (New York: Macmillan, 1934), p. 367.

if the child does not perceive the relationship between the sugar and the trap which it is baiting. Enticement seldom allows a person to recognize what he is really feeling. Coupled with the threat of domination, it almost never does.

When a child says, "Mother, what can I do?" neither parent nor offspring realizes what is happening between them. "Why don't you play with your blocks?" "I don't want to." "What about coloring the pictures you got for Christmas?" "I don't want to." "Perhaps you'd like to go over to Johnny's house?" "I don't want to."

This is a conversation which bespeaks frustration after frustration on the part of the child. "What can I do?" really means, "What am I allowed to do?" and, "I don't want to," is the disguised rebellion of a six-year-old's subconscious saying, "Now it's my turn to say no to you!"

Many a mother thinks it is love which leads her to make decisions for her children. "What shall I wear today, mama?" is occasionally proper. Habitually asked, it is demoralizing because it teaches the child to be dependent. The day mother says, "You decide," will prove alarming to the child. Meanwhile, mother does not recognize her desire to dominate, and the child is unaware of the fear which underlies his attempt to do and to say the things he believes will bring the approval of his elders.

Faced with undisguised tyranny, an individual can correctly appraise a situation. With sugar-coated domination he experiences conflicting feelings. As a result, it is almost impossible to achieve the internal consistency which comes from knowing what one is truly feeling. What we allow ourselves to feel consciously is inextricably bound up in the standards of conduct which were imposed on us as children. In the sugar-coated household, children learn not only to be ashamed of fighting for the right to be their real selves, but to be afraid to be their real selves. They acquire a stylized pattern which they think will win the approval of the significant individuals in their environment, struggling in the end to become an imaginative thinker, a smart business man, an impeccable housekeeper, a devoted wife, instead of just being themselves.

Where there is real respect for life and for the sacredness of personality, pressures are not exerted on children to force them into some predetermined mold. Love provides the conditions in which the child can grow according to his own nature.

Among other things, this will include a certain amount of physical danger. At an early age he will climb to the uppermost branches of a tall tree. He will want to sleep in the woods with his chum overnight. He will ski on slopes that strain his skill; shout in sheer zest at the challenge of keeping a canoe upright in rough water; play in streets where he must dodge automobile traffic; collect all manner of junk from bugs to bottle tops; attempt felling a tree with a sharp axe, despite both tree and axe being a hazard worth the respect of an experienced woodsman; steal rides on the tailboard of a truck; see how far he can walk atop a fence without falling off. All of these involve risks and some of them will be dangerous. But life itself is a hazard! To overprotect the child from hazard is to unfit him for living. He needs to be allowed to undertake whatever risk he has the competence to face, and as a result, to learn much about cause and effect, how to handle the chill wave of fear, and the absolute inviolability of natural law.

This is not to be confused, as many people mistakenly confuse it, with neglect.

NEGLECT

There are parents who think they are modern because they allow their children to do as they please without guidance. This is a far cry from giving the child the intellectual soil and the emotional climate in which he can be and express his spontaneous self.

Where parents busy themselves with outside activities to the exclusion of the home, there is no family leadership, no family goal, no family co-operation; just each going his own way in a situation where things left to themselves lead to disorganization and confusion. Nobody knows quite what to expect because there is no unity, no security, no achievement as a group.

There is usually petty quarreling among the children showing how rebellious, how careless, and how irresponsible children become without leadership. It is co-operative interaction between the members of a family which makes a happy home; the constant sharing of ideas, hopes, disappointments, anticipations, concerning things which range from the trifling to the sacred. Otherwise how can personalities develop? Personality is not an individual thing, it is an interpersonal thing. Every one of us is always a slightly different, and sometimes a vastly different person in the presence of different people because of the diversity of emotional reaction we have toward each other. We hate and fear being made subservient by someone else, but we gladly follow leadership based on superior knowledge and acceptable method.

COMPETENT LEADERSHIP

Where parents have a sound knowledge of human emotions and a sincere desire to achieve solution with others instead of to achieve power over others, the result is a happy home. Children will be kept understanding why. "Fire burns" is a real reason. "Father says" is not a reason; it is an order. Sincere attention will continuously be given to what the children are thinking and feeling. The prerequisites for genuine co-operation (see page 322) will be met because when parents love children they live again in their children, and so feel what the children are feeling.

How can a three-year-old participate in mutual responsibility for the happiness of a home? His laughter bestows something on the household no one else can duplicate. Given the opportunity, he will delight in contributing his share toward maintaining the happiness of a new baby, covering him up when necessary, or calling mother's attention to the baby's needs. Even the new baby has a contribution to make to the home. Parents should find it and provide for it, realizing that the contribution will find expression in different ways as the child grows.

Under competent leadership there is freedom to think and to grow; not the destructive restriction of tyranny or domination, nor the "nobody cares" atmosphere of neglect. Love cannot flourish where there is rigidity in holding to one's own ideas. This is fear, not growth. Love cannot flourish where there is dependence upon or blind following of another's ideas. This is weakness, not growth. Love can flourish only where there is an active, responsive interplay of feeling and behavior.

Under competent leadership there will be a genuine feeling of belonging and being wanted; not the subserviency demanded by a household autocrat, nor the absence of esprit de corps where leadership is lacking. There will be real emotional security; not an existence dependent upon the whim of a powerful parent, nor the gnawing insecurity of disorganization.

Such a family will work together, not just talk about it. Each child will understand his relationship to the rest of the family, and the relationship will change as he matures. He will perceive how what he wants and what he does affects and is in turn affected by what the others do and what they want. There will be confidence in each other, which is far more than merely being emotionally honest with each other. There will be no fear of misunderstanding or of being misunderstood for long, because *every member of the family will honestly believe in his own ability to meet and adequately to cope with his interpersonal relationships.* The child will see at work in his parents, the healing and the hope of trying to find the best answer together. The parents will be careful not to use their position, their superior knowledge, or their religious beliefs as the magic and the incantation for having power over the children. On the contrary, each child will be respected as a thinking, feeling, responsible human being of individual personal worth.

Under no circumstances will the child be placed under the authority of more than one parent at a time.

Each child will have a play-place of his own to be kept as he wants to keep it. If the rest of the household is neat, he will learn neatness easily enough when the time comes that he is ready to do it. The rest of the family will have respect for his desires regarding that place, which in the ideal situation will also allow him privacy in his own right if and when he wishes it. Should a ten-year-old be expected to have thirty-year-old ideas of organization and order? If he has a collection of rocks on a shelf and wants them left alone, not even a New England housewife will disturb them, no matter how badly she thinks the shelf needs dusting. To do so is an attack on his personality.

As the attitude of a child toward his parents changes with the years, so also the behavior of the parents toward the child will change. The infant needs cherishing; the adolescent needs growing freedom with adequate security; the adult needs independence.

There will be moments of impatience and anger. The person who has only creative emotions and no destructive ones does not exist. Parents make mistakes, but it is amazing how easily a child will absorb these mistakes without much damage when he is loved.

Under competent leadership the general atmosphere will consequently be one of family affection, family enthusiasm, co-operative action, children developing into their real selves because the parents provide what the children really need.

What the Child Needs*

(I) A feeling of security:

    (A) Knowing that his physical needs will be attended to with prompt regularity and adequate sufficiency

    (B) Knowing that he is loved, and being loved can obtain and rely upon the help or experience of his parents whenever legitimate need arises, either mentally or emotionally. He needs sincere affection based on a respect for his personality, as much as he needs physical care

    (C) Knowing that he has the opportunity to learn to

---

* This outline was stimulated by a personal letter from Dr. Vannevar Bush of the Carnegie Institution.

practice, and to perfect successful interpersonal relationships. When he has the ability to meet unpredictable social situations without fear of people —including tyrannical people—he will not endeavor to force others into patterns which make him feel safe. He can then be his real self and allow others to be themselves. Success in life depends principally on being able to meet and to cope with people in a friendly way

(II) An opportunity for self-expression:

(A) An area (playroom, cellar, back yard), and a field (stamp collecting, paper dolls, model airplanes) in which he can achieve an outlet for his developing skills without interference. He should be allowed to form his own judgments, and except in rare cases should not be protected from the consequences of his own acts. "See, I did it all by myself," is among the important developmental responses of a little child

(B) As time goes by, both the area and the field should widen and deepen. The basis of self-development and self-respect lies in using one's aptitudes, for a worthwhile purpose, in a way which gives one the emotional satisfaction of work well done, with no need to examine whether one's colleagues are impressed or critical

(C) During adolescence opportunity for self-expression will gradually be separated from the security of the home. Parents will stand behind the children as the children begin to go out into the world on their own. Home will still remain a refuge where strength and courage can be renewed while the ability to face up to life's hard knocks develops, and a faith matures that will transcend the defeats of the moment without discouragement or breakdown. Learning and practice must go hand in hand in the maturing process, for learning is always a function of its consequences. The adolescent needs a growing confidence, because he can feel a growing competence, in his ability to cope with life successfully

(III) Healthy recognition:

(A) In general this should place emphasis on work well done instead of upon the child himself. Teach him to take the job, not himself, seriously

(B) Bribery is not healthy. Tasks which he should do, like good school work or keeping his room neat, ought not to be paid for. He should be as willing to shovel snow or to cut grass as part of his contribution to the family as mother is to get breakfast. On the other hand, he should have reasonable money of his own and be allowed to determine its expenditure

(C) The child will have ideas of his own, or come home with someone else's ideas, which he will try out on the family. If ridiculed or censured, he will soon keep his thoughts to himself. Or perhaps he tries something and fails. If laughed at, the feeling of humiliation may destroy his initiative. We give the baby encouragement in his attempts to learn to walk. The child should have it in his effort to think and to act for himself

(IV) Consistent and reasonable discipline based on kindness without weakness:

(A) Too many parents use their children as a means of working off aggression. For the child this is punishment, not discipline

(B) In the rare instances where punishment is necessary, its sure swiftness is of greater worth than its severity. There are, of course, times when the child cannot be allowed to have his own way. He should not play with a butcher knife or the scissors. But as the dangerous article is taken from him he can be given a block or a ball. Again, beware a bribe! Sometimes he will be bitterly disappointed, in which case the parent can honestly sympathize. Some frustrations are inevitable in every life, but there need not be domination behind them

(V) An opportunity to develop and eventually to live by his own standards of value:

(A) Under domineering parents, a child feels that to the adult there is no confusion over right and wrong. All that is necessary to be omniscient is to be grown up! As an adult he cannot then be free from conceit and prejudice

(B) When mistakes have been made, a child should be encouraged to think out consequences for himself. He should not be made to feel guilty. We resist, resent, and eventually hate anyone who consistently makes us feel guilty, inferior, or inadequate

(C) No child should be forced into a pattern of thinking. Children belong to the future, not to the past, and should not be bound by the limitations of the past. Suppose the physicists were indoctrinated with the idea that Aristotle had the whole truth, and to question his beliefs would be to imperil one's immortal soul! Then why restrict moral progress? To make value judgments for one's self is the sacred privilege—and duty—of each personality. The result, contrary to what those with a vested interest in maintaining power over us often claim, is not moral chaos, but balanced, emotionally mature, co-operative people. Compare the result of freedom of thought in the sciences. Has it brought chaos or scholarly co-operation?*

Thus, the competent parent regards each child as a growing individual, continuously in the process of becoming his real self, and constantly developing in terms of the adequacy of the family environment. The competent parent respects the uniqueness of each child, and strives in every way to protect and to nurture his emotional integrity. Little will be offered in the way of advice, even when asked for, because parental advice often shows lack of confidence. The child's reaction is, "You do not have faith in my adequacy, and this frightens me." Advice is only another person's opinion. What matters is the truth. Consequently, continuous effort will be made to help the child to think for himself in terms of alternatives, and of probabilities, so that he becomes increasingly self-directive and self-responsible as the years go by.

The stages of developing emotional maturity from fetus to mature self-reliance will be:

(1) All my needs are fulfilled for me, and though I am completely dependent on my mother, everything I want is supplied. I do not even have to breathe for myself. Best of all, there is no hostile competition. All I need to do is to take, take, take

(2) Now that I have been born, I experienced feelings of need or of satisfaction which I express the instant I feel them

(3) Most of my satisfactions depend upon the presence of my parents. I try to get from them whatever I want

(4) Most of my satisfactions depend upon the actively expressed approval of my parents

(5) Many of my satisfactions are dependent on my specific behavior. If the significant people in my life are not pleased with me they will not do as much for me

* See G. B. Chisholm, "The Psychiatry of Enduring Peace and Social Progress," *Psychiatry, Journal of the Biology and Pathology of Interpersonal Relations*, Vol. 9, No. 1 (February 1946), pp. 1-11.

(6) My satisfactions are mostly dependent upon my own capacity for discriminating judgments concerning, and capacity for adjustment to, the reality of my environment. This is in terms of my ability to

(a) see the truth about people, things, and situations

(b) adjust to them

(c) bring about their adjustment to me

As a result, I am no longer dependent on other people. I no longer want others to provide for me. I have been able to build my pyramid of desires to the point where I am capable of creative self-expression. Now I can give.

Interference with this development results in an incompleted process. Thus, never wholly getting out of stage three, the excessively dependent person becomes agitated and afraid when deprived of the presence of whoever stands in *loco parentis*. Thus, thousands of emotionally immature people lodge on the fourth step, continually seeking reassurance through the approval of individuals in a position to withhold something they want. There are many examples: the pathetic weakness of, "You do love me, darling, don't you? You know you do," or delighting in a title promotion that has nothing to do with increased responsibility or opportunity. Many of us never get beyond the fifth step, but spend our lives behaving in terms of what we think other people think, instead of in terms of our own creative abilities.

A contributing factor in the child's maturation should be his participation, on the proper level, in the discussion of family problems. At an early age he can express an opinion as to where the family shall go for its summer vacation. Eventually he can be consulted as to whether father's Christmas bonus should go toward a new car, a screened-in porch, or a tennis court. Unless the child has such an opportunity, how can he learn what marriage is like?

Good Discipline

When discipline is resented and resisted there is something wrong with the discipline as applied to the particular individual. In order to achieve compliance with a willing heart, it is only necessary to explain to the child our need to agree on the meaning of a word, or which side of the road to drive on, or which traffic signal means stop. But it often requires great emotional pressure to compel a child to accept the idea that the exposure of his naked body is sin, or that he must not be noisy in the house, or that he should wear a particular article of clothing. This suggests that he ought not to be compelled.

Jack was ten years old. Just before school closed, his mother took him on a shopping trip which included buying sneakers for him. As usual he was allowed to decide on the style, and chose blue because it would not be so difficult to keep clean. He wore them at once, but something happened at school, and the last few days Jack went back to wearing his shoes. Asked why, he said the other children might laugh at him.

All summer Jack went barefoot over the country roads and the sloping shoulders of the hills surrounding the family summer cottage in New Hampshire. The day school opened he wore his Sunday shoes. Mother said nothing until that afternoon.

"You must have misunderstood, Jack. We bought you the sneakers for school wear in order to save money on your shoes."

"Yes, mother, but wearing the shoes saves me embarrassment. It would be unpleasant to have to wear the blue sneakers."

"Very well, Jack, we'll not discuss it further now. I don't want you to be embarrassed. Let's talk about it again when we can find out what Dad thinks."

Meanwhile, mother remembered that Jack had been laughed at in the second grade for wearing sandals, and she reminded her husband of this before they discussed the situation with the boy. Many parents would say, "You picked out the sneakers, and now it is up to you to wear them," never realizing the domination.

These parents talked with Jack exactly as they would have with an adult. What was the matter? Blue sneakers would be looked upon as girl's footwear. White sneakers were for boys. He would be laughed at. Who would laugh? His friends? No. Then who? He wasn't sure. He just knew he would be humiliated.

At this point many parents would say, "That's all nonsense. Now put your sneakers on." Domination again. What Jack's parents did was to suggest that if white sneakers were for boys this should have been considered when the purchase was made. He had not thought his choice through to the end. Furthermore, there was as yet no proof that unpleasantness would result. Was it not fair to wear the sneakers for one day to see what would happen? Yes, that was fair. Very well, on a day of Jack's own choosing he would make the experiment.

Over the next weekend when the crisp tang of late September was in the air, the family went to New Hampshire. The question arose whether to go home Sunday night, or to arise early and return on Monday morning, taking the children directly to school. Edith and Fred were enthusiastic about Monday morning. Jack said nothing. (Observe how good administration functioned in this family by consulting the children's opinions.) When Jack said nothing, mother looked at father with a look which said, "Blue sneakers." Jack finally agreed to the Monday morning return.

Ten minutes later when they were alone mother asked, "Son, why did you hesitate about staying over?"

"I was afraid we might be late to school."

"Oh, come on, why did you hesitate?"

"Maybe we won't have clean clothes."

"What's your real reason, Jack?"

"Well, Mom, I'm wearing my sneakers."

"All right. Don't let that worry you. We'll start early enough to take you home so you can change to your shoes. We said you could choose which day to wear the sneakers."

A trifling incident? Not at all. In such seemingly little things are revealed such tremendous things as a parent's real motives, and whether what is done corresponds with what was promised. So many parents would rejoice in a circumstance which forced the child into the desire pattern and which, incidentally, would make the wearing of sneakers a despised symbol of subservience for the rest of the individual's life. If he is not given an opportunity to discriminate for himself, he will be driven by fear, will power, and rebellion.

If mother had said, "Never mind all this fuss. I want you to wear those sneakers. Nobody is going to criticize you. You'll find out that I am right," Jack's self-respect would have been attacked. With irresponsible use of the values she perceives him to hold in the situation(see table, page 302), she would have been claiming to represent an assumed future part of him in conflict with the presently functioning him. Such irresponsible use is misuse.

Finally, on a day of his own choosing, Jack wore the blue sneakers. Nothing was said. They reappeared the next day, and the next. After a week his parents brought the subject up again. There had been one unpleasant experience: the postman's son had ridiculed him. Did that really matter? No, not really.

Two evenings later Jack's mother read him Aesop's fable about the old man, his two sons, and the donkey, who were criticized no matter who walked and who rode. When she had finished Jack turned a somersault on the living room rug and came up with a merry smile as he exclaimed, "I know why you read me that! I know exactly why!" A month later he said, "I don't understand why I made all the fuss about my sneakers."

Doubtless he did not remember the humiliating experience in the second grade. That was of no consequence. What did matter was:

(1) Respect for his personality, thus
(2) Avoiding the development in him of fear of people, particularly those in positions of authority, and
(3) Above all, the fruitful opportunity to learn that what other individuals think is not so important as what one thinks of one's self.

This experience was far better than any amount of talk. Feelings change only in terms of direct, personal knowledge, not in terms of speculative words imposed without concomitantly living through some event of an appropriate nature. The domineering parent would never imagine that in blue canvas and rubber soles could lie an effective chance to teach the essentials of self-control self-realization, and happiness. Such a parent cannot realize that kindness, loyalty, fair play, unselfishness, love, are all the product of understanding what we really feel. Nor can the subservient person perceive this.

Lastly, the child was allowed to solve his own problem. If we want a child to learn to walk we must take away our hands and not be deterred by his stumbling. When we try to push children too fast we frighten and confuse them. When we try to hold them back, we frustrate them. Because a child is slow in making some adjustment does not mean that he is unable to make it.

There are, of course, times when he cannot be allowed to have his own way. Perhaps, in anger, he wishes to smash a window with his fist. Accepting his desire to do it, because one recognizes the frustration behind the desire and so can understand how logical —though irrational—the desire is, makes it possible to prevent his doing it without at the same time making him feel subservient.

Romping through the living room at full throttle with the dog, as she had been forbidden to do, Ruth broke an expensive vase which was one of her mother's heirlooms. She might have fled from home. She might have lied about it, blaming a playmate. She might have hidden the pieces and denied all knowledge of the disaster. Such procedures lead to nothing but an immense spiritual emptiness. No interpersonal wrong can be mended unless there is direct man-to-man communication.* To maintain a relationship of love Ruth must have the courage to tell her mother the whole truth because she knows she will be understood and forgiven. Mother and daughter can be secure in their togetherness only when they have examined together daughter's grief and shame, mother's disappointment and loss, and their mutual concern for the happiness of both. Forgiveness must come mutually. Hardest

* In this connection people would do well to remember Matthew 5:23-24, "If thou bring thy gift to the altar and there rememberest that thy brother hath ought against thee; leave there thy gift before the altar and go thy way; first be reconciled to thy brother, and then come and offer thy gift." To Jesus, religious living was more important than ritual.

of all will be Ruth's task of forgiving herself. It is many long years since she was a little girl, but she has never forgotten how she cried for two hours before she went to her mother, and the loving understanding with which she was received.

The idea that punishment constitutes discipline is held only by those who wish to dominate. They, in turn, are proceeding on the theory that the desirable pattern of family life is the tyranny they themselves experienced in childhood.

In Conclusion

The only way to have a better world is to have better people in it. The only way to have better people is to do a better job bringing up children. Some of us feel that the only way to do a better job bringing up children is to have a better religion in the home. If we could give one complete generation the right bringing up it would not only rebuild society—for what is done for the family is done for all society—it would actually bring about a comparative heaven on earth. The energy now expressed in hate, prejudice, self-defense (often a disguised form of aggression), inferiority, fear, would be released for co-operative, happy living. But as long as we have unhappy homes we shall make children ruthless, and as long as we raise ruthless individuals the intelligent ones will get to the top to make it a dog-eat-dog world.

Real progress can be made in any area whenever the method of approach is right. Good family administration requires:

(1) A many-sided, comprehensive approach to every problem

(2) The integrity of each member consistently respected

(3) Each person's interests considered and protected because of:

    (a) effective participation by each member on his appropriate level

    (b) solutions reached in terms of the facts of the whole family situation

    (c) an orderly process of investigation, interpretation,

decision, and implementation, based on common understanding

(d) an opportunity for analysis and review of all decisions, which recognizes the need for adjustment to changing conditions.

The fundamental law of the universe is the relatedness of all things. Wise parents strive for right emotional relatedness in the family. No parent can love his children as long as their behavior seems a threat to his emotional security. The ability to vary evaluations as to the appropriateness of noise, blue sneakers, window-smashing, or whatever it may be, comes only with the healthy self-confidence of emotional maturity.

An otherwise intelligent person can be blind and unrealistic when it comes to handling interpersonal relations, particularly with little children, even though for most of us life's superlative satisfaction is the rearing of a happy, healthy, emotionally mature family in which each individual has a personality and a mind of his own.

13

Divorce

MARRIAGES END IN SEVERAL WAYS

ALL marriages eventually come to an end. Beginnings are usually joyful events; endings are sometimes sorrowful ones, and the end of marriage usually involves suffering. Sometimes it involves tragedy. Death has its utter finality; annulment has its exposure of fraud or duress; desertion has its desperation and its cruel uncertainties; separation has its frustration of freedom without being free; divorce has its cold surgery, its implications of failure, its remorse, its bitterness.

Marriages ended by death involve no social stigma. The cause, to use our legal phrase, is presumed to be an act of God. Neither poor judgment nor moral turpitude by either party is involved. But is this always so? If all illness has its emotional as well as its physiological origins, as the experts in psychosomatic medicine are beginning to believe, death is sometimes due to what amounts to slow murder. The only complete defense against life is death, and life can be so intolerable as to make escape into the silent halls of death a consummation devoutly to be wished. We will learn more about this in the next half century.

An annulment dissolves the marriage as though it had never existed, the legal point of view being that the marriage ceremony

382

could not have been performed had all the facts been known. In short, someone perpetrated a fraud by failing to disclose such things as another marriage already in effect, impotency making the consummation and fulfillment of the marriage impossible, or inability to meet the legal age requirement. But the fraudulent representation of wealth or of social standing is no grounds for annulment. Entering marriage for any such reason is considered a fraud perpetrated on one's self, for a successful marriage cannot be bought with money or prestige. Furthermore, the ecclesiastical law expects every person to "use timely and effective diligence to obtain correct information."*

Though there may have been no fraud through concealment, the bringing about of a marriage by illegal compulsion is usually ground for annulment. So is insanity.

Will Durant says that we should "have a decent respect for the hypocrisies of mankind." Certainly all of us soon learn to escape certain disagreeable things by not calling them by their real names. Thus, some people get around divorce by having a marriage annulled.

Desertion for some specified length of time is a ground for divorce in every state except New York, but desertion usually does not end in divorce because it is the poor man's way of breaking up a family. (A divorce is an expensive thing, regarded by the lawyers as "a luxury.") Desertion is particularly common where religious beliefs prevent divorce, no matter how incompatible the husband and wife.

Legal separation is a half-way measure which compels the husband and wife to live apart, but allows neither to remarry. The wife is entitled to appropriate separate support, and to the other legal rights specified in the separation agreement. The marriage tie itself remains unaffected except for the fact that it no longer includes the one privilege which is illegal without marriage—the privilege of intercourse.

Divorce brings the marriage to an end by a legal process which

* T. Poynter: *A Concise View of the Doctrine and Practice of the Ecclesiastical Courts* (Philadelphia: Littell, 1836), p. 140.

is the unhappy opposite of a wedding. Nobody wants this, but people will accept it, in sorrow or in wrath, as the lesser of two evils. Most states require that a specified time elapse, after the granting of an interlocutory decree, before it becomes final. This is the period of engagement in reverse, testing whether or not the husband and wife feel they have made a wise decision, and no reconciliation is possible. It also has the desirable effect of preventing an immediate remarriage, not as a punishment, but as a precaution to prevent committing another mistake on the rebound. A good readjustment takes time.

Numerous as our divorces are, they do not represent the actual number of unhappy homes. Because two people still live together does not mean that they still have an abiding affection. Many unhappy families continue to exist on a domestic battlefield because husband and wife lack the courage, or the money, or the religious freedom, to go through a divorce. Some fear public opinion and its effect on business or professional success. Such marriages hold together for the sake of appearances, and may even succeed in concealing from most of the family friends the misunderstanding, the hate, the deception, and the unsatisfied emotional hunger which have shattered its unity. These are not called broken homes because the pieces are held together by a wire of fear or of false pride, and the cracks are covered with the putty of pretense. But they are, in fact, broken homes with wretched parents and demoralized children, living together in an atmosphere of despair.

Reasons for Divorce

There is always personal tragedy involved in divorce, but there is often greater personal tragedy in staying married. Marriage should be a sacrament, not a penal institution which increases the emotional instability of husband and wife, and produces it in the children. Compelling two incompatible people to continue to live together does not teach them how to live happily; it only sharpens resentment and creates hate.

If divorce is always wrong, then what becomes of the religious doctrine of the gospel of a second chance? Everyone will agree that it is possible to marry for the wrong reason. Then divorce for an adequate right reason is logical. There are forty-nine different legal concepts of an adequate right reason in continental United States, which brings about unfortunate confusion and difficulty, but to say that no adequate right reason exists for dissolving an emotionally bankrupt marriage (as the state of South Carolina did until 1949) is wholly unrealistic.

Marriage is a partnership between two adults. Many adults are not sufficiently mature to carry on a successful partnership in business, say nothing of a partnership which is sexual, religious, social, and recreational, as well as intellectual and financial. Out of unhappy homes come damaged industrial relations, tyrannical governments, international wars, and broken children who will themselves produce unhappy homes with the same old patterns of cynicism, self-pity, drinking, and infidelity.

Death may be the cause of a divided family. Desertion, or separation, or divorce is never the cause, but only the end result. Nor are the legal reasons like cruelty, desertion, adultery, habitual drunkenness, willful neglect, or conviction of a felony, the real causes. Even the quarreling and the unhappiness which preceded the disruption were not the cause, but the antecedents.

Real causes go back to such things as the emotional immaturity of insecure, unfulfilled, dependent, frightened men and women who were not loved as little children. To suppose that the apparent causes are the real causes is to fall into the same superficialities of classification that lead some people to declare the whale a fish and the bat a bird.

Causes

Marriage failures are sometimes courtship failures, but usually they are the delayed consequences of incompetent parents. To examine our divorce record is to realize that either the ideas we have about marriage are wrong, or the way we bring up children as a preparation for marriage is wrong. Divorce is not the cause of unhappy marriage, it is the consequence which comes about because the conclusion has been reached by one or both partners that the legal bond between them should be terminated.

There is no intelligence in attacking consequences instead of studying causes. To raise a clamor about the evil of divorce is not to study causes. Causes lie in the determinants of emotion. When we want to find these as earnestly as we wanted to split the atom, we shall succeed in doing so. But we cannot bring about family unity by ecclesiastical pronouncements, by legal requirements, or even by courses in college. Emotional problems cannot be solved by denying, repressing, or cataloguing the emotions. Our divorce laws have become more rigid, not more lax, since 1890, but the percentage of broken marriages has mounted steadily.

At a recent convention of clergy, the contributing causes of divorce were given as hasty marriage, lack of a spiritual foundation for marriage, easy divorce, alcoholism, and incompatibility. None of these get at the heart of the matter. Why was the marriage hasty? Why do we lack a real spiritual foundation for our lives? Why has our culture demanded that divorce be easy? Why do we endeavor to drown our sorrows in the befuddlement of alcoholism? Why do we marry individuals with whom we are incompatible?

The cause must be our total situation, beginning with what happened to us in childhood. What did we learn through felt experiences about the nature of a deep and abiding love, about sex, or self-realization, or co-operation, or knowing what we were really feeling? Ignorance can ruin a family as easily as it can destroy anything else. Ignorance of our emotions, ignorance of adult responsibilities, ignorance of the nature of love, ignorance of the fundamentals of happiness, ignorance of interpersonal relations. We have plenty of schooling in the United States, but little worth the name of education in these personal areas.

Would there be a hasty marriage if the individual could identify his emotion as infatuation? Would there be incompatibility if we knew that attraction and affection are not the same thing?

One wonders how many couples think themselves incompatible because they never honestly tried to make emotional adjustments. The reason they never tried is not because they did not want to, but because they did not know how. Nobody wants to be unhappy or to be involved in a failure.

Divorce does not come about because we are free to pursue happiness, it comes about because we have not learned how to pursue happiness. Escape from misery is only running away from something which threatens one's well-being. It is not the achievement of satisfaction which comes with the fulfillment of one's well-being.

Can husbands and wives be expected to make the bricks of adult happiness without having first been given the straw of childhood love? Certainly they cannot give until they have received.

The steps in an unhappy marriage follow a fairly universal pattern:

(1) Not being honestly loved as a child, resulting in

(2) Some unrecognized, counterfeit form of love, leading to

(3) A sentimental marriage, without emotional maturity, so that

(4) Dependent or defensive emotions arise between husband and wife, thus

(5) Frustrating any real love, and leaving only the perverted affection which, starved by its own hunger and thirst, ends in

(6) Quarreling, disillusionment, and probably divorce.

Thus, many marriages are potentially wrecked before they ever start. They fail because destructive emotions, created in childhood, wreck the objective of the partnership. The superficial cause may be no more than rebellion against drudgery unrelieved by recreation, but the absence of fun goes back to some compulsion imposed in childhood. Decay never comes directly from outside forces. It is always the result of some internal failure. The superficial cause may be sexual incompatibility, but the truth usually is that because of its delicacy, the sex relation is merely the place where the incompatibility broke through to conscious awareness.

A marriage, terminated on the ground of adultery, was often a broken marriage before the adultery occurred. The significance of the adultery goes far beyond a mere physical urge, to something like a revolt against childhood taboos, a refuge from the spouse, an attack against the spouse, or an attempt at emotional reassurance through new conquest. In any event, just the fact of adultery does not justify divorce except legally. What were the underlying circumstances? It could be that these had little to do with the marriage.

To say that the decreasing economic dependence of husband and wife is a cause for increased divorce, may or may not be true. It might be why family breakdown is more easily possible, instead of a reason for family breakdown. To say that the turmoil of our present civilization is a cause for increased divorce, may be putting the hen before the egg.* Perhaps the uncertainty of society in transition has been caused by the breakdown of the family. Perhaps, also, this has been the reason for the increased independence of women. The modern family began to disintegrate about two hundred years ago. Most of these other things are more recent.

Divorce and the Church

Even the power of high explosives has had less effect on the fate of mankind than the ideas of the clergy, a fact for which many of us are downright grateful. But not always.

The old Roman belief was that so delicate a relationship as marriage must be continuously refreshed by the waters of mutual affection. Streams which have no such outlet soon go salt. If mutual affection had gone, reasoned the Romans, there was no longer a marriage, and all the community required was the mutual acknowledgment of that fact. No court procedure was involved.

The early Christian church changed all this. It declared that

---

* Obviously, in the evolutionary process, the egg came first, because there were many kinds of birds before the hen evolved.

marriage was a sacrament from which the only release was the death of one's spouse. To this day, except for the escape provisions of annulments, the Roman Catholic Church makes few exceptions to this dogma. Most Protestant churches still declare at the end of the wedding ceremony, "What God hath joined let no man put asunder,"* but usually do not live up to it in the narrow undeviating sense. Perhaps it has occurred to few good people that what God actually has joined cannot be dissolved by human effort.

By any standard that makes sense it is a mystery that any man can suppose marriage to be under the jurisdiction of God, and therefore undissolvable by man, because some man has pronounced two people man and wife. It is unthinkable that a loving God could be party to some marriages sanctioned by the church. There are wives who so hate and envy men they have a subconscious compulsion to destroy emotionally any man they marry. There are husbands who do the opposite.

The theory is that when people know their marriage yoke cannot be shaken off, they become better husbands or wives because of the inescapable necessity of remaining together. If only it were true! But compulsion is no substitute for a loving childhood home, or for emotional maturity. The theory further is that divorce robs the family of the security and permanence God and nature intended. What, please, is the supporting objective evidence . . . evidence which would stand up in a court of law, say nothing of in any scientific body devoted to a search for truth, through reason and with integrity? Does enforcing a dogma safeguard the security of the family any more than the famous proposal in the Ohio legislature years ago to legally make the value of $\pi = 3$ instead of 3.14159 changed the relation between the radius of a circle and its circumference?

* See Matthew 19: 3-9 and Mark 10: 2-12. In both reports it is obvious, as Bowman has pointed out, the Pharisees were trying to trap Jesus. The Pharisees were those Jews noted for their insistence on strict, undeviating observance of traditions. Their question and the answer they got pertained to a principle, not to its interpretation in a particular case. The fact that the one-sided privilege of a man's divorcing his wife was being abused at the time is significant.

What right have we to expect all marriages to succeed when no other human relationship is perfect? Can we preserve love by the coercion of religious law? Does not humanity go on suffering many types of needless tragedy because it so habitually clamors for force instead of seeking for deeper understanding? Marriage and divorce should both be based on predominant emotional fact rather than on blindly applied dogma. No one should get married without an adequate, honest emotional foundation, or stay married if it cannot be maintained. We need to act constructively on our genuine feelings, even if it leads to divorce, rather than to tear each other to pieces.

Actually neither judge, nor clergy, nor anyone else except the partners themselves ever decide whether a marriage is to survive. They may stay under the same roof, they may be denied separation by court and church, but if they do not have a loving relationship there is no marriage worthy the name.

To absolutely prohibit divorce results in one of three alternatives: (1) the hypocrisy of false annulment; (2) changing residence or religion to an environment where divorce is possible; or (3) the continued conflict and personality damage to husband, to wife, and most especially to children. The by-products include much adultery and an occasional murder.

Henry the VIII of England did not stop at murder. He did, however, make an unsuccessful attempt to have divorce legalized on the grounds of adultery, desertion, long disappearance leading to presumed death, cruelty, attempted murder of one by the other, and deadly hatred.

When a marriage has become a destructive battle ground, there should be some respectable, dignified way of terminating it. Instead of the continued failure of an incurably sick marriage, divorce can bring the healing of renewed self-respect for facing up to disagreeable facts and at last showing some consideration for each other.

What about separation? This has ecclesastical sanction, but as the English court points out, it "throws the parties back upon society in the undefined and dangerous character of a wife without a husband, and a husband without a wife."* This is often an unjust and a corrupting procedure, but does have the advantage of allowing man and wife to rejoin forces without any court action. To do so, of course, voids the separation agreement.

"Go see your clergyman," is common advice to married people engaged in a private cold war. It will be much better advice some years hence when the clergy are less denominationally minded and know more about emotions. The degree to which a consultant can perceive what constitutes the heart of a problem, how to get at it, what to do to correct it, is the true measure of his value. This is as true of the cloth as it is of a garage mechanic.

Certain it is that an increasing number of thoughtful people agree with Wayland Vaughn when he says, "The higher divorce rate may be interpreted as indicative of a rise rather than a decline in our standards of morality . . . living together in mutual hostility and hatred is no longer condoned . . . evidence of higher moral standards [is] the insistence on mutual affection as the only decent basis for marriage."**

My own conviction is that the real disgrace lies in our lack of emotional maturity because so many of us do not know how to bring up children, and do not know what love is. Let the colleges and the church be concerned with causes. Consequences will take care of themselves.

INDICATIONS OF TROUBLE AHEAD

One test of a bankrupt marriage is loss of emotional unity. The absence of togetherness in any kind of effort—industrial, religious, or domestic—makes the co-operation of willing hearts impossible. There are many little straws of behavior which will show that an emotional ill-wind is blowing. Desertion, chronic alcoholism, continued adultery, persistent neglect, or wanton cruelty all show

* J. Kent: *Commentaries on American Law* (New York: Banks and Bros., 1891-92), Vol. II, p. 128.
** W. Vaughn: *Social Psychology* (New York: Odyssey Press, 1948), p. 804.

that the marriage itself has gone. The little straws show that the common goals, which are the basis of togetherness, are going.

These include:

(1) Belittling the spouse to the children, relatives, friends, neighbors

(2) Making important decisions without consulting each other

(3) No longer doing little helpful things for each other. What someone does not do for an individual is often more significant than what he does do

(4) Not treating each other as equals

(5) Not missing each other's companionship when apart;

(6) Attempts to achieve power over each other rather than endeavoring to find solutions together

(7) Quarrels which leave bitterness instead of the catharsis of forgive and forget

(8) Abusing each other's confidence. Perhaps the wife tells her husband's business secrets, or he spends money she inherited and entrusted to him

(9) Putting other values, like money or social prestige, ahead of cherishing each other

(10) Deliberate deception. Any such situation will surely produce unhappiness and bitterness.

As emphasized in Chapter 6, emotional immaturity almost always produces marital failure, whether it ends in divorce, or not. There is no bilateral approach by which to see other aspects of a situation than one's own; no ability to wait and see, to defer judgment while more evidence is being gathered; no earnest desire to find the facts and to adjust to them.

LEGAL GROUNDS FOR DIVORCE

Marriage is illegal except by mutual consent. In the eyes of the law, except in the states of Washington and California, divorce is impossible if there is mutual consent. In fact, where both parties sue there is practically never a decree given to either, because one party is supposed to be guilty and the other innocent. This idea is a bit bleak in the light of the fact that fault is practically never all on one side.

The theory of no mutual consent is primarily to prevent the kind of collusion where grounds for divorce have been manufactured with premeditation by husband and wife; or where perjury has been committed by the introduction of false testimony concerning some offense, like adultery, which was never actually committed; or where the defendant is discovered in the failure to defend himself when a valid defense exists.

However, honest agreement that no hope exists for saving the marriage should be no impediment, and in actual practice our courts are coming closer and closer to the old Roman idea of divorce by mutual consent. The so-called defendant merely puts up no defense. Ninety per cent of divorces in the United States are uncontested, so that despite the legal fiction there is neither adversary nor contest. Before the trial husband and wife have usually met with their lawyers and drawn up a separation agreement covering the disposition of the property and the custody of the children. Divorce by mutual consent is an actuality, usually granted and always valid so long as:

(1) Both spouses agree to the divorce

(2) The plaintiff appears in person and has actual legal residence under the jurisdiction of the court

(3) The defendant is represented by counsel

(4) The plaintiff has legal grounds in the divorce granting jurisdiction

(5) The legal procedures in the particular state are complied with.

The bona fide residence of the plaintiff is a must, especially if only one party appears. Get a job, establish charge accounts, join the church, buy or rent a house, join a club, register as a voter, and do not depart immediately on receiving a decree.

No suit can be entered until the plaintiff has satisfied the residential requirements of the particular state in which the suit is brought. The time necessary to establish residence varies from six weeks in Nevada and Idaho, to five years in Massachusetts. There are also the complications which arise where the residence requirements apply to both spouses. There may be the question of whether a summons can be served outside the state, as well as how and by whom it can be served.

Each of the forty-eight states and the District of Columbia have their own individual requirements for granting a divorce, thus creating the worst confusion of its kind in the world. So confused is the situation that it is sometimes impossible to be sure, short of a court decision, whether a person is married or not in a given state, or whether the children of a second marriage are legitimate.

Nelson* lists forty-three different grounds for divorce in the fifty-three different jurisdictions of the United States (including Hawaii, Alaska, the Virgin Islands, and the Canal Zone). Adultery constitutes legal grounds for absolute divorce in every state. The only other ground in New York is belief that the absent spouse is dead, but as a result annulment is comparatively easy. Most other states have laws covering desertion, cruelty, the commission of a felony, impotency, continued and wanton drunkenness, willful nonsupport, and incurable insanity for a period of years. The specified time of desertion varies from six months in Hawaii to five years in Rhode Island. In most states it is either one or two years.

Nevada, Florida, Idaho, Wyoming, and Arkansas all have easy divorce laws for which the respective Chambers of Commerce bear some responsibility. Only New York refuses a divorce for willful desertion. Kentucky recognizes fourteen different grounds; Tennessee and Wyoming, thirteen; most states, eight or ten; South Carolina, four; New Jersey, three; and New York, only two.

* W. T. Nelsen: *Divorce and Annulment*, 3 Vols. (2d Ed., Chicago: Callaghan, 1945).

The important question is not who has been a transgressor and to what degree, but whether a tolerable relationship can be reestablished between husband and wife despite the present conflict. The California courts are considering:

(1) The chances of a reconciliation
(2) The danger to life, health, and emotions of a continuance of the conflict
(3) The effect of the parental conflict on the children
(4) The comparative culpability of the parties.

Instead of being primarily interested in guilt or innocence, concern is being shown in the courts of Toledo and Cincinnati over whether the marriage can be saved. A 1951 Ohio law requires professional investigation of the family situation whenever children under fourteen are involved. In the state of Washington the judges' first duty is to be convinced no reasonable hope exists that the marriage can be salvaged. This begins to make sense.

It is the wife who most often gets the divorce, not only because the law favors women over men, and so do most judges, but also because of the chivalry involved in a procedure where one side is traditionally presumed innocent and the other guilty. If a change of residence is involved, this is usually easier for the woman than the man. He has a job. Finally, the aftermath of a divorce is usually both more severe and more lasting on a woman than on a man. She has the greater social adjustment to make, the more malicious gossip to bear, and the larger financial change to face.

The legal complaints for which divorces are granted are distributed as follows:

Cruelty	50.2 per cent
Desertion	33.0 per cent
Nonsupport	8.4 per cent
Adultery	3.5 per cent
Alcoholism	2.0 per cent
Miscellaneous	2.9 per cent

The real causes are unknown, although they always rise from some form of incompatibility. The legally aggrieved partner, who thus becomes technically the innocent partner, may easily be the one actually the more at fault. It would take a good psychiatrist to find out.

As for the legal fight, it seldom is concerned with whether the marriage shall be brought to an end. The difference of opinion is far more likely to center around the division of property, or the custody of children.

Divorce, as has already been said, is based on the assumption that the marriage was valid and without impediment. Annulment is predicated on the existence of some legal impediment which existed prior to the ceremony, so no valid marriage was possible.

The refusal of either spouse to consummate the marriage is one obvious ground for annulment. Concealment of the inability to have children, or the premeditated intention not to have them, constitutes a fraud, and therefore becomes a basis for annulment, providing the defrauded party brings suit quickly and can prove his case. So-called "shot gun" marriages can be annulled providing there is real coercion (duress) and not just the threat of force. A girl deliberately becoming pregnant in order to blackmail a man into marriage is also a fraud, but difficult to prove.

Despite the fact that an annulment says that legally she was never a wife and he never a husband, it is sometimes possible—especially in New York—for the woman to collect alimony.

The law is consistent in demanding that a legal separation be a real separation. It forbids even sleeping under the same roof. If the marriage is dead the couple "cannot litigate by day and cohabitate by night," as one judge said. Any sensitive man, legally separated or not, who in fact no longer loves or respects his wife, shudders at the idea of intercourse with her. No one who has not experienced this can imagine it.

THE STATISTICS

The twin upholders of the family seem to be children and the farm. The divorce rate in the city is twice that in the country, and 71 per cent of all childless marriages end in court. To put it another way, two-thirds of all divorces come from the one-seventh of our families which have no children. But it is dangerous to assume a correlation between statistics just because they apply to the same thing. Even if there is a correlation, can we assume one to be the cause and the other to be the effect, in the hope of bolstering an argument? There is more scientific evidence to show that couples are childless because they are unhappy, than there is to show that they are unhappy because they are childless. (See section on Sterility, page 281.) To say, "Happy homes have children, therefore have children and you will be happy," is often like saying, "Bankers wear striped trousers, therefore, wear striped trousers and you will become a banker."

The length of time required to wreck a marriage varies greatly. Some 5 per cent end in divorce the first year. A few do not suffer the sharp agony of legal surgery until after half a century of living together. About 50 per cent of all divorces occur before the sixth year of marriage, which suggests that the first five years are the most difficult. The divorces which come later are postponed either by hoping for a miracle and refusing to face the facts, or by the absence of any load on the marriage which would bring out the weak places. Depressions, for example, do not destroy happy homes; they merely produce the emotional pressures which show that the husband and wife were not really in love. Perhaps they were only adjusted to a mutually acceptable way of living in which it was easy to tolerate each other. When the way of living was destroyed, the tolerance was gone.

The median length of time, before calling in the lawyers, is about seven years. The most frequent length of time, preceding the final invective and the legal fangs and claws, is three to four years. The approximate distribution of divorce, in terms of length of marriage, is:

Time	Percentage of Divorces
0-5 years	36 per cent
5-10 years	29 per cent
10-15 years	17 per cent
15-20 years	8 per cent
All others	10 per cent

The lowest divorce rates are to be found in the middle Atlantic states. Next comes New England. The highest incidence occurs in the Rocky Mountain and Pacific states. About 3 per cent of the decrees are granted to individuals who go to another state to enter suit.

As recently as half a century ago divorce was considered a disgrace. This attitude has been gradually changing; partly due to a more intelligent concern for the importance of individual happiness; partly to our economic prosperity; partly to the devastating effects of hasty marriages in two world wars, and the loosening of moral standards which always accompanies a war; partly because the ease of transportation now makes for a larger number of marriages between people who have not grown up together. The trend over the past century leaves many with a troubled depth of spirit.

1865—1 divorce for every 36 marriages that year
1900—1 divorce for every 13 marriages that year
1945—1 divorce for every 3 marriages that year
1950—1 divorce for every 4 marriages that year

In 1950 about one in ninety of all existing marriages ended in divorce. Half a century earlier it was one in two hundred and fifty. Any way it is calculated, and there are several possibilities, the divorce rate has increased both tremendously and consistently, with a few short periods of exception. There are now over 800,000 divorces in the United States per year.

The table showing the percentages since 1890 is as follows:*

Year	No. of Marriages	No. of Divorces	Percentage of Divorces
1890	542,307	33,461	6.2 per cent
1895	598,633	40,387	6.7 per cent
1900	685,101	55,751	8.1 per cent
1905	804,016	67,976	8.4 per cent
1910	948,166	83,045	8.7 per cent
1915	1,007,595	104,298	10.4 per cent
1920	1,274,476	170,505	13.4 per cent
1925	1,188,334	175,449	14.8 per cent
1930	1,126,856	191,591	17.0 per cent
1935	1,327,000	218,000	16.4 per cent
1940	1,595,879	264,000	16.5 per cent
1945	1,618,331	502,000	31.0 per cent
1950	1,667,231	385,144	23.1 per cent

This in no wise represents the number of unhappy marriages. The terror of separateness which drives many people into marriage and which denies love to the marriages, is a terror which likewise prevents many a divorce which would end an unhappy marriage, but not the unhappiness. There are many reasons why people do not get a divorce. It costs money. They stay together for what they believe to be the sake of the children, or the effect on family status. Some lack the courage. Others are motivated by business or property considerations. A few are idealistic. Once in a while the reason is spite—or its opposite, consideration.

The incidence of divorce by occupations is worth consideration. Salesmen, actors, musicians, and doctors are in the top bracket. In the middle group are to be found bankers, professors, lawyers, plumbers, and merchants. Those among whom a wrecked marriage is least likely to take place are clergymen, farmers, carpenters, miners, and manufacturers.

In any given year about one person in six is marrying for the

* Computed from Federal Security Agency, National Office of Vital Statistics; *Marriage and Divorce in the United States,* 1937 to 1945; Vital Statistics- Special Reports, Vol. 23, No. 9, September 10, 1946, Table 12.

second time, following a death or a divorce. The men marry spinsters more than the women marry bachelors, but both tend to marry someone who was not previously married.

More than half the people who escape from an unhappy marriage never marry again. Of those who do, not more than half have learned enough to find happiness.

Effects

Divorce involves emotional shock, not only to the husband and wife, but to the children, and sometimes to the relatives. A decree can end, but cannot wipe out the loss of what should have been years of happy married life. The feeling of failure remains to be manifested in self-justification, the self-consciousness of some subsequent chance meeting, the changed and often embarrassing social relationships. Husband, or wife, or both must make new friends. They cannot go on in the old circle of mutual friends. And there is the difficult adjustment to an upset sex relationship, although the upset probably preceded the divorce by a long time.

The husband may attempt to lose himself in work, or in travel, or in some new love affair. The wife may go home to her parents, or get a job, or marry again, or seek solace by becoming someone's mistress. Still the fact of the failure remains. Even if one or the other remarries with great success, "betwixt her lips and mine there fell thy shadow." There is the aching emptiness of secrets and memories and experiences the happy couple should have shared together, but never can because the past is unalterable. This hurts. Lives are saved by surgery, but the scars are always there.

The childless divorces are the fortunate majority of those who marry and are incompatible. (Two-thirds of the divorced couples have no children, the remaining one-third usually have only one child.) Where there are children, many people believe the parents should stay together for the sake of the children. I used to think so. Parents may be able to fool the neighbors as to the tottering condition of the home, but they cannot possibly keep the children from feeling and being affected by their incompatibility.

Children need emotional security as much as they need bread.

Where the father and mother are unable to solve their own inter-personal problems, how can the children learn to do so? Broken homes are not just one-parent homes. Both parents may be present, and yet the home be shattered irremediably.

Whatever happens, there will always be high emotional partici-pation by the children. This is particularly intense in our kind of family organization. But it is far better to live with one parent in peace than to live with two parents on the battlefield of a quarrel-ing home. In an unhappy home, the children will try to reconcile two emotionally immature people who do not understand them-selves or each other. The children will try unsuccessfully to co-operate with two people who cannot co-operate themselves.

Living alternately with divorced or legally separated parents is almost as bad as living with quarreling parents, because neither parent wants the child to be happy with the other. Few of us are big enough to forgive, particularly in a situation where our emo-tional security is threatened. But using a child as a weapon by which to hurt someone else deprives the child of his feeling of being loved. The children of unhappy parents are always insecure, whatever their outward appearance, and when the time comes for them to marry they are likely either to make a failure of the marriage, or to build defenses against being married.

Upwards of 300,000 children are now affected by divorce every year in the United States. "Whenever parents lock horns the chil-dren are gored." Hostile parents destroy every other advantage a child can be given in travel, schooling, summer camps, or social contacts. "My parents did not get along well together," writes a college boy. "We children were still so weak inside ourselves we needed someone to cling to for security. Yet when father and mother treated each other hatefully our loyalties were divided, our sense of any anchorage was destroyed. The situation was somewhat relieved when they were divorced, but the damage was never really corrected."

Where there is any dispute about it the mother usually gets custody, not only because the children are young, but because the father has a living to earn and probably inadequate facilities to take care of them. Even the preference of a child for the father may not be conclusive where a contest is involved. Quite rightly the courts do not like divided custody amid bitterness. The judge knows the litigants will carry on their warfare through the children. Also, the courts like to keep siblings together. But the parent without custody has the right to visit and to be visited by his children.

Then there are questions of property. When the wife leaves her husband to divorce him in another state she probably will be unable to collect alimony. For one thing, the husband is not subject to the jurisdiction of that court. Also, the husband's liability often depends upon who, in the eyes of the law, broke up the marriage. If the wife is unwilling to perform her marital obligations, runs off, refuses to live with her husband, he has no financial obligation, for she must be a wife in order to expect his support. She must, therefore, have a legal excuse to leave him, and be blameless herself.

Any award of alimony is largely a matter of judicial judgment. In such cases the common property is usually divided equally, and the wife given one-third of the ex-husband's present income, so long as she does not marry again. If the income goes up or down, the amount of alimony may be changed if the court so decrees. Men can be jailed for willful refusal to pay alimony. This is not considered imprisonment for debt, which is illegal, but imprisonment for contempt of court.

Alimony originated because for so many years the husband got legal control of all the wife's property when they married, and could use it for his own purposes, in return for which he had the responsibility to support her and their children. All this has been changed in America by the Married Woman's Property Acts. Her property is now as wholly hers as it was before the marriage. Consequently our ideas about alimony are also changing.

REMEDIES FOR DIVORCE

As already pointed out, there is no intelligence in attacking consequences instead of getting at causes. Love cannot be brought about by reproaches, or by legislating against hate and hostility.

It must come by removing the causes of hate and of hostility, and producing the sources of love.

The root cause of all emotional maladjustment goes back to the fact that the individual was not loved in childhood. But unfortunately no one can change his childhood. *We are not to blame for what was done to us, but we have the inescapable responsibility to try to set the situation right.* What then, should a married couple do, when they begin to perceive indications of trouble ahead?

First, they must genuinely want the marriage to last, which I think will almost always be the case if the coming trouble is perceived early enough. Second, they must take intelligent steps toward remedy. As we are our own first diagnosticians in physical illness, calling the physician for a more competent opinion, so we must make the first diagnosis in emotional trouble, leading us to seek professional help. Going at once to a divorce court is like sending for the undertaker before trying a physician.

The initial step should be, "I am unhappy, and therefore there is something the matter with the way I am living my life. What must I do to me?" This should be followed by a realistic plan of action. If the home remedies fail, professional help is indicated—and immediately!

Be prepared to take plenty of time. There are many years of emotional conditioning behind the situation. No one should expect to be able to set emotions right in a few days, or even in a few months. This is not a situation where the house is burning down and action despite emotional upset is necessary; this is a situation requiring calm, considered decisions.

Some individuals feel that a separation is beneficial to a sick marriage. In some instances this may prove true, but in general what the husband and wife learn is how to get along without each other, not how to get along together. Others suggest drawing up two lists: one containing the good points about the marriage; the other containing the bad points. This is largely an intellectual proceeding, as though troubles were to be cured by some magic of bookkeeping instead of through right emotions.

And there is the ever-present, childish plea for, "One more chance." A second, or a third chance is wholly desirable and right where it is intended to implement a realistic plan, entered into by both partners. "Give me one more chance!" is usually only the weak cry of someone with no ideas except to cling in terror to a sinking vessel. This is bound to fail.

Before resorting to divorce, husband and wife should make sure, over at least two years, that no reconciliation is possible. They should try studying appropriate books together; they should try religion, or perhaps some vigorous changes in their religious ideas (Freud thought the trouble always went back to sex. He might equally well have believed that it always went back to religion); they should try a marriage counselor or even a pyschiatrist. They should not resort to divorce without a period of real separation intended to allow the cooling of emotions and the readjustment to living alone. Once they are sure the marriage is really insolvent, that no togetherness exists between them, then there is nothing except unfairness, unhappiness, and tragedy to be gained through lack of courage to face the facts.

Tom was the only child of a wealthy family. His parents were divorced when he was in his teens, leaving him with a severe sense of insecurity, which was camouflaged by beautiful manners. As he grew up, his mother made him her darling.

Sarah also came from a wealthy family. Her father died when she was quite young, but not before the emotional bond between them had become so strong that she idolized him. The mother married again, not happily. This had three consequences: she made a favorite out of Sarah's brother, adding additional strangulation to Sarah's heart; the home atmosphere was continuously beclouded by the smoke and dust of family quarrels; the wife and two children travelled continuously in Europe and America, never getting their roots down anywhere, but trying to forget, since they could not kill, the hurt of not being loved.

At the end of his senior year in college, Tom met Sarah at a summer resort. Three months later they were married. There was a round of gay parties, and a honeymoon trip to Europe. Then Tom settled down to the grind of learning the family business, with its restrictive hours and the small-town surroundings of a branch factory. Sarah rebelled. She complained that he no longer gave her enough attention, yet she grew angry when he did.

The case is now in the divorce court.

Here are two people, each with a good physical inheritance, excellent intellectual equipment, and poor emotional conditioning. They were willing to marry after knowing each other for three months, yet neither was willing to take six months with a competent psychiatrist in the endeavor to straighten themselves out.

In Conclusion

Divorce is only legal. Marriage is not primarily a legal relationship, but an emotional adjustment between two people. A divorce may bring a calamitous relationship to an end, but it cannot confer release from the dark shadows of an unloved childhood. It cannot restore the embittered heart and the cynical mind, except in so far as it allows the embittered heart to find love, and the cynical mind to find truth. (Second marriages are almost always unusually happy, or unusually disappointing.)

The sexual maladjustments, the conflicts in careers, the religious differences, the jealousy, the excessive drinking, the conflicts of desire—none of these cause unhappy marriage. They are only the concomitants of unhappy marriage. For causes we must look deep into the attitudes which keep us emotionally and intellectually adolescent, which deprive us of a realistic preparation for maturity and for marriage.

The physical man-made structures like bridges, and houses, and churches do not collapse. The social man-made structures like governments, and families, and religions sometimes do collapse. Why? Is it because we have used good method with one and expedient guesswork with the other? We diligently experiment to discover how the strength of a beam should be calculated. Our efforts at understanding our emotions have been hopelessly inadequate.

We have not yet learned how to be happy, even though we

loudly proclaim our right to the pursuit of happiness. Perhaps the reason we have not learned is that we lack the courage to throw over many of the old absolutes, as the scientists did three hundred years ago. There are areas of great influence on human happiness, in which it has been considered evil to search for new truth. Happiness as a prerogative of marriage—a right to be enjoyed merely because two people are husband and wife—is a completely modern concept. Even now, the idea is foreign to most of the people in the world, because for them marriage is an economic rather than an emotional institution.

A high divorce rate must be due to inability to recognize during courtship whether or not one is in love; failure to perceive that love is an art to be learned, and that only the baby can expect to be loved without first earning it. Perhaps even more fundamentally the trouble is ignorance of the nature of love. So many people think that love and sex are synonymous.

Be that as it may, the only way to come through the searing blight of a divorce, unscarred by vindictiveness, inner conflict, guilt, or the destroying days that can follow malignant circumstances, is to keep living by two principles:

(1) The tragedy is not the divorce but the necessity for it;
(2) I will try to conduct myself in such a way that if there are any regrets about this, they will not be mine.

One of the magnificent facts about life is our capacity to grow both intellectually and emotionally almost as long as we live. And as the pages of the book of life are opened, they bring us back again and again to a place where, perhaps falteringly, we see more light and can grow in an area which was dark before. One such place may be the page which records the ending of an unwise marriage.

It is tragic that this growth, if it takes place, happens after the inner conflict and the failure, instead of before it, or at least during it. But give thanks that *the chance is always there*. Out of heartache can come understanding. Out of battle can come peace. From the wilderness of hate and recrimination it is possible to reach the Promised Land if only one can learn to love.

14

Religion in the Home

WHY, in a book on courtship, love, and marriage, should there be a chapter on religion in the home? Because life and religion cannot be separated. Because real religion is indispensable to happiness and fullness of life, the only condition in which decency and beauty and goodness can survive. Because the family is the character-forming agent of society, the greatest influence for the strengthening and the improvement of morality. Because the church has rites for birth, marriage, and death—the three most significant experiences in any life—and because of the emotional content and early conditioning of these rites. Because we shall never solve our domestic problems until we solve the dilemmas in our spiritual attitudes which produce them. Any material problem always has a spiritual side, and a right material solution is impossible until the spiritual principles have been discovered on which to base that solution. Otherwise the answer is only an expediency which is likely to include an attack on the consequences, instead of finding the causes of the emotional determinants. Because the religious problem is present even during courtship. Because religion is the result of the unification of our thinking and of our feeling into our way of life. Because the desire to find the truth is fundamentally religious—which is why science stemmed from religion.

Whether we recognize it or not, every home is constantly teaching religion of some sort. Because of the inconsistencies between what we profess and what we do, religion in most lives seems to be set off by itself. Actually that cannot be done. A man's religion is not his church membership but his way of life, his basis of interpersonal relationships, his discriminations as to what is worth doing, his road to peace of mind, his particular way of hungering and thirsting after righteousness. Creeds are important only in terms of their effect on actions. A person does not become religious by some profession of faith any more than he becomes a physician by taking the Hippocratic Oath. It is what he does that matters. Clinging to sectarian practice without possessing religious belief is empty.

We live by what we accept as true, and if it is not true we are penalized—as when we think we are in love but are not. To live religiously is to be constantly aware, emotionally and mentally, of the moral significance of every act. When the individual deceives himself concerning what he feels religiously, he makes it necessary to lie to himself about other things, including love, in order to protect the religious falsehoods from discovery.

If our concepts of religion were right, we could not have so many different opinions.* We realize that there are no absolute and ultimate answers for us. Finite man can have only partial answers. Truth which exists beyond the ways and means by which we are able to observe it, cannot be known, say nothing of proven. But the rewards and punishments of this life result from what we accept as true. We cannot have the whole truth, but we can have better truth. The common religious objective of mankind should be better truth, the closest we can come at any given time being *those imporant ideas which are accepted by the body of competent*

---

* There are over 260 different sects in the United States alone, each wanting to nail down its own narrow creed as the one true religion.

opinion around the world. Truth is universal. Any real morality is as valid for the agnostic as for the pietist. The way to righteousness is available to every man alike, for there must be only one God, not a multitude of tribal gods.

The happiness of our homes will never be saved by politics, or economics, or physics, or biology, although our very lives as well as our happiness may be destroyed by the misuse of any one of them. Our happiness will be saved when we apply to our emotions and to our religious beliefs the same *scientific methods* which have already done so much for the working of our minds in other fields. Only thus can we have a deepening concept of the nature of man. Without this we cannot become better people.

Nothing else can save us, for the only way to find out whether a thing is true or false is to put it to work and see what happens. "By their fruits ye shall know them." This is the basic fact which has been followed by the physical scientists. When a thing does not do what it is supposed to do, they try something else.

Similarly, what the home does always reveals what religion in the home is, and when a home is not what it ought to be, something should be done to correct its way of life. There is great need of a search for real spiritual values in these highly unspiritual times.

APPROACHES TO RELIGION

Traditionally there have been two approaches to God. The first is to regard Him as one might regard a tyrannical father: someone to fear because of his superior power, to plead with, to bribe with sacrifices, to appease as one would appease a touchy and unloving parent. It was this concept which led Abraham in his journey to the land of Moriah for the purpose of sacrificing Isaac. It was this concept which allowed the fanatical citizens of Salem to take eighteen lives on Gallows Hill because the Reverend Cotton Mather, suffocating in the comfort of his own self-righteousness, quoted the Bible verse which says, "Thou shalt not suffer a witch to live" (Exodus 22:18). In Indo-China today, famine and fighting do not interfere with offering the best cattle to placate the Gods.

In America even educated people sometimes refuse to sit thirteen at a table, as though a vindictive deity would punish them for reproducing the number who gathered at the Last Supper.

This is the sort of religion which allows a person to change at a moment's notice from praying for a child's soul to beating him for making too much noise. This is the sort of religion which maintains that man is created sinful by the very nature of his creation. The best such a religion can produce is a coerced and therefore false saintliness, honeycombed with hypocrisy, fear, and guilt. As was said earlier, a frightened person cannot be a sincere person. True religion is faith in God, not fear of God; faith in the inevitability of happiness and self-realization if one finds and lives by the laws of the government of nature. This requires the exercise of observation, comparison, and discrimination. Merely to obey what someone else says is to throw the responsibility for our acts onto someone else. This is essentially immoral, even for an army officer, as the Germans found out at the Nuremberg trials. Thus, to put the emphasis on "believe" instead of on "understand," to preach the submission of "obey" instead of the salvation of "find yourself and be born again," is to impair the value and the dignity of religion.

Why, then, do we believe in a God of fear? For one thing, because it has been to the advantage of men with power over us to devise and to retain these thought patterns. The efforts of the ecclesiastical hierarchy in every religion, as well as of the politicians, have more often been dedicated to the preservation of their particular form and power than these efforts have been dedicated to that most exacting of all disciplines, the pursuit of significant truth. This was one of the characteristics of the clergy which made Christ most angry. Around the world it is still true that men are sometimes the helpless pawns of religious masters to whom I refrain from adding an adjective. The most complete way to get power over someone else is to dominate his conscience. Make him fear disobeying your wishes, but make him think that the wishes are God's, not yours, and your power will be both complete and permanent.

Power over other people—as distinct from competent leadership —can only be maintained through fear, a condition which many religions produce by threatening punishment in the hereafter. This consequence, incidentally, has never been demonstrated, although it is clear enough that wrong behavior results in self-punishment here.

Yet all the time behind this concept of God as an all-powerful, exacting, and absolute deity there has always been the idea that He was also a loving father who offered salvation for the elect. Beside the fear of hell there was the hope of heaven and whoever was worth saving was never wholly lost.

The second approach is to regard God as one might regard a benign father, who nevertheless wants to keep his children dependent, always turning to him as the source of all power. This, as Dean Everett M. Baker said,* is the concept which causes us to think of God as the giver of Grace, the avenger of wrong, the arbiter of justice, the controller of destiny, as though He could end poverty and hate an injustice anytime He wanted to. We thank God for bringing the war to an end, as though we ourselves had no responsibility for bringing it about or causing it to cease. We pray God to save us on land and on the sea when disaster threatens, as though He were what Erich Fromm calls a "magic helper," who could reach down and by a miracle preserve us from the consequences of our own acts.

There are many inconsistencies in such a religion. For one thing there is no scientifically acceptable, objective evidence that the laws of the government of nature are ever momentarily repealed for any cause whatsoever. When my aged mother hastened with undue zeal over a slippery place, the fact that hers had been a life of good works and loving kindness did not bring about the momentary revocation of gravity to save her from a broken hip. Perhaps the planets could move according to some new plan, but they never do, and the soft iron filings of Faraday's experiment never deviate from the same curved lines extending from one pole

* Quoted from a lecture at the Massachusetts Institute of Technology, April 9, 1947.

of the magnet to the other. Insofar as we can discover, God *always* obeys His own laws. It is a childish idea that He can or will follow the impulse of the moment, as children so often feel that grownups can.

Many of us want a God of miracles and of supernatural power to make our personal experience different from the rest of the world, because we were brought up to be subservient. There is a high correlation between the amount of a person's suppressed hostility, and the intensity of religious feeling with which he can say:

(1) God is a magic helper

(2) If He is that kind of being, I can have complete reliance on His taking care of me

(3) Therefore I have security at last!

Such religion is intensely concerned with self-evaluation and re-assuring one's self of acceptability, particularly in some hazy future eternity, as though now were not definitely a part of eternity. Through irrational manipulation of the unknown, people have been given all sorts of positive statements in areas where we possess no positive knowledge, as though it were better to fill the unknown with pleasant and threatening myths, than to label the area "unexplored." To assert that we know things we cannot prove is mere rationalizing.

This is as immature as the thinking of the little boy in the story who said, "I'm drawing a picture of God."

With tolerant surprise, his mother asked, "How can you do that? Nobody knows what God looks like."

"They will when I finish," the lad replied confidently.

We laugh at the child with so omniscient an attitude, and often take with profound seriousness the clergyman who combines the same notions with the dignity, the mystery, and the incantation of his office. This is only because it is impossible to reason us out of irrational beliefs and into more intelligent ones, when our emotions have been conditioned against it in childhood. Instead of asking, "Is this true or is this false?" we ask, "Is this different?" and if it is, we conclude that it is false.

Religious symbols, dedicated to a God requiring appeasement, or to a God who is a magic helper, seem real enough to anyone who has been brought up to respect them. Other individuals will at once see absurdities, as we do in the Chinese prayer mill, or the Hindu sacred cow, and as they must in some of our ideas. All of us know, when we think about it intelligently, that heaven is not a place in the sky, that God does not reside in a crucifix on the wall, and that immortality is only a speculation. Not that immortality is any more incredible than the indestructibility of matter (we know we have chemical immortality!), but there is a difference between what is proven and what is only unsupported assertion. This cannot be faced in an irrational religion of miracles because the moment one starts questioning, the whole structure will topple. If tomorrow it were proven beyond doubt that there is no life after death, the discovery would make no difference to truly religious people.

Approaching God in fear of His power or in want of His protection are not the only alternatives. There is a third: the profound conviction of a togetherness with God, akin to the feeling of a child toward an emotionally mature father. Beside the God of fear and the God of miracles, there is the God of love. If God is love, He does not use the coercion of fear or the enticement of miracles. To love is to cherish, to have affection for, to be identified with.

The value of religion is not clear to many people because they have no sense of participation *with* God. As the important thing in marriage is togetherness between husband, wife, and children, so in religion, it seems to me, the important thing is the togetherness of the individual with God, each contributing on his own level. He created matter and the laws by which it behaves, including the laws which hold the atom together, the stars in their courses, or human beings in a relationship of love. He gave us the freedom to discover and to use these laws. As we can do nothing without the materials and the conscious awareness God gave us, so also there are things which apparently He cannot, or at least He does not, do except through us. The only restriction laid upon us, as Macmurray points out* is that over the years we fail when our motives are evil or our actions unrealistic.

Our responsibility for a togetherness with God is beautifully illustrated by the story of the colored man who bought a tumble down house on a weed infested lot. By diligence and skill he turned it into an attractive home: clean, well repaired, fresh painted, framed with lawn and flowers. His clergyman, admiring the result, remarked on the transformation.

"You and God have certainly done wonders with this place."

"Yes, Sir, Reverend, but you should have seen it when God had it all by Himself."

Of course sometimes we fail, perhaps even suffer. But failure and pain were the chance God had to take and the price men have to pay for the priceless gift of free will. The alternatives are either to lose the reliability of the laws of the government of nature and human nature, or to lose all capacity to grow, all spirituality, all love.

The true rewards come from discovering the facts of helpful, interpersonal relationships and following them. The false rewards come from worship which is mere blind adoration. The way in which truly to relate to God is earnestly to seek and sincerely to follow the laws of constructive human behavior. This recognizes the fatherhood of God as a creator, and the brotherhood of men as inescapably interdependent beings.

Much of our present approach to religion in America is a confusing compromise between the idea of God as fearsome, as magical, and as loving. Some parents say to children in effect, "We represent the source of your togetherness with God. We will decide when you are to fear Him, but if you do as we say, you will be protected. On the other hand, if you want some magic performed, follow the formulae we give you and if you have faith enough the miracle may happen. Of course God is loving too, which is why you can hope to escape the consequences of your own acts, but

* J. Macmurray, *A Clue to History* (New York: Harper, 1938), pp. 58, 59, 61, 94.

don't try to find consistency in all this—just believe and depend on us." This is a far cry from trying to relate back to God through the demonstrable facts of right interpersonal relationships.

Religion would not succeed if parents lined up straightforwardly on the side of a God of fear. The children would rebel against such coercion. Nor would it succeed if parents consistently worshiped a God of magic. The enticement would soon become apparent. Complete devotion to a God of love would destroy domination in the home. So most of us adopt a confusing compromise which keeps both us and the children away from reality. The road to power over other people is to keep truth or the desire for truth out of children's minds. Knowledge leads to freedom.

Perhaps it should also be said that the way to make a good thing bad is to beat it out of shape and to twist it. Because each individual has to live with his own ideals, it is emotionally disastrous for one person to impose his standards on another. I think it is also immoral.

The Consequences of Different Methods

The way to appraise any method of behavior is to examine its consequences. Except for our devotion to money and to the sciences which give us advantages of bodily comfort, emotional security, and physical power, much of what is called religion in America has degenerated into mere parrot talk, and the accompanying inconsistencies between profession and performance. There are several reasons for this.

We have lost faith in the individual's capacity to learn right from wrong by himself, and consequently religion in the home has imposed predetermined answers on children, with little regard for their self-development through adequate experience. When we believe certain acts to be beneficial, we emphasize the act instead of allowing the child to feel his way, through his own experiences, to the meaning of the act—which alone can make an act genuine. We have set up creeds and dogmas which the child can question only at the price of a parentally-imposed load of guilt and fear. Moral instruction never was and never can be a substitute for the true religion of a faith based on one's own experience.

The inevitable result is pretended standards of value, unsupported by that background of honestly appraised experience which is a prerequisite for real belief. The true issues of life must be dealt with honestly. The alternative is shallowness of thought followed by the havoc of dishonest action.

Sooner or later in the child's life, undebatable religious dogma is faced with undeniable objective fact. A fact is a fact. We can deny it, fight it, ignore it, ridicule it, suppress it, but it is always still there, patiently waiting to correct us. The child has been told that he must choose between the material *versus* the spiritual. His experience cries out that life is the material *and* the spiritual. He has been given many affirmations about life after death. His education shows him that in twenty centuries we have learned nothing concerning life after death.

Thus he is faced with many inconsistencies. If he kills twenty Japanese on Iwo Jima, with whom he has no personal quarrel, he is a hero. If he kills one fellow countryman, toward whom he has reason for intense animosity, he is a murderer. One Christian faith teaches Ten Commandments, which include a prohibition against idol worship; another not only has no such commandment, but teaches genuflection in front of sacred images. He is told that lying is sin, and is also told that he ought to be ashamed of himself for saying some of the things he believes to be the truth. He is taught that the meek shall inherit the earth, and his observation suggests that they couldn't possibly have it by any other means!

As his education progresses, he will come to realize that progress in the art and the understanding of human relations is not coming from the church, but from such sources as a Viennese neurologist. Yet, in most of our homes, if he is to remain in the good graces of the traditionally faithful, he must stubbornly defend *in words* what he has been forced to accept or else be condemned. If religion is mere talk, no wonder in 1944 we spent twice as much for tobacco and seven times as much for liquor as we did for our churches.*

But all the time the growing child knows in his heart that it is unintelligent to say "I know" when there is no scientifically objective proof. (No one is more persistent in asking "Why?" than a little child, or as willing to accept a new truth.) All the time he knows in his heart that salvation does not spring from another individual's power to entice with promises of heaven, or to coerce with threats of hell. He knows in his heart that he must think out and feel out his own values for himself. He knows in his heart that rational faith implies full assent of the mind, and therefore certitude, because personal experience has shown that complete trust and confidence are rational. He knows, subconsciously at least, that Erich Fromm is right when he defines as irrational any faith which is an "unshakable belief in a person, idea, or institution which does not result from one's own experience, but from emotional submission to authority."** Without a rational faith to live by, life becomes too much for us.

All the loose talk to the contrary, as the child matures something keeps telling him that the experiences he has through his five senses, incomplete as they always will be, constitute everything he can ever have on which to base a rational belief. All else is irrational speculation. The glorious fact that he possesses altruistic desires and undeviating hopes which the most highly developed knowledge of science cannot always satisfy, does not alter that truth.

Men who want power over him will try to deny it. They sense what a weapon reason is. So they endeavor to cut the props from under it. To impugn reason outright would be to give themselves away. Therefore, they do not say reason is evil. They say reason is limited, that there is something else above reason. Call it revela-

* Figures from a study made by the Golden Rule Foundation.
** E. Fromm: "Faith as a Character Trait," *Psychiatry, Journal of the Biology and Pathology of Inter-Personal Relations,* Vol. 5, No. 3 (August 1942), pp. 307-19.

tion if you wish. Don't try to think, just "Believe man, believe."*

Nevertheless, man's moral as well as economic progress has come because of "I want to know," or "I must find a better way."

"His yearning to understand reaches far beyond the control of nature for his bodily well being. The shepherd on the hill at night views the stars and ponders, not that he can thus care better for his sheep, not just that he is idle and his mind roams, but because he wonders whether, beyond the stars, lies the reason why he can thus ponder."**

When some questing mind invented glass, he made possible a better way to see. Aided by the telescopic lens astronomers have learned enough never again to believe heaven is a place in the sky. They also grew in a realization of the incredible exactness, magnificence, ominiscience of that unknown creative force men like me call God.

Without the emotion which says, "I want a better way," men would still be living in caves, hungry, cold, ignorant, miserable, and naked. Despite all the ignorance, wrong unbringing, sin, hatred, and war, humanity does progress. Still, we wonder why, down through the ages, religion has so failed to teach people how to live together in love that our rapidly increasing knowledge of destructive weapons has now reached a point where all humanity is threatened.

The answer is *we are talking love but not living it*. Many of us who talk about love do not even know what love is. Nobody knows enough about it. To say that all we need to know about love is in the Bible is to be unaware of so simple a point as that every generation has altered its interpretation of the Bible to suit its own concepts.

The way we are taught to wrap up in separate little packages our

* See A. Rand: *The Fountainhead* (Indianapolis: Bobbs Merrill, 1943), p. 692.
** V. Bush: *The Search For Understanding*, an address delivered by the president of the Carnegie Institution of Washington to its staff and trustees on the occasion of its fiftieth anniversary, December 11, 1952. Privately printed, p. 15.

religious beliefs and our search for truth, has produced a terrifying self-betrayal.

The result is a desperate effort to find certainty in irrational ways. One method is to ignore the real problem of understanding one's self and one's relation to the universe, but to fly to the hoped-for protection of an imagined magic helper. A second is to deny one's true feelings, smothering them in idealism. This never quite accomplishes complete suffocation, but does fill the individual with guilt, not only because he has not performed things which he is completely unable to perform, but because he has feared to do things his true self feels are right. We often try to solve our inner problems by means which will not solve them.

Thus does religious dogma get people into as many emotional tangles as it seems to get them out of. Poor anguished and bewildered souls. When the attempt to create certainty is not in accord with the facts, the result is unrealistic. A serious consequence of this training in unreality is emotional immaturity. It contributes to the idea that marriages are made in heaven; that in all the world there is a "one and only" for each of us; that suffering is God's way of developing character instead of being the consequence of some wrong act.

But suppose the family approaches God with a conviction of His love, and of His desire for man to grow into an emotionally mature stature enabling him to be and to express his spontaneous* self. Suppose the family accepts the need for beliefs developed from experience, and rejects compulsive affirmations imposed by authority. Suppose the family has a conviction of togetherness with God, and of responsibility to discover and to abide by the laws governing human nature—as we have already done with the laws of nature, after first persecuting those who began the attempt. Here is a religion which gives each individual, from the youngest child to the oldest grandparent, a sense of moral purpose in the self, bigger than the self; a deep and an inescapable sense of personal duty to work for those things which are of supreme good

* It might be well to reread what is said about spontaneity on page 8.

to all men; a respect for the sanctity of personality; the discovery of our true emotions; the achievement of individual peace of mind; the abolishing of war—domestic, industrial, or international.

Family quarreling now becomes an evidence of family failure to discover and to obey the laws of good human relationships, and the subsequent family unhappiness is seen as just as much a punishment for that failure as a stomach ache is punishment for failure to obey the physical law. Both are God's way of showing us that something we have done is wrong. When we have suffered enough from wrong behavior, we usually try something better. *True goodness is a joyful thing.*

Thus the atmosphere of the home becomes inevitably a reflection of the family religious experience, and how honestly that experience has been dedicated to the discovery of the significant truths concerning good individual and interpersonal emotional relationships. Religion cannot be separated from behavior, nor can the family be stronger than the spirituality of its character-forming base. And the children can only be as sound as the family. The child who cannot find God in his parents will not have an easy time finding God anywhere. The parent who cannot see God in the face of his child has never known God. Where the family has found a group way of life which gives adequate emotional motivations and satisfactions to each individual, free from mere leaning on symbols which constitute only a way of hope, it has a strong religious foundation. Where the family is individually and collectively in a continuous process of objectively examining the results of its human relationships, a progressive revelation of the laws and purposes of God will take place. Those who do not evaluate the past are compelled to repeat the mistakes of the past.

As the physics laboratory is concerned with the discovery of the laws of nature, so the truly religious home becomes a research center for better interpersonal relations. Each member of the family will act cautiously but courageously in trying to discover and to resolve the inconsistencies in his beliefs and in his behavior. Each will commit himself to the best he knows, but constantly assume that there are better ways to be found. There will be an intellectual and emotional atmosphere which accepts doubt concerning the old absolutes. There will be no blind following of authority, but the same freedom to theorize, to test, and to revise premises which has brought such spectacular progress in physics, chemistry, electrical engineering, or any other field where it has been honestly applied.

Is everything worth knowing in religion already known? That is exactly what was thought about physics in the medieval world!

Science is a method, not a body of doctrine, and the only reason science has formulated no moral values is that we have not yet tried to be scientific in our approach to religion. Consequently our knowledge of the physical sciences has become a two-edged sword, used both to develop and to destroy. Scientific conclusions in any field are always partial and sometimes wrong, but the refusal to accept a given piece of evidence as final, the unflagging quest for more evidence, soon shows error to be error, thus leading to further discoveries. This can be true morally as well as physically.

Have the scientists fallen into undisciplined thought because they were free to think and to experiment for themselves? Certainly not. With a total lack of authoritarianism they have developed the most rigorously self-disciplined thinking in the world. Is there any reason to expect less of scientific methods applied to religious truth? Religion, indifferent to research and to new truth, is mere superstition and dogma, exactly as the belief, held inviolable for a thousand years, that Aristotle was right when he said a heavy body would fall faster than a light one, was erroneous guess work. The Galileos of physics are no longer persecuted for disproving old myths. We need to stop crucifying the explorers who would lift the horizons of religion, most particularly those who are trying to find and to tell the truth about what we really feel. To be a living thing, religion must be a growing thing. To maintain the old absolutes is to deny progress.

"But God wrote the Bible," some Christian insists. "Shall we not follow holy writ?" "Excuse me," says his Jewish friend, "God wrote the Torah." "You are both mistaken," the devout Hindu declares, "God wrote the Rig Veda." To them all, the thoughtful searcher after truth replies, "Give me a telescope, give me a flower, give me a microscope, give me a little child, give me a mountain range, give me a loving family, and I will show you the book God really wrote. Come, let us study it. The Ten Commandments and the Sermon on the Mount are such great expositions of truth we call them divine revelation. We might say the same thing about the law of gravity or the conservation of energy. Surely through study we can learn much more about this book God really wrote."

There was once a carpenter, despised, rejected, reviled because he continuously proclaimed in effect, "The Old Testament says . . . But I say unto you. . . ." He was a man of sorrows and acquainted with grief because he wanted men to become conscious of their irrational ways and the consequences of these irrational ways; to find better ways through better understanding. That hope is slowly beginning to be realized. He had more to say about fear than he had to say about sin. We, too, are gradually finding out which is cause and which effect.

But we cannot change to a dynamic concept of morality until the family feels the need for change. We have resisted recognizing the need for change, despite the evidence of family breakdown, until we could see some promise of improvement. Many of us are finding this promise, together with an enlightening realization of the implications in some old religious truths, in contributions outside the church which should be coming from the church. When a person can say correctly, "Here is evidence that if you do so-and-so, such-and-such will happen," he is talking about truth.

The past should be a guide, but it must not be a ball and chain. New wine still bursts old bottles. We must always remember that we are dealing with a *specific* situation. To enter any situation with an old generality is to learn nothing if we use the generality as an axis of revolution instead of a point of departure. We must doubt the "obviousness" of many things, including "spare the rod and spoil the child." A conclusion, based on what appears to be evidence, may not prove to be warranted if enough additional evidence is gathered. Whipping the child may bring about immediate compliance, but long-run rebellion and character damage. Truth is always an incompletely known thing. We must vigorously seek to know it better, and to make fruitful application of what we learn.

To admit new truth accomplishes nothing until it has been acted upon. "Good" means little unless accompanied by a realistic plan, and followed by sincere activity. Self-examination will lead, through growing self-knowledge, to self-realization. The result of any given behavior pattern will become more and more predictable in the case of each individual. *If the results of behavior are not predictable, then there is no reason to prefer one course of conduct to another.*

In a family with this kind of religious beliefs there will be no blind following which makes false what the individual feels and hyprocritical what the individual does. There will be no beliefs imposed on anyone by someone else. The only reason for valuing any concept will be because one's own experience has shown it to be true. "Ye shall know the truth, and the truth shall set you free." Growing knowledge of the whole self will lead to growing obedience to the whole law, with no protecting screen of idealism or of sentimentality to hide some unpleasant truth.

No child will learn to repress his desires, to deny, even to himself, the existence of his baser impulses. To be his real self is not to allow unrestrained impulse, however. The child will recognize a base impulse without shame. They come to all of us. Then he will release creatively the energy behind the impulse. Exactly as man has not conquered nature, but has learned to understand and co-operate with the laws by which nature operates, so, in such a family, the members will not try to repress their evil thoughts, but to perceive, to understand, and to redirect them. To be free from feelings of guilt does not mean that one is free from self-restraint. But it is self-restraint without fear.

Each member of the family will live in a continuous process of becoming his real self. Because, for him, religion will not involve trying to become what he thinks someone else thinks he ought to be, religion will never prove a source of self-torment. No one will become discouraged as a result of his inner self having been squeezed into something drab and cold and empty. There will be times when it will be necessary for members of the family to forgive themselves (as distinct from excusing themselves), but they will have inner peace despite mistakes, and despite the lack of absolute certainty in the outer world. The fountainhead of inner peace has always been the exclusive property of those truly religious individuals who understood and had confidence in their own underlying goodness. These are the individuals who can take the responsibility for themselves. This is a different thing from a pious anaesthetic, or a memorized set of reassuring answers, or a magic formula, or an intellectual sterility and an emotional cowardice masquerading as faith.

A good life is always founded on right human relations. So is a happy family. Thus, it is essential to emphasize and to reemphasize the fact that the important task of religion in the home is to teach people how to live happily together. To want this is the only true hungering and thirsting after righteousness. Enforcing the old rules is no more a live answer in spiritual things than it is in physical things. The humble acknowledgement that all peace of mind and all good interpersonal relationships issue from understanding and obeying God's laws concerning human behavior, and to find these laws, as the physicist does—instead of trying to define God himself, which is presumptuous to say the least—has been the basis of all great religious leadership.

Understanding emotional relatedness in the family and respecting it, is just another way of saying that the spiritual and religious life of each member will inevitably affect and be affected by that of the others. This is not a false morality of enticement or coercion. This is not a ready-made faith, piously mouthed but not really accepted because not proven in one's emotional responses. Religion must be something worth living by, not an attempt to solve life's problems through talk. Words are not a solution. Right solutions come through a right emotional approach to purposes which lead to action.

Observe that this has nothing to do with blame or condemnation. The great religious leaders have not been interested in punishing or in judging men, but in improving our grasp of the realities of human relationships. The home ought to function on the same ideals. If we believe in the fatherhood of God, how can we participate fruitfully in the activities of His household unless we try to understand what the principles and the purposes of that household are? "The respect* of the Lord is the beginning of wisdom." Being afraid interferes with wisdom.

The consequences to our family life of worshiping a God of punishment or a God of magic help, instead of seeking to discover and to follow the laws of behavior established by a God of love and logic, have been disastrous. We have:

(A) Denied our own real natures, maintaining that there is a difference between desire and morality. All behavior is motivated by desire. Wrong desires are merely right desires perverted by frustration. Do our true desires want quarreling, deception, exploitation, thievery, domination, feelings of inferiority? Why are we not our real selves? Because we have been taught from childhood to pretend to be what we thought someone else thought we ought to be

(B) Thus we have betrayed ourselves, condemning ourselves to disintegration from within. We are, of course, subconsciously aware of it, and hate ourselves as the result

(C) The inevitable consequence is loss of integrity; emotional self-destruction because of refusing to be ourselves, but accepting spurious motivations which are not true to ourselves. Even if the final behavior is right, our inner consistency has been sacrificed.

* Proverbs 9:10. "Fear" is a poor translation. The Hebrew is, "Techelat chochmoh Yirat Adonoy."

"It follows that wherever man rejects the discovery of himself he will be committed to a line of action which is attempting to achieve what cannot be achieved. Every such effort will, in the course of history, defeat itself."*

If God is a god of love, those who say that following our honest emotions leads to sin are in danger of impious irreverence. A god of love but not of miracles must have a passionate desire to work with us, that we may create *together* the conditions under which each can be his spontaneous self. If this is not true, then God must be a god of sadism, who delights in creating something fundamentally bad, and in calling virtue the pain of overcoming one's true nature.

There are so-called religious ideals which imply exactly that, and they result in homes of comparable cruelty, however the cruelty is disguised. The idea that we are born evil and "must be saved" no doubt came from someone who had been cruelly rejected by his parents.

Religious ideals of this kind are always accompanied by fear. A life of fear has no choice but to become a life of self-defense, and desperation leads to anarchy. Was this the kind of God the Apostle Paul had in mind when he said, "God hath not given us the spirit of fear; but of power, and of love, and of a sound mind."**

Following a God of love, who made us whole and wholesome, if only we know how to be our real selves, leads to:

(A) Developing personalities with a right perspective as to their place in and their relation to the universe. These individuals will possess a sense of togetherness with God because they will seek to play a dynamic part in bringing about a better world through better self-understanding. As human beings in a finite world they will not expect to escape trouble and suffering, but they will feel clean and right because they will feel honestly that goodness, and self-realization, and growth are practically synonymous

---

* J. Macmurray, *The Clue to History* (New York: Harper, 1938), p. 59.
** II Timothy; 1:7.

(B) Better interpersonal relationships. Relieved from the fear of coercion and the dishonesty of externally imposed religious affirmations, these individuals will seek emotional satisfactions in ever improving, right relatedness with others

(C) The realization that we must find religious answers *together*. In no other way can we learn to:

(1) Love the government of nature and human nature "with all our hearts, with all our souls, and with all our minds"

(2) Love ourselves, because we are self-comprehending and lovable

(3) Love our neighbors as we love ourselves, because we can understand them, and live happily with them.

Where religion in the home is built from personal experience and a dynamic concept of morality subject to a continuous examination of results, there will be no need for the fantasy security deriving from some magic helper. This will have many consequences. The little child will not grow up afraid of people, nor will he learn to be afraid of death. During courtship, infatuation will not be mistaken for love. The individual will not need the false reassurance of how some other individual makes him feel, and he will know what he himself is really feeling. In marriage there will be no need for dependence or coercion, because the absence of a God of wrath and power—often served by father acting out an identical role—will make unnecessary the struggle for power which develops when people are seeking certainty in irrational ways. How can we hope to compel certainty where there is uncertainty?

In Conclusion

The only absolute certainty we have is that the government of nature always operates in accordance with natural law. One of these natural laws is that all life leads to death. But man wants more out of his stay on earth than just a grave. Religion should give him the sure feeling of personal significance, not in some speculative hereafter, but here and now because of the happy creative, interpersonal relationships with his fellow men, which it is the proper task of religion to teach him.

When a crisis comes with its content of grief, what the individual has been doing to his character is always revealed. The secret emotional dishonesties may have been hidden from other people, but their effect cannot be hidden. Conversely, the result of right relationships within one's self and with one's God is magnificently obvious in any situation where the individual is faced with the dismaying task of picking up the scattered pieces of life, and going on.

Religion in the home is not a gush of sentiment or a ritual of worship. It is the underlying philosophy by which the members of the family live, and without which they have a sense of moral incompleteness. It should rest on an unshakable conviction that God has created us good, and wants each one of us to find and to cherish his own goodness first, and then the goodness in others. This truth does not lie in mysteries, or in someone else taking responsibility for us, or in salvation purchasable by any other means than honest self-realization.

What we accomplish is always in terms of where we put our energy. The end point of *all* behavior—chemical, physical, or emotional, from the solar system, to the factory, to the individual—is energy. We do not yet know much about the nature of energy, but in that nature lies the riddle of the universe.

If we would stop using our intellectual and emotional energy in a figurative attempt to bail ourselves out of a sacrificial pool of blood, shed to redeem us from our sins, and expend that energy on research for the improving of moral group-relatedness—which can be improved only by improving individual character, and which would result in a lot less sin—we might come closer to the feelings and to the intentions of Jesus. Religion is what we do, not what we profess. Christ did not ask to be worshipped, he asked to be followed.

There will be those who feel that a scientific approach to religion is impossible; that science and religion are incompatible. Could God be consistent and yet have made them incompatible? What has seemed to be a struggle between science and religion has only been the struggle between reason and ignorant prejudice—on both sides. Science has usually won, because the scientists have consistently refused to accept anything that did not rest upon objective experiments which could be duplicated. But the test tube and the laboratory alone are inadequate. Man lives by something more than bread or chemicals.

There will be those who feel that any criticism of worshiping in the home suggests a lack of proper adjustment to the faith of our fathers. Perhaps those who believe themselves well adjusted to the modern world would be willing to consider whether or not they have adjusted themselves to a fairly wretched state of affairs. We humans will part with almost anything before we will give up those prejudices which make us feel secure. Remember how the men, chained to the back wall of Plato's cave, wanted to go back to the wall instead of out to the sunlight when they were freed?

There will be those who feel that any criticism of worshiping the kind of God who would be a magic helper is sacrilegious. If the criticism has put them on the defensive, they will become aggressive and abusive, which has nothing to do with hungering and thirsting after righteousness.

Despite all the sorrow in the world, and perhaps in the universe, there is an unquenchable tendency toward growth, goodness, understanding, truth, freedom. Man has solved most of the serious problems except his own unhappiness. But we are beginning to apply the methods of scientific investigation to an understanding of human behavior. Rightly followed, this should be a truly religious effort because it will reveal to us more of the character and nature of mankind; how to love ourselves better; how to love each other. Men still die with ignorant courage to give some little Caesar power over other people. Gradually, we are acquiring equal courage to overcome the ignorance which prevents us from living to become our true selves.

God grant that, through a rational religion in the home, the next generation may more effectively release the great resources for happiness which lie within each one of us . . . Or do you believe, as I believe, that God gave us the potentialities, and upon *us* lies the responsibility of developing the happy homes? Are we to prevent moral evolution as we tried to deny biological evolution, or are we to gird up our loins with prayer and humility and hard experience? Are we to recognize that under every material problem is a spiritual problem, and to seek a better religion for better human relations within the family, exactly as we seek better physical things for better physical comfort in the home? Real happiness and real goodness cannot be far apart.

If the kingdom of God is to come, its starting point must be in the home.

Appendix

Over the last quarter century it has been my bright and precious opportunity to lecture on preparation for marriage in thirty odd colleges and universities scattered across America from Maine to California, and from Florida to Oregon. Many times I gave a series, and sometimes an entire course.

College students hunger for authoritative information, reverently presented without taint of self-consciousness, mental reservation, or dogmatic assertion. They know instinctively that attitudes are an important part of information, and in matters of delicacy often the most important part.

Always each student was supplied with pencil and paper. This accomplished two desirable ends. It protected each questioner in a way which made it possible for him to ask what he really wanted to know, including on occasion some intimately personal facts about me. Sometimes these were so intimate and so personal as to produce a many-throated gasp from the audience. I would explain that the question was legitimate for a number of reasons. To begin with, every man's opinions are colored by his own experience, and here was someone who wanted to know what my experience had been. Furthermore, if I failed to read the question aloud its author would know I was not being completely straightforward, thereby perhaps throwing doubt on the sincerity of my whole presentation. After that I would try to answer the question honestly and with appropriate humility, no matter what it was.

The second desirable end stemmed from the fact that these written questions gave me an exact and permanent record of what had been asked, to a present total of some 1500 separate queries. When duplications are combined and a few irrelevancies omitted, the result is the 427 questions which follow. These should, it seems to me, be of value. I am not thinking so much of others who are engaged in teaching the subject. If they are worthy, they already know. I am thinking of the lessening battalions of parents, college administrators, and others who still mistakenly believe there should be no place for this sort of instruction in an academic curriculum. The proper place, they say, is in the home. This ignores altogether the obvious truth that before parents can teach, future parents must be taught, especially when there is so much ignorance and such an earnest desire on the part of most students to learn above the content of the bull session and the level of the ribald joke.

Often, as is the experience of every teacher, questions were asked which had already been discussed in the lecture. These were painstakingly answered again. Some questions could be answered by a simple "Yes," or "No." Always there were questions which should be matters of personal good taste, questions which revealed appalling ignorance, questions indicative of mature reflection on the part of thoughtful, well-informed individuals, questions which were sophistical, questions molded in delicacy, and questions testifying to the coarseness bred by parental diffidence.

Once in a while I did not know the answer. I preferred to admit it rather than to demonstrate it. Many times, as should be obvious to the reader, questions were such that no reputable person would dare try to answer. The information was too meager and the situation too serious. Unhappily, students often fail to realize this. Their perception has been somewhat corroded by men who give positive answers over the radio amid hazy clouds of facts which do not warrant even an enlightened guess. To have only one or two bits of information, and hearsay information at that, in a situation which needs to be thoroughly investigated with professional objectivity, is no basis for competent judgment concerning any problem in human relations. Nevertheless, young people suffering pangs of uncertainty, hope for positive answers from a professorial oracle instead of diligently seeking the fundamental principles by which to guide their own discriminations.

To replace this shocking simple-mindedness, especially on the college level, instruction is needed which will provide enough facts and teach adequate good method by which individuals can think concisely, penetratingly, and inclusively for themselves. They especially need to *think a problem through to the end* instead of in terms of the moment.

There will inevitably be individuals who feel this appendix should have been omitted. Some of them will even be shocked, not realizing that being shocked is their subconscious attempt to be identified by other people as among the virtuous. I know full well what I must suffer from their criticism and from their organized opposition, as I have suffered before. This seems to me unimportant when balanced against the rewards of even a small contribution to better preparation for marriage.

The truly noble person will regret the anguish, the ignorance, the mistaken evaluations, the tragic bringing up, the overwhelming evidence of parents' inhumanity to children, which is reflected in some of these questions. He will say, as Karl Compton once said to me, "If this is the truth, we better face the truth." He will be undisturbed by any lingering legend of impropriety, or the unwarranted suspicion that my mental fig leaf is out of place. He will be seriously concerned with giving our youth a better start toward adequately fulfilled marriage, unspoiled by ignorance, impulse, or ignominy. He knows full well that keeping things under cover always results in wrong answers. Nothing is evil but man's attitude makes it so.

What is it then that youth most wants to know? The question I have been asked most often (51 times) is, "Can an interfaith marriage (usually Protestant and Catholic) be happy?" Obviously the words were not always the same, but I have been careful not to distort the meaning. The modern Juliet is saying, "Oh Romeo, Romeo wherefore art thou denominational? T'is but thy sect that is my enemy. Thou art thyself though not a Protestant (Catholic, Jew)." The young Montagues are saying the same thing to the Capulets.

The second most frequent question (48 times), saturated with sadness and yearning, is, "How do you know when you are in love?" Is there any more important question the ordinary person is ever called upon to answer? Underneath it lie tremendous questions concerning self-knowledge and self-fulfillment which must precede any well lived life.

Practically tying for second place (47 times) is wanting to know what, if any, are the demonstrable reasons against intercourse out of wedlock. If such questions as, "How far should an engaged couple go?" (30), "What about trial marriage?" (7), "How do you know you are well mated unless you experiment before the wedding?" (15), "Isn't it true that the groom will do better on the honeymoon if he has had previous sex experience?" (13), and "Does previous sex experience lead to more happy marriage?" (7), are included in this category, the total soars to 119 times.

A Jeremiah should arise in America to cry out in the wilderness of our academic thorns and sandhills the need for attention to the fourth most frequent question (37 times). "How can I learn to be emotionally mature?" Add to this such queries as, "Will you please define emotional maturity?" (5), "What is emotional honesty?" (5), "How do you find your real self?" (15), and "How can I overcome the emotional scars of growing up in an unhappy home?" (16) and the total becomes 78 times.

The fifth most frequent question (33 times) asks for instruction concerning a good method of birth control. This question cannot be answered in Massachusetts because to do so is against the law, which perhaps explains why it is asked there more often than elsewhere. Include the inquiry as to when the so-called "safe period" occurs (13), and the number of times the question has been asked me becomes 46. My personal belief is that it is better to leave such information for the period of planned parenthood.

There are in all 76 questions which I have been asked five times or more in almost identical words. In the list which follows they have been identified by an asterisk. In addition to combining duplicate questions, an attempt has been made to classify them and to arrange in some semblance of order. Only questions which are not pertinent to this volume, and a few personal questions about myself, have been omitted.

EMOTIONAL MATURITY

* Did you say that emotional maturity is the single most important factor in a happy marriage?
* How can I find out what my real self is like and what kind of person I was intended to be?
* What is emotional honesty?

How can you be emotionally honest in the kind of world we have?

At what age is a person emotionally mature?

* What is emotional maturity and how do you know when you've got it?

Is an emotionally immature person incapable of love?

Is a person who cannot make decisions for herself emotionally mature?

* How can I learn to be emotionally mature?

Does emotional stability make a person independent?

* Will you please define emotional maturity?

From the questions asked it is apparent that many students have been made to realize that they are not emotionally mature. If true, haven't you done more harm than good?

Will a person's emotional maturity be improved by marriage?

* How can I overcome the emotional scars of growing up in an unhappy home?

Can you love someone else if you don't like yourself?

* If you don't like yourself what do you do?

How can you distinguish liking yourself from smug self-satisfaction?

What is happiness?

Is it wise for an emotionally immature person to marry?

Please explain how love and hate are close together?

What are the elements of character?

Who and what should determine how anyone ought to live his life?

What is jealousy and why?

How do you overcome jealousy?

How do you get out from under parental domination?

Why don't they teach high school students these things so everybody could have the advantage of knowing how to make more successful marriages?

Courtship and Criteria

* At what age should we start going steady?

  At what age are people capable of falling in love?
* What is the best age to get married?

  Is it true we are too young to know when we are in love?

  Is the opinion of our parents more likely to be right than our own in choosing a mate?

  Do older men and women do a better job of mate selection?

  How successful are professional marriage counselors in predicting a happy marriage?
* How does one go about finding a mate?

  How can students in a girls' college meet eligible men?

  How can you arouse the interest of someone who seems to be indifferent to you?

  Is being afraid, being in love?

  What do you do if you are afraid of marriage?

  Please distinguish between marital and parental love.
* Please define love again.

  Is there such a thing as love at first sight?
* Is there such a thing as unrequited love?

  What is the best way to find out whether someone you're in love with likes you?

  What can a girl do to let a boy know she likes him?

  Should a girl ever propose, even if it is leap year?
* Is there more than one person with whom it is possible to be happily married?

  How can you convince yourself that someone else can be the right one when the person you loved for ten years marries someone else?

  When you find someone you can love will the feeling be mutual?

  What can be done if the girl you like is going steady with someone else?

  Can I be in love with a boy who fascinates me but who I know is dishonest with me?

  A girl I like won't go out with me because she thinks I like her roommate. Is this fair to herself or to me?
* Is it true that opposites attract?

  I have never met a girl I would want to marry. Is this abnormal?

* Is it possible to be in love with two people at once?

Should you court only one person at a time?

What is wrong with an individual who just goes out with one person after another as they come along?

Is an only child a bad bet?

How long can infatuation last?

If a boy who says he's in love with you suddenly cools down, what does it mean?

Is heredity important in mate selection?

Suppose you don't look forward to seeing him when he is coming, but hate to see him go?

Can you be happily married to someone you dislike at first sight?

* Can you build a happy marriage on respect without love?

Can you be aware of someone's faults and still love him?

* How long should a courtship last?

After three dates can you know whether you're in love?

* How do you know when you're in love?

Won't careful scrutiny such as you suggest spoil romance, cause quarrels, and even prevent ever being married?

* What are the chances of being happily married to a foreigner?

How important are good looks in a wife?

* Do age differences have any important relationship to happiness in marriage?

Is it true that a girl will turn out like her mother?

Is love strong enough to make up for diverse interests?

Should wanting or not wanting children affect the kind of person to marry?

Do you think romance is essential to a happy marriage?

Is it wrong to kiss someone you like?

Should you kiss your date good night?

Does a boy lose respect for you if you let him kiss you on your first date?

If you tire of a person's kisses does that mean you could not be happily married?

How can you evaluate another person's emotional maturity?

* How is it possible to really find out much about another person when you never see him for long in his natural environment?

What are the chances of a successful marriage with an emotionally unstable person?

* If a person has grown up in an unhappy home does that mean he or she is incapable of happy marriage?

Should a person from an unhappy home select someone from a similar background to insure happiness?

Can you be happy with an individual dominated by his parents?

How handle a mother who allows no social contacts with boys and who opposes classes like these as "unnecessary for girls so young?"

Could an individual's unpleasant laugh be cause for future unhappiness?*

What are the chances of being happy with a war widow?

* Can a woman have a profession and at the same time bring up a family? Will she do both jobs well?

Can a girl change undesirable characteristics in a boy by marrying him?

Can a girl acquire the necessary culture to marry a man of higher social station and better upbringing?

Should you completely trust someone with whom you are in love?

* Isn't physical attraction necessary before love is possible?

Is it possible to think you are in love when all that has happened is sex attraction?

Is it true that sex alone is not a sound basis for love?

Is "love at first sight" purely physical?

Is infatuation harmful because the emotions are not honest?

Is it harmful for people who don't go steady, but who are in love, to neck to a great extent?

Should you make a date for no other reason than necking?

Is it true that if you neck you soon will pet?

Will a girl be more popular if she pets?

What should a girl say to a boy who wants to go too far without offending him so she can still retain her popularity?

* Don't you think people who are in love are entitled to petting?

Is heavy petting during courtship detrimental to emotional stability?

* Does petting cheapen love?

Does a boy lose respect for a girl if she pets?

---

* This question should not be dismissed as silly. Neurotic people often have strident laughter.

In my lover's arms how can I know how far to go and when to stop?

How long should you know a boy before you go the limit?

Should sex be considered part of courtship?

Should we have frank sex discussions with the opposite sex during courtship?

* Is it possible to be in love and yet to have no sexual feeling toward the person?

Are you marrying the wrong man if intercourse with him seems repulsive?

If a girl and boy don't have intercourse they build a mental block between them. Will just a marriage license break this block?

If you enjoy sex with a person more than conversation, can you be in love?

Can a moral man be happily married to a girl who has had an illegitimate child?

Can a man be happy with a woman who has a past?

How can a man tactfully ask a girl to have a physical examination before he proposes?

* Can a college graduate be happily married to someone who only went to high school. (Asked by 9 boys and 7 girls)

Is it true that men do not want to marry intelligent women?

I feel from practical experience that you are all wet. To attempt to develop sensible reasons and common interests with modern girls is to invite their avoidance. Why?

* Should a couple marry while the man is still doing graduate study and the girl works to support them, or should they wait?

* Will being married during college hinder education?

Should two students marry if they are so much in love it interferes with their studies?

Should a married woman stay in college?

* Should first cousins marry?

What is the best way to break up with a girl you thought you wanted to marry?

Of what value are statistical studies of marriage when statistics are general and not applicable to the individual?

How much do you think anyone will actually be influenced by the points you have made if he is already in love with a girl?

Pre-marital Sex Problem

My parents told me nothing. How can I get a dignified, authoritative sex education?

I have tried to give my mother a little intelligent sex education so she would understand me better. I get nowhere. What do I do, or must I give up?

Is a college bull session on sex of any value?

Will sex education make for immorality?

* What is the difference between love and lust?
* Isn't it possible for what started as only sex attraction to develop into genuine love?

Does suppressing sexual desires make a person inhibited?

* How do you get self-control?
* What is the best thing to do when you are sexually aroused out of wedlock?
* Is petting wrong outside of wedlock?
* Does pre-marital petting have harmful effects later?
* Does petting without intercourse lead to frustration?

Is frustration physically harmful?

Does pre-marital petting diminish subsequent sexual activity?

Does almost going the limit have serious consequences?

How far should just plain friends go with necking and petting?

Is petting a natural expression of love?

How can you break the habit of petting?

What is masturbation?

What per cent of college men and women masturbate?

* Is masturbation harmful or sinful?

How many times a week can a person masturbate without injury?

Is it unnatural to have never masturbated?

Do you approve mutual heterosexual masturbation?

With our postponed marriage isn't a normal sex life impossible for the college student?

How can you stay virginal in a society which postpones marriage for years beyond its natural age, and still not become inhibited?

What causes homosexuality?

Should a fellow with homosexual tendencies marry?

Years ago I was attacked by a sex fiend. I have never overcome the fear it instilled. Can you help me?

What should an emotionally immature person do? He still needs sex even though he's a poor bet for marriage.

What percentage of college freshmen and college seniors have had intercourse?

How reconcile Freud's dictum that all emotional upset stems from sexual inhibition with the idea that intercourse should be reserved for marriage?

Isn't man naturally polygamous?

What is your reaction to the phrase around here, "Sexual intercourse will make a man out of you?"

What should you do if the girl you are going with wants sexual intercourse?

If you refuse sex relations with a boy will he lose interest in you?

Can a man tell whether a girl is virginal?

Will a gentleman marry a girl with whom he has had pre-marital relations?

What do you think of legalized prostitution?

In all our bull sessions we seem to agree that we prefer to marry a man who has already had intercourse. What is there about the actions of a prostitute different than those of any normal female?

Girls I respect tell me they'd rather marry a man who has had sexual experience. Are they kidding themselves?

Is it true that promiscuity gradually destroys a man's ability to love a woman?

When a boy says, "I thought you were sophisticated enough to have an affair," should an old-fashioned girl try to win him over to her point of view, or wait to find a boy who already has it?

Will a girl who will go the limit with you be slack with anyone else?

Can you be really in love and yet sexually attracted by someone else?

If the boy friend knows you are not virginal will it make a difference to him?

Men seem to expect their brides to be virgins. What should the women expect of the men?

If sex is an appetite what's wrong with being fed when you are hungry?

* Why isn't it all right for two people with strong physical attraction but no intention to marry, to have intercourse?
* Is there harm in having intercourse with someone beside the person you are going to marry?
* Do you believe in pre-marital sex relations? To what extent? Why or why not?
* How do you know you are well mated unless you experiment before the wedding?
* Isn't it true that the groom will do better on the honeymoon if he's had previous experience?
* How can you be assured of mutual, lasting sex attraction?

   If intercourse before marriage is harmful, how come so many second marriages are successful?

   Do you believe in the double standard?

   Is it necessary for a boy to have intercourse before marriage? Isn't it true more brides than grooms are virgins?
* Does previous sex experience lead to more happy marriage?

   Can you be happy if you have intercourse before marriage with your future spouse?

   Does pre-marital promiscuity lead to infidelity?

   Is it true that a man prefers that his wife have previous sexual intercourse?

   Does a virgin make a better wife?

   Ought not the extent of sexual activity before marriage be left to individual conscience?

   Should the physical standard be the same for all married couples?

   How much sex experience can you have and not have too much?

   How can one compensate for the fear of discovery which accompanies intercourse?

   If a girl is pregnant out of wedlock and the couple do not want to marry, what should they do?

   Is there an age when a person should give up hope of a happy marriage and seek extra-marital relations?

PERIOD OF ENGAGEMENT

Should you get engaged if you are not quite sure you have found the right person?

How essential is parental approval?

What things should an engaged couple decide before marriage?

What is the ideal length of an engagement?

Is a long engagement better than a short one?

How can you avoid a long engagement when you haven't any money?

Is a long engagement likely to end in a broken engagement?

Is a period of separation a good test for love?

How long should a girl be willing to wait for a man?

* Is it OK for an engaged person to go out with someone else, especially if the betrothed is living miles away?

Does becoming engaged give the man privileges he did not have before?

Should engaged couples discuss sex?

Is petting all right during the engagement?

Should couples who have petted heavily during their engagement stop and take stock of what prompted their engagement?

* My fiancee and I have gradually gone as far as heavy petting. How can we keep from going further until we are married?

* If you are not virginal should you tell your prospective mate?

* Will intercourse during the engagement lessen love, particularly if you have a long engagement?

* How far should an engaged couple go?

What is the best way for an engaged couple to keep from going too far?

Wouldn't the absence of intercourse during the engagement tend to break down love?

If an engaged couple lost control once, can they return to the original restraint?

* What about trial marriage?

How can I know whether my fiancee is faithful to me?

Should an engaged couple have a physical exam to determine whether they are sexually suited?

Before marriage is there information an engaged couple should get from a doctor, or should they let circumstances guide them?

If you are engaged to a boy who will probably be killed in the war, is it better to marry him and become a widow at age twenty-two, or wait, or give him up entirely?

Do you think a girl who cannot have children and is engaged to a man who wants them should tell him before the wedding?

I am engaged to a man who does more than what I consider moderate drinking. How can I know whether it will have serious consequences?

WEDDING

Is there anything wrong with eloping?

What place in the menstrual cycle does the bride set for the wedding?

Is it natural to be nervous and uncertain as the wedding approaches?

Once a couple in love are married can they ever get over being in love?

I think it is practically impossible to know and to love someone fully until long after the wedding. It takes years. Am I right?

HONEYMOON

My mother thinks that just before marriage is time enough to be told these things. Why do you disagree?

* If good bedroom manners are important why isn't everybody taught something about it?

How soon after marriage should you have intercourse?

* Should you have intercourse on your wedding night?
* What is good procedure on the wedding night?

Should the husband use a prophylactic on the honeymoon?

Should the man who is not virginal expect his bride to be?

* What should you do if you find out you've married someone who isn't virginal? Should it make a difference?

How does the gentleman avoid discovering whether his bride's hymen is intact?

Does intercourse hurt a woman the first time?

If your bride is a virgin, how should the hymen be broken?

Does a bride who is a virgin feel more secure with a man of previous experience or of no experience?

Will most brides forgive their husbands for not giving them an orgasm the first few times?

How many times should a couple have intercourse on their honeymoon?

THE SEX RELATION

Are sex relations necessary for a happy marriage?
* Is a good sex adjustment necessary for a happy marriage?
Is sex adjustment ever impossible, and if so what do you do?
Can a marriage be happy when one person is sexually vigorous and the other is not?
Is sex maladjustment responsible for failure in marriage?
Do emotional upsets, not between husband and wife, affect intercourse?
Is intercourse a good way for husband and wife to rid a marriage of antagonisms and tensions?
* How often should normal married people have intercourse?
How do you handle the fact, without hurting each other, that husband and wife are not always sexually interested at the same time?
What is the proper emotional preparation preceding intercourse?
Is there any incentive to pet after marriage? Isn't the spirit of conquest what motivates it?
* Do you think a "French-kiss" is wrong?
Is it vulgar to kiss a wife's breast?
* Is a genital kiss immoral in marriage?
How do you know what is allowable and what is vulgar?
What are the psychological dangers of practices considered vulgar by the other person?
* What constitutes good procedure in intercourse?
How long should the sex act take?
At what time during her monthly cycle is a woman most sexually active?
* Does a woman get as much enjoyment from intercourse as a man?
Do different individuals find different positions in intercourse the most satisfactory?
How does a woman achieve an orgasm?
How can a man control his orgasm if the wife is slow in reaching hers?
* How can a husband tell when his wife has reached her orgasm?

How can a wife slow a husband down so she can achieve total pleasure?

If a woman does not have an orgasm does this mean that she does not love her husband?

* Is intercourse evil when conception is not intended?

Are twin or double beds preferable?

* What is the most satisfactory method of birth control?

* What is the so-called "safe" period?

Without birth control what would the birth rate do to the future of America? Famines like India and China?

* Does the use of a contraceptive spoil the enjoyment of intercourse?

Is artificial insemination moral?

How should you tell your husband that you are pregnant?

Isn't sex less important after middle age?

Can you be happily married and have a lover or a mistress?

Is it all right for a wife to commit adultery if she knows her husband does?

Is there any situation in which abortion is justified?

My wife is not passionate. What is wrong?

Biological and Medical

What effect does intercourse have on physical well-being?

What is the beauty or aesthetic value in intercourse?

What is the relation between alcohol and sex?

What are the causes of sexual incompatibility?

Do men have more sex desire than woman? If so, why?

Is it true that intercourse is sometimes impossible between two people? If so, can a physician remedy the trouble?

Does a physician have to break the hymen in order to give a thorough physical examination?

Does a considerable difference in height indicate probable difficulty in making a sex adjustment?

Does sexual stimulation, like petting, without subsequent intercourse, lessen a woman's chances to have children?

Does a girl who masturbates have a difficult time reaching an an orgasm? (ambiguous question)

Is a woman a virgin only if the hymen is unbroken?

Does bleeding occur when the hymen is broken?

Please explain the process of menstruation.

How is menstruation possible when there is a maidenhead?

Does a woman menstruate during the first or the last of each month?

Are women emotionally upset during menstruation?

Do males have some form of monthly like women?

Is it true that a woman can become pregnant only at a certain time during the menstrual cycle?

Is intercourse possible, desirable, or harmful during menstruation?

For how many days is conception possible between menstrual periods? When does this come?

Does menstruation stop during pregnancy?

What is the process of fertilization? How does the spermatazoon get to the ovum?

When does ovulation occur?

Is it always the same ovary that discharges?

Do the two ovaries eject eggs at the same time?

How do husband and wife know that intercourse takes place at a time when both sex cells are mature?

Is it true that if one drinks alcohol it will kill the weak sperm so only the strong ones live?

After an emission how long will it be before the next fertile emission?

Between what ages should a woman have her children?

What is the best time of year to have a baby?

What is the best interval to have between children?

Does the practice of birth control interfere with having normal children when you want them?

Is it possible to become pregnant without breaking the hymen? (Yes.)

Does pregnancy always follow the first intercourse?

Does pregnancy always follow intercourse?

Does conception take place only during menstruation?

What is the average number of intercourses required to get a woman pregnant?

Must a woman have an orgasm in order for conception to take place?

Is it true that thoughts or physical condition during the intercourse influence the character of the child?

How soon after conception can pregnancy be determined?

What is the first sure symptom of pregnancy?

Is intercourse permissible during pregnancy?

Are contraceptives necessary during pregnancy?

What is the effect of smoking and drinking during pregnancy?

What determines whether it will be a boy or a girl baby?

How soon after the intercourse can the sex of the baby be told?

How are twins conceived?

Why, if true, can only two eggs be fertilized when conception takes place?

How should a husband help prepare his wife emotionally for child-birth?

What should a young husband know about prenatal care?

A pregnant woman may have trouble with her teeth. Does it follow that a man's teeth are damaged by intercourse?

Should a pregnant woman have a special diet?

How long before birth should intercourse stop?

What does an ordinary person need to know in order to deliver a baby in an emergency?

How long does it take for a baby to be born?

What is the fluid which is discharged during birth?

What is the function of the umbilical cord?

Explain the process of disconnecting the umbilical cord.

What happens to the umbilical cord inside the mother after birth?

How difficult is delivering a baby feet first?

What is a miscarriage?

Can a miscarriage take place at any time during the pregnancy?

What causes premature birth?

What are the causes of death at childbirth?

If a woman has a very small pelvis, does that mean she should never become pregnant?

How is a Caesarean operation performed?

How many children can a woman have by the Caesarean operation?

How soon after birth may intercourse be resumed?

Is it true that a woman goes through a change after which she cannot have children?

What is the effect of the menopause?

What happens to a woman's sexual satisfaction after her menopause?

Why are men sexually potent longer than women?

Are abortions really extremely dangerous?
What is a frigid woman?
What causes frigidity?
How do you cure a frigid woman?
What is the positive evidence of sterility in male?
What is the process of sterilizing a female?

EMOTIONAL ADJUSTMENTS

What is the most important single contribution to a happy family?
Can two people who start out without love develop it afterward?
We married in haste. How can we save our marriage?
Can two selfish people ever adjust so they can be happily married?
Obviously no two people are the same. How can you compromise to satisfy each other?
Should a woman try to cultivate interests she does not care about just to make her husband happy?
What do you think about a husband reading the newspaper at the breakfast table?
How can you keep a husband from walking all over you when he is being annoying and you are being kind?
How do you handle a wife who cries and makes scenes?
Can a man who feels he must have one night a week out with the boys love his wife?
Should a wife mind if her husband kisses another woman good night?
Who are the competitors you should know about after marriage?
What is the best way to make up after a fight?
What makes a person say that if you love them you'll do what they want?
How can the problem of over-drinking be solved?
How important are in-laws in marriage?
How can we handle a smothering mother-in-law?
Is it possible to conduct family affairs as a democracy?

RELIGION

* To what extent should religion be part of family life?
Do you think religion differences ought to interfere with love?

* Can an inter-faith marriage be happy?
  Can a Catholic and a non-Catholic be married by a priest, and yet allow the non-Catholic to retain her own religion?
* Will our generation ever see the day when religion unites people instead of separating them, and when even inter-racial marriages will meet with social approval?

MONEY

What is the minimum salary on which two middle class people can get married?

Should you expect your betrothed to wait three or four years while you pay off your college debts?

What about students still in college marrying on a parental allowance?

Will adverse economic circumstances destroy love?

Should people marry without waiting for absolute financial security?

Would I be foolish to marry an artist who may never earn much of a living though he is fine in every other way?

How can you tell whether someone loves you for yourself or for the money you have?

* Can people from families of different social standing and financial means be happily married?
  Should I marry for "practical reasons" only?
  What difference will it make if the wife works and earns more money than the husband?
  Should the budget be handled jointly by husband and wife or by only one of them?
  Should a husband share his financial affairs with his wife?
  How handle the finances if each partner thinks he should have control?
  How much does it cost to have a baby?

CHILDREN

* Must a married couple have children to be happy?
  What would be the reason for a girl not wanting to have children?
  Is it important to space your children by planned parenthood?
  How long should a couple wait to have children, especially in the

light of the fact that it takes several years to find out whether a marriage is successful?

What is the ideal number of children?

Why are children from the same family different?

Does alcoholism affect one's children?

What are some of the common causes that make it impossible for a man or woman to have children?

Should you adopt children if it is impossible to have your own?

Do parents bring up children the way they were brought up?

Is sex information harmful to a seven-year old?

* At what age should a child be told the facts of life?
* What is the right way to tell a child about sex?

Do you believe in spanking children?

What can be done to give one's children emotional maturity?

Divorce

When two incompatible people are married is there some other reasonable alternative than divorce?

If all attempts at adjustment have failed, should you get a divorce or try to make the best of it?

Should unhappily married people stay together for the sake of the children?

Are the lawyers right when they say that sexual incompatibility is the principal reason for divorce?

My parents parted without rancor. Do you mean to say that because they no longer live together marriage will be more difficult for me?

* Isn't it true that children of divorced parents will make a more happy marriage because they have suffered from an unhappy one?

Don't you feel that a girl brought up in an unhappy or a broken home will work harder for a happy marriage because of the terrible things she experienced with her parents?

I come from a broken home that was hell. Can I live it down or am I doomed?

Isn't the increase in divorce merely due to the ease of divorce?

Can a second marriage following a divorce be happy?

Is it a hazard to marry a divorced man with children?

What is the right way to go about getting a divorce?

Index